Nola

A Memoir of
Faith,
Art,
and Madness

BY

ROBIN HEMLEY

GRAYWOLF PRESS

Publication of this volume is made possible in part by a grant provided by the Minnesota State Arts Board through an appropriation by the Minnesota State Legislature, and by a grant from the National Endowment for the Arts. Significant support has also been provided by Dayton's, Mervyn's, and Target stores through the Dayton Hudson Foundation, the Andrew W. Mellon Foundation, the McKnight Foundation, the General Mills Foundation, the St. Paul Companies, and other generous contributions from foundations, corporations, and individuals. To these organizations and individuals we offer our heartfelt thanks.

Published by Graywolf Press
2402 University Avenue, Suite 203
Saint Paul, Minnesota 55114
All rights reserved.

www.graywolfpress.org

Published in the United States of America

ISBN 1-55597-278-0

2 4 6 8 9 7 5 3 1
First Graywolf Printing, 1998

Library of Congress Catalog Card Number: 98-84451

Cover design: Scott Sorenson
Cover photograph (background): © 1997 by Paul Elledge Photography

A lie can only thrive on truth;
lies heaped one upon another, lack substance.

ISAAC BASHEVIS SINGER
from "A Tale of Two Liars,"
translated from the Yiddish
by Joseph Singer and Cecil Hemley

The reason of God is most often the wildness of men.

NOLA HEMLEY

Why do we utter letters and move them around?
I, a fledgling, will tell you what I experienced.

The Essential Kabbalah

FOR OLIVIA AND ISABEL:

When they understand

And when they don't.

Table of Contents

Prologue: Larceny

My parents seemed to believe in letting everyone do whatever they wanted until they became very good at it or died. My father, Cecil Hemley, was a poet, novelist, editor, and translator of Isaac Bashevis Singer's work. He was also a good smoker and that's what he died of when I was seven. My older brother Jonathan used to be good at everything, from languages to sports to the sciences, but over the last twenty years he's specialized—in Orthodox Judaism, and lives with his eight children and wife in L.A. My sister Nola was good at everything, too, art and language, but especially things of the spirit—and that, in a sense, is what she eventually died from. My mother Elaine Gottlieb is a short story writer and teacher. She's good at surviving. As for myself . . . I've always had a larcenous heart.

As I get older, the thief diminishes, but still there is something inside me essentially untrustworthy, someone hard and calculating, egged on by the deaths of my father and sister, someone who will not always accept responsibility for his actions. I remember a camp counselor at Granite Lake Camp in New Hampshire telling me one night that he was on to me. He called me conniving. I pretended I didn't know what he was talking about, and was silent. He was one of the only people who saw through me like that, or at least one of the few who ever told me directly. I wonder about confession, this nagging need. When I confess, I make myself vulnerable. Some people will like me for it and others will arm themselves with my admissions and hurl them back. One time I told my mother what this counselor had said about me and the next time we argued, she said, "Your counselor was right. You are conniving." After that, I resolved to bury myself deeper, to hide this other person where even I wouldn't be able to recognize him. Sometimes I think it's too late, that he has already stolen away the things my sister gave me—things of the imagination and spirit that he pawned to support his habit.

Inadmissible Evidence

I'm looking through a drawer of a desk in my room at my grandmother's house. I'm seventeen and I'm looking for something to steal—loose change would be great or an antique paperweight or letter opener.

Inside one of the drawers, I come across a legal-sized document with a rusty paper clip attached. It's titled POINT OF ERROR #1 and reads "The Finding that 'No marriage between Elliot Chess and Elaine Gottlieb (also known as Elaine Hemley) was ever entered into at any time or at any place' is contrary to the evidence and against the weight of the evidence. Appellees proved the contract of marriage." That's as far as I read. I'm not sure what this document is or how it pertains to me, but I know I have to have it, and I know that I can't tell anyone about it. It has something to do with Nola, who's been dead three years.

Discovery

Uncovering the facts, not even the facts but the feelings of my sister and mother's lives, has become a detective story for me. It started out before I even knew it was a detective story, when I was seventeen and found some court documents about my mother and Nola's father, Elliot Chess, in a drawer at my grandmother's house. The remarkable thing about finding these documents was that I never told anyone I'd found them and never read them until now. For years, I kept them in a box and never looked at them. But now that I've read them, now that I understand things about my mother's life, things perhaps that she wouldn't want me to know, the revelations follow quickly, one upon the other. And the more I uncover, the more I realize that one of these days I'm going to have to tell my mother about the court papers I found. Eventually, I'll confess. But the documents keep multiplying. Everyone in my family, or connected with it, it seems, has written about the events I want to write about—although not in a way that gives an overall picture of who we are. Every day, I seem to learn about new documents. I'm drowning in them. My mother tells me little by little about their existence, almost as though she's teasing me. But this is how she's always been. Rarely does she volunteer information about her life, although if asked a direct question, she'll sometimes answer. She's known a lot of famous writers and artists: Isaac Singer, Joseph Heller, Robert Motherwell, Weldon Kees, Louise Bogan, Conrad Aiken, John Crowe Ransom, but she almost never mentions any of them: It's not important to her.

My mother has kept a journal for years. I never knew this until I stumbled upon the fact New Year's Eve, 1994, when I asked her nonchalantly whether she'd ever kept a journal.

"Sure, I've been keeping a journal since I was sixteen."

I was stunned. "Do you have anything from your time in Mexico with your first husband?"

"Sure, I have a lot about Mexico."

"I need it all," I told her.

She laughed.

"Do you know where it is?"

"I was just looking at it the other day."

"Mom, I'm always amazed how I just find out these things about you by chance."

She laughed again.

That night, she and I sat on her bed and sorted through her journal, hundreds of loose-leaf typed pages dating from the thirties. She let me have whatever I wanted, but she also said, "I don't think you should know everything."

"I have to," I said, half laughing. "I want to know everything."

I keep thinking that it's my right to know all this, that she should volunteer everything she knows, as though this is a court case and she'll be accountable for what she doesn't divulge. It says something new about my relationship with my mother that for years everything was too painful to divulge to me, but now nothing is. My mother, since learning about my project, has been sending me steady streams of old photos, journal excerpts, letters.

The Present

My mother is working on a novel, two novels really, a mystery about a trip we took to England when I was eighteen and another one whose subject I'm unsure of. She's been working on a novel for years, ever since I can remember—her second novel. Her first was published in 1947, the year of my sister Nola's birth. Almost every time I speak to her she's working on a new novel, having abandoned each previous one after a couple of drafts or a few chapters. Every few years she rediscovers her old novels and realizes they were pretty good. She'll work feverishly on a rediscovered novel with renewed vigor until another loss of faith, and then she's off to a new project. In between she writes short stories. For many years they were published in some of the best literary journals and anthologies.

I find myself trying to make time to read her new stories between my busy teaching schedule, doing my own writing, spending time with my own family. Everything produces guilt. I look at my daughters and realize I'm not spending enough time with them. I try to give everyone encouragement. "Just keep sending them out, Mom." "Why don't you just finish this one before moving on? I like the idea of this one."

"I'll get back to it," she tells me.

But I know that after she dies, I'll find a dozen or so novels in various stages of completion, and I won't know what to do with them. Should I find the best ones and try to edit them? Should I send them out as is? Why am I worrying about this now? It's strange to think of your family leaving you documents, but that's what my family leaves behind: stories, novels, poems. Documents. Half-truths. Fiction. It's what my family was built on, what we've always believed in. We've always been suspicious of fact, frightened of it. My grandmother, on her deathbed, delirious, asking for the impossible—to just go home and sit outside for a while on her porch, started ranting, according to my mother, about a supposed case of incest in a branch of our family that happened two hundred years ago, and begged that the family line be stopped. Facts, even two hundred years old, haunt our family.

"Fictionalize it," my mother says. "Why don't you fictionalize it?"

THE PAST

My father has been dead six months. Heart attack. I'm spending the summer with my grandmother Ida, and she enrolls me at Atlantic Beach Day Camp a few blocks from where she lives. I hate swimming, so during swim period I organize a pickpocket ring. I don't know how I learned to pickpocket, but I'm pretty good, so I teach a small group at the camp how to do it. At first, we lift combs from back pockets, but then we start taking wallets. We're finally caught and lined up by the pool where the head counselor interrogates us.

"I know you're good kids," he says. "You wouldn't do this on your own. There's one bad apple among you. Tell me who it is and I'll let the rest of you go."

I turn to the boy in line next to me, a fat kid named Bernard who reluctantly joined the ring, and who seems to think I'm cool. "Why don't you tell them it's you?" I say to Bernard, as though this would be a very good thing for him to do.

He blinks at me and tugs his hair.

"*Tell them it's you,*" I say.

"*Why?*" he whispers.

"*You'll be a hero,*" I say.

The counselor waits. He moves down the line, looking at the tops of our heads. More than anything, I don't want Ida to know what I've done. She wouldn't be able to believe it. She thinks I'm a good kid and so does my mother, and I can't bear the thought of them being told what I've done.

Bernard glances over at me and gives me an unsure and suffering look. "*Go ahead,*" I say. "*Be a hero.*"

He raises his hand.

"*What?*" the counselor says.

"*It's me,*" Bernard says. "*I'm the ringleader.*"

The counselor looks a bit surprised, but then a smug look replaces the other and he grins. He reaches over and yanks Bernard by the arm. Bernard cowers in front of us.

"*I thought so,*" the counselor says. "*I knew it was you.*"

The counselor takes Bernard away and that's the last I ever see of him. Another counselor dismisses us. No one says a word to our parents, or in my case, my grandmother, and those of us involved never speak of the pickpocket ring or Bernard again. Maybe they think they've scared us enough or maybe they don't want our parents to think Atlantic Beach Day Camp gives its campers enough idle time to organize pickpocket rings.

The next day I'm idling by one the buildings listening with a whole group of idlers to a transistor radio. We're entranced by a new Beatles song. Someone has called me over to hear it, and we gather around the radio as though hearing the first transmission from a distant universe. Across from us, the good campers, the nonidlers, the Boy Scouts, the Penny-saved-is-a-penny-earned boys are playing softball. I glance up for a second and see something white coming down on me. It knocks me flat. The other idlers laugh at me and the softball group runs over to where I lie, mildly concussed. They argue whether or not it was a home run or fan interference on my part. I don't care. I know it's punishment. A knock on the head from heaven.

A counselor named Herman takes me under his wing. He thinks I'm a good kid and he feels sorry for me that my dad has died. He spends extra time with me, even after the day camp has closed. With my grandmother's permission he takes me to the boardwalk one night. We ride the Ferris wheel. He buys me cotton candy and a potato knish. It's a strange night because there's been a tidal wave the night before, and it's flooded the normally wide beach all the way to the street under the boardwalk.

The boardwalk is fine, but you can hear the small waves roiling against the support beams, even catch glimpses of the water through the slats. As we're walking along he picks me up and dangles me over the railing. I see the water, the ocean right beneath me, a dark slapping sea.

He laughs. "Should I drop you over?"

"No," I say, laughing, too, confident that he wouldn't dare.

"I'm going to drop you," he says, and for a moment I can feel it. I'm lost. I'm gone out to sea, pulled far from anything solid. I scream.

Still, he holds me over.

"Don't you wish you learned how to swim?" he says.

Does he know, I wonder? Does he know that I was the ringleader? I'm dangling over the railing by one foot. "I've got you," he says. "I've got you," and I wonder what he means by that.

THE NONFICTIONAL

My mother returns my call on Thanksgiving. I left a message on her machine. I know she's there—probably upstairs in her study writing, but she can't hear me because she's turned her hearing aid down. One of her former students invited her for Thanksgiving dinner, but my mother declined, preferring these days to celebrate holidays by writing.

"Did I tell you I'm working on a mystery?" she asks.

"Yes." She's told me a dozen times already.

"With Nancy Cowgil," she says. "It's about our trip to England."

"I'm writing, too," I say. "I hope Jonny won't hate me when I finish this." But that's not what I really mean to say. What I really mean to say is, "I hope you won't hate me."

"Why's that?"

"I'm not holding anything back."

"You can always soft-pedal the facts," she says. "I found a photo of Nola for you, but it's from when she was twenty."

"I'm going to be writing about you and Elliot Chess."

"What do you know about us? I haven't told you much."

"But that's part of it. I've done a little . . . investigating." I think about what she said about soft-pedaling. I think about the document I have that she doesn't know about, what I found when I was seventeen. I didn't even read it until this summer. While preparing to write this, I remembered the papers and started searching for them, tearing through my files, coming up with nothing, thinking with despair, "I couldn't have thrown them out. Why would I throw them out?" Finally, I found them in my attic, in a corner, at the very bottom of a file box filled with assorted papers. There's so much in these papers that my mother doesn't know I know. I keep hinting that I know more than she's told me, but I just can't make a clean confession. I think about what she said the last time we spoke about this, "God, I'm going to have to become a hermit after you write this." I want to confess. I want more than anything to tell her what I have, but I know that she'd want to see it, that she'd say, "Fictionalize. Don't embarrass me," and I'd have to say, "There's nothing to be embarrassed about. It happened fifty years ago. These things happen every day now." But I know that wouldn't do a thing to diminish her pain, the pain of abandonment and betrayal. And now, here I am—am I betraying her? Do I have any right to say what I know, to tell the facts, private facts from public documents? I know that if I had grown up in a different family, a family of architects, the answer would have been no. All of my writing friends urge me to wait until the manuscript is done before I show it to my mother. One of them tells me, "Thomas Wolfe never would have written *Look Homeward, Angel,* if he'd sought his mother's approval first."

The Fictional

I come from a family of writers, and the pain that comes from words is not diminished, necessarily, by a fictionalized stance. I grew up as the subject of or a character in my mother's published stories. I was told that I shouldn't be angered by this, that fiction transforms. And I wasn't bothered, except by momentary twinges when I saw revealed in a story, my late thumb-sucking, for instance. I still believe we have the right, the obligation, to write about the world as we see it. Of course, it's always transformed. There's a story by Donald Barthelme, "The Author," in which a famous writer uses her children as the models for all her stories, and when they come to complain to her about telling all their secrets, they ask what gives her the right and she blithely answers, "Because you're mine." But the flip side of that is that they own her, too. The children own the mother and father, whether they know it or not. At times, I want to cry as I'm writing. At times, I want to do wrong, knowingly, to get at what's right.

The Lies

In Ida's room while she's in the kitchen, I open the clasp of her pocketbook and start digging for her purse. The pocketbook is stuffed with sugar packets she's taken from restaurants, salt and pepper packets, moist towelettes, tissues, combs, her compact, and finally down at the bottom, the little cowhide change purse where she keeps her bills crumpled up together in a wad. I open it and feel the bills. All of them come up in my hand together. I've done this many times. The money is for comic books. I'm fourteen. I don't plan on taking all her money, just a few dollars, maybe five, depending on how much she has and how much I think she'll miss.

As I'm sorting through the mass of wadded bills, Ida walks into the room.

"What are you doing?" she asks. For some reason, she doesn't look surprised.

"I was looking for something," I tell her.

"In my purse?"

I'm holding the wadded bills still, gently, as if I don't know what to do with them, like they're some wounded bird I've found.

"A pen," I say. "I was just looking for a pen."

There's a bit of a whine in my voice, even a threat, not physical, but emotional. I'll do whatever necessary to protect and preserve this lie. I stare at her. I hate her right now for finding out about me. And this is something she can't stand. She looks afraid for a second and says quietly, "I'll help you find one." Only then do I put the money back where I found it and neither of us say a word about this to anyone nor to each other, nor, I'm sure, to ourselves.

THE SPOKEN

Nola was my half sister from my mother's previous marriage, eleven years older than me, a brilliant young woman who graduated Phi Beta Kappa and then studied for her Ph.D. in philosophy at Brandeis. She was also interested, obsessed actually, with spiritual and psychic phenomenon and apprenticed under her Guru, Sri Ramanuja.

Sometimes I still miss Nola keenly. I miss her most when I'm with my daughters, Olivia and Isabel, and it's just us, and I wish they could know their aunt, someone who played the Irish harp, who knew Sanskrit and Greek and French and German and Hebrew, who would teach them Shakespearean songs and sing with them—someone so impractical and imaginative that nearly anything seemed possible to me in her presence.

Anything that had to do with the hidden, with the magical, Nola was interested in, and she cultivated this interest in me. I was her darling baby brother, and she wanted my life to be rich with what was hidden and most inaccessible about the world. In the summer, Nola made a garland of flowers and placed it in my hair, then danced around the yard with me.

She was always telling me stories, Irish folktales, Tolkien, Greek myths, or we sang folk songs, and her songs, like her stories, brimmed with possibility—even to say brimmed, suggests a container, but there was none that I could see. She learned to make animals out of balloons for me and birds out of paper. She loved transformation. She loved metamorphosis. Everything was changing and vibrant in her world, and she tried to show me that in all she made for me. The most ordinary earthbound thing could be made into something that could fly away.

In 1973, she died.

The last several years of her life were spent in and out of mental hospitals, where she was diagnosed with schizophrenia.

She and I had been close until her illness manifested itself and I started to detest her. Before I had a chance to grow up, to mature, to understand, she vanished. It wasn't suicide, I was told, although she had tried to kill herself before. It was a horrible accident, a doctor's mistake. He'd prescribed too much Thorazine and her body had shut down, kidney failure. She went into a coma and died two days later.

THE UNSPOKEN

I've never written about my sister, except in the most oblique way. Every time I've tried head-on, I've failed. For some reason, I can't seem to recreate on the page who my sister was. The people I know the best elude me when I try to describe them. The writing friends whom I admire the most are those who seem to be able to write completely recognizable portraits of their sisters, their fathers, their friends. I've never written about my closest living relatives—never touched my brother or my mother, not even in a fictional way, even though I could avoid issues in fiction that I can't avoid in this. I wonder if you can feel bereavement for the living as well as the dead. That's close to what I feel for my brother.

Jonathan boycotted my wedding because I married a woman of Scotch/Irish/German descent, not Jewish. A couple of weeks before my wedding a rabbi from L.A. called me and told me he was an emissary from my brother. He wanted, he said, to fly to my home and spend a day with me to "tell me the great spectacle of Jewish history."

I thanked the rabbi and told him that the spectacle of Jewish history, while interesting, I'm sure, would not affect the outcome of my marriage. Finally, the rabbi gave up, but before he left me he extracted a promise I'd tell my brother that he'd tried. For some reason, he also seemed intent that I remember his name, which I repeated three times, like something out of Rumpelstiltskin, and promptly forgot the next day.

I know I have not always been the best brother myself. I have often been neglectful. I never bought him a wedding present when he married in 1980, for instance. I wonder if bereavement and guilt are inextricably linked, if in some way you have betrayed the memory of the one bereaved simply by continuing on your own without them. My brother, who is five years older than me, became my father figure after my father died. I always followed his lead until he chose his Orthodox path. He's hurt me as I'm sure I've hurt him. What hurt me the most was a conversation my mother reported to me last year. She said that she had told Jonny she wished we could become close again and Jonny replied, "We were never that close." I wondered if that could be true, if my memory could be so misleading—if his version of the truth or mine is the right one, or if the years of silence between us have stolen the truth away from us forever.

NOT GUILTY

I try not to feel guilty about any of this, any of these thefts. I've felt guilty in the past, but not now. In a way, I feel proud. I'm telling you "Look what I got away with." I cheated death. I escaped madness. I stole before I was stolen. I want you to know that this is what it's really about. This is about the stories we're allowed to tell and the ones we lock away. I'm telling you this is what I've become good at. The other morning I saw that word "Larceny" scrawled in a dream like a film title. The words scrolled in front of me like the beginning of an old movie that establishes a different time and place through words, not images: "Paris, 1797. Anarchy reigned in the streets!" But these words wouldn't have made sense to a movie-theater crowd, wouldn't have set any scene: "Stolen property. Your sister Nola. A search of many years ensued."

An acquaintance of mine, another writer, recently suggested that all writers should be virtuous. He was drunk at the time, but I'll assume it was an honest sentiment. I guess I don't believe it in any case, at least not in the traditional sense of virtue. Outwardly, I'd like for people to think of me as virtuous, but inwardly, I don't care. There's something inside me that still wants to be the thief. For me, the truth is not a matter of virtue. It's something to be stolen, co-opted, appropriated— hot-button words that make the virtuous cringe and yell, "What gives you the right?" The answer is nothing, no right, but what's best about the world did not always spring from the brow of virtue. Pat your pocket. Show me the location of what you value most.

Nola Hemley

Nola

The Invisible and Quiet Hand

We believe and disbelieve a hundred times an hour,
which keeps believing nimble.
EMILY DICKINSON

My sister and my brother inherited most of the spiritual genes in my family—I suppose by way of our maternal great-great-grandfather Abraham, a village mystic in Lithuania, a colored photograph of whom graces the wall of my office.

According to legend, he lived to be 117 or 105—accounts vary. My grandmother Ida told me that his secret was a cup of hot water with lemon every day, and that's the regimen she followed, religiously, but she only lived to be 90. Ida used to tell me that people would come from all over Lithuania for Abraham's advice; in the picture, he wears a *yarmulke* and has a full gray beard and mustache.

My father comes from a family of atheists, but he was always fascinated by philosophy and by Eastern religions, and he and Nola would have long conversations about Buddhism and Hinduism toward the end of his life.

My mother and I are, I suppose, the agnostics of the family. For my mother, writing is her religion. Although her maiden name, Gottlieb, means "God love," I don't remember her ever saying a word to me on the subject—with one exception—when I was seven and announced to my mother that fairies were real but angels weren't—my sister's influence, no doubt. My mother thought this was a hilarious assumption, and made me repeat it to my father. But that's the only conversation on any religious subject that I can recall.

I can't presume to think that my mother is without spiritual yearnings whatsoever—but we treat it the way other families might treat the subject of madness perhaps. In some ways, for me, it's closely allied to madness. A large percentage of people classified as schizophrenics see visions and join cults. In my limited experience, that's true. Nola was always seeing visions, and while my mother has steadfastly claimed to be a skeptic, I always felt she wanted to believe. In the early 1970s, the Hemley household was Psychic Phenomenon Central. At eleven, I was doing automatic writing, a kind of spiritual advice column for my family and my mother's students, and I signed the columns "Shiva." My sister was communicating with her Guru Sri Ramanuja, whose Centre of Being was located in Queens, New York, sometimes by way of letter, sometimes by telepathy. I remember my mother hosting a séance in 1971. But now she dismisses all of that as a kind of game, or as her attempts to try to understand what was going on with her daughter.

Still, someone accused my mother of being a witch—some disaffected student, she thinks, who received a low grade, and she wasn't reappointed. That's part of the reason, in any case. At the time that my mother was coming up for reappointment at Stephens College, Nola suddenly disappeared (one of several times), drove with an acquaintance to New York to be closer to her Guru, and wound up in the psychiatric unit at Bellevue chained to a bed. For weeks, my mother had no idea where Nola was, and when it came time to give the tenure committee her teaching evaluations and other documents she just handed them a sheaf of papers and said, "Here. I can't do anymore. Nola has disappeared. I've got to go to New York." The committee made no excuses for her and she wasn't reappointed.

Here. I can't do anymore. Nola has disappeared. These are words I'm tempted to repeat, to shove the couple hundred pages of her journals in someone else's hands and say, "You make sense of them. I'm going to New York to look for her." Gone for almost twenty-five years, run away for good this time. I know that eventually I'll have to throw away the crutches of other people's voices, their words, and even throw away Nola's own words. To rediscover her, I'll have to look into those wordless places I've turned my back on.

Sept. 1, 1994

Dear Robin,

Here's Nola's "Journal." As you will see, she wrote in an extremely exaggerated style. I tried to edit the manuscript—with her consent—but I gave up. It was too much, and she couldn't do it herself.

She also distorted facts. WHEN SHE QUOTES THE little speech to God that she made as a child, she says it was her "stepfather" who was with her—but it wasn't Cexcil, ixt was I. What actually happened was that we

were climbing the stairs of the brownstone where I first lived in the
Village, and as we came to the top floor, mine, she looked up at the small
skylight and said: Oh God, I love you God, if I could see you now I would
hug you, but I can't because you're invisible, aren't you, God?——Quite
remarkable for a five year old, I xxxx

thought.

    Of course, Cecil and I were married when she was five (on her birth-
day, actually, but she wasn't with us that time).

There are other things she dxistorted—but you won't know until

you've worked your way through the flourishes of her sometimes unread-
able handwriting. She did type some of it, which may help.

Love, Mom

What my mother refers to as my sister's journal isn't a journal at all,
but a memoir of sorts, titled "In Search of God, An Autobiography."
It's about 150 pages, half typed and half written in my sister's script,
and it was written the last year of Nola's life, when my mother thought
that writing might be therapeutic for Nola. I have to keep reminding
myself that my sister was twenty-four when she wrote her memoir, that
I'm nearly fifteen years older than she was when she died, and that
Nola's aims were high ones. She didn't merely want to tell the story of
her life—the book seems as much of a book of spiritual instruction as
anything else. Events are foreshortened and skipped over lightly in
Nola's telling—much of the text is addressed to people in general, ex-
horting them to give up material things and self-love and follow her
spiritual master, Sri Ramanuja. I also have to remember the year in
which she wrote this, 1972.

What immediately strikes me as I read through Nola's memoir are
the crossed-out passages. These are the crossing-outs of my mother,
not censorship exactly, but my mother's higher calling always: to turn
the overwrought into art, to tone down, make something subtler, find
exactly the right word. My mother edited Nola's manuscript with
Nola's permission, she says. Still, there's no denying that my mother
was exerting the same kind of control over Nola's words as I'm exerting over her own. Even in her letter to me, she wants me to know the
truth, that she (not my father) was standing with Nola on the steps
when Nola cried out to God at age five. And my reaction: Why does

that matter? Why is it important that I know of my sister's "distortions," certainly ones so trivial? Perhaps there are some distortions of fact in Nola's autobiography, but not distortions of the spirit. My sister, as she claims throughout her book, hungered for things of the spirit. Her writing begins, "I have always been obsessed with God." Here, my mother has drawn a line through the rest of the sentence, "and with the hidden." That seems like a perfectly fine sentiment to me, even a connection between Nola and myself, and I feel almost resentment at it having been crossed out. While I have not been obsessed with God, like Nola, I have, like her, been obsessed with the hidden, and perhaps my mother, even in the crossing out of such a simple line is stating that she prefers to keep the hidden crossed out? Nearly every paragraph has something crossed out, or a replacement made. In some cases, the editorial changes my mother made were good ones, but I prefer to put the versions side-by-side, to compare the choices of my sister with the choices of my mother. When I first read the memoir, I felt my sister's presence more strongly than I'd felt it in twenty-five years—despite the rhetorical flourishes my mother writes of, my sister's voice, or how I remember it, comes through. The only way I can truly describe my feelings from reading Nola's memoir is "drunk." My head reels with strange connections, almost explosions, stumblings of possibility.

The first page and a half sets the tone for the rest of the memoir. The italicized words are my mother's substitutions:

> I have always been obsessed with God ~~and with the hidden.~~ Nature has appeared to me, even as a child, to be a veneer; the product of erroneous vision which should in some *way* ~~manner~~ be corrected. As a child and adolescent I *immersed myself* ~~was submerged~~ in the occult, reading the imaginative ~~most bizarre~~ stories of I.B. Singer (who was a friend of my parents, also writers), hypnotizing friends to see whether they had latent psychic powers ~~and doing so well in certain forms of school work that it seemed to rush from some higher center of the brain rather than the ordinary process of laborious thought.~~ Very early in life I *was reading* ~~immersed myself in the most outrageous and~~ mystical ~~of fairy tales~~ *stories*, preferring George MacDonald, Lord Dunsany, Lewis Carroll and L. Frank Baum's Oz series to something like Hardy Boys. Age made no difference to this preoccupation with the fantastic ~~toward which I was pushed as if by an~~

~~invisible and quiet hand. My life, accordingly, took on a more~~
~~and more miraculous character, and~~ I began to frighten my
friends by intuiting their private thoughts.

My earliest yearning for God was inspired by an Irishwoman
who used to sit *with* ~~for~~ me when my parents went out. She was
a devout ~~but simple and unfanatical~~ Catholic; I remember one
Christmas kissing a little effigy of the Christ child when she told
me that he had once lived to redeem the world. I was about five
when I learned about *Padre* ~~Pope~~ Pio, the Italian saint who was
said to bear the marks of the cross on his hands and feet in com-
memoration of his great predecessor. My parents were agnostic
Jews, and completely unsympathetic with my thirst for the divine in spite of their own *artistic temperaments* ~~bohemianism~~
though I recall one incident which seemed to belie this. I was
five, and I stood in the dining room watching my stepfather,
~~Cecil Hemley~~ *chatting* ~~speaking~~ with someone in the hall. A copy
of Buber's *I and Thou* was on the buffet. ~~Naturally,~~ I had never
read this before, and I was mystified by the title. I ~~writhed in an
effort~~ *wanted* to understand what it meant; "Thou," a word which
I had never heard before, sounded like a term for someone of
immense importance. "Mother," I asked. "Is 'Thou' God?" My
mother, who at that time was preoccupied with her writing, answered ~~carelessly~~ that it was. I could not get that book out of my
mind, ~~however,~~ and kept wondering what strange conception of
God a grown man could have, and why it was necessary to write
a book about Him when He was so apparent everywhere. ~~I had
not yet been initiated into the twisted habits of the world, which
has to read books before it will see what it has always inwardly
seen, and which requires proofs for the obvious~~. My stepfather
caught me one afternoon in a kneeling position on the ~~nursery~~
floor, with my arms wildly outspread, crying out "Oh God, I love
you and I wish I could shake hands with you, but then I'd only
be shaking hands with nothing." He always made a joke of my
piety; he was a Greenwich village intellectual and a cum laude
graduate of Amherst, a kind of twentieth-century Faust, who
thought he had exhausted the world's secrets ~~with his own half
diabolical mind, and refused to question the limits of his intellect; it was especially strange because~~ Most of his poetry and
prose were profoundly religious, though from the point of view
of postwar America God had died. He used to recite me nonsense

poetry about little children being devoured by lions and the Jumblies, who had green heads and blue hands ~~playing mercilessly with my imagination until I had nightmares and~~ I began to see real devils' heads peering out of the dark ~~when I tried to sleep~~ . . . *I had nightmares* and screamed so terribly that my parents often had to put me to bed by force.

I have to resist being an apologist for either my mother or my sister, in the same way I have to resist being critical or patronizing to either—although this is an impossible task I've set for myself. How can one be objective about one's family? How can one resist the urge to edit, to become the family spin doctor? There are old scores to settle, I'm sure, ones I'm not even consciously aware of—although, if I become aware of them in the telling, I'll let you in on them—perhaps. We are constantly, as we read, looking for conclusions, judgments to be made, sometimes villains. I suppose I am the villain in all this for writing it down, manipulating the texts I choose to uncover for you, the juxtapositions. I am playing God, manipulating. I suppose some might look at it that way, and it's true in the sense that any writer manipulates. My sister manipulates. My mother manipulates. Even the reader manipulates in the conclusions she draws.

Many of my mother's edits in my sister's manuscript seem entirely justified to me. The places I wince are those where Nola sounds too self-important, a little pompous and self-congratulatory. Yes, I know those are qualities that fit me as well right now—criticizing my dead sister, for heaven's sake, who wrote those words nearly thirty years ago never knowing that her kid brother would pick them apart. And patronizing. I know, but that doesn't stop me from having those feelings, from wincing in certain places. Too much the writing teacher in me, I suppose. Too much of my mother, whose religion is writing, who has an alliance to the facts, but shudders at the truth, and to my father, the modern-day Faust with his "half diabolical mind" who feels he's discovered all the world's secrets. That's where my father and I separate company. My mind, three-quarters diabolical, has not even uncovered one of the world's secrets, although sometimes a secret feels close.

I would have cut "I writhed in an effort," just as my mother had cut it from my sister's text, but there are other choices, other substitutions that I wonder about. For a moment, I'd like to put those questions aside, and instead question my sister's views of events—did she really have such a sophisticated notion of God when she was five years old?

Asking my father about Martin Buber? Seeing God in everything? A young pantheist? I don't doubt it—not in Nola's case. I wasn't born yet, and so have no way of knowing whether Nola was truly this precocious, although my mother corroborates the story of Nola's talking to God—albeit in a different setting. But of course, my sister must exaggerate in places, as my mother warned in her letter. Nola was sick when she wrote this. She was hallucinating at times, talking to invisible beings who surrounded her. How could she remember events straight-on? But I wasn't there and neither was my mother, not all the time, and so maybe everything Nola says *is* true, or at least no more exaggerated than anyone else's memory.

We are not invading her privacy by asking these questions, by challenging her stories. Clearly, she meant for this book to be seen by others, just as my mother expected her journals to be saved for posterity—the voice, the stance, is a public one. We are her reviewers.

I couldn't imagine my own daughter, Olivia, at the same age, asking about Martin Buber, but I can imagine the kindling of an interest in metaphysics. Recently, my wife found a Canadian coin on a path in the woods. The coin was dated 1929 and had a portrait of King George on it. Olivia wanted to know who King George was, and Beverly said he used to be the King of England.

"What does he do now?" Olivia asked.

"He's dead," Beverly said.

"Who killed him?" Olivia asked.

"No one," Beverly said. "He was probably very old and sick when he died."

"Where did he go?" Olivia asked.

We had not really discussed this issue in our family, and so Beverly said, somewhat uncertainly, "I guess he went to Heaven."

Olivia, sensing Beverly's hesitation, said, "Or maybe he went to college."

I laughed when Beverly told me this, and recounted this anecdote to several friends, as well as to my mother—it's the kind of ready-made story one might expect to see in *Reader's Digest,* as one friend suggested.

Still, I'm bothered that Beverly and I were so unprepared for her natural curiosity. If Olivia had asked me where one goes after one dies, I might have answered, "The bookshelf."

I suppose that no story is entirely innocent when you examine it—I wonder what signals we've been sending Olivia about the life of the mind versus the spiritual nature of things. Heaven and college, in some schemata, could be seen as polar opposites. The intellect, I acknowledge, is a miserable failure when it comes to transcendence. Instead, the intellect traps us where we know we shouldn't be; knowledge, perhaps, was forbidden by God for our own safety, for our own sanity. And yet, we keep after it, doggedly, toward our own self-destruction. That is the diabolical side of the pursuit of knowledge, the pleasure of it, disobedience, having a hand in what we know is wrong for us. A kind of intellectual leap of faith, if that's not a complete contradiction in terms; there must be something in it, we reason, we reason, we reason.

What you must have noticed, as I did in the above passages from my sister's memoir, were those places my mother crossed out that were not so much edits of style as edits of content. Why, I wonder, does she cut out these words: "I had not yet been initiated into the twisted habits of this world, which has to read books before it will see what it has always inwardly seen, and which requires proofs for the obvious." This seems like a perfectly intriguing and possibly true statement, although rife with interesting contradictions. I want that passage kept in my sister's book simply so I can argue with it. Nothing is obvious until we write it down, I want to say, defending words. The Koran, the Bible, *I and Thou*, your own words, Nola, the words of your spiritual master, Sri Ramanuja. Whatever is "inwardly seen" requires all the more proof because who can trust what one sees inwardly? For my mother, crossing out these words must have been an easy decision—heresy, as she saw it, as I see it, even.

And it's interesting that my mother crossed out the criticisms of my father, " . . . his own half-diabolical mind, and refused to question the limits of his own intellect . . ." Not that my mother is protective of my father's memory—although she might have been in the early seventies when she made these editorial changes. More than once, she's told me he was an egoist, and that many of Nola's problems might have been less severe if he'd treated her more kindly—she was not his daughter, and he could not bring himself to truly care for her. Perhaps my mother crossed out these words because she thought they were overwrought, or perhaps she simply thought they weren't true, that he *did* question the limits of his own intellect. Still, this was Nola's version of my father, and she should be allowed her say. And, I have to remind myself that these changes my mother made were with Nola's consent. Nevertheless, I want the original.

My mother, too, felt conflict over letting my sister speak for herself and retaining some control over the story. When my mother first told me of the autobiography's existence, she said, "Her mode of expression was so flowery. I began cutting things out and I decided I didn't want to cut anything out. I wanted it to be the way it is. It's very hard for me to face anything about Nola. So I never did anything with it."

Almost every page in my sister's memoir has a revelation for me, but it's these opening pages that I choose to examine right now—another crossed-out passage, "the invisible and quiet hand." Who hasn't felt that quiet and invisible hand, even if we call it coincidence?

Coincidences—things fall into place in a way that most writers are used to—intuition is a word I might be comfortable with. Unlocking the unconscious? That's a little too tainted, like the jargon of a late-seventies workshop. Fate? That's a word the whole twentieth century renounces. I'm as skeptical as anyone else. I'm as gullible as anyone else. Synchronicity? I need to call this phenomenon something. Little miracle. I go to the edge of belief and pull back before I'm caught in it.

Flipping through Nola's memoirs I find this quote:

> That which is passes away, but being does not pass away. That which knows passes away, but knowledge does not pass away. That which loves passes away, but love does not pass away.

The quote moves me, because Nola wrote it, typed it, in her auto-biography. Of all the pages of the text, it's this one quote that I take note of. It seems almost a message to me, that I shouldn't mourn, but this is too egocentric, the thought that my sister could have written something twenty-five years ago, secretly addressed to me. I read every text in this way, especially the texts that my family leaves behind. I mull over the quote and then consider using it as the epigraph of my book. Months later, my mother sends me a box of Nola's papers . . . I find the quote again, although I wasn't looking for it, written on the back of a pamphlet from Nola's guru. Yes, I know it proves nothing. I'm not try-ing to prove anything. Quite the opposite. I'm afraid of proofs. Let's mock proof, mock the obvious. (I had not yet been initiated into the twisted habits of the world, which has to read books before it will see what it has always inwardly seen, and which requires proofs for

~~the obvious.~~) Nevertheless, the quote is exactly the same (That which is passes away/but being does not pass away . . .), although broken off into lines like a poem, with these added lines:

> True Vision comes only to the seer
> Who sees beyond himself and his desires

Sure, that's the basis of most religions, opposite of most art (except perhaps religious), setting its faith in expression of the self. What's remarkable to me isn't the idea so much as the juxtaposition, the fact that I have lifted it out of Nola's text once, on my own, and then, months later found the same quote, in her hand, in another batch of papers.

Another passage in Nola's autobiography that stands out describes the summer of 1967 when Nola traveled alone through Rome and the Middle East. In Rome, she went to the Sistine Chapel and stood "for three hours in suspension under the Sistine ceiling, trying to recognize among those luminous forms something in relation to my own vision and that of Michelangelo." Just imagine a young American woman who has visions standing beneath the Sistine ceiling for three hours trying to see if her visions matched Michelangelo's—searching earnestly for sublime expression, confident that it can be found.

And then, in that same box of Nola's letters and school papers and report cards my mother sent, I come across a three-by-five manila envelope with a clasp. The envelope is bulging with something, more papers I figure. When I undo the clasp, more than a hundred blank postcards from my sister's trip spill out—four postcards of details from the Sistine Chapel on top. I study them looking for a vision other than Michelangelo's, looking for my sister in the portraits of the saved and the portraits of the damned.

I'm torn between my mother's view of the world, salvation through art, and my sister's, salvation through the spirit, not that the two are mutually exclusive. My mother reminds me that literature's roots are in the spiritual—the Dionysian mysteries, or the spiritual stories that every culture shares. And even these books have gone through many versions, many differences of text and interpretation before an official text was agreed upon.

I have kept a journal since I was sixteen, like my mother, and now I have a collection of about twenty hardback journals of various sizes, not ordered in any way. Sometimes I flip through them, making discoveries, rediscovering a story idea, an outline, an overheard snatch of dialogue. After my grandmother died, I found among her belongings a blank journal with yellowed paper—a gray cover with the printed word "Journal" written in a kind of nineteenth-century script, although the journal probably dated back only to the twenties or thirties, maybe the forties. I claimed this blank journal as my own, although this time I did not have to steal it, as I did with the court papers about my sister I found when Ida was still alive. After my grandmother's death, we also discovered that she had saved every tax return she had ever filed, dating all the way back to the first year a federal income tax was imposed. I almost wanted to save these documents, too.

Of the few possessions of Ida's I claimed for myself, this blank journal was one of them, and I used it as my own for several months, until I realized that its yellowed pages were only going to become yellower, and if I wanted to save my words for more than ten or fifteen years, I had better find something else to write in.

Yesterday, I was scouring all of my journals, looking for an incident I had recorded in one of them around 1981. I never located the passage I was looking for, but instead stopped in this yellowed journal, the words in it dating from my early twenties. I found an outline, or the beginning of an outline, of a story that I had started then abandoned, about Nola. The outline consisted mostly of questions:

What is the story?

Is it about Nola going mad? No, too long a tale.
Is it about death? ~~No, because the~~ No
Is it about Change? No
or is it about love?—Yes

If it is about any one
of these four things,
then the others must be
removed.

Cut out the madness
Cut out the death

These instructions seem to me now not so much the recipe for a successful story as instructions to myself, what I was telling myself to remember when I remembered Nola.

Tearsheets

My mother has never wanted much more from life than to be an artist. Money has never mattered to her. She taught her children to scorn it, and always told me, at least, that the most precious commodity I had was time, that time was the only true currency of value.

In 1941, she decided to move from Brooklyn to Manhattan to become a writer. She had grown up in a large extended family on Bay 26th in Bensonhurst, with her younger brother Alan and their mother Ida, who had been widowed in her early thirties. Ida was a teacher in the public-school system of New York, a woman who swung between extremes of practicality and extravagance—who, in the midst of the Depression, thought little of taking her children on a trip across country or down to Cuba, and who fed hungry children in her classes, a practical but fun-loving woman who had helped her family weather the Depression with her steady teaching income and presents from her married boyfriend. She knew, I suppose, the right ways to save money, but also the right ways to spend it. Ida was the most frugal person I ever knew, investing, over her lifetime, in stocks, saving everything, helping out my mother when she needed it. In her eighties, she helped design a new house, saw it built, and moved into it from the house she'd owned in Long Beach, Long Island, since the late 1940s.

The only unwise thing she ever did concerning money, as far as I knew, was to share some of it with me. When I was thirteen, she presented me with a wonderful collection of silver dollars, Franklin half-dollars, buffalo nickels, and Indian head pennies, which I kept for maybe a year before pawning the collection for twenty-five dollars to buy comic books . . . my comic-book collection would be worth thousands of dollars today, but I sold it when I was nineteen. Unfortunately, I inherited my mother's money sense, not Ida's.

My uncle Alan was his mother's son, and today is a wealthy retired dentist in Calabasas, California. And all of my great aunts and uncles, gone now but the youngest, Carrie, saved and invested and had money in their old age. My mother, though, rejected their, what she deemed, bourgeois values.

One of her journal entries from the forties:

> In America one is constantly adjusting oneself to the viewpoints of opposing societies . . . for example, no sooner does one come to the sad knowledge that in bourgeois groups everything is justified by personal material gain . . . than one is swept into a group of naive communists who think that humanity is good and one works only for the enlightenment and elevation of society . . . or else one swerves from a group of individual materialists into one of intellectual moralists . . . or from those who are emotional and lusty to those who understand only intellectual discourse . . . How can one who has known the viewpoints of these various groups fail to retain some residue of the preceding one as he passes into the next . . . so that adjustment is always difficult, always surprising? Yet how can such a person take sides, when he sees, as he inevitably must, that there is something valid in each? What happens in the end? Does he become philosophical, partisan, or merely neutralized?

This uncertainty, this apprehension of what's valid in opposing viewpoints, and the fear of becoming neutralized, is something I've inherited from my mother. It's something I don't think I'll ever defeat, this profound uncertainty and attraction to contradiction. It's most clearly what makes me her son.

Part of the summer of 1941, my mother spent at the Cummington School for the Arts. My mother's love of both writing and visual arts fit well with the school's credo, as they wanted students who were active in more than one art. But it was for writing that she primarily attended the school—to study with Katherine Anne Porter, who, at the last minute, was unable to attend. Still, there were plenty of other writers to work with: the poets Delmore Schwartz, Marianne Moore, Allen Tate, and critics R. P. Blackmur and Malcolm Cowley. She had met Delmore Schwartz before, and he was to keep surfacing in her life, marrying one of her good friends, the writer Elizabeth Pollet—and Schwartz was also friends later with my father. But they met first in the late 1930s when my mother wrote Schwartz a fan letter for a story of his she'd read in the *Partisan Review*, "In Dreams Begin Responsibilities." He apparently thought she was a man, as she signed her letter, "E. S. Gottlieb," and invited her to meet him at his attic apartment off of Washington Square. "I sat on a chair and he sat on his bed, or crouched on his bed. It seems to me in retrospect that he was in shadows all the time because I couldn't hear him." My mother has had a lifelong hearing problem, and Schwartz was a mumbler, so she couldn't hear a word he said. "He kept talking to me and I didn't know what he was saying . . . I don't know what he asked me and I don't know how I got through that but sometime later he met Jean Garrigue and mentioned having met me. And he said, 'She's a strange girl.'"

*   *   *

Sept. 15, 1941

Dear mother,

I do appreciate all you have done for me . . . but it is impossible for you to do any more, for I have turned into an entirely different person from what you expected. This is not your fault . . . it does not even mean that because you were indulgent I have become so-and-so. What it means is that certain traits which were always part of me, even in my childhood, traits I was born with, have become strengthened, have learned to assert themselves . . . and I want them always to be strong . . . I cannot be anything but what I am, and since it clashes with what you would like me to be, I think I had better move away. If I stayed here any longer I would lose time . . . that is all I am afraid of . . . losing time. I am a writer, before anything else, and my life must form a pattern on that theme. By living in the city I shall have a better chance to know the people who will help me, people like myself who are interested, as much as I am, in those things that mean most to me . . . people who see life in an entirely different light from the way you see it. It is even possible that they may help me find work . . . I have had offers . . . but I must be near them, accessible. I am aware of all the flaws in living alone . . . and I am only too conscious of the need for money . . . but I want to take a chance, because it means so much to me. You don't know how important it is for me, from now on, to think and write and act exclusively as myself, with no imposed identity. I must concentrate on writing, I really must . . . it is the only way for me to save this precious thing, my talent. It sounds selfish, I know, and it is completely out of form with your attitude toward life, but I must be that selfish, I must act that way, I must be unconventional, if you think of it that way, for it is the only way for me to live, and I must live my own way, not yours or anyone else's. My need for self-fulfillment is as powerful as your need for your own way of living.

Please try to forgive me. I don't want to hurt you. I never did. I only want to be left alone to live as I must live. God knows, there are difficulties enough in just being a writer, without the added conflict between child and parent.

Love,
Elaine

My mother doesn't remember Ida's reaction to this letter, so maybe it was never delivered. But if it was, then I can guess Ida reacted with silence, or a sigh, the sigh of the martyred parent who has done everything for her child and is repaid with what? She wants to be a writer in New York.

She was twenty-five in 1941, old enough, it seems to me now, to live on her own where and how she chose. But three months before Pearl Harbor, the country was still slogging through the Depression, and where were the jobs? And nice young women didn't go off alone to live in Greenwich Village and become writers.

My grandmother had just purchased a beach house in Long Island.

Why don't you go there to live, to Long Beach? You could write there. No one would bother you. I wouldn't bother you—since you think I'm such a nuisance.

It's not that at all. You're missing the point. Anyway, there's no one in Long Beach, no one . . . oh please, mother, this isn't easy for me either.

Yes, that must be how my grandmother reacted. I know this, not because I asked my mother and she told me word for word, but I know all the same . . . . Still, was it that year that Ida bought the beach house in Long Beach? *I* would go there to write, to be alone for a while. But the beach house has long since been sold. The last time I saw it was almost ten years ago. I walked past the white stucco wall—saw the tin G again embellished on the screen door—G for Gottlieb. My grandmother's garden had not been well tended in years. I cried a little bit as I walked by. The giant fir tree still crowded the front stoop and the juniper bush was still there where Nola had fallen in when she was a toddler. Not my memory, but my mother's. A family legend. And Nola, around that time, started calling our grandmother Ida, not Grandma, and that's the name that stuck for all of us.

I know how that conversation went. I was there in a way. I don't want to know all the facts, after all. The facts are boring . . . bourgeois, not my currency.

Actually, my mother tells me that Ida bought the beach house in 1947, the year Nola was born. So the beach house was not an option. The facts keep pulling me under.

My mother's journals can't be trusted either. Her journals from this time are full of yearnings and longings and nameless fears. I think my mother knew that someone would read these journal entries someday, or at least she hoped they would. Maybe not her son, but a critic per-haps. The entries seem written with an eye clearly peeled toward pos-terity, and for that reason they don't seem completely natural to me, like one of those old author's photos with a guy holding a pipe, caught, it seems, in a pure moment of brilliant reflection.

When America entered the war three months later, my mother was certain that Hitler was going to come to America. In 1942, this seemed like a distinct possibility, and my mother, a young Jewish intellectual, was justly terrified by Hitler's seeming invincibility as he invaded and colonized most of Europe over the course of a few short years. She was terrified of death, terrified of the war, and so decided to take a war job, to face her fears head-on. Her dreams of becoming a writer in New York were postponed as she took one war job after another, not terrifi-cally suited to any of them, first inspecting radios in Chicago for the Signal Corps, then being trained to teach photography to the Army Air Corps in Denver.

She had always been interested in photography, so the job seemed right for her. Unfortunately, a measles epidemic swept through the camp, and my mother caught the virus just as Ida was coming to see her for a visit. Ida took care of her in her hotel room, but didn't want to pay the rate for a double. So every time the maid came to clean the room, my mother, feverish, jumped out of bed and hid in the bathroom behind the shower curtain, while my grandmother found ways to keep the maid at bay.

When my mother finally recovered, the army didn't want her back. She'd told them she was sick, but they didn't believe her. Someone reported seeing her in downtown Denver with an officer on each arm.

But that's such a cliché. If they'd only allowed my mother to tell her version, I'm sure they would have at least been entertained by the image of her hiding from the maid so Ida wouldn't have to pay double occupancy. Who could make up such a detail? It calls up all kinds of associations, not all of them humorous, but other types of clichés appropriate to the time. One can call up the same scene being played out in various apartments and houses throughout Europe, someone huddled in a bath, hiding, but not from the maid. One can read this as an illustrative story, as Hitler might have, or Goebbels, of the mind of the Jew—the stereotype of the Jew as someone who will go to extremes to avoid payment of a bill.

So my mother, a civilian who couldn't be court-martialed, was "washed-out" of the Army Air Corps, the civilian equivalent of the court-martial. She was not believed.

In 1946, a story of hers appeared in Martha Foley's annual anthology, *The Best American Short Stories*. I own a copy of this anthology, and thumbing through it yields, not exactly secrets about my mother's life, but sequences—her biographical note, for instance, at the end of the book gives me an encapsulated history of her life until that point, some of which she might have mentioned in passing, but never in such succinct detail:

> Gottlieb, Elaine. Miss Gottlieb now lives in New York City, where she was born. She has a degree in journalism from New York University and has studied art at The Art Students' League and Columbia University. Various jobs have taken her all over the country, and as a result, she has lived in California, Florida, Wisconsin, New York, Illinois, Colorado, Massachusetts, and North Carolina. Her occupations have included book-selling at Macy's, window dressing, secretarial work, photography for the Army Air Corps, cable writing for The Office of War Information, and radio inspection for the Signal Corps. Since 1940 her book reviews have appeared in *The New*

Republic, New York Herald Tribune, Poetry, Accent, Decision, and others. Her short stories have appeared in *Chimera* and *The Kenyon Review.* At present, she is at work on a novel.

When I read this encapsulated biography, it surprised me. I didn't know that my mother had jobs in Wisconsin and Illinois, nor that she worked for the Office of War Information. I wondered why she thought that none of these facts were important for me to know. I wondered if she neglected to tell me because I didn't need to know. But, if so, then she was wrong, because everyone's life, I believe, is a kind of detective story, every clue of our forebears' lives, every decision, missed opportunity, guessed motivation, a part of the solution to our own existence.

I asked my mother if any of this information was fictionalized, if she had embellished any of these facts to make her life sound more exotic. She laughed as I read her what she had given fifty years earlier as her supposed biography. "Oh boy, what an embellishment. I didn't live in Massachusetts. I went to the Cummington School one summer. I must have included every summer vacation I ever took."

My mother's story, *The Norm,* is about an affair between a couple of college students, Donald and Muriel. Muriel is Jewish and Donald is a blond Midwesterner, although this isn't a Jewish *West Side Story.* It's a story about accepted norms of behavior, and how the two of them struggle against these norms, especially Muriel, but eventually drift off into the preordained patterns of their lives, a kind of mutual betrayal of one another by default.

It's a moving story, written in an unabashed romantic style, more suited perhaps to the 1940s than today—but more importantly, it's my mother's story, written over and over again in her life and her writing—a young woman or an older woman seeking an escape from the norm, from the expectations of parents and society, makes some bittersweet choices, searches for love and meaning, finds it briefly, and then sees it slip from her grasp.

For me, every bit of writing I read by my mother is somehow prescient, somehow reflects the future—each sentence a kind of family prophecy.

In the beginning of their relationship, Donald and Muriel are invited to a psychology lecture at a local mental institution. The lecture turns out to be more of a brutal sideshow, a callous demonstration of a patient's dementia that has the other students laughing, but horrifies Muriel.

> "Isn't it strange," she said, "that for all those college students any deviation from the norm is laughable as if they didn't believe it, as if anything outside their world were part of a show, unreal?"
>
> "They're stupid," he said.
>
> They put their arms around each other's waist, and there on the sunny path, surrounded by cultivated flowers and healthy trees they became a happy unit, blessed by sunshine and alive in time.

Muriel, annoyed and unconcerned with rules of behavior and norms, eventually goes to live with Donald in his apartment, but, needing money, she tries to pawn a ring that her parents gave her for her twenty-first birthday.

> Here it was, the perfect little ring, a symbol of bourgeois waste, of misplacement of values. What did it mean to her that a certain brightness shone on her little finger? How important was her little finger?
>
> She remembered again her shameful journey, the trip to the jewelry store in town. She wished to trade in her family's sentimentality and misjudged values for something more logical . . . love. If she could change the ring into money, she could stay here with Donald . . . . Why was any worldly effort necessary so that she and Donald might live together, why did it not just take care of itself? And she had been ashamed that she must do something so vulgar, so humiliating, as to try to pawn this worthless ring for her love.

This is fiction obviously, and I've grown up in a family of fiction writers, believing and telling everyone that fiction is not the truth—or, is a different kind of truth, ultimately more valuable than any odd assortment of facts. Most writers, including me, caution anyone from reading a work of fiction as akin to the author's life. Yes, we try to convince the reader that what we're saying is true while we have the reader within the borders of the story we're telling. But as soon as we've released the reader, and he or she wants to know what really happened, we shy away. What really happened is beside the point, we say, with a slight attitude of superiority. And yet, maybe what really happened is important and shreds of biography remain in even the most altered piece of fiction.

But when I read that story of my mother's, "The Norm," I wonder if she ever did have such an affair. Maybe not before she wrote the story, but there's something in the story that seems to foretell her brief life with Elliot Chess, Nola's father. And in the scene of Muriel's disgust with the treatment of the patients at the mental hospital there's a reminder to me of Nola's time in the mental hospital in Missouri, of Nola's voices and demons, and my mother's unwavering compassion and love for her. Like the writings of Nostradamus, I suppose one can see whatever one wants in here. I even see myself in this story—I see this attempt to capture my sister and mother's life as necessary, but potentially dangerous. I'm not sure what I'll uncover. In the psychology class that Muriel and Donald visit, the professor explains one form of dementia:

> The child's daydream is a comparatively harmless form of the escape from reality that later, if allowed to develop, absorbs the entire personality, so that we finally see the individual becoming his own escape, utterly incapable, in more advanced cases, of remembering the real past, which was to him distasteful . . .

But there is no real past; it's all a daydream, it seems, or an endless series of clues and discoveries that seem circular, that can naturally, inevitably, drive one mad.

The Valley of Ednah[1]

> When Rabbi Meir came to Rabbi Ishmael and gave his profession
> as a scribe (of the Torah) the latter required of him the utmost
> care, "for if you leave out a single letter or write a single letter too
> much, you will be found as one who destroys the whole world."
>
> ERUV. 13A

. . . My one great friend of childhood and adolescence was Isaac
Singer, with whom I got into long discussions about the nature
of the afterlife, and read from his small library of spiritual and
psychic books. I communicated to him all my dreams, with
which he was much ~~more~~ in sympathy ~~than my parents, and
was later to hypnotize him at fifteen in a very successful exper-~~

---

1. The following is a portion of the first "chapter" of Nola's memoir, which I
have broken off at, what seems to me, a natural stopping place. The chapter
heading is my own invention, and I, like my mother before me, have done some
editing of Nola's original—not for style or content, but for the sake of brevity.
Nola sometimes records page after numbing page of her dreams, and while a
couple of them are crucial, I believe, to an understanding of who she was, I
didn't think the reader would have the patience to wade through them all, nor
through the sometimes lofty and tangential descriptions peppering Nola's
memoir. So, knowing full well that I am perhaps tainting Nola's text, I shrug my
shoulders finally and say, You'll have to trust me on this one. My edits are indicated with ellipses. I have also included, after much deliberation, my mother's
edits and Nola's edits. I had originally thought I'd expunge the text of all edits
and present the reader with a "clean" copy, but discovering such a copy is nearly
impossible, and this story is as much about editing as it is uncovering the original. The crossed-out passages are, to me, often as interesting as the passages that
have been kept—why they've been crossed out is the question, and by whom, my
mother or Nola? I believe that the earlier substitutions are my mother's, although not exclusively. Later on, when my mother gave up, finding the task too
difficult, too tiring and painful, Nola took over, and now finally, I'm trying to tell
her story again, although perhaps not in a fashion she or my mother anticipated.

iment aimed at discovering his psychic potential. He seemed to
know much more about the psychic than I did, and took me once
to an obscure shop in Manhattan where we tried unsuccessfully
to get e.s.p. cards. After a while, though, he too could not *comprehend* understand why I was more concerned with the afterlife
than with the present one, and kept telling me that an excessive
interest in the spiritual was "unhealthy," and why didn't I get
interested in other things, until the two of us finally parted company, since he was unable to understand me.

I continued to experience my solitary visions, until they
moved me to discover their source and cause, and I could think
of nothing else. At the age of twelve I left the Bronx with my parents to live in Manhattan, and attend the New Lincoln school. It
was a private, progressive institution and we were indoctrinated
into Eastern culture at a very early age, since it was the school
policy to provide its pupils with a training in disciplines that
were generally ignored in the majority of public schools. When
I was twelve, therefore, I began reading the teachings of the
compassionate Buddha, the works of Lao-Tze, and Pearl Buck;
the latter inspired me to write a poem which attempted to di-
vinize the earth . . . like Blake I began to compare the cosmic
forces which had invaded my life and dreams to the music of
human breath exhaled upon a flower . . . .

It was at this point that I had the most critical experience of
my *childhood* life, and the precursor of a vast chain of mystical
visions which were at last to lead me to my guru. It was the
night of December 26th, the day after Christmas. The year was
1960, and I was still thirteen. I began to have a fantastic dream.
I was walking on a dense, grey and rocky terrain with a group of
friends, many of whom I recognized as classmates. We were
chattering to each other in as unenlightened a way as possible,
discussing our possessions, what we had gotten for Chanukah,
and exchanging words with the most greedy and self-absorbed
overtones imaginable. There was a red-haired woman among us
whom we could not help regarding as very mysterious, since she
would not take part in our gossip but preserved on her face the
most incongruous smile, which never altered with any of the
things we said but seemed to carry on an existence of its own,
and required no outer encouragement . . . .

The landscape throughout this initial stage of my dream was

dull, wild, and barren, without pattern or design in the shifting plains, insensitive-looking and pointless . . . corresponding to the state of our own minds. Suddenly the entire group stopped in terror and disbelief. Without our conscious knowledge, but nevertheless, very steadily, we had been led up a steep hill to a pass between two towering mountains, and found ourselves on the brink of a great cliff hanging over a bottomless abyss. White fumes reeled up from its depths, as if enticing the air on which they rose to consume itself and become fire. As we stood there paralyzed with fright, trying to reconcile ourselves to the scene by pretending that it was a "tourist attraction" of some kind, our leader, who had thus far been elusive and fairly silent, looked at us with a terrible ecstasy in her eyes, and *threw* us, with almost superhuman strength, one by one over the cliff. The whole herd of travelers, terrorized, shrieked in a single *agonized* voice ~~whose tone of agony it was death to hear~~, and the memory of which I afterwards repressed. One by one we shot down over stones and stubble, ~~with despair on each side and~~ *into* a vast nothingness ~~below.~~ Again, I was certain that I was going to die, and prepared for a loss of consciousness. Suddenly, without any warning or intimation that this was going to happen, we found ourselves descending at a steadily decreasing rate, and when, miraculously, we were nearly at the bottom of this interminable drop, we were floating as gently as feathers ~~sporting~~ in the wind. When we had nearly reached the bottom we were submerged in a wide, dark lake ~~whose profound dampness melted into our souls until we felt that we were in purgatory and were being washed by the vast waters of the spirit~~ *whose waters seemed to purge us*. Finally the waters dispersed, and we were floating over a low, ~~gentle~~ *misty* plain ~~whose greenness could scarcely be separated from the nets of rain that had been thrown upon it as if from a recent shower~~. The landscape had become transformed, and now even the rocks ~~which stood at~~ the farthest ~~distance~~ from ~~where we stayed~~ us pulsed with a continuous rhythm ~~in sympathy with the currents of our own thought, which had just undergone a drastic change~~. From the moment we had begun our descent into the valley a force so tremendous it caused unspeakable pain had begun to press its way ruthlessly into our souls, until we were crushed by its power and our sense of self ~~utterly~~ destroyed. That, we knew, was the real death, and our horror had sprung from an apprehension of nothing but this.

By the time we had reached the base of the valley the murderous Will of we knew not what ~~had completely butchered our own and now~~ possessed us ~~mercilessly, holding us hostage like flies in its perpetual fire~~. When the force had overtaken us beyond all hope of self-recovery, and our spirits had undergone a complete inversion, we experienced a shock. ~~A terrible~~ Ecstasy rushed into us ~~in the midst of our liquidated state~~, until we realized ~~by default~~ that perception of truth ~~can come~~ *comes* only to those who have made a void of themselves, ~~that true vision comes only to the seer who sees beyond himself and his desires~~. In order to possess anything, we found that we had to relinquish all we possessed, and that by canceling ourselves we were preserved. Our enslavement had become our liberty, the object of our dread our highest bliss. The chief property of this valley was that it rejuvenated both body and soul, and now, annihilated and reborn, we floated transfixed, enraptured, stung by each other's beauty. We had indeed died the most fearful death, the only death from which it is possible to fully awaken, to follow the steps of the joyous Dance for which we had been intended . . .

I ~~began to see~~ *noticed* a solitary form in the center of the valley who somehow looked out of harmony with his surroundings, although I could not tell why. I went up to him and discovered that he was the only aged person in the entire valley; his white hair extended to his shoulders, and his skin was pale. (I later made the discovery through a professor of philosophy at a college in New York that the very same motifs which had been prominent in my dream—the fall over the cliff, the death of the ego, the bliss that followed, and the meeting with the old man in the center of the valley, are the exact themes which appeared in the dramatic sequence of the Eleusinian mysteries and other ancient mystery cults, and were the characteristic themes for the rebirth of the soul). He seemed to have been in the area for a long time, and to know all its secrets. I asked him quietly if he would explain to me the origin of the valley, how it and its beautiful properties came into being. He nodded graciously . . . in acknowledgment of my question and answered: "The Lord Jesus flew over this valley years ago and blessed it, and since then it has retained the property of rejuvenating the body and soul." He then revealed to me the name of the valley, which sounded like ~~an atrocious~~ common name, but which was spelled very differently: E-D-N-A-H. I looked at him in astonishment, since no one in my family or among any of our friends had that name, especially with that particular spelling. I considered it a lousy title for *such* a place ~~which bore such exquisite features~~. When my conversation with the sage (which I assumed him to be from his appearance) was finished I awoke, with an inexplicable feeling that somehow all this had really occurred, that my soul had traveled to another plane during the night and received an invaluable lesson from the Beyond. The whole day I experienced ~~the most violent transcendental~~ *a great* bliss, which I could communicate to no one because it would have been met with denial and suspicion. The one memory which ~~was engraved in my thought the minute~~ *I retained when* I awoke was the kind of rejuvenation which had occurred ~~im-plied~~ an absolute freedom from possessions or material impediments of any kind, which were simply nothing, having no lasting substance and therefore absolutely fruitless . . . My materialism ~~had~~ vanished overnight, and I now saw clearly what my soul would be seeking beyond anything else, although I had no idea at the time how I could obtain it.

A few days later I ~~grew curious~~ *began to wonder* about the name which my aging friend had given me, since I had never attached any importance to it or heard it with that spelling before. I searched in the Dictionary of Common Names, and finally found my word, with the same spelling, which was apparently the precursor of the present female name. It was of very ancient Greek and Egyptian origin, probably used at the time of Christ, and it was the only name in that part of the dictionary which meant rejuvenation. I later discovered that some other friends of mine (in college) had had the same dream at about the same age (puberty: ~~although~~ the ancients regarded the ceremony of puberty as significant of a far greater metaphysical rebirth. My own guru became a realized soul at the age of thirteen, and the number in general is said to have a profound esoteric vibration; Christ, for example, originally had thirteen Apostles). A few months afterwards, I related my dream to Isaac Singer, who told me that the "pass between two mountains" is the Biblical symbol for death. I then told him the name of the valley. "But that is the old Hebrew expression we use to signify the turning point of one's life," he gasped. "How in the name of God did you ~~come to~~ know ~~it~~ *that*?" . . .

The Ghost on the Staircase

I've seen a ghost. The sentence throws suspicion on my credibility immediately. One either believes or doesn't believe. There seems to be little room for an in-between stance. "You *think* you saw a ghost," someone says. "You're making it up," says another. "You believe you saw a ghost, and that's the important thing," another says in a patronizing tone. Or, "I've seen one, too. I see them all the time." And then I doubt *your* credibility, and wonder about your sanity. Or, "I wish I could see one." But that's not something to wish for. Don't wish for that. Even though it was one of the defining moments of my childhood, it was not a pleasant defining moment, and has thrown the rest of my life into turmoil, made me doubt myself, my perceptions, my memories and beliefs.

And I wonder what about that simple statement threatens some of us so much (and I'm including myself here because I'm threatened, too), why we want to dismiss the seer so immediately. I suppose such a statement backs us against a wall, makes us stop and consider limitless possibilities, and we're used to limits; the supreme comfort of the material world is that it does not demand anything but our tangible bodies creating a tangible wake of cause and effect around us.

I've seen a ghost. Or, I think I saw one. No, I'm sure of it. There I am, doubting myself again, wondering whether even the text of my own life is something I can agree on.

And, I have a witness, someone else who was there as well. My older brother, Jonathan. Jonny and I agree on so little these days, it's amazing we still agree on this, that we both saw a ghost when I was five and he was ten.

This was 1963 and we were living in Athens, Ohio. We lived our first year in Athens in a rambling broken-down home that was over a hundred years old. It had bricks missing from its foundation, and seemed to sag everywhere.

Athens impressed me from the start. In fact, I recall the moment I set foot in Athens as a kind of quasi-religious experience. My parents and the rest of the family had gone ahead while I stayed with Ida in Long Beach, and then, when things were set up, Ida and I took the train down from New York to Columbus, and then we took a Greyhound from Columbus to Athens.

When I stepped out of the bus, my grandmother right behind me, I stood in front of the Greyhound station for a moment, wondering where I had landed.

"Robin, this is your new home," Ida told me.

Nothing around me looked familiar. My family could tell me a thousand times where I was going and how much I'd like it when I arrived, but until I experienced it myself, I could not know. I had no real expectations at five, or hazy ones at best.

There was a tree planted in the sidewalk, not unlike trees planted along sidewalks in Manhattan, so I don't know why this particular tree seemed suddenly so remarkable, but I looked up in its branches and saw the sun sparkle through it. Certainly I'd seen the sun glitter through trees before, but this time was different. This time the light seemed to lift me up through the branches and the green was of such a beauty as I'd never experienced, and all I know was that I was going up and up through those branches without a scratch. What does a five-year-old know or need of ecstasy, but five-year-olds know much more than we sometimes assume, more than they can communicate. The problem is communication, that's all, and the long forgetting and learning of our lives.

I do not remember the breaking of that dream, the moment at which Ida called my name and pushed me ahead of her, the moment at which I fell back down and saw that tree as only another tree, or noticed the dog running on the sign in front of the station, and the familiar concrete sidewalk beneath my feet. What I remember is that feeling, although only dimly now. What I remember is that light through the branches burning into me, engraving itself inside me.

That Halloween, I was a ghost. The previous Halloween, my first, I had been something else, Prince Valiant, I think, wearing a stiff plastic mask the entire afternoon and into dinner, refusing to take it off, pushing food into the round hole of the plastic mouth, observing everything like a spy through the eyeholes. During dinner, a neighbor came to the door and told us that her apartment was on fire, and so all of us rushed outside and watched the flames shatter the windows of her apartment and leap outside as we waited on the sidewalk for the fire department to arrive. I assumed this must be what Halloween was all about, watching a fire engulf someone's apartment while wearing a mask. I had been coached by Nola and Jonny to say Trick or Treat, and so I did. I chanted it over and over, "Trick or treat, trick or treat, trick or treat," as I watched, impressed by this Halloween activity, which was a lot better than bobbing for apples, something I'd done in the park across the street that afternoon.

But the next year, the rules changed. We were in a new town, and this time, we were going to take empty bags and return home with our bags filled with candy, an activity that seemed like a fair replacement for a fire. My mother, never much of a planner, cut out a couple of eye-holes in a sheet, and that was my costume. This suited me fine, too. I didn't know what a ghost was, and I didn't much care. What I liked most was this feeling of being covered, wearing a mask, and seeing the rest of the world around me while being at least partially hidden myself. If I ever become a ghost, I'm sure I will be a good one, not a midlist ghost, but one who really gets into his job—not to scare people, but to observe and stay hidden, and only make myself known in order to cast doubt in those who see me, delicious ambiguity and uncertainty, which, after you're used to it, is really what makes life interesting.

*　　*　　*

Nola ran away early that first year—we were all always running away, not to escape a dreadful home life, but out of peevishness, because we were spoiled and expected too much, and also because we were in a hurry to see everything in the world we could see. When Nola suggested that I run away *with* her, I couldn't refuse. I knew that she would take me somewhere I wanted to go.

I don't know how long we walked, but we crossed the muddy Hocking River away from town and walked along a country road in the dark. The sky was brilliant with stars, and Nola knew all of their names and their stories. She told me their stories, archers and bears and frozen lovers, and both of us were so happy with the evening and the stars and the dark shapes of the trees and the gravel under our feet, that we didn't care where we were headed. I remember a car approaching and us climbing inside again and being driven home, but I don't remember the driver this time—my father probably, although it doesn't matter. We were brought back down. I wanted to keep walking. There were so many stars she hadn't yet told me about. I didn't know all their names.

Kennedy was assassinated that fall, and Nola wanted immediately to get in touch with his spirit—she always aimed high. The night she decided to try to contact Kennedy was only a couple of days after his death. My mother and father had gone off to a faculty party and left me and Jonathan in Nola's care. Not long after our parents left the house, Nola took out her Ouija board and asked us if we wanted to help her try to get in touch with Kennedy. I only vaguely knew who Kennedy was. I knew he had been killed, primarily because all of my regular TV programs had been preempted, including *Truth or Consequences,* my favorite, and someone who had been sitting on a flagpole for fifty days in a car lot had to come down as soon as Kennedy was shot, and the TV kept showing people crying on the street and in stores or coming down from flagpoles or the steps of churches where the camera showed everyone crying except for one woman who smiled at the camera. The announcer asked, "Who is this woman and why is she smiling? Could she have had something to do with the assassination?" And that's all I really knew about Kennedy, that whoever he was, he was causing a lot of unhappiness. And now my sister wanted to get in touch with him. Neat.

Nola told us to put our fingers on the planchette, LIGHTLY, and not to move it, that it was supposed to move itself. I didn't ask the normal questions one might expect of a five-year-old, like, "How does it move by itself?" I just accepted what Nola had to say as fact, and waited. Slowly, the planchette moved toward the number 1 and then stopped. A number formed and Nola became excited. What I remember is that the number was Kennedy's birthdate, and that Jonny and Nola looked it up in an encyclopedia, and the number turned out to be the right date. Nola insisted that she had not known this, but Jonny said she must have known, that she had probably heard it on the news within the last couple of days and simply forgotten.

In the memoir that Nola wrote during the last year of her life, she mentions this incident, but in such a way as to cast doubt on everything she says before and afterward. She writes:

That was the year of Kennedy's assassination, and I remembered attempting to contact his spirit through a Ouija board, which was at first entirely unsuccessful. After a few attempts at communication I stopped, and turned my attention elsewhere. Five minutes afterwards, when my mind was no longer what we like to describe as "consciously" directed at the board, I was seized with the compulsion to write two dates on a slip of paper that lay on the desk. One of them was 1948, and the other was 1963. I spat out the words, without knowing what I was saying or why, that the famous PT boat rescue had occurred in 1948 and Kennedy's marriage to Jacqueline in 1963. I had never consulted any histories of United States presidencies and at the time I never read the paper, so there was no normal means by which I could have known of the accuracy of these dates. An hour later, I confirmed them in one of my brother's history texts.

Here I am, left with a passage that's so inaccurate as to be almost ridiculous. But also, I must remember that Nola was sick, suffering from hallucinations and voices. To achieve any clarity at all must have been a supreme struggle for her. Of course, 1948 was not the date that Kennedy's PT boat was sunk. The war had been over for three years by then, and he and Jackie were certainly not married in 1963, the year of his death. I was compelled, at first, to find out the correct dates and substitute them, but I realize that would be terribly wrong, the worst kind of manipulation, to make Nola seem infallible. What's important to me is the essence of what she says, not the accuracy of every date, the exact order of things. The essence is accurate, and what I want to capture are her perceptions, even the maddest, because, what's lucid, what's presented clearly and accurately can be the baldest of lies, and what's confused and illogical can sometimes lead to revelation.

Maybe Nola was referring to a different incident than the one I remember, because I don't remember her spitting out any words or writing them down on a piece of paper. It could have happened. I'm not saying it didn't, but my memory of that evening is pretty vivid, and what I remember is her asking for the date of Kennedy's birth, not anything about PT 109 or Jackie.

Nola, in her memoir, didn't mention something else that happened that night, something that I alone remember, and that everyone in my family told me was impossible when I told them. It's remarkable that I haven't forgotten, but the memory is stuck back there, stubborn, refusing to be dislodged.

Nola and Jonny had their backs turned to the Ouija board. They were looking up the dates that the board had given them, and as they argued about something, I was spacing out, my eyes focused dreamily on the planchette. I looked at the round window and it seemed as if there was a light inside. The center started glowing.

I jumped up and tugged at Nola. "It blinked at me," I told her. "There was a light inside it, and it blinked at me."

Neither Jonny nor Nola believed me. They told me that it was just a little window, and there wasn't any light inside. And so, with the resignation of a child who knows it's futile to argue with older people, especially older siblings, I said, "Oh," and dropped it. Jonny and Nola knew so much more than I did, and if they told me I didn't see what I didn't see then I didn't see it. But I thought I did. They didn't see it. How could they tell me I didn't see it? But they seemed so sure. They said it was probably the reflection of the overhead bulb. I looked up at the bulb. Nope, not unless the whole bulb dropped for a moment right smack in the center of the planchette.

Nola kicked us out of her room. She said she wanted to try the Ouija board alone. I remember her physically pushing us out, and then locking the door behind her. Nola's room was on the second floor of the house, and in order to get to our room, we had to walk down a hallway past the staircase landing. As we turned away from Nola's door, Jonny suggested we go watch TV, and I started across the landing a little ahead of him. As I walked, I noticed something down the stairs, something coming around the corner of the staircase. A hat is what I saw first. My mother had worn one out that evening. So I called, "Mom."

I stopped and Jonny stopped. What we saw was a man coming around the corner, an elderly man with a cap on of some sort, and the oddest thing was that he was wearing a kilt. How could I make that up? Why would I want to make that up, as it makes the image slightly ridiculous, and I'm as afraid as anyone of being called a fool or a liar. The image of a man I didn't know walking up our stairs was enough to make me stop, but a man in a dress was even stranger. And I say, a dress, because I had no experience or knowledge of kilts, and to me, it looked like an old man with a gray beard and knobby knees, walking towards us wearing a dress. At first, I stared at him quizzically. I had no expectations, so I looked at Jonathan, whose eyes were big, and he forced out the words, "It's a ghost."

Now I was terrified. A ghost. Jonny and I started pounding on Nola's door and screaming, and when we looked back a moment later, the ghost had vanished. Nola let us in, but reluctantly. She thought naturally that we were making everything up, that we were playing a joke on her, but when she saw how terrified we were, she told us to tell her calmly what had happened, and we couldn't. So she called our parents, and they came home right away from their party. It was a strange reason to be called back from a party, because your children have seen a ghost, but our parents came home, understanding at least, that we were very frightened.

This story has been told many times in my family. I'm sure I have it memorized, that my memories of this evening are memories of memories, and to get at the real truth of that evening is nearly impossible.

I remember this night vividly, but I have always worried that maybe none of this happened, that perhaps Jonathan made it all up. I have always worried that someday Jonathan might tell me that this was an elaborate ruse on his part, that he knew how suggestible I was, and just invented the whole thing as a joke. I know that's not true, but if it is, I don't want to know it, because it would be too manipulative, too diabolical, and I think my brother is neither. There were times he played practical jokes on me when we were young: the time he told me to close my eyes and stick out my tongue, and then he poured Tabasco sauce in my mouth, or the time he lined up my GI Joes against the wall of our house and executed them with his BB gun, and I could go on, as I'm sure he could detail a list of old grievances against me. But this event is too important. It made too much of an impression on me and my view of the world, and the only other person who knows whether it happened or not is my brother, and he has always insisted, always, that it happened that night, that we both saw this apparition. He has even brought it up on his own, to his own children, in my presence, and although they didn't believe him, they thought he was telling a joke, I knew he was telling the truth.

Whenever he mentions our ghost, I watch his face. I study him, and I see the faint trace of a bemused smile and I wonder, as the announcer wondered of the woman on the steps of the Washington Cathedral the day after Kennedy's assassination, why is he smiling? Is there something he's not letting on? Is he partly responsible for this crime?

Recently, I asked him via e-mail what he remembered of that night. Matter-of-factly, in five terse lines, he recalled the Ouija session, but not the particulars. Of the ghost, he recalls a man with a beard, kilt, cap, and bagpipe. A bagpipe? I hadn't remembered a bagpipe. He says we saw the man climbing the stairs and disappearing in front of us. Bewildered, we looked at each other and asked if we had seen the same thing—not the terrified response I remember, but a calmer version of this same ghost story.

Did you see what I saw? Do you believe what I believe? The same questions we're asking each other today, ones we'll never completely answer.

Paging through Nola's memoir, I find a mention of my ghost on one of the later pages, a brief mention, and again, it's distorted, reported in an impossible way. The distortions embarrass me, but they also interest me. When my mother sent Nola's book to me, she warned me of the various distortions, but at that time, I wasn't bothered, not by distortions of things my *mother* remembers, only distortions of things *I* supposedly remember. Why, I wonder now, do we care so much? I suppose this all reflects on the credibility of our own memories, mine and my mother's, and I have always prided myself in having a good memory, at least long-term. My short-term memory is wretched, but if something makes an impression on me, I'll never forget it. Or, that's what I think, what I believe.

In 1972, only nine years distant from the experience, Nola wrote of me:

> He always had been very sensible about ghosts, having entered my room one night years ago, looking at me with a deadpan countenance, and said, "I just met a Scotsman on the stairs. He was in plaids, and he looked pretty mean. Jonny (my other brother) saw him, too. He just disappeared."

But I didn't know what a Scotsman was. I didn't know what plaids were. I never said those words, but does it matter? I'm not sure. Perhaps it only matters to me, and my aim, after all, is to convince you that I saw this thing, to convince myself as well. But, that is impossible. As soon as something happens, it's lost to us forever, as it happened. Then it becomes a new creation, forever renewed and transformed. We live in a time, alternately desperate for and derisive of experience that transcends what we think we know. We are so territorial about our own revelations. I believe in mine, but you, whatever your story, you saw Jesus on a blue flour tortilla or on a screen door, you were kidnapped by aliens who looked like Dolly Parton, your dog spoke and told you to watch your step, buddy—you're crazy. One card short of a full deck. But so what? So what if you're crazy. Why are we afraid of crazy? Still, I worry. I worry about the safety of my perceptions. And maybe I'll patronize you, say, it's not important whether it happened. What's important is that you believe. Like hell. What's important, you

say, is did it happen? Did ... it ... happen? Enough of this polite speculation, this intellectual meandering, this approach to life like it's the
New York Times crossword puzzle and we're cheating, using a pencil instead of a pen. I want to know, DID IT HAPPEN, did I really see what I
think I saw, and if so, then what does that mean? So, even though I was
there when I saw this ghost, I still wish I'd been there.

For children and people who are considered unbalanced, there
seems to be no shut-off valve between the empirical world and the
world of possibility. But I have one. It almost has a physical location,
somewhere near my sinuses, I think, and maybe that's what gives me
headaches, not the dampness in the air. My shut-off valve is twisted
tight, and in the evening I open it up for my dreams, and in the morning when I write, all I need is a little twist, and it's released, partly,
almost unnoticed, but annoying, bothersome with its steady and dis-
tracting drip ... drip ... drip.

Even a liar wants to convince you to shake off your skepticism, and
I have to say that perhaps I'm lying here, that this whole memoir of
Nola's is my own invention. And I say that not to manipulate you, but
so that we may question together how truly or falsely words can ever
relate an experience, and to say that it is not only the truth of an experience that matters, but the telling, the transformation that happens
in the telling, the power of words sometimes to create a new experience, a new truth, that the distortions are not what matters, or at least
not for the ordinary reasons. It is precisely the distortions that tell us
who we are. It is not the event itself that matters, but what we do with
it, how we make it our own. It's not simply a matter of belief—I believe
I saw a ghost when I was five tells you nothing about me, and there's
no way for you to enter into that experience. But I let my sister tell you
the story and I tell you the story in different fashions, and somewhere
there, in that space between contradictions, lies a kind of truth that
perhaps you can enter into and wonder about. It's not belief I'm after,
but wonder, the opening up of possibility.

When I was eighteen or nineteen, my mother took me to a hypnotist to be regressed and try to get to the truth of that night. My mother
had long been intrigued with my ghost story, and thought hypnotic
regression was worth a try. I still have a tape of that regression, although it barely survived the years. A particularly destructive dog of
mine, a brute named Angus (named after the cow because of his looks
and the power of his mind) tried his damnedest to chew it up one
night. He came awfully close. I found him happily gnawing the case off

the cassette, and snatched it from his jaws just in time. Although the casing was destroyed, I managed to re-record the tape, and except for some distortions at the beginning, the session survived. Angus was the kind of happy monster whose goal in life seemed to be to eat through the material world.

Now, I like what he did to my tape, the distortions in the beginning that he created, unconsciously, through his happy gnawing. The voice of the hypnotist and my voice sound, at times, like an old record played at slow speed. These physical distortions serve as a playful reminder of Angus and of the distortions in my own mind that I must not only acknowledge but celebrate. The tape starts with the regression in progress:

> *Hypnotist:* Up at the f . . . oo . . . **theeeeeeere iiiiiss** . . . probably
> . . . aladystanding . . . I waAANT to **Looooook** in direCTION. And,
> **Ta-heLLLme** who she is.
> *Me* (Very softly. A whisper. A mumble. My voice throughout
> sounds slurred and tired): My teacher.
> *Hypnotist:* Can you tell me about her?
> *Me:* She . . . has blond hair and . . . she's young . . . in her 20's . . .
> and boutveryly pretty.
> *Hypnotist* (Distorted, as though a gas pain is rippling through her):
> Do you kn**ohohoho** anyone **el—se** in class?
> *Me:* Um, there's . . . . a boy . . . a boy named Mark. He . . . I don't
> really like him very much.
> *Hypnotist:* Why?
> *Me:* He's . . . sort of stupid . . . and there . . . some girls around.
> *Hypnotist:* You like girls?
> *Me:* Yeah, sure . . . but . . . except . . . **Woooo** we go on the play-
> ground . . . they try to kiss me.
> *Hypnotist* (Amused): They try to **kiss** you?
> *Me:* Uh-huh.
> *Hypnotist:* Do you run away or do you kiss them?
> *Me:* I run away.
> *Hypnotist:* Why?
> *Me:* I don't want them to catch me.
> *Hypnotist:* Oh, are you a fast runner?
> *Me:* Mmmm.
> *Hypnotist* (Much louder, closer to the microphone): Do you like
> school?

Me: Mmmm . . . yeah, it's all right.

Hypnotist: Are you frightened?

Me: No.

Hypnotist: How did you get to school today?

Me: I walked.

Hypnotist: Have you ever been here before?

Me: . . . Yeah.

Hypnotist: When?

Me: . . . In . . . in . . . kindergarten.

Hypnotist: And how old are you?

Me: Six.

Hypnotist (Businesslike): All right, thank you. We're going back even further now, Robin. We're going to go back . . . to a time in the past, even a little bit more distant . . . when you think or maybe you remembered or dreamed or read, we're going to find out for sure about what you saw. We're going to go back to that time and I'm going to count from one to three and you will be there. And you will describe to me *exactly* . . . what is occurring, exactly what is occurring, *everything* that is occurring. One . . . we're going back to that time now . . . two . . . in a moment we'll be there, and you'll describe it to me exactly . . . three . . . back again . . . to that time. What's happening, Robin?

Me: I'm . . . in . . . my . . . I'm in my sister's room . . . and my brother and my sister are there . . . And my sister has the . . . Ouija board . . . and we're . . . playing with it. And asking questions.

Hypnotist: You and she are doing it?

Me: . . . N . . . my brother and her . . . are doing it. I'm watching, and they . . . they're asking questions. . . and . . . my . . . sister . . . asks about . . . President Kennedy . . . about when he . . . was born . . . and . . . the board points to some numbers and they say it's right. They go to the . . . to the . . . dictionary or something and look it up and find that it's right. He's just been . . . killed. But my sister wants to . . . do the Ouija board . . . alone.

Hypnotist: She wants to work it alone? How old are you now?

Me: Five.

Hypnotist: Go ahead and tell me what's happening.

Me: My brother . . . doesn't want to leave . . . and I . . . I . . . I want to watch TV, but she tells us to get out. So we leave, and . . . . we . . . we go out . . . we uh weuh . . . go out the door, and Jonny and I . . . are . . . walking to our room . . . the second floor of the house.

The house is . . . really old and there's a hallway carpet, and . . . and our room has a curtain instead of a door, it just has a big curtain and we have two bedrooms, and . . . and . . .we're going to the room. We look down the stairs . . . and there's . . . from around the corner . . .

Hypnotist: There's what?

Me: There's something . . . coming around the corner.

Hypnotist: Did you say there was a fern? Something coming around the corner. All right.

Me: And I think it's Mom. She's at a party. But . . . well, I call her name . . . and there's no answer. So I call again. And there's no answer. And . . . there's something . . . walking up the stairs, and it's not Mom, and . . . it's a man.

Hypnotist: A man?

Me: Yeah.

Hypnotist: Can you describe him to me?

Me: . . . He has a hat on . . . it's green . . . and a dress.

Hypnotist: A what?

Me: A dress.

Hypnotist (Dumbfounded): A hat and . . . a dress.

Me: And he has . . . a shirt on also. And he's . . . walking up . . . the stairs. And he's not talking or anything. He's going very silently towards my brother and I.

Hypnotist: Does he look the same as you and your brother?

Me (Perplexed): No.

Hypnotist: How is he different?

Me: He's older. He's a . . . a man . . .

Hypnotist: I mean, does he look all right? Is he healthy and is his complexion good? He looks normal or is . . . what does he look like?

Me: He looks very . . . um . . .very . . . he looks like . . . like . . . like . . . um, like my father does when . . . he's . . . um . . . angry oror notnot-not angry, butbut . . . almost angry . . . when he's . . . he looks . . . not my father . . .

Hypnotist: Does he look angry, this man?

Me: No, no. He looks almost angry. Just sort of.

Hypnotist: He's coming up the stairs now, tell me what's happening.

Me: He's around the corner and he's coming up the stairs . . . and my brother . . . tells me . . . that . . . mymy brother isis frightened . . . and he says i. . . he says that it's it's it's a ghost . . . and I get scared and we run to my . . . sister's room and knock on the door, scream, yell, and . . . she doesn't let us in . . . we go back and look, and . . . he's not there anymore. And then my sister opens the door and asks what what happened, what's wrong . . . and . . . we tell her . . . we saw someone, my brother says it was a ghost . . . and I'm . . . scared, but I want to watch TV . . . My sister wants me to tell her about it, so we . . . talk . . . and then . . . I go to my room. And, scared, but I go to my room, and Jonny and I watch TV. We . . . watch . . . um . . . um . . . a . . . it's a comedy show.

Hypnotist: Did you ever see this man . . . before?

Me: No.

Hypnotist: Have you ever seen him since?

Me (With anxiety, a whisper): No.

Hypnotist: Do you think if you did see him again you'd be frightened?

Me: Yeah.

Hypnotist: What would you be afraid of?

Me: . . . His . . . silent anger. Sort of.

Hypnotist: That was scary to you. All right. Now relax. Very, very relaxed now as I count five, getting very very relaxed, four, very, very relaxed, three, still deeper relaxed, two, and one, very, very relaxed . . .

The thing about being in an hypnotic trance, at least for me, is that you kind of know you're in an hypnotic trance, and so how can you really be in a trance if you are aware, on some level of what you're saying? But I've heard this is true of other people as well, that they think they're conscious and in control while they're in a hypnotic state. It's a strange feeling, like being awake and not awake, or the moment in a dream, when you suddenly become aware that you're in a dream. That's what surprised me about being hypnotized, that I thought I was in control, I was aware of what I was saying, I was aware that I was under, and so I couldn't really be under. Or maybe I could. Just as I'm conscious of talking, but not sure what I'm going to say until the words form on my lips. Or writing. Maybe, in some ways, we're always, or often, in a trance, and think we're in control when, in fact, another portion of our mind, like the hypnotist with her questions, directs our thoughts—gently probing, backing up, making sure we're in the right place.

I don't like to lose control completely, so I was never much of a drug-taker in college. My three housemates one year dropped acid every weekend and invited me to join in the fun, but I never did. At the time, I mistakenly believed that Nola's psychosis had been triggered by a bad experience with LSD, so I didn't want to risk triggering the same illness in myself. I'm not sure where I picked up this notion, but everyone in my family, including Nola herself in her memoir, denies that drugs had anything to do with her altered perceptions. The most Nola admitted to trying a couple of times was marijuana. The truth is much scarier to me than any easy explanation. The truth is that perhaps Nola was always a little out of control, if that's what you want to call it, although that puts a negative spin on her perceptions. But maybe that's what I want to do. I don't want anyone to think I'm crazy, too. No, not that.

I don't like losing control in the way I perceive the world. I don't like to lose control in this way because I can never be sure whether I'm indeed having a paranormal or religious experience or merely a nervous breakdown. I don't necessarily want to see ghosts or fairies or visions of Jesus in the clouds above Six Flags over Georgia. I'd rather lead a comfortable life and admire the real wood console of my Lexus (if I could afford one), and the only pain I might feel would be the tiny prick of the Novocain needle. But, of course, that's not true either. The truth, like everything, is somewhere in between, in the space between contradictions.

When I awoke from my trance in the hypnotist's office, I remembered it all, everything that I'd told her, and yet there were details that I remembered that I hadn't thought about in years, like the curtains that separated the bedroom my brother and I shared. That doesn't prove anything, of course, and I'm amused a little by the hypnotist's assertion, as she brought me back, that we were going to find out *exactly* what happened that night, that now, we'd know for sure. But we don't and we never will.

I remember being surprised by how close the hypnotist held the microphone to my mouth, less than an inch away. She told me that hypnotized people are very lazy and that when they speak, their speech is very soft. That startled me because it suggested that I was like everyone else, everyone whom she so easily hypnotized, all those others who thought they were calling the shots.

The other night I saw my ghost again. Not in a physical sense but in my mind. I had listened to the hypnotist's tape for the first time in years, and I could see him again, coming up slowly toward me. His silent anger. I saw his gray sideburns. I saw his gray hair and his hat again. I saw that he was a short man. I don't know if any of this is true. I don't know what I saw that night. Just as sometimes, I can see my sister Nola, dead now for twenty-five years, and sometimes I can almost hear her voice, hear her singing, in a region not so far from the one in which I think I dwell.

Her Soul's History

. . . I had decided to put I.B. Singer in a state of hypnosis to see whether there was a possibility that he might have latent psychic powers. I had originally picked up at least the basics of the hypnotic technique at a beach near San Francisco at the age of ten, where I observed a professional put two girls into a trance in broad daylight and cause their hands to interlock so tightly they could not separate them. I began experimenting afterwards on my cousin, and on friends with little success; the first fruitful session occurred with Singer. I decided—how I intuited this I cannot be sure—that the best method of inducing parapsychological experiences, which involved the sensing of objects hidden from ordinary perception, was that of first causing the subject to see what did not exist at all, simply to accustom him to seeing non-sensory objects. I took him through a series of hallucinatory visions—from canaries (his favorite bird) flying at him through the parlor window to huge distended green fountain pens floating about in midair. When he had finally become completely credulous in the trance state and was able to touch, feel, and see every object I suggested, I decided that it was time to take the step from the purely imaginary to the paranormal. I picked up a red book which lay on the floor in the other room out of his range of vision, brought it in behind my back and his chair at an angle from which it was definitely impossible for him to see, and asked him what the object was that I held in my hands. After what appeared to be a profound struggle with his unconscious he told me that it was a red book. During this experiment, besides the precautions I took to conceal the object, I induced in him a temporary hypnotic blindness so that he was incapable of seeing even the most obvious of objects. I chose another article to experiment with and asked

him what it was. After another period of strain, he said that it was a blue sock which he had carelessly thrown on the floor that morning (his preoccupation with writing seemed to leave him oblivious to appearances); this was also correct. When I was about to look around for more sophisticated subjects to experiment on, the phone began ringing frantically, putting Singer in a very ~~tenuous~~-*slippery* state between sleeping and waking, during which he ~~let~~ *gave* out the most unliterary snorts and groans, until I was obliged to awaken him completely, and restore his critical ~~mind~~-*faculty*. The moment he opened his eyes, Singer looked at me with an expression of amazement, asked me who I was, and looked as if he were about to collapse. When I demanded an explanation for his behavior, and he had come out of his initial stupor, he told me that when he had looked at me at the moment of awakening I appeared to him very old, as if my spirit had revealed itself to one whose vision had artificially been coaxed into a clairvoyant state, in which my soul's history had become suddenly transparent to him, and had displayed itself in its full antiquity in this child of fifteen. I thought his comment very strange, since I had always felt that in some inexplicable way I was very old, and seemed to carry memories of previous births in India, the Middle East during the time of Jesus, Tibet, China, South America, and perhaps once among the North American Indians. I remember once getting up for class at thirteen and thinking about my . . . teacher, who was always stressing that it was his divine right to rule our lives and thought[s], because he was much older than we were and therefore far more competent. I had awakened one morning in a state of intense illumination about I knew not what; I looked in the mirror and suddenly observed: "Mr. C (my teacher), if only I could tell you how wrong you are! My soul is much older than yours!" I have never lost that sense of my soul's antiquity; last year when I "tripped" on marijuana with a friend (a practice I have since completely stopped because of its crippling effects on my mind) I had that same sense of long-forgotten lives, as an Egyptian or Delphic priestess, a devotee of Christ, as life [sic] among yogis in India and Tibet. My spirituality, in fact, did not seem to be simply incidental, but the product of many previous lives of suffering.

I had spent the remainder of my school year covering the walls lovingly with paper scenes . . . valleys, mountains, angelic souls that had reached the highest bliss through the ~~old~~ paradox of finding freedom through enslavement to God; constructing wishing wells for the school leprechaun in one of our plays, creating Greek costumes for our production of Dido and Aeneas by Purcell; I remember the choral singing one of the final songs in the opera: "Great minds against themselves conspire, and shun the cure they most desire," with which I deeply identified, since my whole life at the time consisted of absorbing very beautiful impressions which I was afraid of transforming from within and giving out in art and was mingled with the light of God . . . even though my soul's happiness depended on it so desperately.

The Exploding Pen

My mother sent me a couple of new stories of hers to read. The first one, she has already warned me, is about me when I was an adolescent. It's called "The Habit of Loving," and it's to this one I'm immediately drawn, of course, when I open the manila envelope. There are times in midterm, when I'm swamped with student stories, and I don't even have enough time for my own writing, when my mother sends a story for me to critique. Some of these stories have gone unread, uncommented upon, until my mother calls and complains, "I shouldn't ever send you anything. It's no use. You never read it."

At least, I tell her, when friends or acquaintances call to complain about the same thing, I can tell them in all honesty, "Look, I don't even have time to read the stories my mother sends me."

Someone who can't find the time to read his mom's stories, now that's low. You don't have to tell me. In the guilt department, I'm a professional. I have vast guilt reserves, untapped Alaskan fields of guilt, that lie in wait for plunder and exploitation.

But I started this one because it was about me—admittedly when I was much younger. The story begins:

> Something in him says he doesn't love me. He is lying alone in his room and has shut me out. I think: It is because I am not young, because my face says: Loss.
>
> He is reminded of that day when he had to know that his father died. He did not like my tears.
>
> (Everyone has to die, he said. Don't cry.)
>
> Now he remains in his room with the door closed and the radio on or the small TV, and "does things." He has comics stacked on cast iron shelves (that I used to have for plants)—up to the ceiling. He says he is sick, but the doctor can't find anything wrong. One of Chris's reasons for hating me is that I called the doctor.
>
> I knock on his door, but he won't open it.
>
> He refuses to go to school.

47

That's as far as I get for now. Maybe it's fiction, but it seems pretty accurate. My comic-book collection, my father's death, the time I refused to go to school, the way I hid out in my room, even my adolescent cruelty toward my mother. I don't remember telling my mother, "Everyone has to die. . . . Don't cry." Maybe I did, maybe I didn't. This all happened when we lived in Columbia, Missouri, when all the horrible things were going on with Nola, and then I seemed to catch her problems, mutated to fit my own psyche. But I haven't come to that part yet. My mother has, but I haven't. I'm not ready for that particular pain.

For months now, I've been letting my mother know a little bit here and there about my project, this book. I have not shown it to her, and I won't until it's finished, but I've shown bits and pieces to friends, who have given me encouragement. I'm not trying to taunt her, "Ha ha, I'm writing about you," but more to prepare her and also to assuage my own guilt, I suppose. Now, I see that's a little unfair, and she has, in effect, retaliated—preparing me over the phone, "I've written a story about the time you refused to go to school," the same way I've prepared her for writing about her life. "I'm writing about you and Elliot Chess now . . . I'm reading his novel . . . I'm writing about your time in Mexico now."

I leave the story she's written about me and look at her letter:

The letter begins by saying she stayed up all night worrying about my memoir. She tells me not to use real names, that even though some events happened in the past, they're still painful. She ends by asking the impossible:

> *"Please ASSURE ME YOU WILL NOT publish anything that I might consider offensive to me or anyone else."*

She's clearly upset, but even so, she still wants me to read what she's written.

> *"P.S. I am sending the two stories I said I'd send."*

This letter alarms me—I realize I have told my mother too much, and that for both our sakes, I should have waited until the book was farther along. Now I've caused her to lose sleep, but of course, I can't give her the assurances she wants, at least not now, not while I'm writing. I might try to second-guess her, might find myself poised over the keyboard, wondering if my next sentence could possibly offend her or someone else.

I try calling her, but her line is busy, so I hang up and try again and again.

My wife calls from downstairs. "Are you ready?"

We're going shopping with the kids, so my call will have to wait until we return. In the car, I tell Beverly about my mother's letter.

"You had to expect this," she says. "Your mother's not the most forthcoming person about these things, and you're writing about painful events, showing them to the world."

"But she's written about me before," I say, lamely. "I've never said anything."

"That's different," she says, a little exasperated, it seems, by my lack of understanding of my own craft. "That's fiction."

"It can still be painful."

She gives me a look like she's not buying these goods.

Still, it's true. I know who Chris is in her story. Anyone who knows me and my mother knows that Chris is me. Simply changing a name doesn't make it less true . . . or less painful. And my mother is right. The fact that something happened way in the past does not diminish the pain it causes. I'm not saying I'm bothered by my mother's story, at least not by her having written it. I don't mind the fact that others might see me as having led less than an exemplary adolescence, and I don't mind letting people see my faults now—not out of a kind of exhibitionism, but because the real fiction is that any of us are saints, that our motives are always pure and unselfish, that we never hurt others.

"Don't worry," she adds. "You're lucky. Your mom is a writer. If anyone should understand, it's her." I hate my wife's reasonableness at that moment. I won't let it go. I want a fight and by the end of the ten-minute car ride, I've goaded Beverly into one. She calls me "selfish and superior," and I call her "anti-intellectual." Beverly tells me she's always been uncomfortable with the way writers "use" experience. But what else are we supposed to use? And there are so many different ways to "use" experience in one's writing. Don't one's intentions count? I imagine Beverly sees me as one of those cold-hearted technicians at an animal laboratory, pulling apart monkeys for the sake of an abstraction. And I'm deeply offended by Beverly's remark, in a way that I can't at that moment articulate—but of course, I worry, too that she's right. Still, I wouldn't write if I didn't think it mattered, and I suppose that *is* selfish. Can't a kind of selfishness and even superiority coexist with what is good and true about art, about the process of discovery? By superiority, I mean the necessity to cast aside self-doubt, if even for a moment, and will oneself to believe that the journey inward is at least as important as the journey outward.

At the store, we each take a shopping cart and a child and fume separately, buying the things we need to buy. By the end of our shopping trip, we have reached a truce, negotiated in part by our daughter, Olivia.

At home, there's a message on my answering machine from my mother. She wants me to know that a favorable review of my latest book has appeared in the *Chicago Tribune*. She wants to read it to me. And I know that things will be all right between us. I call her, thinking it's a good thing her line was busy when I called before because now I've had time to reflect, to realize that this isn't a life or death moment, that Beverly was right, I'm lucky that my mother is a writer.

"I got your stories," I tell her after she's told me about the review (which I already knew about), "and I read your letter. I don't know that you should be worrying about this right now . . . But I can't change the names of you or me or Nola or Jonny. I can change minor names. Like the journals you gave me, when you write that you love Herbert, I can change his name."

"Yes!" she says. "Definitely change Herbert's name. But look, Robin. You don't have to give me a lecture. I understand. If anyone's going to understand, it's me." I wonder if somehow Beverly has beat me to it and called my mom first, but I know that's not true. Beverly hates telephones.

"When the book's done," I say, "I'll show it to you and treat you like any other editor. Some things I'll take out, but some things I'll keep, and other things we can reach a compromise on."

"You know I always cave in to you," she says. "You'll have your way."

My mother is being too good about this. It's time for me to come clean. It's time for me to tell her about the court documents about Nola. I tell her what a little thief I used to be, and how I found the documents at Ida's house years ago while rifling through her drawers. My mother laughs. I go on and tell her that I took the papers because they had something to do with Nola, who had only been dead for a couple of years, and that I knew I needed to have them, but I didn't know what for. I never read them, I tell her, until last summer. And I've been feeling guilty ever since. I've been waiting for the right moment to tell her.

"That shouldn't bother an experienced thief like you," she says, and laughs again. "I'm glad you took them. I would have given them to you anyway."

I let that sink in. She would have given them to me anyway. Really? I'm not sure. I remember Jack and the Beanstalk, the giant clomping after him as he steals the goose that lays the golden eggs. I imagine the giant yelling, "Wait, Jack, the goose is yours. Just stop a second. I've got a new story to show you."

"Have you had time to look at the stories yet?" she asks me.

"No, I just received them, Mom," I say. "Just today."

*   *   *

I go into the laundry room and find Beverly with her head in the dryer. "I'm not talking to you," she tells me.

"Why?"

"You left a pen in your pants pocket. This is going to be a three-hour job."

She has a sponge in her hand and ink is splattered all over the inside of the dryer.

"I wouldn't talk to me either," I say, and I give her a guilty and apologetic look, but I don't actually tell her I'm sorry, and so now she's *really* not talking to me. "At least you could say you're sorry."

"I am sorry," I tell her, although I know that an apology after one has been reminded to apologize does not cut it with Beverly.

My only way of making amends is to get in there and scrub, so I try to convince her to let me help. "You won't scrub. You'll just wipe," she tells me.

"I'll scrub. I'll put some elbow grease in it."

"Okay," she says, disgust in her voice and she walks out of the room.

I start scrubbing. Olivia comes into the room and asks if she can help. "You can keep me company," I tell her.

"I want to help," she says.

"Okay, you can get me some paper towels."

"They're too high," she says. "I've got to go potty."

When she returns, she's carrying a stuffed bear. "I love this bear," she says. "Here, you can have him, Daddy. He'll make you company. His name is Revley. He's imagination."

"He is?"

"When you want something, just say his name."

"How do you spell it?' I ask.

"A-O-X."

"What's his name again?"

"Prolly."

"And how do you spell his name?"

"T-Y-F-D."

"And what's his name?"

"Creemoss."

"He's imagination?"

"Yes, and you spell it Y-N-B-G."

Olivia turns and leaves me scrubbing, scrubbing away, my head and half my body in the dryer.

Walk Away from Them

I can tell you this for sure: Nola was born July 3rd, 1947, in New York City, the daughter of Elaine Gottlieb and Elliot Chess. She never knew her father. He died at the age of sixty-three in El Paso, Texas—drunk, climbing the stairs, he had a heart attack. My mother, on learning of his death, went to Nola's room. Nola was sixteen, the difference in age between Chess and my mother, perfect, it seems to me now, that he should die when she turned sixteen. Nola was the gap between my mother and Chess, the physical cause of their separation, the difference in their humanity. My mother said, "I'm sorry I have to tell you about it. I hope it doesn't make you unhappy," and Nola said, "Why should it make me unhappy? I never knew him."

The only thing my mother ever told *me* about Elliot Chess while I was growing up, was about the bus trip they took together to Lake Chapala in Mexico, never another word about this man who saved her life in 1946 and then nearly destroyed it. Whenever I brought up the subject of Nola's father, she would say firmly, "I don't want to talk about him." If I pressed her, she said, "It's too painful," and that's when I'd be quiet. The last thing I wanted was to cause my mother more pain since pain had been a constant in her life, from the death of her father when she was six to the death of her husband, my father, in 1966, and finally my sister's death in 1973. I don't want to diminish the importance of my father's death or the death of her father, but it was from Nola's death that she could never recover. She made this clear to me once when she told me that after Nola died, she thought of killing herself, and might have if not for me. I was fifteen when Nola died, sixteen when my mother confided in me her thoughts of suicide. This knowledge of my mother's vulnerability and my importance to her, that if I didn't exist she wouldn't either, was a burden for me, something that made me feel guilty. I don't think she was consciously trying to manipulate me, but I thought it was a terrible thing to be given this much responsibility for my mother. She seemed to be saying that

I was her last chance. I know that's self-centered of me, but that's how I took it at the time. I felt that I couldn't have any pain because any pain of mine would be immediately transmitted to my mother, become her own, and finish her off.

It's never been easy for my mother and me to talk about things that hurt us—she suggested after Nola died that I might like to talk to someone, namely a psychiatrist, but that was the last person I wanted to talk with, not after Nola's experiences with psychiatrists, nor my own. But even though we didn't talk about such things, I slowly picked up pieces of who Elliot Chess was, and of my mother's brief life with him. Here and there I'd ask her a question, and she'd give me a tidbit before telling me she didn't want to say anymore. For a long time I didn't know anything other than that he was her first husband. For years I didn't know what his first name was. I just knew his name was Chess, that he was a writer, and I thought he owned a ranch in Texas. My mother told me they had met and married in Mexico after the war, but that he didn't like children, and when she became pregnant, she went home to New York, and he never followed, although he had promised he would. I knew he was now dead, and that when he died my mother tried to have Nola declared as an heir, but that his sister prevented it, claiming that my mother and Chess had never been married. My mother could not produce a marriage certificate and so she lost the case. Those are the facts I knew then.

Here's a story he could have written, the only one my mother ever related to me as I was growing up about this time in her life. While on a bus to Guadalajara, Elliot spied someone outside pointing a gun at the bus and shoved her down on the floor. Bullets shattered the window where her head had been a moment before. Shots flew from both the front of the bus and the rear. As she and Elliot lay on the floor of the bus, hearing the pops of the guns and the screams of passengers, the bullets seemed distant and bizarre to her, and she was concocting a story about them. She had heard and believed that there were wild Indians in the hills, cannibals, and she thought it was this mythical tribe attacking the bus. Actually, it was a rival bus company.

I suppose my mother allowed me to hear this story when I was growing up because it *was* such an Elliot-like story, full of physical but not emotional danger. It was the kind of story he would have told, about dramatic, potentially life-shattering events, but not about him or her. The focus is on my mother, not him, and when she told me this story, I could only imagine a faceless man, arms shoving her to the floor. Even the embellishments, what she was thinking lying there, are something she only revealed to me recently. And when I asked her to describe Elliot to me, she wouldn't. Instead, she referred me to a story she'd written and published in the 1950s, called "Passage through Stars." "I describe him in there," she told me flatly, and of course, I didn't press her. But even this story's existence was a revelation to me. Until then, I hadn't realized she'd written about him, since I assumed, if it was too painful for her to talk about, she wouldn't be able to write about him either.

In the story, a fictionalized account of my mother's time in Mexico and the circumstances surrounding my sister's birth, she leaves out her terror on the bus completely, leaves out talk of marriage. Instead, she focuses on the pain of separation and the joy of a newborn child. Like many of her stories, this is one of reflection, in which the narrator, standing almost outside time, wonders how events pass, and where she fits. This is not a story Elliot Chess would have told.

I have four documents in front of me now that tell me something about my mother and Elliot Chess. The court papers I discovered in my grandmother's drawer, "Passage through Stars," a photocopy of Elliot Chess's 1941 novel, *Walk Away from 'Em*, and transcripts of taped interviews I've been conducting with my mother for several years.

These relics almost complete a picture of my mother and Elliot Chess's time together, but not quite. What's missing for me is the dust jacket of Elliot Chess's novel. My mother says she used to have a copy of his novel, but that it vanished in the sixties. "Maybe Nola took it," she says. She gave all her pictures of Chess and all their letters back and forth to my great uncle Morty for the court case, but those, too, have vanished. "Morty probably burned them," she says. I have a vision of Morty building a bonfire on the beach—my mother has used these exact words several times: "He probably burned them." Maybe he lost them or threw them away, but my mother prefers to dramatize. At least I have excerpts of the letters, preserved in only one place in the world, I think, these legal documents. But no pictures. I still have no idea of what Elliot Chess looked like—I imagine Gary Cooper. I've toyed with the idea of contacting the paper in El Paso, Texas, where Chess lived most of his life, and where he died, or even flying down there and digging up his obituary, retrieving a picture of him.

The other artifact I'm missing is my mother's 1947 novel, *Darkling*, which, I confess, I've never read in its entirety. I used to own a copy, but like Elliot Chess's novel, my mother's book somehow vanished. Maybe, sleepwalking one night, I burned it behind my house. I, too, like to dramatize.

* * *

Mexico was Robert Mother-well's idea. My mother used to visit him and his wife in East Hampton, where she lived after studying art with him at Black Mountain College. The English have the Continental Tour to round out their education—for my mother, it was Mexico. Motherwell suggested that she go down to Mexico to write, because wartime travel restrictions had been lifted, and living there was inexpensive for American artists.

An eighteen-hour plane ride to Brownsville, Texas—and my mother and her traveling companion, a woman named Tess who was "working on her third divorce and relaxing between hearings," collapsed in a hotel room and slept for two hours before traveling on. Tess was friends with Herbert, my mother's boyfriend of a few months whom she had met when the men returned from the war. Until recently, I'd always thought of Herbert as nothing more than a family friend. I remember visiting him and his family, how Nola and his daughter were friends, and him taking me to museums. Knowing that he and my mother were romantically involved, however briefly, makes me reevaluate every time I saw this man in the past. This knowledge changes all my memories, however slightly, as in those sci-fi time-travel stories in which a hero or villain goes back in time and changes something—and the entire future of the world is transformed. ("Oh, Herbert was nothing," she insists now, but then I read in her journal: "Feb. 17, 1946: I love Herbert. I would give up my book for him." Which one of you is telling the truth?)

There was no need, after all, for my mother to give up her book for Herbert. By the time she and Tess were sleeping off the effects of their eighteen-hour plane ride in Brownsville, the book was complete and her romance with Herbert was over.

My mother left on her own for a little resort she'd heard about, a place called Casa Heuer on Lake Chapala in Ajijic, Mexico. "You say it as if you're giggling," my mother says. "Ajijic." The Casa Heuer had a main building where all the guests ate on the porch, and around it were various cottages where the different guests stayed. It was here she met Elliot Chess. She was thirty. He was forty-six. At sixteen, he'd been a pilot for the RAF in World War I, and had also been a pilot in World War II, and in what his aunt refers to in the court documents as the "Polish War,"—whatever that was. He had done and seen everything, and had stories to tell about it all. He'd been a boxer for a while. He'd been an actor in Hollywood. He'd been in publishing in New York and had written a novel. At dinner, everyone at Casa Heuer was fascinated by his stories, including my mother. After all, she loved stories, was a storyteller herself. As the court documents blandly phrase it, "They found they had much in common." But really, beyond the fact that they both wrote, they had little in common, it seems. What really attracted them was probably how unlike they were. I imagine my mother's fascination. She was Jewish and had grown up in Brooklyn. He had always lived, except for his war stints, and his brief times in Hollywood and New York, in El Paso. And they were different types of writers. My mother wrote for the literary quarterlies—quiet, lyrical stories, full of introspection and conflicts of the soul. The conflicts in Elliot Chess's fiction were the large ones that could take a person out of himself, with little introspection, full of corny dialogue and larger-than-life actions, a stunt-pilot hero named Nick Wayne and a bombshell babe named Toddy Fate.

The central metaphor of the book, *Walk Away from 'Em*, is that of the plane crash, the crack-up. The metaphor is mentioned on almost every page of the book. The book opens with a crack-up that Nick Wayne is able to walk away from, and we soon learn that this event encapsulates his philosophy of life, that you'll be all right, no matter how bruised you are, if you're able to walk away from your crack-ups, and that goes for broads, too. Nick has already been married and divorced, and his ex-wife is still in love with him, as is another woman for whom he left his first wife, although he's left her, too. It's only Toddy Fate, the daughter of his stunt-pilot partner, recently killed in a crash (or so it seems), that he can't walk away from.

The book is hilariously bad, and perhaps I have some stake in saying that, some family honor to reclaim—but I have no animosity when I read this book—more like curiosity. As with every other document I possess, I look for clues, for ways into the personality of the author. The book is a kind of cross between bad Hemingway and bad Bogart dialogue, a compendium of thirties clichés, the Irish cop, the Jewish lawyer, a character named The Greek. A New York cabby seems to fall in love with Nick, too, and follows him around, half-puppy, half-butler for much of the book, and New York is referred to as . . . the Big Town. But it's Nick's relationship to women, especially Toddy, that interests me.

> She brushed back her hair with a trembling hand. I saw the tragic look in her eyes.
>
> "I'm really slipping today, Nickie. I was on my good behavior last night; but today, I'm really slipping."
>
> "Well, you know the answer to that one."
>
> "But don't you care? Don't you? . . . There's still a little bit to salvage."
>
> That did something to me inside; so I turned and looked out the opposite window.
>
> "I know—" Her voice was far away, distant. "I know. Any crackup's all right, if you can walk away from it. And I'm just about ready to crack up so you're walking away from me. And there's nothing to salvage . . . Listen, isn't there anything to salvage?"
>
> It was brutal the way I took hold of her arms, drew her up close to me, and said:
>
> "You're shaking and you're all shot to hell. You've cracked up all right. And anything that's cracked up—"
>
> "Oh, maybe with a little patching, why—" Her voice was almost a whisper now, and pleading. "Why I might be as good as new . . . I've got the panic, Nickie . . . Kiss me. Just once!"
>
> "Here?"
>
> She said helplessly, "All right—some other time . . . ."

I think my mother should have read this book before she fell in love with Elliot Chess. She, apparently, was not his Toddy Fate, although he was her Nick Wayne.

One thing odd about Elliot Chess's book is how obsessive Nick Wayne is about women's clothing. He's constantly telling Toddy Fate how to dress, and my mother says that this was true of Elliot, too, that he was always telling her how to dress, always concerned with fashion.

> We taxied around ... shopping for gloves and hosiery and a bag and a tricky little hat. And up at Hilgram's we found a dress with green trim. The green seemed to turn on the lights in Toddy's hair. I wasn't so sure about the red evening frock, though. It didn't have any shoulder straps, and that worried me ...

Elliot Chess seems to have been a person concerned with the physical, with image, with appearance. My mother says that when he arrived at Casa Heuer, he was dressed unlike anyone else, in natty urbane attire, not shorts and casual shirts like everyone else. And it's also interesting to me that my mother insists that his physicality was not what attracted her, but his stories. And yet, in her own story, "Passage through Stars," she focuses on his physical appearance, his body as he dove and swam in the lake.

In the story, the Casa Heuer is renamed the Casa Unger, and Elliot is called Claude. Instead of Elaine, the character based on her is called Emma.

> She would see him in the mornings, going down to the lake for his pre-breakfast swim; a shining maroon robe flapped around his narrow legs. He would walk briskly, towel in hand, remove his robe in two swift movements, step out of his slippers, and chin erect, approach the lake. Deliberately, he would plunge his head in, shake it vigorously, stand waiting a moment, and then plunge boldly. A little later he would return, hand passing through his wet mahogany-colored hair. Frowning against the light, he would continue to walk, martially erect, his head high and handsome, the face still young, eyes like the eyes of tigers .... He had always seemed to convey an air of the miraculous. Handsome, bronzed, square, he bore his head at an angle that eluded the mundane. In referring to his past, he would enumerate famous people, mention exotic places .... In Paris, Claude said, he had met Hemingway; in Brooklyn, Hart Crane; and in Majorca, H.G. Wells. In awe of the world he described ... she had thought: He has come to conclusions .... She, herself, could sum up nothing, not even to afford as negative a philosophy as his. He had read many books, had done much—lived everywhere .... All he could say was that nothing mattered except "one's personal happiness."

* * *

I knew only the barest of facts about this time in my mother's life before I interviewed her when I lived in North Carolina. My wife and children and I were getting ready in 1994 for a move across the country to
our new home in Washington state, and my mother was down for a
visit. I took out my tape recorder and found out that the facts I
thought I knew about my sister were not facts at all, but garbled memories of mine, mistranslations of fact. I had interviewed my mother before, but never so extensively, nor with any real purpose in mind besides a family chronicle of sorts. And I knew how hard it was for my
mother to open up, that it would be difficult getting her to bring up
the past, that she might at any moment look inward and announce,
"It's too painful. I can't talk about it anymore." Sometimes, when I hit
on something from my mother's past that she doesn't want to talk
about she'll just as soon tell me that it's something that she wants to
write about—something to keep from my grasp. So, often, it's either
too painful or she makes us out to be writing competitors, a thought
that makes me uncomfortable. But this time when I talked to her, I
tried my best to be as gentle as possible, to give her as much time as she
needed to talk about painful subjects, to come back to them later if
she wanted, and I pointed out that we were mother and son, not two
writers feuding over the same material.

For whatever reason, my mother opened up to me more than ever
before on the two days over which I interviewed her.

In the court papers, the bus trip in which Elliot saved my mother's
life became the catalyst for Elliot's proposal of marriage, this near
brush with death. He wanted to marry her, the court papers assert, but
she would only agree to be engaged. But after they arrived in town,
they were both so shaken up that he told her she should not delay the
marriage any longer.

This marriage, in fact, never happened, nor any talk of marriage.
This could have been something from one of my mother's stories, but
I didn't learn that until recently. I'd always believed that Elliot Chess
was her first husband, but somehow, I found out they never really were
married. I say "somehow," because exactly how I learned the truth is a
great mystery to me. Strangely, I couldn't remember who gave me this
information that Chess and my mother never really married. Perhaps
I just guessed.

Casually, as we were talking, I decided to drop in my mysterious information about her fictional marriage to Elliot Chess.

"It was his sister who kept Nola from inheriting anything?" I asked.

"His sister?" my mother said. "He was an only child. It was his mother's sister."

His aunt. I'd always thought it was his sister. How many other things had I transformed? I'd also always believed that Nola was partly Native American, through her father's side, but my mother dispelled that myth, too. "He was English," she told me. "But he had high cheekbones. I always thought he looked Indian."

"And you had all this trouble because you weren't married?" I said, after a long pause. How smoothly I inserted this question, as though I'd always known, but just needed some clarification, like one of those TV detectives who gets the suspect to admit his involvement in the crime without them realizing their admission.

As my question was trailing off, my mother started in. "I didn't want him to marry me for the sake of any laws. I was very idealistic. And Ida, of course, insisted on trying to get something out of him. And she and Morty initiated this whole thing. I felt very helpless. I didn't know what would be right to do."

"But he was willing to marry you?" I asked.

"What do you mean?" she said.

"I thought you said you didn't want to marry him."

"I didn't want to press anything. His mother thought I should go out to El Paso and face him. And if I had been a stronger person I would have. I guess I sensed that actually the two of us were not meant to be together because he had led a very different life. He was about sixteen years older than I."

"You were thirty?" I asked.

"Thirty. Just thirty. And his values were different. He had done some writing, but it was all very commercial. He wrote a book that was sort of pulpy. We just had very different values altogether."

"What attracted you initially? A handsome guy?"

"Well, he was very . . . No, I wouldn't be attracted to someone who was just handsome." We laughed.

"I know."

"He had all kinds of stories to tell about his life. He'd been everything and done everything and been everywhere. He was a pilot."

"In World War II?"

"Yes. He'd also been a pilot at the age of sixteen in World War I with the RAF. He always had something to tell. Everybody at the place where I was staying in Mexico was fascinated by him."

So these court papers and the fictional marriage they tried to prove were the doing of my grandmother and my uncle Morty. In their version of the way stories should go, my mother had married this man named Chess and then he'd deserted her after she became pregnant. But in my mother's version, marriage had never been in the plan. Still, it's curious that the version she adopted, the one I learned as I was growing up, was my grandmother and uncle's version. The court papers, my mother tells me now, were an elaborate concoction, an embellishment as great as any a fiction writer might employ. The bare facts were true: the bus ride, the letters between them, but the vows of marriage were part of a romance novel written by my grandmother and Uncle Morty. My mother tells me now that she was confused, that she let Ida and Morty do what they wanted, from the moment in 1947 when my mother returned from Mexico, pregnant with my sister Nola, to the early 1960s when Elliot Chess died. She says now that she thinks that if Ida and Morty hadn't hounded Elliot, he might have come around and accepted some responsibility for Nola—but he was stubborn. He wasn't going to be forced to do anything.

I want to call him Elliot now, although I dislike him for the way he treated my mother. Of course, had he treated her any other way I wouldn't have been born, or I would be half myself and half someone else, a child named Nick perhaps.

I want to call him Elliot, not because I like him or want to know this man especially, but because for years he was known only as Chess, and we seem somehow related. My brother, Jonathan, according to my mother, asked her when he was young, "How am I related to Elliot?" The question itself doesn't surprise me so much. What I wanted to know from my mother was how my brother, at a young age, came to know who Elliot Chess was. I'm jealous of this knowledge, as I am jealous of any knowledge kept from me.

I want to call him Elliot because I cannot call him by his full name. It sounds made up, another fabrication, so close to Elliot Ness I can almost imagine him in an alley toting a tommy gun—which I suppose, is not too far removed from the violence of his real life.

My mother has taken to calling him by his first name in our conversations. It's as though I'm familiarizing her again with her life, reacquainting the two, and not all of it is painful. Sometimes, she even calls up and volunteers information. She calls me one night and tells me how she and Elliot walked around the lake one evening, talking half the night, and they paused by a tree and sat down and didn't get up again.

What has made her volunteer this information to me now? I wonder. Perhaps she wants me to understand her life fully now that I have uncovered a part of it—another writer friend of mine tells me that this is a common problem for biographers—their subjects by turn volunteer information and then want control of it. Yes, but most biographers don't write about their mothers.

*   *   *

I have to tell you several stories in several forms in order to piece one together. This is a story of documents, and, as such, each one has its own weight—the ones that purport to tell the truth are full of lies and the fictionalized ones have nuggets of truth. I wish you could feel the court documents in front of me now, typed out on thin and brittle legal paper by an attorney in El Paso. I hardly know what to do with them, where to store them where they'll be safe, they're so precious to me.

STATEMENT

NOLA ELIAN CHESS, the infant-claimant, appellant here-in, testified by deposition substantially as follows: (tr. p. 48)

She was born on July 3rd, 1947, in the city and state of New York. That she claims to be an heir of Elliot Chess. (tr. p. 50) That she is the daughter of Elliot Chess. Her birth certificate was admitted into evidence. (Exhibit A-1) (p. 59) Said birth certificate states that Elliot Chess was her father.

Claimant's mother testified as follows:

Claimant's mother, a resident of New York, met the decedent, a resident of Texas, on September 2nd, 1946, at the Casa Heuer, on Lake Chapala, Ajijic, Mexico. (tr. p. 99, 106). She was an author and he was an author. (tr. p. 106, 348). Both had written and has [sic] published books. (tr. p. 105, 106). They found that they had much in common, (tr. p. 111) as both were in Mexico, working on their writings. They were in constant companionship (tr. p. 112) and on September 14, 1946, (tr. p. 118) decedent proposed marriage to claimant's mother. She agreed only to become engaged to him. (tr. p. 118, 122). They went to Guadalajara to celebrate their engagement (tr. p. 118). While on the

bus to Guadalajara a shooting of guns caused much bloodshed and injuries to the passengers and greatly unnerved and upset both claimant's mother and her father
(tr. pp. 119, 120, 121, 122). He refers to, in his letter dated January 11, 1947, this bus incident saying:

> "and I think of the episode in the bus again, and
> how quietly our personal destinies could have
> ended." (Exh. A-22)

They proceeded to Guadalajara and celebrated their
engagement. (tr. pp. 122, 123) Because of their haz-
ardous experience in the bus, when they could have been
killed, (tr. p. 349) he told her that they should not
delay their marriage any longer. He pleaded with her to
marry him immediately, (tr. p. 349) stating that as a
Texan they had a right to be married by the exchange of
mutual vows without further ceremony. (tr. p. 350) She
had faith in him, loved him, (tr. pp. 113, 349, 477)
relied upon him, (tr. pp. 350, 475) and agreed to marry
him as he wished. (tr. p. 350) He told her to repeat
after him these words: "I take thee, Elliot, to be my
lawful wedded husband" which she did. (tr. p. 350) He
vowed, "I take thee, Elaine, to be my lawful wedded
wife." (tr. p. 350) They embraced, kissed each other,
announced their marriage to the proprietor of the
hotel, (tr. p. 350) celebrated their marriage with him
with a drink he offered, (tr. p. 350) and she moved
into his cottage and commenced living with him as husband and wife. (tr. pp. 126, 350) This occurred on
September 15, 1946. (tr. pp. 126, 350) She believed she
was married to Elliot Chess on September 15th, 1946.
(tr. p. 253) They lived together until November 16th,
1946. (tr. pp. 126, 475)

The first time I read this elaborate reconstruction of a marriage
that never took place, I had to call my mother to ask her once again
about the truth. I was bothered that these might be her own words,
that she could construct something so false just for material gain, even
for her daughter rather than herself. And what even seemed worse to
me: It read like a lie, like a piece of amateur fiction, not believable for a

second. His explanation of Texas law seemed too convenient, and why couldn't they wait until morning? My mother could do better than this, I thought. So I went to her story, "Passage through Stars," published in the fifties before the court case. The character based on Elliot Chess tells the woman in the story, "You won't lose me, darling," words that are almost identical to those in the court papers: "You will never lose me." I wasn't sure what to believe anymore.

(Mr. Broaddus)

1. Q. "How did it (the marriage) take place?" (tr. p. 349)

A. "He said 'You will never lose me. I want to marry you and marry you right now.' I said, 'How is that possible?' He said, 'We can marry each other by agreement,' and I never heard anything like this, but I was very much in love with him and he was sixteen years older than I and I thought he knew a lot more than I did and he asked me if I would go through with it. He said that in Texas, where he came from, you didn't have to appear before anyone; that two people could just agree themselves to be married and I believed him. He said 'Repeat after me: I take thee Elliot to be my lawful wedded husband.' I said that and he said, 'I take Elaine to be my lawful wedded wife.' He kissed me and said, "I adore you,' and he put his arms around me. **** then I moved into Elliot's cottage that night."

I called her up, ready to believe whatever she told me at face value, ready to coach her, if necessary to give her my own prepared script.

Q. "I'm kind of confused about a couple of things. Let me see if I can phrase this right . . . I'm going to quote from the court papers and your story, 'Passage through Stars.'"

A. "Why do you have to quote from those crazy court papers because they're not . . ."

Q. "Accurate?"

A. "Yeah."

Q. "Now you didn't actually. . . all your testimony was by deposition, right?"

A. "Yeah."

Q. "So you didn't appear in court."

A. "And I was coached by Morty."

Q. "Okay, that's what I was wondering. There's a section here that basically says, 'How did the marriage take place,' and then your answer.'"

A. "Well, that's embarrassing, Robin. I wish you wouldn't put it in. I was just being pushed around by Morty."

Q. "I'll say that."

A. "And they kept saying, 'You have to do this for Nola.' It was completely against my stand in this whole thing. I mean, I had a baby because I wanted a baby. I didn't want to involve him."

Q. "So they were just pushing you to say all this. So Morty coached you and told you what to say?"

A. "Yes."

Q. "And you just wrote it down."

A. "Yes."

Q. "Okay, that's what I wanted to know because . . ."

A. "Because you couldn't imagine me saying those things."

Q. "Well, it's just so elaborate and it just made me wonder. I had a hard time because you said you didn't want to push him, but basically they pushed you."

A. "Well, I was so confused."

Q. "I know, I know."

Still, she had to lie under oath in order to participate in the suit against the estate of Elliot Chess. According to her, Morty told her she had to do this. He said, "Here's the story," and she memorized it. I can almost imagine my mother sitting at a table, as in some spy film, a single lamp illuminating her, while above her, Morty holds a pen in his outstretched hand. "Sign," he says. "It would be better for you both if you did." In this version of events, my uncle Morty plays the role of villain. What story isn't full of lies, half-truths, and misperceptions? Everyone lies, and sometimes they don't even know it. Sometimes, they're embarrassed by the truth, and sometimes they know what they say is a lie, but they lie to spare someone's feelings, to save someone's life, to protect someone they love.

Morty is no longer alive, nor is my grandmother, Ida, so I can't ask for their versions. But one thing I remember about Morty and Ida: They were sure of themselves, and of what was owed them. They lived in a certain, deliberate world in which one remade the truth, if necessary, for the greater good. My mother and I have never lived in that world—I am like her in this respect, easily pushed around, caring too much what others think, believing that others have the keys that we've somehow lost. From the very beginning, when my mother returned from Mexico in 1947, until the court case in the early sixties, my grandmother and my great uncle agitated for something, some recognition, some acknowledgment of responsibility from Chess— now I'm back to calling him Chess. In the early fifties, after my mother had married my father, Morty tried to have the fictional marriage annulled, to leave a paper trail. Nola, in their minds, should get something, even if it was simply recognition. This, I'm sure, motivated my grandmother more than money. On the last page of the court documents, my grandmother's fears and concerns, as I imagine them, are voiced:

> Because the marriage was not registered in the small village of Ajijic, Mexico, despite the mother's belief that she was married to decedent, the Court in effect held the innocent offspring of that honorable relationship, a bastard.

Ida would have wanted them married, if not in truth, at least in the eyes of the law, to hold on to the family's respectability.

According to my mother, my father wasn't really invested in these proceedings, nor was Nola. Everyone just went along. Morty was the expert, the lawyer, the orchestrator. He told her this was the only way. But what am I saying? He wasn't the villain—if there was a villain here, it was clearly Elliot Chess. So my mother lied. So what? The law of the time was wrong, that a child could only be declared an heir if a legal marriage document could be produced.

One day in the early sixties, when Nola was in her teens and I was five or six, my mother went into a law office in New York to be deposed, her family in tow: Morty, Ida, Nola, my brother, father, even me (although I remember none of this), and gave her testimony.

> . . . She became pregnant and soon developed the usual symptoms of pregnancy, (tr. p. 126) of morning sickness and such. (tr. p. 127) A skin rash appeared and she learned it was also due to the bad food and milk obtained from tubercular cows. (tr. p. 127)

They decided on the 15th of November, 1946, to go home. He would go to his home at El Paso, sell his land that he owned there, (Exh. A-17, A-18) raise some money and join her in New York. (tr. p. 148) She would go to New York, where she could get proper food and take care of her pregnancy and her illness. They journeyed together to Guadalajara and stayed at the Hotel Phenix there. (tr. p. 131) He registered there, in his own handwriting, in her presence, as husband and wife. (tr. pp. 132, 133)

He left the next morning for El Paso. (tr. p. 139) He left early in the morning, kissing her goodby and promised her that she would have a letter from him upon her arrival in New York and that he would join her in two weeks. (tr. p. 139)

Many letters were sent by him to her thereafter explaining his delay in not coming sooner to her. He refers constantly to her pregnancy and tells her that he will join her as soon as the land is sold which is taking longer than expected. He tells her to get an apartment, with another person, to defray the expense, with a limitation on time.

She got an apartment, in her married name, Elaine Gottlieb Chess. She also used her maiden name, according to his wishes, because he told her he was a "feminist" and that she should continue to use her maiden name. (tr. p. 175) She used her maiden name because she was a writer and always used it. (tr. pp. 98, 469, 470)

In his letters he also explains his delay in joining her by stating that he must finish his book.

November 30, 1946—"At the moment circumstance is against us. For my own survival, I must do this thing I'm on and in my own stride. And this pathos of distance is no aid. And circumstance with you helps little. Yet my personal ego is involved, so it conflicts—conflicts, conflicts within me. Just sit down and think a moment—as you have not—we should have more moments of freedom, without concern of an ultimate,

```
that is the consolation I feel at the moment—my
adorable—tell me." (Exh. A-15)
```

```
    Her excluded explanatory testimony would have ex-
plained that "my personal ego" referred to his desire
to have the child.
```

```
    December 9, 1946—"Of my funds this. I have some land
which is being sold, parceled out in lots, and I'd sunk
everything I had in it—almost—but now it looks like the
stuff will be turning. Any day now something should
happen, and then things will be as they should be." (Exh.
A-18)
```

```
    (NOTE: His letters are couched in words that are am-
biguous and the refusal of the court to permit her ex-
planations as to what the words meant to her is
assigned as error.)
```

The letters that Elliot Chess wrote to my mother *are* certainly vague, and it's easy to see why—he was being cautious, he didn't want to write anything that could be used in ... court. There's an aspect of this caution that reminds me of myself—none of us want to be pinned down by the truth later on.

But some of the lawyer's interpretations are completely wild—the word "feminist" appearing in association with Chess is ludicrous. No opponent of women's rights could come up with a more perverse notion of feminism. And to say that "my personal ego" is a reference to my mother's pregnancy, seems like a bit of a stretch. Yes, there's a section in which Chess seems quite clearly to be upset that my mother didn't choose his "solution" to the problem, but "personal ego" seems like a fairly straightforward statement.

```
    Your judgment about the other perplexes me deeply.
I know there is an inherent need inside of you for
it, but to dismiss everything else as a secondary con-
sideration is a tough one. But you know your personal
demands ***** I spoke of caution, but you'd have none
of it. There were considerations, sure. But there was
[a] solution. (Exh. A-26)
```

In his defense, if that's what it is, I have to point out that the voice of his book and the voice of his letters to my mother are completely different—that his letters were not spiced with references to "dames" and "big palookas," that something approaching sincerity could be discerned in them.

> Although she continued to write to him, this was his last letter to her. His letters stopped just after she advised Elliot Chess that she did not intend to have an abortion but was going ahead and have her baby. (tr. p. 362) Letters to him from her were found in the effects after his death. The court refused to allow them into evidence, together with a letter written to him after his death, received by the administrator of his estate. (tr. p. 481)

. . . Now, I see, of course, that this document is only part of the story. I don't have the entire transcripts of the trial, and I have no idea where they might be, or even if they still exist. The other document I have, forty more pages typed on the same brittle legal parchment, has little of personal value, and is simply a point-by-point rebuttal of the case to have Nola declared as Elliot Chess's legal heir—a case which, by this time, was already lost. What I have are the papers of appeal. And what they make me feel are an odd mixture of confusion, sadness, and outrage.

Whether Elliot Chess and my mother were, in fact, married, seems moot to me, but not to the courts of the time, not in El Paso. In the forty other pages of court documents I have, the term "lawful issue" keeps popping up. And that, apparently, was all that mattered, that Nola wasn't Elliot Chess's lawful issue—not whether he had some responsibility to her.

In my fantasy, I imagine myself going down to El Paso and looking up the remaining Chess's, even finding his aunt, over a hundred and twenty perhaps, and confronting her, making her see that she was wrong in denying my sister her birthright. It's a fantasy—why not take it further—somehow, we'd reopen the case—and the land he owned, no matter who owned it now, would be given back, given over—hell, why not turn it into a home for unwed writers? Why not? It's my fantasy. They're just words.

And maybe I'd look up all those addresses in the court documents, all those names, see what exists and what doesn't. Elliot Chess doesn't. My uncle Morty doesn't. Not even my sister, Nola. There's nothing left to fight for in El Paso, not even family honor.

That's the source of my sadness, that there's no way to change outcomes, no way to bring anyone back, no way to change defeat into victory, to make people responsible for what they've done.

. . . About 1951, claimant's mother commenced an action in New York to obtain an annulment of her marriage to Elliot Chess, on the grounds of his failure to continue to cohabit with her as promised. (tr. pp. 356, 365) She had met her present husband and that was what actually brought out the feeling of her suit for annulment. (tr. p. 357) She filed the annulment suit because she thought it was necessary before she got remarried. (tr. p. 467)

In a memorandum of law submitted by the attorney for Elliot Chess in opposition to her application for leave to sue as a poor person, a summary of the marriage laws of Mexico was submitted that indicated what the requirements were for entering into a marriage and indicating that the absence of conformity therewith would render a marriage void. (Exh. B-19) An affidavit made by Elliot Chess averred that there was no record of the marriage in the office of the registry in Mexico. (Exh. B-19)

She did not continue the annulment suit based on the point brought out by Elliot's lawyer that since the marriage was void in law there was no reason to. (tr. p. 465)

Based upon this advice of her attorney she deemed her marriage to Elliot Chess null, as a matter of law, and thereafter remarried. She did not mention her null marriage in her application for a license to marry. (tr. p. 360) She accordingly did not deem it necessary to proceed with her action to obtain a judicial decree of her marriage to Elliot Chess. (tr. p. 360)

The logic of my mother's case is so odd, no wonder she lost: The marriage took place and should be considered legal even though no documents support it, but on the other hand, no annulment was necessary when she married my father because no marriage, in fact, legally had taken place.

> Appellees, through their witness McKim, proved that Elliot Chess had been previously married and divorced, (tr. p. 385) was eccentric, did not like routine or regimentation of any sort, and liked to go and come as he pleased without interference from anybody. He had a very strong aversion to being tied down. He disliked it immensely. He walked away from them. (tr. pp. 383, 384)

When I read that line for the first time, I shivered. How strange that the documents should make an oblique reference to his novel, *Walk Away from 'Em*. The reference seemed dropped in, casual, not something that the judge or anyone else might take note of, unless, in the original transcripts, more was made of his novel, and some connection was attempted between the independent and eccentric Nick Wayne and the real Elliot Chess. I've always thought that if I were arrested for some major crime, all the authorities would have to do would be to read my fiction, and they'd know I'd done it. Likewise, I'd have that guilty look on my face.

But isn't that what I'm trying to do here, putting people on trial for the words they've written—I hope not. I don't need to conduct a trial because sentence was passed on Mr. Chess by Mr. Chess himself. The messenger was my mother when she wrote her final letter to him announcing the birth of his daughter:

> . . . On July 3rd, 1947, Nola Elian Chess was born in New York, at which time Elaine Gottlieb Chess wrote him: (tr. p. 182)
>
>> "Dear E,
>> In a way it would be preferable to avoid writing this. But in another way I cannot avoid it. You have a little daughter, born July 3rd, named Nola Elian Chess. I love her very much and would not

for any reason have foregone the experience of
bearing her. She looks a great deal like you.

    E"

(Exh. A-26) (tr. p. 187)

The name Elian is a combination of the first name of
Elliot and Elaine. (tr. p. 171)

    May White, the mother of Elliot Chess, (she prede-
ceased him) made many visits to New York when she saw
and played with the claimant. She wrote letters to
claimant's mother (tr. p. 208) and sent the child
gifts. (tr. p. 376) In one letter, dated April 4, 1949,
she wrote:

> "My dear child,
> I can well understand what you mean about Elliot,
> because his father did the same thing, and I did
> not know why. I was seventeen and had been married
> one year and six months. Elliot always wanted to
> know his father. In the end his father longed for
> him, but too late; he died of a heart attack."
> (Exh. A-36)

Elliot Chess never knew Nola, as his own father never knew him,
and whether he came to regret this choice in his life, as his father did, I
can only speculate. But what he was working on, a play about an
American dictator, was never produced, and he never published another book—one assumes he lived off of his land, selling it parcel by
parcel until his death.

*   *   *

My mother, clearly upset by the memories I've probed, calls me, nearly
in tears. She tells me again that she never wanted anything from Elliot,
that she knew he didn't want the baby, although she did. Ida told her
she'd take full financial responsiblity for the child, but then she got
hold of Elliot's address, and changed her mind. She wanted *him* to pay.
"I felt betrayed," she tells me. "I was confused."

And those words of his, "You won't lose me, darling," written in her
story and repeated in the court documents—he really said them, my

mother tells me, but she's not sure when. Was it after the events on the bus? I want to know.

"I don't remember," she says, and her voice sounds so weary, so fragile.

I remember my first philosophical dilemma, being asked when I was a young adolescent, or even younger, if I would lie for my family to protect them, and I would always say yes. And would I lie for my country to protect it? That issue seemed more abstract to me, and Vietnam was raging, and so I would always say no. The second question seems unimportant to me now because I know it's a dilemma I'll never face. The first question, though, still nags. Now I don't think I'd lie for anyone, not even myself, except for the lie that is always inherent in the telling, in the imperfection of it.

And so, what was the end result of this court case? Nothing material, except for fifty pages of brittle documents that tell a skewed story, like all others. Morty, as I remember him, would not see the value in this document, would say, like everyone else in my family, "That's a sad business. Let's not revisit it." He would not see the good he'd done ultimately, that he'd given us another story to retell and transform.

For further reflection, I refer you to the actual court transcripts, which have long since been destroyed by my uncle in a bonfire on the beach, or sit moldering in an El Paso warehouse, or have been passed down from one generation to the next in the Chess family, part of the history of their world.

Interior Shot

"In Dreams Begin Responsibilities," the story by Delmore Schwartz that prompted my mother to write him a fan letter, is one of my favorite stories, too—one of the finest stories ever written, I think. Of course, my mother and I are not the only fans of this story. Nabokov called it one of the finest half-dozen contemporary stories, and it was published two years after Schwartz wrote it (at the age of twenty-one) in the first issue of *Partisan Review,* as the lead story, before works by Edmund Wilson, Lionel Trilling, and James T. Farrell.

I need to give a synopsis of this story, which, like many great ones, breaks the rules. In it, the narrator watches a film of the day of his parents' engagement.

> I think it is the year 1909. I feel as if I were in a motion picture theatre, the long arm of light crossing the darkness and spinning, my eyes fixed on the screen. This is a silent picture as if an old Biograph one, in which the actors are dressed in ridiculously old-fashioned clothes, and one flash succeeds another with sudden jumps. The actors too seem to jump about and walk too fast . . . . It is Sunday afternoon, June 12th, 1909, and my father is walking down the quiet streets of Brooklyn on his way to visit my mother . . . .

The film, seen initially from the father's point of view, follows him as he walks the streets of Brooklyn to the house of the narrator's mother; he's pondering whether he really wants to marry her or not. When he arrives at the house, the father is greeted warmly but with a little amusement by the family, because of his awkwardness. We see, in succession, the narrator's aunt, a young girl, who answers the door and takes his hat, the narrator's uncle, a boy of twelve in the film who runs in from outside, the grandfather, who engages the father in conversation, and rubs his beard thoughtfully when his daughter comes down the stairs and he wonders what kind of husband this man will make. At this point, the film breaks, the audience claps in impatience, and when the film is repaired, we once again see the same scene over.

Throughout the story, we are not allowed to simply view this as unadorned narrative. Schwartz makes sure that we know that we are watching a film, that the self-consciousness of the story is an integral part of the story.

> My father tells my mother how much money he has made in the past week, exaggerating an amount that need not be exaggerated. But my father has always felt that actualities somehow fall short. Suddenly, I begin to weep. The determined old lady who sits next to me in the theater is annoyed and looks at me with an angry face, and being intimidated, I stop . . . Meanwhile, I have missed something, for here are my father and my mother alighting at the last stop, Coney Island.

The narrator, after becoming strangely moved by the sight of his parents strolling along the boardwalk and watching the ocean waves crashing, gets up and goes to the men's room to calm himself, and when he returns his parents are riding the merry-go-round. At dinner, the father finally proposes, the mother breaks down in tears, and it's here that the narrator jumps up in his seat and yells, "Don't do it. It's not too late to change your minds, both of you. Nothing good will come of it, only remorse, hatred, scandal, and two children whose characters are monstrous."

The audience, of course, treats him like a lunatic. He's shushed, people stare, the lady beside him tells him he'll be put out, the usher flashes his flashlight at him. And so, the narrator, dejected, closes his eyes, unable to watch. But eventually, he emerges from his sulk and begins to take an interest in the film again.

The young couple go to a photographer, who, interested not in money but only in art, keeps readjusting the poses of the lovers until the father grows impatient. His son in the audience feels sympathy for the photographer, knows how he feels, but it is the father's implacable will that must be obeyed, and finally, he cajoles the photographer into snapping the photo, which, when it is developed, shows the father's face in an unnatural grimace.

The mother drags the father to a fortune-teller, but now he's grown impatient and hostile, and storms out of the fortune-teller's tent. The mother starts to go after him, but the fortune-teller grabs her arm, and urges, begs the young woman, not to follow. It's at this point that the

narrator goes berserk—several scenes earlier he urged his parents to forget the whole idea of marriage, but now sees the alternative as unbearable. He starts to scream, "What are they doing? Don't they know what
they are doing? Why doesn't my mother go after my father?" And, of
course, the narrator is dragged yelling from the theater by the annoyed
usher, who chides him for acting so irresponsibly. "You will be sorry if
you do not do what you should do. . ." the usher tells him. ". . . you can't
carry on like this, it is not right, you will find that out soon enough,
everything you do matters too much . . ." and with that, the usher
throws the young man out of the theater into the bleak snow, and the
narrator awakes on the cold morning of his twenty-first birthday.

A dream, and we don't even learn that until the end!

*   *   *

In *my* film, I see my mother in Delmore Schwartz's cramped garret in a
boarding house off of Washington Square, she half-deaf, he mumbling
out of embarrassment because he thought her letter was from a man.
And neither understanding the other, so that later he remarked to a
friend that my mother seemed strange. I suppose he was speaking
from experience. Here was a man, however great a poet and short story
writer, whose strangeness, actually madness, fit him like a tailored suit,
and who is at least as well known for that as his writing. Paranoid and
delusional, he eventually drove his wife, Elizabeth Pollet, into hiding,
and once, according to a family friend, went into my father's office in a
murderous rage, seeking her out, and emerged an hour later, somehow
soothed and made rational once again. But that was the exception.

What I see next is my mother and sister, only an infant, in 1948. For
me, like the character in Schwartz's story, the future always looms. I
know the outcomes and can do nothing to stop them, just as his character mentions an uncle "studying in his bedroom upstairs, studying
for his final examination at the College of the City of New York, having
been dead of rapid pneumonia for the last twenty-one years."

My family's reaction to Nola's birth was, as far as I can tell, surpris-
ingly cool headed. If there were recriminations, gnashing of teeth, I
haven't heard of this. My mother, by that time, was in her early thirties,
and the family knew that she was a little different and would lead her
own life regardless of their approval or disapproval. When I asked my
uncle Allan what the family's reaction to my mother's pregnancy was,
he laughed, and said, "Rene and I were a little annoyed. Your mother
stole some of our thunder. No sooner had Rene announced she was

pregnant then here comes your mother and says, 'Guess what, I'm pregnant, too.'"

I'm drawn to a letter, undated, written from my mother to my grandmother in the late forties, when my mother, unwed and living with Nola at my grandmother's beach house in Long Beach, seemed as happy as I've ever known her—although, of course, I didn't know her.

Tuesday night

Dear mother,

All doors are locked. The water heater
is unlighted. The baby is sleeping
angelically. And I have had three
anxious visitors. Grandma. Morty.
And Bill.

Don't you think you worry foolishly? I
am not the helpless child. Nola is.
And at that, she is not so helpless.

Try to get a green lampshade.

It looks as if tomorrow will be a
beautiful day. Maybe one of my friends
will come. I'm beginning to feel
afraid they will come. It's lovely to
be here alone with the baby. Really
very pleasant. I've been very happy
all day. Nola and I slept a lot. I
did a little reading.

Relax.

Love,

E & N

I am not a credits watcher, but when I walk out of the theater, I want to try to come to terms with what I've just seen.

I show the letter to Beverly, but Bev, who has scruples, unlike me, is at first hesitant to read it. "It's kind of private, isn't it? Would she want me to read it?"

"She sent it to me," I say. "Go on," I urge her, the devil on Beverly's shoulder.

She reads the letter and hands it back. "What's she talking about, a green lampshade?"

A green lampshade. For heaven's sake, Beverly focuses on the green lampshade.

"I don't know," I say.

"It's funny that she's telling *her* mother not to worry," Beverly says. Of course, that's true. My mother is a great worrier, as my grandmother was, as I am. I head back upstairs to my study and leave Beverly as Isabel trots out of the family room as if chased by some invisible being, her arms stretched out ahead of her. "Boobie now!" she yells, her war cry and hops into Beverly's lap. I leave this mother and daughter scene, which perhaps I take for granted, for another one that played out before any of us were born. It's impossible for us to always be moved by the same events, the same passage in a letter. I focus on the tenderness of mother and child. Beverly sees the green lampshade. But she understands wordless things between mother and daughter that I'll never know.

*   *   *

The film of my parent's meeting starts forty years after Delmore Schwartz's film, on December 31st, 1949. I wouldn't presume to try to equal Schwartz's achievement by copying it, but this is how I naturally see my parents' meeting, too, cinematically, although my film is quieter, less dramatic, and, as far as I can foresee, I have no reason to stand up and protest, nor to be dragged from the theater. But Delmore Schwartz was present, and I imagine him as one of the ushers, an anti-usher really.

The scene is a New Year's Eve party given by a couple of people my mother knows, the Goldsmith brothers. Mary Goldsmith, the wife of Dick Goldsmith, is bringing in little snacks for the guests. She sets the avocado dip in front of my mother, who takes this as an invitation. Then Mary sets down some cauliflower, and my mother starts dipping the cauliflower in the avocado dip. Delicious. She asks Mary for the recipe. She's bored and eating like crazy. No one else to talk to. All the early guests are friends of the older Goldsmith brother, fraternity types my mother disdains. Just as she's thinking of leaving early, a crowd of her friends walk in: Jane Mayhall and her husband Leslie Katz, Elizabeth Pollet and Delmore Schwartz, a woman named Toshka—the owner of the Four Seasons Bookstore, and her husband Bob. Delmore is smiling, charming people with a story, because at this time, he's only a little crazy, like most of us. Years later, he'll call my mother on the phone, looking for Elizabeth, and just ramble on and on. But now, he's happy. It's New Year's Eve. You can't hear his story, but he's making big gestures. "Make noise," his gestures say. Everyone is laughing around him. "I won't throw you out. You *have* no responsibilities." There's a young woman named Norma, whom my mother doesn't know, and a man with her, Cecil Hemley, who reminds my mother of a Brazilian surrealist painter she has a crush on.

They all sit down and Toshka introduces them. "Have you met Cecil Hemley, the poet?"

My mother waits to be introduced as Elaine Gottlieb, the short story writer and novelist, but Toshka doesn't seem to think this is important. At this time, my mother is a brighter literary light than my dad is. She's published a novel and short stories in some of the best magazines and anthologies. My father has a few poems and stories here and there. My mother feels a bit irked by Toshka's introduction—at least irked enough so that she never forgets the remark and mentions it every time over the next forty years that she tells her son the story of how she and his father met.

If I were to stand up now in the theater, and I'm not saying I would—in fact, I hate it when people make the slightest sound in the theater; I'm one of those people who would have hushed the narrator of Delmore Schwartz's story; he was acting crazy, and yeah, now I know what was going on in his mind and that makes his actions sympathetic, but in real life, you don't get that chance, you're trapped in your own consciousness, and when you see someone standing in front of the screen yelling at it, you yell back, "Down in front," or you huff and wait for the manager to do something, but they never do because theaters don't have ushers anymore.

I'm not the type of person to make a scene, but if I were, I suppose now would be as good a time as any to stand up and not yell, but interrupt as politely as possible, say, "Excuse me, I'm not saying you shouldn't get married, because I think it's not a bad idea. Still, I think there are issues here between the two of you that need to be explored—look Dad, even though I respect you a lot (I can't really say I love you anymore because I don't know you), you have to admit, from the very outset your career is taking precedence over hers. I know you didn't introduce yourself that way, that Toshka did, but you're complicit. I saw how you puffed up. And Mom, maybe you should just say something instead of stewing about it. Okay, I know it's the dawning of the fifties, not the most enlightened age when it comes to gender roles, and you are both just products of your times; hindsight makes judgment too easy. So we shouldn't blame anyone in particular, maybe just the times, but here's what's going to happen. Remember what Delmore said in his magnificent story? "Everything you do matters too much," he said, and it's true. So is the opposite. Now you've set the ball rolling, as they say. You've started a pattern. In a couple of years, after the two of you get married and Dad starts Noonday Press, your writing is going to come last. You'll be expected to work at Noonday, to help with the latest Singer translation, to help Dad edit his own work, to take care of the kids, and then maybe, if no one else makes further demands on you, you might have an hour or two to write. It's not the end of your career, but it won't help. And some of this resentment will be borne past Dad's death (yes, Dad, you'll die when I'm seven, sorry to be so blunt about it, but maybe you should put out that cigarette now) and will be transformed into pride in your son, and a residue of competition with him. We share, after all, the same material, as it were. And Dad, Dad, listen, look please, she has a little daughter. Her name is Nola, and she's an inventive, imaginative child who never met her own father, and you're not going to pay much attention to her either. So maybe you should just think about that. Just think about it. Show her a little affection."

And in my film, unlike Delmore Schwartz's, the characters can see me. At least a single character can see me. My film has been influenced by Woody Allen, not only Delmore Schwartz. And Delmore himself gets up and faces me, addresses me—he's the one who can see me, he's crazy after all, and the other people at the Goldsmiths' party look at him, but he says, "Louder, kid. No one can hear you. We're a long way off."

And my mother tells me now that it wasn't avocado dip.

"But I have it written down, taped transcripts. That's what you told me. Avocado dip."

"No, it wasn't avocado dip. I asked her mother for the recipe."

"Her mother?"

"Her mother. She was there. She was helping out with the dip. Let's see, it had sour cream and mustard and what else?"

"It doesn't matter. I'll say avocado."

Despite the slight, my mother feels attracted to Cecil Hemley, who comes over to talk with her. But she's shy. He's with this woman, Norma, although my mother doesn't know Cecil and Norma were only paired up for the evening by their friends. My mother doesn't talk much. Later, much later, he tells her he thought she was a snob that night. But we don't know this. We can't see their interior thoughts, although we might intuit them from a gesture, a glance. This is film. She's seated in a stuffed chair and he's on the floor beside her. She balances a plate of snacks with some dip on her lap, leaning forward to hear him better. The audience can't tell what kind of dip it is. It's greenish, but yellowish, too, like stone-ground mustard. The camera zooms in on her plate, as though the dip holds some special significance.

He sucks on a cigarette.

"Excuse me," he says. I'm going to get some more champagne. Can I get you any?"

He stands up and she shakes her head, mouth full, she smiles awkwardly.

JUMP CUT

The Four Seasons Bookstore some months later. Interior shot.

My mother is at the counter chatting with Toshka, and Nola stands beside them restlessly. Cecil Hemley enters the store and my mother and father recognize each other. He gives Toshka a wave and glances at Nola. He comes over to say hello, and my mother tells Nola to go look at some books, and Nola, three years old, happily runs off to the children's section . . . oh, who am I fooling? This isn't a film, it's a story, no not even that. What I want to tell you next is a brief scenario, the next time my mother and father met, how he bought a Babar book for Nola and my mother didn't even notice the book until she returned home . . .

In college, I was a film major, not an English major. I studied film criticism—although I was attracted to English I didn't want to be an English major and follow too closely the lives of my parents. The Great Rebellion. One of my teachers told me that film was the art form of the twentieth century, and that literature no longer had a function in society. I resisted that notion then, told her that she was wrong, that literature would always be important. But *sometimes* now (in my more cynical moments), I think she was being too optimistic, that film is also a dying art form. The new art form is the home page.

I don't resist change. I embrace it. The Internet, at least, is closer to memory, to the associative properties of memory, than even film. One thing leads to another and another and another.

Click on the underlined words for more information or links to other sites.

My mother and father in the Four Seasons Bookstore.

Did he really buy the book for Nola?" my mother asks Toshka on the phone.

"Come on over for a beer," my mother says to my father. "Bring your own."

Translators

First I thought I was a writer. Then I realized I was a Jew. Then I
no longer distinguished the writer in me from the Jew
because one and the other are only torments of an ancient word.

EDMOND JABÈS

It's Yiddish, not Hebrew, that I'd like to know. The words I know are so
few. *Gay kacken afen yam,* go shit in the ocean, is about all my relatives
taught me, and I have only one book written in Yiddish, *The Yiddish
Teacher,* published in 1939. I open the book up to the copyright page
and can get no further than the starkness of that date. I have little desire to learn Hebrew as my brother has. He has always had a facility for
languages, and speaks Hebrew fluently now. It's Yiddish, such a useless
language, that I want to know, in part because this language was so important to my parents and their careers, although they barely spoke a
word of it either. I think somehow the cadences of Yiddish, the bleak
deprecating humor of the *shtetl,* the schtick, survives somehow like a
genetic imprint in me.

The word, "translator," is used by radio stations for a kind of relay
station that picks up a weak signal from the mother station and trans-
mits it to a broader audience than might pick up the original signal.
Words are perhaps the best translators we have for actions, emotions,
and ideas, but still not powerful enough to capture the original signal
in all its invisible and swift complexity.

My father was Isaac Singer's editor and both my parents were his
translators from 1953 until my father's death. But to call what my father and mother did translation is a bit of a misnomer. It's no less important than translating, but my parents didn't know Yiddish.

Singer would do a rough translation, or his nephew Joseph would
do this, and often these translations were quite rough, the words jum-
bled or in the plainest English, and my father, my mother, Saul
Bellow, Elizabeth Pollet, or his other trans-editors, would go over the

manuscript, polishing the prose, making it not merely sensible, but artful. Trans-editing might be a more appropriate term. When Singer won the Nobel Prize, the judges had not read his work in Yiddish, but in the English translations, and one of the works the Nobel Committee cited in its presentation was Singer's novel, *The Slave,* which my father trans-edited. My father had won a Shadow Nobel Prize. They were Singer's thoughts everyone was reading, but my father's words.

*   *   *

Another translation:

> August 8, 1976
> Elaine Gottlieb Hemley is a serious, intense woman of middle age, the mother of two sons and the widow of Cecil Hemley, the poet and translator. In the 1950s both of them played a significant role in the next stage of Isaac Singer's career.
> Mrs. Hemley wears her dark-brown curly hair short. Her brown eyes peer out solemnly through dark-rimmed glasses. Dressed informally in a purple T-shirt, lavender slacks, and white summer shoes, she relaxes on a sofa bed in the living room of her mother's home in Long Beach, Long Island.

So begins a section on my mother, my father, and the Noonday Press in Paul Kresh's 1979 biography of Singer. When this biography appeared my mother was upset with Kresh because he'd revealed things she'd told him "in confidence." She calls the biography "unscholarly." She says that there were many inaccuracies, and warns me that I'd better check with her first before I quote anything from Kresh's book.

She was also worried what Singer would think of her comments when he read the book—I remember her worrying about this, just as I worry about her reaction to my words.

But if Singer was upset with her, I don't think he ever said anything.

What my mother told me of the starting of the Noonday Press and what she told Paul Kresh for his biography of Singer are slightly different, but only in tone. With Kresh, she gave him unadorned facts, except what she says she told him "in confidence." I wonder if she thinks she's made a similar assertion with me, although the only thing I know I've promised is to show her the book when it's done. With me, she sometimes lets slip things that I can't possibly report, things that I might report, but that might make her seem petty, or me seem petty, although they might be true. These are mostly aspects of color, what a translator would want to bring from the mother language to the new text—as when my mother says that one of my father's partners at Noonday was there for his money, not his talent, when she says of him that he had "literary pretensions." This is the kind of thing best left out of my telling.

What she told Kresh was this:

> My husband and Arthur A. Cohen founded the Noonday Meridian Press, and they were on the lookout for quality writers. One evening in 1953 Cecil went to visit Dan Talbot . . . . In the course of the evening Dan read to us Saul Bellow's translation of 'Gimpel the Fool'—the story which had just been published in the May issue of *Partisan Review.* We were all mad for it. I think another of Cecil's partners, Bill Webb, was there that night.

And so on.

The student who typed up the transcripts of *my* interviews with my mother has no idea who most of these people are, and continually misspells their names. Arthur Cohen in my version has been transformed into Arthur Colon. Everything is transformed, even a word-for-word transcript. There are places that have been written as "unintelligible" or simply ? I love it when I happen upon a question mark. It makes the search seem more genuine.

So, in my version, a Mr. Arthur Colon, whose father had made a lot of money in the clothing business, was approached by my father and several others. Mr. Colon had LITERARY PRETENSIONS and money, and this enabled Noonday to start publishing. Noonday never did very well financially, but it published some of the best writers of this or any era. Besides Singer, they published Boris Pasternak, Herman Hesse, Jean-Paul Sartre, Machado de Assis, the philosopher Karl Jaspers, the poet Louise Bogan. My father was the driving force behind Noonday, and later when Noonday was bought by Farrar Straus, Roger Straus brought him to Farrar Straus as an editor.

Isaac Singer's first book was published by Knopf, *The Family Moskat.* One would hope that Singer, if he were starting to write novels today, would be well received by any number of good houses, but one can't be sure. The Family Muscrat? The Family Mascot? Satan in Goray? Where's Goray? *Satan* sells, but maybe you should put him in

Montana. *Satan in Montana.* Yentl the Yeshiva Boy? Our fall list is al-ready too heavy with books about yeshivas.

Singer was unhappy with the cuts Knopf had made in his novel, and so he went to my father and cast his fortune with the struggling Noonday Press. In a literary sense, it was probably the best thing Singer ever did. Singer, of course, was also the best thing that hap-pened to Noonday.

*   *   *

Several years after Singer's death, nothing approaching a comprehen-sive biography has yet been written, although at least one person I know of has tried. The father of one of my good friends was autho-rized a few years ago by Singer's widow Alma and a major publisher to write a biography. This man set about interviewing everyone who was still alive who had known Singer, including my mother, and he was given unprecedented access to Singer's letters and papers. I even photo-copied letters from Singer to my father and sent them to him. My friend's father hired her to type the transcripts of these interviews, and every once in a while she'd call me up and tell me what a horrible man she thought Singer was. She said her whole opinion of him had changed. I didn't press her for details because she was sworn to secrecy by her father, and I admit, I was more interested in what people had to say about my father in these taped interviews. She told me that over and over people talked about my father in glowing terms, saying how tirelessly he worked to promote Singer. "You know, Robin," she told me once, "the one name that keeps coming up is your father's."

Strangely, there was one transcript that my friend's father would not let her transcribe. This was the interview he had done with my mother. He knew that his daughter and I were good friends. What could be on that tape? Why all the secrecy? My first thoughts run to the mundane and improbable. For a fleeting second, I think maybe my mother had an affair with Singer or something of that nature. But I know this is un-true. How do I know this is untrue? My mother wouldn't volunteer such information to me—okay, I don't know it's not true, so I'd better just call her up and ask her. My friend says her father, whom I've only met once, is the chivalrous type, and she thinks that my mother simply said some things about my father that he thought might be unpleasant for me to hear—that my father, for instance could be influenced by Singer in ways that were unflattering, that around Singer, his attitudes toward women became more negative. Perhaps, but then he's being too chivalrous because this knowledge wouldn't shock me. I recently ran into a friend of the family, a poet, and I told her that I thought maybe my father had stymied my mother's career. "Your father *was* a wonderful person," our friend told me. "But human. I know you're too good a writer to judge him." I definitely don't want to judge him, I told our friend. "Your mother probably didn't even know any better back then," she told me. "None of us did. We hadn't had our consciousnesses raised." I related this conversation to my mother who told me, "I certainly *did* know better, and I resented it!"

"I was a little annoyed with your parents," our family friend tells me. "They didn't tell me about Singer. They brought him for a reading to Athens, and he seemed so . . . charming, and then when I went to New York to visit him, well, he just started in." She laughs and says, "No one warned me." According to my friend whose father was writing the biography, Singer would sometimes quiz women about their menstruation and how and when they lost their virginity.

"That must have been when he was losing his marbles," my mother tells me.

"What? When did he lose his marbles?"

"Maybe when he was older. He never said anything like that to me."

"Did he ever make a pass at you, Mom?"

She laughs, maybe at the archaic term, or more likely, at the thought.

"A verbal pass, once. It was after your father died, when I brought him out to Slippery Rock (Slippery Rock, Pennsylvania, where she had her first teaching job). On the way to the airport he said to everyone in the car, 'I consider Mrs. Hemley a very desirable woman.' I didn't know what to say. It was embarrassing."

A strange remark, but not what I'd consider a pass. But now I know that at least Singer isn't my real father.

But my mother agrees that Singer did not hold women in high regard. He used to say, "A woman is long on hair and short on sense," and apparently he regarded feminists with even less esteem. When Singer said these things, my father would agree, and my mother would feel "uncomfortable."

Of the biography my friend's father was writing, I can tell you this: One day, his source dried up. One day, Alma, Singer's widow, would no longer give him access to her letters. My mother always liked Alma and felt that Singer treated her terribly. Alma is dead now, and I'm sure that a new biography is in the works, and that maybe this one will approach a certain truth, will demystify the man, because that is what we all want, isn't it? None of us are immune to the need to know everything, to pry into the darkest corners and topple our heroes.

There are things I want to say, but can't.

But what does it really matter anyway? There are some things in the translation that can't be spoken, certain gestures and looks that accompany words, certain words that have no exact meaning. And didn't I mention that this is all a translation? My sister's memoir is written in Sanskrit. The letters I have from my family are in Yiddish. My mother tells me her story in church Latin. And I say my own words in tongues, languages that aren't human. I can't even understand them before rendering them in English.

The Pattern of Her Dreams

The dream instructions which I was receiving with increased frequency bore a significance which carried into ~~the events of~~ my waking life. Their quality was ~~without exception~~ so ~~vivid~~ *in-tense* that I never ~~seemed to be afflicted by the forgetfulness ex-perienced by most~~ *forgot them.* My dream perception sharpened until ~~my~~ *I acquired the* ability to function in a higher intuitive consciousness than what is accepted as normal ~~crept into me, and made it increasingly difficult for me to find any common subject of discussion with my classmates or friends, who were actually operating on a different frequency than I, although I could not yet put it in those terms, and endless misunderstand-ings arose as a result~~.

. . . . I [began] to read, and derive a strange fascination from, the chapters of the Bible on the conversion of Saint Paul, whose blindness on the Damascus road I felt as I would my own,[1] whose self-annihilation and rechristening I read with ~~a~~ delight ~~so interfused with pain that it became a symphony of ethereal conflicts~~. Whenever I read about the blindness, the shock of four days spent without sight ~~in a constant state of disintegra-tion of the petty self~~, my whole being would tremble with ~~a ter-rible~~ joy[2] which I was as little able to explain as the sensations

---

1. "The men who were traveling with him stood speechless, hearing the voice but seeing no one. Saul [later called Paul] arose from the ground; and when his eyes were opened, he could see nothing; so they led him by the hand and brought him into Damascus. And for three days he was without sight, and neither ate nor drank."—Acts 9.

2. She often uses this construction: "a terrible joy" or "a terrible ecstasy," and just as often crosses out the word "terrible" (or else it's my mother who has crossed out the word. I can't be sure). Both the acknowledgment of the pain and terror of religious ecstasy and the negation of that pain seem contained in those phrases, those erasures.

of my original experience. That year (I was fourteen) I wrote a research paper on Saint Paul, as well as the esoteric deities of the Zoroastrian and Babylonian religions. I must have read them with considerable ~~identification and~~ emotion, since it seemed to have a peculiar effect on the class, who ~~greeted~~ *re-acted to* it with ~~a kind of silent~~ shock. It was never possible for me to tell them the sensations I had felt in my research and writing connected with saints, or the peculiar method of intuitive study I had developed over the years by which I was able to apprehend the answers to questions on examinations through an almost extrasensory skill . . . .

At the age of fifteen I began reading Bacon and Spinoza, and grew fascinated with a passage in the *Ethics* concerning the dimensions of space-time, and their intersections which created the framework of human activity, that matter and mind were only two aspects of one substance. This I felt without a doubt to be true, although I found it impossible to explain to others. My philosophic perceptions were just beginning to grow to maturity, and I began to realize that it was somehow my destiny to unravel esoteric mysteries. I had a dream at that period that I was standing before the mouth of a pitch black cave; behind me were crowds of frightened people, who looked into it furtively and refused to enter. I stepped into the cave without hesitation. This has been the habit of my life ever since.

The Unbridgeable Gap

My father and mother . . . were in the world and not of it—not
because they were saints, but in a different way: because they were
artists. The integrity of an artist lifts a man above the level of the
world without delivering him from it.

THOMAS MERTON, *The Seven Storey Mountain*

My father's story will be short, in part because I've reconciled with him
what I needed to reconcile a long time ago. I suppose there's anger in
the statement, "My father's story will be short." I know, of course, that
he did not plan on dying when I was seven—if he had he might have
done a better job of it, left us more prepared—but anger doesn't have
to be rational. This much I share at least with everyone else in the
world. But my anger isn't as dramatic as rage, nor self-pity, just a dull
blue flame near my solar plexus, like a pilot light.

Let me start with his death and work my way backward through his
life, and what he shared briefly with me—no, not his death but his
afterdeath. For years, in my dreams he'd appear to me—in the dark suit
we buried him in, standing by the retaining wall of our house in
Athens, Ohio. This house has come back to me in many dreams, usually emptied of our belongings and in disrepair, which isn't far from

the truth. It's the only house my parents ever owned. Situated in a small valley on the outskirts of town, surrounded by farms, ours was one of the first houses in a development, and for most of the years we lived there, seemed more a part of the country than suburbia.

The house had originally been built at the top of one of the hills, but had slid down in a rainstorm, and the developers rebuilt it where it stopped. The first story was built into the slope of the hill, and most of this story was subterranean, except for the front, which had a large picture window facing the road. The retaining wall was directly outside this picture window, perpendicular to it. The wall did a very poor job of retaining. Unsurprisingly, in light of the house's checkered history, the builders had not fussed over structural niceties, and as a consequence, the hill was slowly reclaiming the house. I doubt it still stands.

It was in front of this house, against the bulging wall, that I often saw my father in my dreams, looking lost and retarded. His eyes looked vacant, his suit was wrinkled, and flecks of earth clung to him.

My father as a zombie, as Marley's Ghost. Come back to haunt me and tell me what? Someone in the dream, usually my mother, would explain that my father had been "cured" of death, but it wasn't a complete cure. While he was still my father, there was something missing—perhaps a soul. That's not how it was explained to me, but that's how I see it now. He was physically there, but that was all, and I was instructed that he was to receive the same affection I had always shown him. But how could I?

*   *   *

My father had his fatal heart attack on my brother's thirteenth birthday.

That, of course, is a loaded sentence. This, in a twisted and terrible sense, was my brother's Bar Mitzvah, his introduction to manhood. Years later, my brother told me that my father had given him a watch for his birthday—to Jonathan, there could have been no more appropriate or symbolic gift. My brother was definitely my father's favorite, as I was my mother's; we were each under the protection of these respective parents. Whatever Jonathan did was excused by my father. Whatever I did was defended by my mother. On the night my father had his heart attack, he and my brother had a bad argument, and it's likely that my brother felt enormous, though unnecessary, guilt for this, just as I had guilt, and believed I had killed my father. A couple of weeks before, my father had angered me for some reason, and I remember standing in front of the dinner table, biting my right-hand ring finger—a very strange and aggressive habit of mine when I was a child. Whenever I was enraged, I would bite this finger, and I had calluses from constant biting throughout much of my childhood. As I bit my finger, I'd shout three nonsense words—a kind of battle cry, and I have no idea where they came from. "Hama! Peemo! Hong Kong!" I'd shout, and my family would know I'd gone off the deep end. My brother thought my display was hilarious, which further enraged me. My sister was always trying to figure out the meaning and origin of these words. Hong Kong was obvious, but Hama and Peemo were more elusive, and she always suspected these words had something to do with a past life.

After I shouted "Hama, Peemo, Hong Kong," at my father, he told me to sit down and finish eating or I'd be punished.

"I hope you die," I yelled at him. He chased me into the living room where I hid underneath a Victorian loveseat, thinking I was safe. My father lifted the loveseat, amazing me that anyone could be so strong, and I became hysterical. I don't remember what happened next, but I probably cried out to my Lord Protector, Mommy, and she came to the rescue.

Within two weeks, my father was dead. But my father was the only one who killed himself. He smoked three packs of cigarettes a day, never exercised, ate meat and potatoes, was overworked and overstressed.

*   *   *

My father died during Nola's freshman year at Ohio University. For a while she lived with us at home, but then she transferred to the dorm. She and my father did not get along. He was not able to show her the love he showed his biological children. More than this, he was cruel to her, even brutal. I know this only because of another notebook Nola left behind. This one came into my possession in an odd way. My mother told me on several occasions of its existence. "I have another notebook you might be interested in," she said, "from when Nola was seventeen or eighteen. But I'm not sure I want to show it to you. She wrote in it that she hated me, and that hurt me very much." Perhaps I didn't want to read this either, because I knew that Nola loved my mother. But on my mother's last visit, she brought it with her and left it on the kitchen table where she knew I would find it. But even then, I didn't look. Beverly pointed it out to me. "Your mother left some papers on the table," and so I picked it up and started reading. Perhaps I thought I didn't need any more documents, that anything new would simply confuse the issue. And that's right—this new document my mother teased me with confuses the issue entirely, and that's why I'm glad I have it, why my mother left it on the table for me to find by accident.

> I do not know if God has ever heard or helped me, but if he has, he has a pretty underhanded way of going about it because I have received no external signs. The only hope approaching this is my Ednah dream at 13, which my mother regards as a joke. Damn her! Is she compulsively blind? But then I ask, as always, is my soul-search any more significant than her forced repressions? She is too, too critical; if she bites once more, I shall go mad—as I have too often in the past. My innumerable fits—what else spurred them but complete isolation and an incomprehensible, critical mother who always attests she is sane and I am not. Cecil I will not mention. Whoever reads this, out of curiosity, spite, or hellish impudence I know not—can read of Cecil in the Tuesday Times, or The Saturday Evening Post. His private life is surely subjected to this nonsense; if it were not, he wouldn't be such a damn lousy father. Enough of him. I don't want to be forced to burn this paper, so better say no more . . .

I wonder if my sister was writing this notebook to my father, hoping he'd find it, this document attesting her confused love and hatred for him. Perhaps we can see in this notebook the roots of all her problems. Obviously, she was furious when she wrote this. Who knows how much she'd disavow if she could? But perhaps I just want her to disavow it. My mother says Nola was being melodramatic, but still, I see truths here: my mother's sometimes critical nature, for one. Her forced repressions. And what did Nola mean by "my innumerable fits?" My mother tells me that she meant ordinary temper tantrums, not bouts of mania as *my* melodramatic imagination would have it. And my mother claims she didn't treat my sister's dream of Ednah as a joke, but treated it as something "more ordinary, because I didn't want her to go off the deep end . . . which she did anyhow." My mother wonders why Nola expressed such hostility to her in this notebook when they had always been so close, except that "she would rather that I had not been married to Cecil."

I can see why when I read a little further.

I must get out into some vast and immutable space where I can begin *pure*. I am tortured here. I cannot bear the suffocation of the dorm. And here—I cannot help it if I'm not his daughter—he is rude, cold, brutal and coarse with me—and flies into a psychotic rage when I assert my individuality apart from himself. Yesterday, I said I was tired when he said he was tired. "Ya lousy bitch," he yelled and loosed a fork at me. This barely grazed my head. "what are you but an eighteen-year-old squirt?" In the process of this denunciation he toppled countless objects about the table—which came flying toward me as a Lewis Carroll pack of cards. He then haughtily sipped his tea and left. I couldn't bear it and dissolved into depression and tears.

I work *so* hard and practically break my back—and then return home to have this terrifying mad egoist fall at me because I am not his child. When he does not do this, he ignores me—taking care to coddle Jonny and Robin (mostly the former) because they *are* his children. On top of this, mother tells me not to yield so much of my emotions. I must hide them before this almighty lunatic. He cannot be reasoned with—she assures me that he is not discriminating. If this continues I will crack utterly and make my eternal home in the asylum.

"Is this true?" I ask my mother after reading my sister's notebook.

"It's true," she tells me. My mother clearly remembers the scene Nola describes, and she tells me that Nola, in helpless retaliation sailed a cup across the room, not toward my father, but away. My mother gestures, flinging her hand open, and we follow the invisible arc of that cup across the room and time, where it shatters.

"But I thought people remembered him . . . everyone remembers him as so kind."

"They didn't know that side of him. He *was* kind most of the time, but not to her. He had a temper. He used to swat at her."

I wonder now, as I reread the passage above, if I've found the murder weapon, if it's as simple as that, if all my sister's problems come down to this fractured relationship between her and my father. I know

now I will never see him the same way. But I don't want to put all the blame on my father because cause and effect are too complex to be reduced so easily.

"I don't know why he treated her this way," my mother says. "Here was this sweet-natured girl who only wanted love, and he was incapable of it."

"Did you try to intervene?" I ask.

"I did," she says. "I tried to take her away from him, to stand in the way, but I know if I had pushed it, the marriage would have ended in divorce. I married him because I wanted Nola to have a father."

"But . . . I thought you loved him."

"I did. I learned to love him. By the end, we were inseparable. And he and Nola started getting along toward the end of his life, when she could talk to him about philosophy."

"But this notebook," I say. "Wasn't it written during the last year of his life? It doesn't sound like they were getting along."

"Yes," she says. "I don't know," and I don't pursue the subject any further. I think of the family friend who told me, "Your father was a wonderful person, but human. I know you're too good a writer to judge him." I still don't want to judge him.

Later, my mother and I are discussing the time late in Nola's life when she was at her sickest and she tried to strangle me.

"You know why she did that, don't you?" my mom says.

"What?" I say, not understanding because it seems so obvious—she was trying to kill me. "What do you mean?"

"Cecil did the same thing to her when she was a child."

"What are you talking about?" I say. "You never told me this."

"Yes, he tried to strangle her. It was before you were born and Jonny was just a baby. Cecil and I were planning on going out for the evening. We hadn't been married that long, and Cecil loved to go out, but Nola was acting stubborn. She didn't want me to leave. She kept running up to me and hugging me and she didn't want me to leave. She said she wouldn't look at the baby-sitter and that she'd just wait on her window ledge until we returned. Cecil finally went up to her and put his hands on her neck. I was so stunned at first. I couldn't believe it, and then I stepped between. Nola barricaded herself in her room, and you know, she *did* wait by her window ledge until we came back. She told me she never forgot that. And she told me when she was strangling you, she was trying to get back at him."

"But that doesn't make any sense," I say. "I wasn't Dad."

"You were his child, and Jonny wasn't around."

"But I'm your child, too."

"She wasn't thinking that way. She wanted to strike back at him."

"Why didn't you ever tell me this?" I say.

"I thought I had," she says.

On a visit to *her* house, she shows me the cup Nola threw across the room after my father's tantrum. She has saved it all these years, a broken-handled handmade mug in shades of green and brown that Nola gave to my mother as a special present because she thought "it matched my eyes. It reminded her of me somehow. I wonder why she chose that cup to throw."

*   *   *

Last year, I was at a conference where I met Sandra, a family friend. I told her about the book I'm writing. I told her that I was afraid my mother might be upset when she read the book. "Maybe she'll never read it," our friend said.

"Oh, she'll read it. If I wrote it."

"She might never talk to you about it. Your mother has a way of avoiding painful topics. I suppose you don't know how she acted the night your father died."

Of course, that hooked me.

She told me that the night my father died, the doctor had told my mom not to leave the hospital, that Dad was gravely ill and most likely wouldn't survive the night. Sandra had driven with my mother to Columbus. But after my mother talked with the doctor, she came out and said she wanted to go home to Athens. Sandra knew nothing of what the doctor had told my mother. So they left and drove the sixty miles back to Athens. "We sang the entire way home," Sandra said. Then she added, "Nola must have been with us . . . if we were singing. Funny, I don't remember her there, but she must have been."

She was. Nola recounts the trip in her memoir:

> I visited the critical room with a friend of my mother's; as I had suspected, his face was tinged with a horrible green, which had crept insidiously over the lines and crannies of his face, as if death had already made its root and home there, and had only to be acknowledged. My mother refused to recognize the mor-

tality in his eyes, kept telling herself that it couldn't happen, not
to one she had depended on emotionally for so long. That
evening I drove home with my mother's friend and began to
sing a song I had learned from *Camelot:* "Far from day, far from
night," intoxicated by the deathlike lure in its lines and
rhythms, as if the song itself were carrying me with it into that
sweet deadly land of night . . . .

Later that night, our family doctor, Dr. Goldberg, called Sandra and
said, "Where's Elaine?"

"What do you mean?" Sandra said. "She's at home."

"I told her not to leave Columbus. Cecil is dying."

Dr. Goldberg drove to my mother's house and banged on all the
doors. My mother was sitting inside with all the lights blazing, her
hearing aid turned off.

It's a painful story and a remarkable one. My mother was alone with
her grief. I was away, staying with family friends, and so was my brother.
Thirty years distant from that night, I wish I could reach back and comfort her. In her story, "The Habit of Loving," she has me, or the character based on me at seven, saying, "Everyone has to die. Don't cry."

$$* \quad * \quad *$$

There was a visitation at the funeral home. I could see my father in his
casket surrounded by flowers as we stood in the lobby. He was in an ad-
jacent room, and people filed through it slowly while my mother stood
in the hallway talking. I didn't want to go in at first to see him. After
all, I had killed him, I thought, and someone was going to find out. My
mother told me I had to go see him, to say good-bye. Nola took my
hand and Jonathan led the way. The casket was low enough so that I
didn't have to be lifted to see him. I see him clearly now, his round face
and dark hair, thinning toward the bald side. I was scared and bewildered, but fascinated, too. I looked at him in death. He had a gentle
face. He was in front of me, but he was gone.

The visitation room emptied and eventually my father was left
alone in the room with the flowers. There was something private I saw
in death. A dead person took up the entire space in the room. For
some reason, I decided to go back into the visitation room. I was the
only one in there, and I approached my father's coffin again, slowly. I
wanted to see his face again, to remember it surely, but also just to

study it, to try to figure it out. As I approached the coffin, his arm lifted out and flopped back down. I ran out of the visitation room screaming.

"Mom, Mom, he moved his arm!" I yelled.

Someone, maybe Dr. Goldberg or a family friend, took me aside and said, gently but firmly, "Don't bother your mother now, Robin."

I don't remember what Nola's reaction was, but no one wanted to hear this, so I quickly shut up. Truthfully, I can't say for sure that this happened, although I absolutely believe it did. I remember his arm lifting out of the coffin and settling back down again. I remember thinking that my father was really alive, that he was just asleep, and that they were making a terrible mistake. Perhaps this caused in part my dreams of his return. On several occasions over the next few years, I asked my mother if they could have possibly been mistaken. She said no, it was impossible, that they'd done an autopsy, that I was imagining things. But I don't think I was. I know that such things happen, that there are involuntary muscle reactions that occur sometimes long after death.

*   *   *

I used to think that I became a writer in part because of my father's early death, that in some way I was trying to earn his approval by choosing his profession. That's often what I told people. It seemed like a comfortable lie. It fit and seemed true, but I don't think it is now. I think, now, that it's simply in my disposition, in my makeup, as it was in his, as it was in my mother's, that's there's no one answer, no simple reason for anything, just as I can't reduce my brother's spiritual quest, or my sister's madness, to one simple reason. I'm tempted to use the knowledge that my father had his heart attack on my brother's thirteenth birthday as a simple reason for Jonathan's turning to religion, but once, when I asked him about his beliefs, Jonathan said he'd simply done some studying and Judaism made sense to him. The same is true with me. Writing made sense to me and still does.

When my father died, a posthumous collection of his poetry and prose was published by Ohio University Press. My father's literary obituary ran in the *New York Times Book Review* a year and a half after his death, on November 26th, 1967. To me, there's so *much* of me in this review. So many of the conflicts my father explored in his poetry and prose, I'm still exploring. His whole precarious position between God and nature and art, an impossible straddle, is the position in which I find myself today.

The Papers of a Poet

Dimensions of Midnight. Poetry and Prose. By Cecil Hemley. Edited by
Elaine Gottlieb. Foreword by Mark Van Doren. 233 pp. Athens: Ohio
University Press. $6.

By CHAD WALSH

Still in his early fifties, Cecil Hemley died last year. The director first
of the Noonday Press and later of the Ohio University Press, he was
a versatile writer, novelist, poet, playwright, and critic. He was also,
from all accounts, a gentle and compassionate man—I remember
the letter in which he rejected a book of my verse with the consoling
postscript, "I see you and I both continue to believe in iambic pentameter." Now his collected verse (including many poems previously unpublished) and his selected prose—minus the novels—is
made available.

What the book reveals is a craftsman of a high order, but a writer
to whom content and moral sensitivity are even more important
than craft alone. He is a civilized man, viewing a world of mixed
comedy and tragedy and pathos, but gravely observing the brief
players on the stage and giving them the same courteous due that
he accorded himself as another player on the same stage.

His stories are full of ironical twists that reveal how far separated
are appearance and reality. "At the End of Summer" is the account of
a young faculty wife bored with her pedestrian husband and lured
by a strong-willed cynical scholar; it is the husband who proves to
have understanding and depth when the showdown comes. "In a
Great Tradition" tells of a second-rate but incurably buoyant artist
whose skill at procreation compensates for his maladroitness with
paint and canvas. The one-act play, "An Appointment with the
Master," ironically presents the reverse meeting of East and West,
when a Hindu swami decides to give up holiness and get a job in the
secular city, and the employees of the agency where he applies insist
that he become their spiritual director and lead them into the serenity of Oriental mysticism.

Hemley reveals himself most of all in his poetry. He wrote that
kind of verse which is least in vogue today. It is neither roughhewn
and raucous nor dutifully intellectual and technically involuted.
His favorite meter is indeed iambic pentameter, though in his later
verse he experiments with wilder and more rugged rhythms. But for
the most part, he feels at home in traditional forms. The nearest
parallel might be E.A. Robinson at the height of the "modern poetry" revolution, when his sonnets and blank verse contrasted
equally with an Eliot or a Sandburg.

The tone even more than the technique gives Hemley's poetry a special quality. He writes as a Platonist by temperament. He sees the shadows on the wall of the cave, and yearns to behold the original figure face to face. But he does not deprecate shadows. The things of this earth—nature, love, moments of religious intuition—while not the unreachable ultimate, are still good and real in their own light. Always, however, there is the sense in his poetry either of paradise lost or paradise rumored and yet to be grasped.

The sense of things hoped for but not quite seen is strong in one of his longer poems, "Seas and Seasons," with its vividly drawn pictures of nature's changing moments, but ending:

> *Is there such perfume? Are*
> *there such floods?*
> *Do you, my dead, enjoy such*
> *calm,*
> *Freed from your loves, freed*
> *from your hates,*
> *At last that beauty you*
> *sought to become?*

The subdued tone of the above contrasts with the greater violence—of language and meter—in a later poem. "August Storm.":

> *That jealous god of storm and*
> *lightning*
> *Scattering the fleet*
> *Of trawlers busy in the gray,*
> *Yahweh, dressed as whirlwind,*
> *Kicking up the sea.*

Hemley's poetry, in fact, stands in a perennial tradition of meditations upon the broken beauty, the mingled glory and pathos of the tangible world; the unbridgeable gap between that world and the world sensed by imagination or faith. Part of the power of his poetry is that he does not opt exclusively for one or the other; even while yearning for the unseen he celebrates the present world and its inhabitants in perceptive and loving verses. It is not the kind of poetry likely to receive much attention in a period marked by poetic eccentricities and strident personal assertions. I am equally convinced that some of it—particularly certain of the later poems—will steadily establish themselves in that small anthology of common consent, compiled by sensitive opinion as the winnowing process goes on through the decades and centuries.

Mr. Walsh is a poet, critic and chairman of the English department at Beloit.

When I was born, according to my mother, Isaac Singer visited her in the hospital and seeing me in the nursery, said, "He looks like he'll be half poet and half publisher," exactly what my father was. But what hits me now is not the bald fact that we both chose the same career, but that our writing involves the same tensions between the irony of the intellect and the yearning for things of the spirit. This seems to me the exact dilemma that my family as a whole has always been bound by. In what do we put our faith, holy texts or secular ones? Nothing can be read literally, nothing is that simple. Everything is open to interpretation and revision.

To me, the unbridgeable gap is not, as Mr. Walsh put it, between nature and things of the imagination or faith, but *between* imagination and faith. Imagination is about possibilities, potential, faith is about acceptance, finally, and that is too much of a commitment for some of us to make. Imagination can be used in the service of faith, and faith can find its outlet in a thing of imaginative beauty—but still, I see the worlds of art and of spirituality as separate ones. One can have a foot in both worlds, but ultimately, one must step over into one world or another—imagination, I believe, is solipsistic, relativistic, and faith is not. Imagination, for me, is a constant series of explosions, of firework bursts that shine brilliantly and then disappear as they fall to the ground. At some point, faith does not explode any longer but rockets into the clouds and disappears from view. It is there that imagination cannot reach.

The sense of things hoped for but not quite seen . . .

Though I acknowledge my limitations, I am ultimately a relativist, if not a solipsist. I cannot help but see relations between things. I cannot make up my mind. I cannot help but see the beauty in that helplessness, that lack of commitment, but that doesn't stop me from yearning for certainty. This is exactly how my father's poetry speaks to me, speaks for me, this is where I feel so close to him I know I could have come from no other.

What splits me off from belief finally is irony, the twentieth century's curse, my golden calf. I cannot throw it away, cannot repudiate it because it seems almost a birthright. And here, I see another split in my father that signifies the split in me—the split between the irony of his prose, "An Appointment with the Master," "At the End of Summer," contrasted to the vulnerability of the poetry. The stance, the voice is completely different. In his poetry, he is a supplicant. In his fiction, his concerns are still spiritual, but tinged with irony. His novel, *The Experience,* for instance, concerns a midtown-Manhattan lawyer, who has a religious experience and becomes obsessed with it. The book is told from the point of view of his cynical partner:

> It has been as I expected; I accomplished nothing this morning. At eleven o'clock he accosted me in the hall and work ended. He had a copy of the Bible under his arm and he wanted to read me a passage. I noticed that it was the New Revised Version and that is characteristic. I cannot imagine George Huber having last year's model of anything.
>
> We went into my office and I pretended to listen. George has a soft, somber voice with an authoritative lilt. It is a voice that assures you it possesses the truth, and one might accept its pretensions, had it not been the instrument of so many contradictory dogmas. But it is a pleasant voice and there have been instances when I have enjoyed listening to him. This was not one of those occasions.

Phillip Lopate, in a recent interview, said that in his writing he strives for honesty but also a kind of worldliness so that he will not be perceived as either a "fool or a naïf." But what if, I posed to a graduate class of mine, in your heart that's exactly what you are, a fool and a naïf? They laughed at this, and I laughed, too, at my own joke.

* * *

My mother sent me a last unpublished poem of my father's that she just discovered, and through this poem, he seems to speak to me, to tell me of his uncertainty, and mine as well:

JOB

They did not know this face
Where the chin rested on the sunken breastbone,
    So changed it was, emptied, rinsed out and dried,
    And for some future purpose put aside.
Expecting torment, they were much perplexed.

His world had gone
And he sat isolated, foul and flyblown,
    Without a world, with nothing but a mind
    Staggered to silence since it could not find
Language to utter its amazing text.

For where was Job?
In some strange state, unknown and yet well-known,

A mask that stared hollowly in God's breath,
Mind that perceived the irrelevance of death,
And the astonished heart unmoved, unvexed.

They did not see his soul
Perched like a bird upon the broken breastbone,
Piping incessantly above the ashes
What next what next what next what next what next.

She also sent me a photo that she took of me and my father when I was four and we still lived in New York. It shows him sitting on a wall, turned sideways, but looking down at me as I reach up, holding onto his leg as if to keep him with me, to keep him from suddenly vanishing. The photo looked familiar to me, although I couldn't place it exactly, and then I remembered. I went to my father's novel, *Young Crankshaw*, and opened it to the back, to the author photo. There was his face, there he was sitting on the wall, not the same photo exactly, but one taken on the same day, the same pose, except this one was cropped so that you could not see what he was sitting on, and you could not see me, although I am certain I was still there, still clinging, unable, unwilling to let go.

The Nonexistent Robe

Great minds against themselves conspire,
And shun the cure they most desire
HENRY PURCELL, *Dido and Aeneas*

Until recently I couldn't have told much of what Nola did the summer of 1967. I didn't know about her married Irish/Jewish lover, Martin, until my mother sent me letters from Nola to Martin and to my mother, and of course, Nola's memoir.

Likewise, I couldn't have said what Nola saw in the Middle East and Europe and how she viewed her trip as a kind of pilgrimage, how two years before she was first hospitalized, she was not only open to spiritual transformation, to visions, she actively yearned for these experiences. Did her sickness come, in part, from this spiritual fervor? As she writes in her book, Isaac Singer told her that a preoccupation with the spiritual is unhealthy, and this was what caused their friendship to sour. Or, did her sickness come in spite of her spiritual yearnings? Or was it sickness at all? Yes, it was sickness—it was destructive and made Nola into someone miserable and lost, something she had never been before. But just because someone sees visions doesn't necessarily make them sick—it doesn't, unless one puts all one's faith solely in the physical world, and faith, in any case, isn't really needed for that kind of commitment. Of course, it's the physical world that is often as brutal and irrational and absurd as even the wildest visions of the most dubious seer. What I'm saying is that the fact that we don't understand something doesn't make it irrelevant to our lives, the fact that some people lose their reason, lose their sense of logic, shouldn't make their truths less important.

Until recently, I could have admitted none of this. I would merely have had a few innocuous memories: the photo of me wearing the psychedelic kibbutz hat Nola brought back to me from Israel, on which Jonny pinned a button with Timothy Leary's famous phrase, "Turn on,

Tune in, Drop Out," (a completely unthreatening and amusing slogan to my mother, undoubtedly, since her children were consumed by their educations, both traditional and spiritual) and I pinned on another, "Make Mine Marvel," with drawings of all my favorite superheroes.

Or, the Irish harp that Nola brought back, and which she learned to play, that my mother still keeps. Or the fake newspapers, which I loved, reporting Biblical happenings in the style of modern journalism: Reuters reporting on Moses dividing the Red Sea, a UPI story on Jonah being swallowed by a whale. Fragments. Souvenirs. The physical possessions one keeps or loses or cherishes, whose value only increases over time, over which there can only be one dispute: Who owns it? Not, did it ever really exist?

A year after my father died, we were in *some* financial need—my mother had gone back to school to earn a master's degree and wasn't bringing in much money. My father's insurance wasn't stretching very far. He had died with a lot of debt, and there wasn't much for us to live on. But Ida came to our rescue. The summer of 1967, she paid for Nola to go with a Jewish youth group to Ireland, Israel, and Greece, and for my brother and me to go to Camp Blowing Rock in the North Carolina mountains. My mother paid for her own return to Mexico to work on her writing.

My mother didn't go back to Casa Heuer in 1967, but to San Miguel de Allende, where she spent a good portion of the summer worrying about us, especially Nola who had the good fortune to land in Israel on the heels of the Six Day War, and who spent much of her time in a kibbutz near the front lines. My mother wrote to Ida in July:

> *I don't know why they keep those kids so near the battlefront . . . I'm not crazy about this place but am still hoping to settle down to work—when I know Nola is safe I'll feel better.*

If my mother met another Elliot Chess in Mexico, she hasn't told me, and I don't think she liked San Miguel, a town crawling with expatriate Americans, half as much as she liked Ajijic in 1946. Of course, her concerns were different and the same. She was still working on a book, but her husband was dead and her child from that earlier union in Mexico was in no small mortal danger in Israel—almost shot by border guards on one occasion, smuggled into Gaza on another, although I doubt my mother knew of these particulars at the time.

As for Jonny and me, I can see why my mother sent us to Camp Blowing Rock, the perfectly crazy summer camp for the children of neurotic New York intellectuals. Camp Blowing Rock was run by a lesbian poet named Clara Sachs, a refugee from Nazi Germany, whom we all loved because she read us a chapter of the *Iliad* every night before bed and also because she wore no underwear, and whenever the campers were on a hike, we all tried to keep up with Clara, marching briskly in front, so that we might look up her dress (which she wore rather than pants) as she clambered up a rock face.

The things I remember the most from that summer at Camp Blowing Rock are:

1. The epic games of Capture the Flag, staged over acres and acres of North Carolina woods, like reenactments of battles from some great war.
2. A fragment from a J. S. Bach chorale:
   Gott ist Zeit, Gott ist Zeit
   Ist die alle beste
   Ist die alle beste Zeit.
   Die alle beste
   Ist die alle beste Zeit.
3. That Clara did not hate all of German culture, that she celebrated parts of it by letting a hundred mostly Jewish kids lift their thin voices up to God in the German language, and it was so beautiful that I remember our final concert as one of those moments in life that almost crystallize into something permanent, something palpable that can be reclaimed by singing in my deeper, changed voice as far as the words will carry me.

My favorite counselor was a boy who was going into the Green Berets after the summer, named Billy Buttons. Billy looked like a cleaner, cheerier version of GI Joe, and the campers treated him like a movie star.

I still have a picture of me standing beside him proudly, as though some of his goodness (for that's what it was, goodness, clean and ever-

victorious, a giant game of Capture the Flag, pressed uniforms and no blood, but maybe a telltale scar) might rub off on me.

At Camp Blowing Rock, we had our own borders, our own war to contend with. The Camp was in a heated dispute with a family named the Yams—again, a real name—who had supposedly attacked the camp the previous summer with hatchets and shotguns loaded with salt-peter. I didn't know what saltpeter was, but it sounded unpleasant. According to camp legend, a hatchet had been thrown at no less a per-sonage than Billy Buttons and stuck in a tree trunk inches above his head. We were warned never to venture near the Yam property, that they were ever-vigilant with their shotguns loaded. Once, I chased a snake onto the Yam property and clambered over the barbed-wire fence separating our warring camps—I heard something rustle in the bushes, and ripped my palm open on the fence trying to get back over, sure that the Yams were in pursuit. My wound became infected and had to be lanced by a doctor in Boone, and I nearly missed the camp outing to Grandfather Mountain and the Tweetsie Railroad as a result.

Jonny, too, had his medical trials. Stung by a bee, he had an allergic reaction and spent the night in a Boone hospital, next to the bed of an alcoholic going through delirium tremens who died in the middle of the night.

Undoubtedly, this is not what my mother would have wished for any of us, but appropriate, it seems to me now, for 1967, a bellicose year, that I would become infected by my imagination, that Nola would pursue visions in the war-torn Holy Land, and that Jonathan, in the fashion of a prophet from the Torah, would see God's vengeance visited upon the sinful.

I recently came upon a loose piece of paper among Nola's belongings, undated, but probably from a year or so before her death, on which she'd written a list of family members and friends, and what each of us wanted. To me, they're still uncannily amusing and appropriate:

> Ida wants family.
> Elaine wants flowers → myths? winged Pegasus which is the
>   flight into creation, something like it.
> Robin wants Egypt ↘ dig deep and delight of the imagination
>   ~~angels give him a spanking~~
> Jonathan wants Mexican color and saints in anguish about him.
> [all in love]

Angels give me a spanking, indeed. I'm glad she crossed that out, but she needn't have. I know that I am the disobedient, sometimes conniving son, that it's true when she says Egypt is what I want—what's hidden, forbidden knowledge, and places where the imagination alone will take me.

The only person she leaves out from this fanciful list is herself, what she wanted, and I suppose that wasn't necessary, because what she wanted, what she always wanted was transcendence, to speak to God directly, to shake His hand, to make Him visible from the air surrounding her.

*   *   *

Nola met Martin, a Jew from Belfast, in Israel. She was twenty, and he was thirty. She was there clearly expecting to be transformed by her journey, and she was, although I'm not sure in the ways she anticipated. I don't mean to be dismissive or patronizing here, but the sixties were the time of a kind of forced transcendence, when India became overrun by young Americans and Brits, and Israel was another spiritual proving ground—the world, in retrospect seemed equally torn by the Red Badge of Courage and The Saffron Robe of Transcendence. My sister, whom I see leading a kind of spiritual, doomed Charge of the Light Brigade, was ever ready to go into the breach. In other words, she saw visions wherever she went—but she had a passion for life and love as well. She didn't lead the ascetic life; after all, she was twenty years old:

> Israel, it seemed, was not as Holy as I had believed; bullet shards and waste lay strewn around us as we passed, for the Six Day's War had just ended, and the nation was still in its shadow. We spent the initial weeks hearing lectures at a labor college, and were then abruptly thrown into one of the most

perilously located kibbutzim on the edge of Gaza. All night and far into the morning we overheard the rifle fire of desert guards searching for snipers or murdering the dogs that fed off the Egyptian corpses in the desert and had wandered, rabid, into our cabins. We slept on hay, in huts that had the consistency of paper, and were nightly invaded by a garrison of rats . . . I was awakened one morning at four o'clock by a huge . . . rat, who insisted on leaping in triumphal arches from the bed of one of my roommates to the other until, overcome by the ecstasy of its own motion, it hurled itself almost suicidally under the shelves on the opposite wall; our screams awoke some of the more humane members of the settlement . . . who tried to eliminate the creature without success, although they were fully armed, and had great expertise in killing men. The following night we were obliged to cultivate the interest of those men in the settlement who had the safest cabins. I myself did not resort to flirtation, but became very ill at the appropriate time, and after the first fits of intestinal virus found myself lying on a couch between a battery of live bullets on the overhead wall and an assortment of rifles beneath. The room was occupied by two Semitic guards and an Irish Jew from Belfast, who had a habit of appearing continually lost in whatever situation or with whatever associations he had entrenched himself. He spoke with constant confusion, as if the patchwork of personalities that usually constitute men, but in most cases are concealed by an appearance of unity, were always embarrassingly present, and never even seemed to cohere . . . When several days had elapsed he decided that he was in love with me, although I knew it was not myself, but the very eloquent and godfearing mood that a week of cotton weeding in the heat among warring barbarians had placed me, that he loved. He was always infatuated with moods rather than persons, in spite of his insistence that I should "see things as they are;" when we had ourselves smuggled into Gaza in an Argentine station wagon he watched me with the most desperate, impassioned expression . . .

I later discovered that upon his return to his wife in Belfast (of whom he had never told me until openly questioned by one of the guards in my presence), his self-transcending passion had declined.

We developed a habit of wandering out of the immediate

borders of the settlement among the orange orchards and
deserted grenade-strewn kibbutzim . . . one evening we made
the momentous decision of venturing past the barbed wire gates
into the neutral terrain which separated Israel and Egypt in the
middle of the night, and were instantly greeted with a rifle barrel that protruded not too graciously from the window of an ar-
mored truck, with a grim mustached officer at the other end,
who congratulated us on our good fortune at not having been
shot at once, since he had suspected us of being Egyptians, and
would have fired if we had tried to run.

Our affair strangely coincided with that of the daughter of a
famous comedian, who had accompanied the group to Israel out
of boredom with Kenya and California, where she divided her
time between her divorced parents. After the first vain efforts to
make a success out of weeding cotton she had managed to en-
gage the affection of a French student from a group of hashish
and wine addicts from the Sorbonne; within days she had reduced him to weeding all her cotton as well as his own, and at
the end of one and a half weeks they had eloped to Cyprus,
where it was her lover's secret intention to make her write home
for money to finance the wedding. When her father unexpect-
edly refused this request, the romance dissolved; Angela left for
England, her lover for his aunt in France, where he prepared to
spend his days off the leavings in her will . . .

My lover was full of assurances that such transience was impossible for us . . .

He accompanied the group to Tiberias, where we left the
group in the hostel and went at night to a cliff by the Galilee,
where Christ had walked upon the waters; I began to speak to
him of very sweet and mysterious things, until he looked at me
in amazement, and wondered aloud whether I was a woman or
a spirit from another place, for I spoke in a trance, as if I wished
to seize the objects of my speech and make them palpable. I
began to tell him everything from my vision of thirteen, of the
tyranny of God for which I desperately longed, which in the
words of Charles Williams "restored beyond belief everything
that it had taken away . . . except the individual will." The night
wind swept past the waters, and there was a silence, and then
out of teeming things visible and invisible which oppressed my
mind, I heard his voice, raised against the sea and surrounding
darkness, saying, "You are fantastic."

What Nola saw in the valley at Galilee was a version of the valley of her dreams, the vision she had at thirteen of the valley of Ednah, the pass where she had confronted the aged man, what Isaac Singer had told her was the passage into death. Isaac Singer had a healthy fear of this mountain pass, and tried in his own way to warn Nola away from it when he told her that a preoccupation with the spiritual was unhealthy, but Nola was nothing if not persistent, was not afraid of death, saw self-negation as bliss, would go into the valley alone, although she thought she could take Martin with her.

. . . Something dark overpowered us, and I knew this was the same, Tiberias the echo of the valley in my vision, the Galileean cliff my mountain pass. I loved him with a love that asked for nothing, of a quality that he could not comprehend. For that time, and for a few succeeding days, he loved me with a depth that was unconsciously divine; the object it sought was not me but the Light which our strange passion had become. He watched me with an expression of the most incredible softness, as if his little self had suddenly ceased to imprison him, and now he faced me with the Love that desires only death, and birth out of death. We were lost in the close and lingering darkness, and passed into that self-destroying shadow, and discovered ourselves when we had ceased to be.

I wish I could feel that earnestness, but irony overwhelms me always, my self-consciousness, my fear of being a fool. Nola didn't care. She didn't care who believed because she was not trying to convince anyone of the truth of her story, least of all herself. I think I am part Martin/part Nola. I identify with him when she writes, "He spoke with constant confusion," and "who had a habit of appearing continually lost in whatever situation or with whatever associations he had entrenched himself." The man seems, from her description, befuddled like me, unsure what to make of Nola. When he told her, "You are fantastic," he meant everything contained in that word, "beyond belief, wonderful, strange, otherworldly." And we cannot be wholly transported all the time by the fantastic, most of us anyway. Most of us want to spend some time not having visions, doing ordinary things, shopping, going to movies, venturing on the briefest flights into fantasy. There are other times when we reject the fantastic, when we repudiate it. Nola found it easiest to identify with Paul and his self-annihilating blindness on the road to Damascus. But I identify most with Peter in the New Testament, Jonah in the Old. I believe and repudiate, want to hide, seek shade under a gourd that withers, curse God for creating things over which I cannot control.

Nola writes, almost unabashedly, that before going to Israel, she read *The Robe,*

> a sentimental narrative of the conversion of an imaginary Roman soldier to the faith by the accidental acquisition of Christ's garment, and decided that it was my holy duty to visit Golgotha as soon as possible. I actually went to Israel with the intention of finding the remains of a seamless cloak lying somewhere near the Via Dolorosa. What I found instead was not at all surprising considering my total lack of realism in the situation, but somehow as holy, for the time that it lasted, as the cherished nonexistent robe.

As always, I retreat into the shade of irony and disbelief, of healthy denial. Nola inherited my mother's romantic nature, and she was only twenty. I'm embarrassed by the twenty-year-old I was. I'm embarrassed by the thirty-year-old I was. I'm embarrassed by the forty-year-old I'll soon be. But Nola, only twenty-four, embraced her twenty-year-old self, even her naiveté, when she writes of her "cherished nonexistent robe." To me, that word "cherished" contains all that I want to keep and hold of my cherished nonexistent sister, the fact that she could admit something so foolish as her original expectations, and not only accept these expectations, but cherish them, not for what they gave her, but where they led her.

Skeptics like Martin and me abound. And skepticism arises so often out of fear. Can you hear the awe, which is not so far from fear, in Martin's voice when he tells Nola, "You are fantastic." And what we are in awe of we fear because it confuses us, makes us want to reject, repudiate, betray. We are in awe of the fantastic, and in fear of ourselves, our tentative place in relation to the fantastic.

I can hear the awe loud and clear in Martin's voice, just as I hear it when he tells her to "see things as they are." Beware of people, I think, who tell you this, because they are invariably hiding something. They mean you harm, or harm you, by putting a mask on their uncertainty and calling it certainty (like those searchers for Noah's Ark, who are missing the point completely; even if they found the ark miraculously intact, sitting on top of Mt. Ararat, that would show us nothing. It's the story, not the artifact that's important). In Martin's case, he was hiding the fact that he was married, but by that time, it was too late for Nola. She was either in love with him, or as she puts it at one spot in her narrative, "the Robe in him," the very thing that terrified him, that made him seem so lost.

Everything here is a parable, in a way. The story of the comedian's daughter and her tryst with the materialistic young student from the Sorbonne versus the supposedly more spiritual liaison between Nola and Martin. But both ended badly. It just took longer for Martin and Nola's romance to dissolve. For Martin, in his confused state, it must have been easy for him to disavow Nola, just as it was easy for Angela's lover to disavow her when her dad wouldn't pay up. To disavow is the most human thing in the world. Betrayal is the most human thing. I can't blame Nola for falling in love with Martin, for thinking that she'd find the robe of Christ along the Via Dolorosa. What she was looking for was that fragile part of the soul that doesn't repudiate, that doesn't "see things as they are."

*   *   *

This was the first time my sister had been in love, and love has the force sometimes of a spiritual awakening. My sister's frame of reference was entirely spiritual, and she could see love as nothing else, she could see the physical world as nothing else, the love of God made real by his desperate spoken word—anyone who has felt the desperation of first love, knows something of the terrible ecstasy of spiritual transformation. And if we are truly made in God's image, then I imagine Him in love with us like first love, a kind of desperate longing that can never be fully reciprocated, and if He repudiates us, it's only out of self-punishment at ever having loved so deeply.

Nola wrote Martin a long letter, over twenty pages (which she apparently never sent, and that's why I have it), after they parted in Tiberias, and she went on with her tour group. Nola seemed to see Martin as some kind of spiritual incarnation, a soul mate, with the emphasis on the word "soul." She didn't care for the other women in her group, whom she saw as frivolous and light-headed, interested mostly in souvenirs and boys. But Nola was interested in much the same, just different kinds of souvenirs and different kinds of boys. She wanted religious relics, the robe of Christ waiting for her along a dusty road, and a boy on whom she projected all of her spiritual and physical desire. Still, the accounts she wrote to Martin seem much more reliable to me than the accounts in her memoir. In the first place, she was much closer to the events as they happened, and secondly, her mind was still clear, unmuddied by the Thorazine given to her later by her doctors. She wrote to Martin of the religious sites she saw, and for her, Martin became almost inseparable with these sites.

From Tiberias we proceeded to Tabgha, on the 23rd of July. When we approached the nave of the Church, the group suddenly asked me to read the New Testament passage printed there in English. I must have read with a great deal of feeling, for I was singularly moved not merely by the pious atmosphere of the place or by the extraordinary animal mosaics which were largely concealed by a makeshift wooden floor, but by the profound emotion which thinking of you inspired. I have never really loved as I have loved you, Martin, notwithstanding the fact that I have revered certain parts of the New Testament ever since that spiritual shock I received at thirteen, every word of that writing at the altar seemed so much more thoroughly impregnated with meaning. A thousand barriers may sever us for good—we may be unable to see each other ever again, but I shall never forget that bright hot morning in Tabgha when I read aloud those passages on the feeding of the five thousand with you in my heart. It was one of the most exalting experiences of my life.

Her accounts of the various shrines she visited are almost breathless—I can hear her voice and the wonder in her words, the way an ornithologist might feel, I suppose, if camped out for days in search of a presumably extinct bird, she sees one swoop by and then another and then another, so fast and in such a winged frenzy of splendor that she might lose sense of herself completely. But Nola, unlike me, expected it all the time—she saw these creatures around her always, even when the rest of us couldn't even detect the slightest movement of air.

She writes, in reverent detail, of one holy site after another, and the particular religion hardly matters to her: a Cabbalist synagogue near Mt. Meron, the Jazzar Pasha Mosque, the Bahai shrine in Haifa ("That golden dome overlooking groves of cypress and exotic flowers, is a vision of almost unimaginable beauty"), the Abbey of the Dormition.

Nola was moved by the physical beauty of these man-made shrines, but they were all the more beautiful to her for the sacred beauty of the words they contain, for it's always words Nola comes back to, not simply the shell of the word, the mosque or church or temple surrounding it, but the Word itself, the communication of the holy that Nola yearns for. This is perhaps why Nola was so interested in language, and why she knew so many: Greek, German, French, Yiddish, Hebrew, Gaelic, Sanskrit. Each language yielded its own version of the Word, one no less holy than another, one no less imperfect than another. Of the Abbey of the Dormition she writes,

> The basilica is comprised of a high arched nave [on the roof of which is represented eight white-robed saints, and above which two mosaic figures (Virgin and child) rise out of what appear to be the waves of the sea—the child holds out an opened book reading in Greek: 'I am the light of the world'] and eight smaller arches on the sides, containing altars to innumerable saints, sages, and spirits formed out of glowing tiles.

Even parenthetically, Nola mimics what she saw, what dazzled her, the capture of the Word within its structure, the basilica.

All around her were remnants of the war, and she did not ignore these. A passage of the war's devastation is juxtaposed to her rapture at seeing the Dead Sea Scrolls.

> I was shocked, incidentally, to discover that of the nine windows painted by Chagall for the Haddasah Medical Centre synagogue, *six* had been shelled during the war and temporarily removed. That knowledge, in addition to the tearful account we received from the guide of the behavior of one soldier who had had his arm amputated, impressed me more profoundly than anything else in Jerusalem.
>
> That afternoon we were admitted into the Shrine of The Book. An indescribable emotion surged through me when I penetrated the anteroom, touched one of the jars in which the Great Scrolls were saved from oblivion in 1947, and finally stood, half-paralyzed with awe before those wondrous writings I had waited *years* to see. I had known of and revered those Essene documents long before I dreamed of coming to Israel, and to see the *Manual of Discipline* (I bought a facsimile of it on Mt. Zion), *The War of the Sons of Light with the Sons of Darkness*, the *Habakkuk Commentary* and particularly the great *Scroll of Isaiah* spread out before me was too much to bear. I don't know how many times I returned to that latter scroll long after the group had filed indifferently out and gone I know not where and cared less, and just gazed at it in unmitigated wonder; at length I realized I had lost the group again . . .

It's a wonder she ever made it home, that she didn't lose herself completely. Of course, Americans going to Israel to find their spiritual identities are so common as to be a kind of cliché now. In Jerusalem, there's even a syndrome associated with this often-disappointing search for the holy—dozens of people who think they're Jesus or Moses or Mary wander the streets. The hospitals are full of them—a Palestinian student of mine even wrote a story for my class about one of these women who goes into an Arab shop and confuses and annoys the shopkeeper, who's only trying to eke out a modest living, and doesn't want to be bothered with the woman's self-deluded religious babble. These people are often tourists, who've sometimes shown no particular religious fervor in the past, and then one day, they simply lose themselves in the crowd, and the next thing they're trying to turn loaves into fishes.

Perhaps they, too, secretly expected to see the robe lying along the Via Dolorosa, and they cannot find their way past that initial disappointment. But Nola, I think, went beyond her cherished nonexistent robe. She had done her homework, as it were. She knew the languages, except for Arabic, and what she found in the words spoken to her and which she spoke was as holy as any word can be.

*   *   *

And they crucified him, and divided his garments among them, casting lots for them, to decide what each should take, And it was the third hour, when they crucified him. And the inscription of the charge against him read, "The King of the Jews." —Mark, 15

There was also an inscription over him, "This is the King of the Jews." —Luke, 23

... And it was written in Hebrew, in Latin, and in Greek. The chief priest of the Jews then said to Pilate, "Do not write, 'The King of the Jews,' but 'This man said, I am King of the Jews.'"
Pilate answered. "What I have written I have written."—John, 19

Pilate did not care. He was certain of his words, but not because they seemed true; the words themselves did not matter to him, nor did their meaning. "What I have written I have written." But even the subtlest variations in stories interest me, the inevitable gaps between versions. How can we be dispassionate where words are concerned?

*   *   *

The words Nola searched through did not necessarily have to be words written on ancient scrolls. Secular stories could move her as well: the account of the soldier whose arm had been amputated, or on another occasion the conversation she had in Yiddish with

an old Nazi refugee from Belgrade, Yugoslavia, who related to me the course of his family's history since their survival of and escape from a concentration camp. You have probably discovered this already, but it amazed me how much of an advantage one has over the casual tourist in Israel by being able to speak Yiddish (or German). The people open themselves up to you immediately. I was tremendously relieved to be able to communicate with someone outside of our light-headed and often pretentious group. It was a momentary vacation from their empty company.

I do not want to paint a sentimental portrait of Nola, one in which I present her as only good and noble and so holy as to be beyond belief, because that is not the truth of anyone's life, and we all do things that are wrong and silly and put us in a bad light.

The group lingered at the Wailing Wall for about an hour; I removed a fragment from one of the stones to take back to the States—an act which struck the women weeping on my right as very odd and impious. They were not ecstatic when I wrote my name on another of the stones either—which, although I'll admit was a childish thing to do, I did deliberately that I might for once see provoked (but genuine) expressions, rather than those pointless grins, on the faces of my companions. I succeeded admirably at this . . .

It's a small-minded moment, compounded by her patronizing attitude toward the women at the Wall. Of course, here I am, so many years later, comfortably judging her. Maybe it's not so small-minded— incredibly irreverent and immature, yes, for one so seemingly godly.

It's clear from her letter that she and Martin both viewed the girls in her group as petty and small-minded, not much above peasants, and they, undoubtedly, viewed her as weird and snobbish. I can't be *sure* of their attitudes toward Nola—my only clues are her own denunciations of the others in her group peppered through the letter, and one cryptic passage in which she discusses a conversation she had with a woman named Sarah, whom I take to be the group's Israeli chaperone:

That night I had a strangely intimate talk with Sarah about one of the members of our group who had developed into a problem. As might have been expected, the subject drifted to my relationship with the others. She con- . . .

And there, the letter has a one-page gap, and I don't know whether Sarah confessed or confronted Nola or conjectured. The page numbers jump from fourteen to sixteen and Nola is swimming in the Dead Sea, or at least I assume it's the Dead Sea. The sentence starts ". . . moving in a depth of forty feet of water without having to exert a limb was a most extraordinary experience." It's frustrating, of course, not knowing what Sarah "con-ed," or even really knowing for sure who Sarah was, or knowing exactly what Nola's relationship to the others was. But it's also strangely satisfying to me to have those gaps, so deep and necessary, between my life and my telling of my sister's life. I am reminded that whatever I say condemns her, romanticizes her, lies about her, idolizes her, but never, never recreates her in all her complexity. And I resist simple judgments. She was a good person. She was a holy person. She was deluded. She was pompous, self-important. Of course, it's those things in myself that I most easily recognize and condemn in her. My own self-importance, my own snobbery.

Nola was far too different from the others, otherworldly, odd, unable to occupy her mind with ordinary, everyday problems. And so, she thought Sarah was strange for trying to involve her in the everyday workings of the group. But I think she tried to connect with the other women in her group—she just wasn't terribly successful. When she did her book report on St. Paul at the age of fourteen, as reported in her memoir, the kids and teacher didn't know what to make of her—they just stared ("I must have read them with considerable emotion, since it seemed to have a peculiar effect on the class, who reacted to it with shock"). Unsurprisingly, she wasn't able to form many friendships with children her age at sixteen, and it seems the same was true of her relationships with others at age twenty. They wanted to have fun, and who could blame them? She made them uncomfortable. They were suspicious of her.

> When an hour had elapsed we returned to a slender beach over-looking the harbor, and I sat next to Riva, trying to draw her out of herself with questions which I framed as pleasantly as I could—but it was impossible. She was cold, impenetrable, and horribly suspicious. I felt that I was a spectator to my own un-doing, and memories of the behavior of Dostoevsky's "Idiot" on the train to St. Petersburg flashed endlessly through my mind. It seemed that every word I uttered she was converting into a weapon with which to harm me; the brief dialogue was cur-tailed, and I resolved never to speak to her again. I understand perfectly what you went through with her. I hope we both for-get her as soon as possible.

Again, perhaps I'm wrong about Nola, because most of the time, she was likable and friendly and full of vitality, and if you didn't mind talk of fairies and mythical beings and philosophy, a lot of fun to be around. The next section of her letter describes her befriending a cou-ple of Israeli girls, and now I remember that Nola easily befriended people. I don't want to be like Riva, suspicious and impenetrable, using Nola's words to condemn her. There's so much I don't know, and never will.

*   *   *

When Nola returned to Ohio University to resume her studies in phi-losophy, she left behind the Via Dolorosa and her cherished nonexis-tent robe, and she left behind Martin, her cherished nonexistent fellow supplicant, and, in a letter she wrote to my grandmother from school, thanked her for funding the trip:

> Whatever happens . . . I shall never forget the magnificent thing you've done for me by sending me to Israel and Europe. You will perhaps never know how much it has transformed my life. But, you'll know that I know, so that's a beginning, at least.

I'm sure she was referring to both a spiritual transformation and a coming-of-age in her love for Martin, whom she devised to see somehow over the next year. Perhaps, she meant the former more than the latter, but I can't see much of a spiritual transformation—you can't be transformed if it already exists within you. Here's a young woman who'd been having discussions with God since the age of five, trying to draw him out of his natural reticence, saying, "Why are you invisible?" and "Is 'Thou' God?" and why do people need books to tell them what they already know? And having dreams of the Valley of Ednah and going to occult bookstores with Isaac Singer, and the robe, so familiar on the street, that no one bothers to turn it into the Lost and Found in Jerusalem, and it's laying there for her, ready to claim. There's no transformation there that I can see. I expect such a young woman to study ancient scrolls, to find rapture in the arms of a lover while looking over Galilee, to study the Sistine Chapel for hours, trying to match one man's visions with her own.

But, Martin, I think, transformed her. She was desperate for him, obsessed by him. "You are fantastic," Martin told her that night as they looked into the valley of Tiberias, and in that, he condemned her—she thought he was recognizing the fantastic as part of himself, but awe soon sours into fear, and the word "fantastic," to me, implies inevitable rejection.

A year later, she went back to Europe. She had graduated from Ohio University and had been accepted into the Ph.D. program in philosophy at Brandeis, but for the summer was attending Edinburgh University to study the Philosophy of the British Enlightenment.

In her memoir, she claims that Martin had been so desperate to see her the entire previous year, as to

> found an international airline association which transported Irish families to their relations in Canada and the United States at a discount, with the hope of boarding one such flight himself; as it happened, the moment he was ready to board the plane for Canada I was boarding one in New York for London, with the result that we completely missed each other in a tragic-comic error that must have had in its artistry something divine.

Perhaps. Cosmic irony often seems much greater than the feeble human variety—God, up there with Supremely bad taste, perhaps surrounded by His various collections of kitsch and memorabilia (God has to be a collector), playing one practical joke after another on us. Of course, Nola's statement about this mix-up seems tinged with irony. She seems bemused in the telling, partly because, when she wrote the above, several years had passed since she was in love with Martin. In the moment, she was much less cool.

Martin told her that whatever hopes she had for a relationship were futile. In any case, his wife was pregnant, and he was looking forward to the baby. From Scotland, Nola wrote my mother a letter with a desperate plea at its conclusion:

> If all goes well, Martin and I will meet in August after summer school ends; he says there's no hope for us and I'm profoundly upset because I am really in love with him. *Please Please Please see* him for me in New York (if possible) or Chicago (if necessary); try sifting and reasoning with him in whatever way you can, and see if *something, anything* can be worked out. If there is anyone who can talk to him sensibly it is you. I will be eternally grateful.

Even in desperation, she couldn't help starting her letter with a moody description of the Scottish countryside, transforming it into a living thing of imagination and melodrama:

> The clouds sit brooding on the hills like partners in some conspiracy of Heaven, whose moroseness is breathed with exquisite irony into a land of tame hedgerows and fields. These are hills and valleys of the reflective soul, a patterned madness exhaled by the dreams of poets and Calibans . . .

I think my mother's children have always been so conscious of the stories and dramas they find themselves in, that they can't help but think of the guiding hand, of authorship, of audience. We can't help but embellish and think dramatically. It's a self-inflicted curse, I suppose. For Nola and me, my mother was the Saint, the one we went to for intervention. For my brother, our father filled the role of divine author, I suppose, but he died when Jonny was thirteen, so Jonny was always much more self-reliant than the rest of us. He had to be. His protector was dead, until he found the protection of an even firmer father than the one he was born with, the God of the Torah.

I can't imagine asking my mother to talk to a lover for me, to convince her that she was making a mistake. I suppose that's because I'm so far removed from that feeling of confused desperate first love. Love, obsessive love, like obsessive spirituality, inspires the best and worst mistakes of people, and they're often one and the same, and it's that irrational edge over which we topple that seems to bring us, for a moment, so close to God. The thought is ridiculous, I know, but I think of a cartoon, the coyote, treading air for a moment, staying afloat until he realizes there's nothing beneath him, and only then does he fall.

In love, out of love, it hardly mattered to Nola. She was always in love with the spirit of things, and so she always acted as though she was crazily, insanely in love with something, although the object might change. In her memoir, she writes of traipsing around the Scottish countryside, full of a kind of vitality and foolishness I've seen in few people since, and which I most loved in her:

> I must have developed a very controversial reputation at that period, since it was my habit to sit only with the male dons at the director's table, and read Sanskrit love poetry to my friends after meals. I became so sentimental over the poetry that I began wandering around the dormitory gardens after dark looking for Scottish poppies . . . We (the students) visited the home of Francis Bacon, and made one trip to Edinburgh Castle at midnight, where we were admitted by the night guard because it happened to be my birthday; on a third occasion we drove out to Arthur's Seat, and the Firth of Forth, where I was so overcome by the beach air that on the way home I started doing Irish jigs in the foliage, and landed in the University hospital with a swollen foot.

I asked my mother a couple of days ago whether she agreed to Nola's request to see Martin for her, and to my surprise, my mother said yes, she had. They'd walked around New York together (my mother was teaching for the summer in New York at City College), and I don't think she tried to convince him of anything, but simply listened. All my mother saw was a superficial young man, no robe in him, nothing but a man around thirty, who talked about Nola a little and then Ireland, telling my mother that things were about to blow up there. She must have met with him right before he returned to England to see Nola—the next communication on the subject of Martin is from Nola, dated September 19th, and reports what happened upon Martin's return. The letter she wrote to my mother is remarkable to me in what it confides; it's the kind of relationship I'd wish for me and my daughters, that they could tell Bev and me anything, even things we might not want to hear.

September 19, 1968

Dear Mom:

I had to write to you as soon as I had the opportunity because your reaction to Martin was precisely what I expected in the light of what I have most recently seen of him. As far as his limitations are concerned you have hit the bull's eye. I have matured considerably this summer because I could not choose to do otherwise after the experiences I was confronted with—which was my intention in going to Europe in the first place. Whether I was deluding myself or not, whether Koons was right or not I had to somehow master this phantasmal passion that was destroying my life by encountering its object in the flesh. This was vital because I could no longer let his imaginary presence prey upon me and I longed to shrink and conquer it somehow. I believe we met on August 12. He had to get on a stand-by for the plane to London and consequently had me waiting for him up at Canterbury Hall (London University dorm) until a quarter of two a.m. . . . He finally drove up in a rakish-looking white Jaguar or something, looking utterly dazed and lost. I was so tired I was stupid, but decided to compliment him on the car when I was seated. "What's nice about it?" he snapped. I stared at him. He had aged and grown bald since I had last seen him, and his face bore not a single trace of the delicacy of feeling I had so hastily ascribed to him. Is this the creature I loved for a year? I asked myself. We drove around for what must have been 3/4 of an hour because I had no place to stay. Nothing much was said, perhaps because I felt a curious void sitting next to me which would not be filled. At last he hit upon a bed-and-breakfast place a few blocks from the dorm. The proprietor took one look at me and charged him double without a second thought. We went upstairs and I started to get him to talk. He told me what I expected and a couple of things I hadn't. I can remember nothing he said that did not impress me with an appalling naiveté. He said that he hoped the child would completely heal the situation between Judith and himself ("to be perfectly frank with you, Nola, I'm looking forward to the baby") because he had seen other families with children that were "pleased as punch." He had grown more considerate of Judith because she was pregnant and he thought things might consequently improve between them. He continued to tell me that my problem was that all my life I had been surrounded by a bunch of nuts and that he thought the reason I was so attracted to him was that he was completely different from anyone I had ever met (i.e. normal, which might be true by his standards). He did, on second thought, say one sensible thing that night: "Are you sure you are in love with me and not just the idea of me?" But he went on to tell me how callous he had grown last year ("Because of me?" I asked, but he couldn't say and continued to jabber) and how I would "always be there" whether things worked out between himself and Judith or not—if I continued to wait for him to change his mind I would more or less be at his disposal, and perhaps even if I didn't wait (what he meant was very unclear). After an hour or two of this kind of interchange, when both of us were too depleted to talk, he surveyed the room and remarked with righteous disgust that the owner had provided him with two sets of washcloths and towels ("He expects you to stay the night."). I prepared to leave. Suddenly quite a different sort of emotion overpowered him; he gripped me tightly and a few seconds later bolted the door. It was too late for me to try getting home that night, and I knew this was going to happen anyway, so I decided to stay although I was already smiling at myself for having fallen for this bundle of inconsistencies. His hands were all over me; he told me to tell him when I was "ready." For what? I wondered, having no idea what this pious little father-to-be intended (he's now shorter than I am). I told him I was on the pill although I didn't know what was up. "You shouldn't a done it," he murmured in shock, and accused me—again in a different tone—of having "had it all planned out" because I "knew we'd wind up in bed together." His horror of the whole situation was only too apparent. At this point I no longer cared what happened to either of us, turned away, and slept fitfully for an hour or two. . .

Martin and Nola's relationship reminds me of a joke I heard once. A guy is walking through Belfast one night when he feels a gun in his back and a husky voice says, "Quick, tell me what religion you are?" and the guy thinks, Gee, if I tell him I'm Protestant, and he's Catholic, I'm done for. But if I tell him I'm Catholic, and he's Protestant, then he's going to kill me, too. So he says, "I'm Jewish," and the voice behind him says, "Great, and I'm the luckiest Palestinian terrorist in all of Northern Ireland." I suppose I'm reminded of the joke because Martin seems to me both victim and terrorist at the same time, holding a gun at his own back, confused and lost and self-hating—ultimately the unluckiest soul in all of Ireland.

Today is Nola's birthday, as I write this. At midnight, twenty-eight years ago, I know where she was, what she was doing. It's an overcast day, not unusual for Bellingham, Washington where I live now. The climate here is so similar to the British Isles—the foliage in which she did her jig was probably not too different from the foliage around Washington—almost everything that grows in Scotland grows here: heather, rhododendrons, saxifrage.

Downstairs, I can hear my two children, Isabel and Olivia, playing, pounding on something. The TV is off now—it's past ten, and the program Beverly likes to watch in the morning is finished—it's a program on which people bring heirlooms or finds from garage sales and have them appraised, and then decide whether they want to submit them for bids to a live national audience. Sometimes I watch the program with Beverly, and we always groan when someone sells an object that belonged to their grandmother or mother. And yet, I've done it, I've sold off heirlooms. I've pawned away things that should have been precious to me.

My mother is visiting, too. She called up one day and told us when she'd be visiting. That's how she does it—and I think she chose this week in particular because today isn't only Nola's birthday, but also my mother and father's anniversary. Of course, we haven't mentioned any of this. She's down in her room now, waiting for me to finish my work. And then we'll go off somewhere together, maybe with Olivia or Isabel, probably not with Beverly, partly because our car is too small, partly because Beverly and my mother don't understand one another—and why should they, they're such opposites? I know I need them both, two sides of me, that too much impracticality or practicality, too much thoughtlessness or too much thoughtfulness, makes me feel unhappy.

Today, I want to be all thoughtlessness and impracticality. What crazy, impulsive thing could we do to commemorate Nola's birthday? But thinking about it makes it planned—if I could, I'd declare the day before Independence Day, July 3rd, Impulsive Day, a day we allowed ourselves not to fit in, to act foolish, to be spontaneous: take a piece of the Wailing Wall instead of praying, do an Irish jig and land in the hospital, but not for long. Anyway, that's the chance you take by acting foolish. Maybe no one else needs that day, but I do—and this is as good as any.

Crazy

To be human is to be part God, part sickness
Always wondering which is which.
SUZANNE PAOLA

I love the word but I fear it. Of course, I can't say it without hearing Patsy Cline or Willie Nelson singing so melodiously about something so dissonant. I suppose when Willie wrote the song, he didn't aim for verisimilitude. If he had, he might have brought in a little of Stravinsky's *Rite of Spring*, which isn't crazy in itself, but caused riots when it debuted in Paris, and would definitely sound crazy if played in tandem with "Crazy." I know there's good crazy and bad crazy and what makes us insane at any given time can change, and what the culture defines as crazy can change, too. When Alfred Jarry's play *Ubu Roi* opened in Paris in the late nineteenth century, the main character Père Ubu, a grotesque figure with a bull's-eye painted on his fat stomach, uttered the word "merdre,"a nonsense word that sounds like "merde," but isn't, and sparked another riot. Those are the only two instances *I* know of works of art inciting riots, making people crazy, and really, the emotions they felt as they shouted and bashed each other with their concert programs or let chairs fly (as I imagine, like a barroom brawl in a Western) were real. I'm sure they weren't thinking, How ironic of us—although some of them might have thought this, the ones who fled across the street and watched from a safe distance. Perhaps *they* thought, How bizarre, how ironic. In the moment of acting crazy, one does not reflect. That extreme lack of self-consciousness would not have afflicted any passersby. They would have seen themselves in relief against the riot—they would have wondered, been in awe, but not part of that spectacle.

I know from Jarry's example that a word can be a trigger, and I suppose I don't really mind being driven crazy, if it's only for a little while, if I can eventually find my way back, if, like the audience, I can clean up, comb my hair, straighten my tie, and hurry off before I'm detained and held responsible for some of the damage.

We're all constantly being transformed, and our perceptions of others are just as inaccurate as our perceptions of ourselves. The less we know of another person, the more apt we are to consider their unexplained actions crazy. I remember the story of a woman who lived in a small town and who walked the streets talking to herself. The townspeople all thought she was nuts until they discovered that she was an author, well-known outside of their town, who figured out the plots and characters of her stories as she walked, and said her characters' words aloud to make sure they sounded plausible. Not crazy but secretive, unconcerned by appearances. In the same way, perhaps my sister was fashioning stories, too, rehearsing the afterlife, and to say she was crazy, simply is to say that we are observing her from across the street, that we are not a part of her life, that beyond our borders what she does makes perfect sense.

In the spring of 1970, Nola returned home for Passover break from Brandeis, and said to my mother, "I have something serious to tell you."

"What is it?" my mother asked.

"I'm very sick," Nola said.

From that point on, Nola was changed, different, for the three years until her death. Years after her death, I had succeeded in almost forgetting that I had such a sister, had come to believe that all was sickness, that her life had ended badly, that there was nothing of value I could glean. Now, I sometimes have to make a conscious effort to remember her in any other way than this.

I was going through my own problems at the time, and perhaps didn't notice at first the change in my sister's personality. We were living in Slippery Rock, Pennsylvania, where my mother found her first teaching job after my father's death. Part of that year, I spent in Hollywood, Florida, with my grandmother, and that's when Nola made her announcement to my mother, so that's why I don't remember any of this. I was away. Of course, I was only eleven, and no one would have confided to me that my sister had gone through a fundamental personality change. Actually, no one ever did. I was left to observe and draw my own conclusions, a dangerous thing.

I remember Nola coming through Hollywood, Florida, later that spring with a friend, and the two of them showed little interest in me. They lay out on the beach and sunburned so badly their skins were bright red and their eyelids burned shut. I remember this physical agony of my sister's but not her mental agony. She lay in bed for two days, prone, her friend in the other bed, on top of the covers, their arms outstretched, as though they were being crucified. When she visited in Florida, she seemed remote. That was the only change I remember. She seemed indifferent to me (before her sunburn. *Definitely* indifferent after the burn). But I attributed this change to the fact that she had finally decided that I was just a kid, unworthy of keeping company

In her memoir, Nola, too, writes of the incident:

One day in the middle of January, I and a friend of mine from school got disgusted with the New England winter and impulsively jumped into a Volkswagen on our way to Florida. We

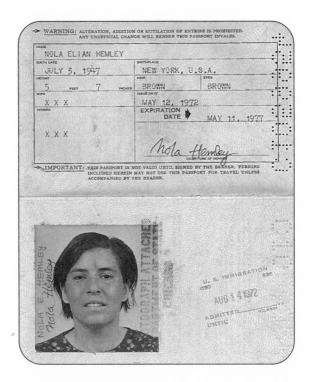

stayed in a room near part of my family in Hollywood where we proceeded to fast, pray, and meditate and contract a dangerous sunburn for two weeks. Somewhere near the end of the first week after consuming a whole jar of honey in five minutes after attempting to reach God through partial starvation, I fell asleep and had the most wonderful dream . . . .

It's not the sunburn that seems so dangerous to me here, but the self-destructiveness that follows, attempting to reach God through partial starvation.

I resist the notion that there was nothing wrong with Nola, that she was not terribly and irrevocably changed after the winter of 1969 to 1970. I suppose the simple answer is to label her, to satisfy myself with the catchall term of schizophrenic. Yes, I know that schizophrenia's onset occurs often in a person's mid-twenties. A psychotic break. I've seen it—twice now—with my sister and later with my girlfriend in graduate school, and I know it explains nothing. I know that many schizophrenics see visions and are obsessed with the spiritual, and this was certainly the case with Nola and later with Rita. But I find the suggestion somehow offensive that everything is explained by this meaningless term and the notion that the mind can somehow be treated like a carburetor—there's simply a chemical imbalance. How trivial, how easy it is to end our investigations with this smug statement that still tells us nothing of the mind's workings. We know the physical locations of many of our desires in the brain, but that's not the same as understanding. Perhaps you can show me the spot in the brain where our yearning for God resides. Perhaps you can even remove it, but that doesn't change the notion of God; it only makes you a kind of monster.

I don't think my sister's madness lay in her irrational acts, her voices, her visions, her jigs in the Irish countryside, her yearnings for something besides the material. At least, I don't feel this way anymore. Those are what distinguish her to me, what make her memory alive and wonderful—but madness is our own self-suffering, when we become locked in an unending and impossible battle with ourselves, when we scar ourselves physically and emotionally, our thoughts caught in an impossible loop, when joy becomes a thing of the distant past. That's my definition, at least, and where I see the break in who my sister was to what she became—from a person who loved life and sought the miraculous in the everyday to a morose and grim ghost haunting the world, afraid of her own thoughts, unable to control her actions against herself.

At first, Nola seemed to love her philosophy program at Brandeis. At the end of the letter she wrote to my mother about her disastrous reunion with Martin in London, she adds this hopeful paragraph:

> I cannot tell you how glad I am to be back in the States. I got pretty fed up with Europe for several reasons and it is a great relief for me. Especially being in Massachusetts. I have never seen a lovelier state. The Brandeis campus is a sheer idyll. Fantastic. And the people are so warm, so alive . . . I am among my own people and I can feel it. I met Henry Aiken last night and found him charming and completely unassuming although I didn't exactly know what to say to him. All day yesterday I was with my cousin Liz Hemley (who looks a lot like Cecil) and I discovered that Susan Hemley, a graduate student in and teacher of physics, is living in Cambridge so I shall probably meet her soon. I think the Hemleys are going to take over this town at the crazy rate we're discovering each other. The Hinduses just called to invite me to dinner on Tuesday and I'm looking forward to meeting them. You really have to come out here; it's an incredible place. Absolutely beautiful. I just enrolled in two very novel courses (of the four minimum we must take): "Conceptual Change" (in the philosophy department) and a new sociology course called the "Social Psychology of Consciousness" which discusses Gurdjieff the first semester and yoga the second. It's going to be an exciting year. I'm crazy about the Christians and I have no asthma troubles. The dog and I are great friends.
>
> All my love,
>
> Nola

Who were the Hinduses and the Christians, I wondered when I first read this letter. Crazy about the Christians? Invited to dinner by the Hinduses? To me, it's slightly comical and ironic, at this quarter-of-a-century remove, that my sister's landlords would be Christians, if only in name, but that the Hinduses (close to Hindus in my mind, at least) would be looking after her, inviting her to dinner. I know it's silly of me, but I can't help concocting cosmic plots, to think that everything has too much meaning rather than too little—call it inherited, one of the basic character flaws running through my family.

I suppose I need to consider another explanation for my sister's sickness, not that I'd try to reduce it to one cause—but the academic pressure she was under must have contributed to the weakening of her mind's defenses against itself. Nola's futile quest for affection from my father, when he was alive and after he was long-dead, drove her, at least in part, to an obsession with intellectual achievement. Of course, one of the treasured Jewish stereotypes is of the bookish and education-obsessed Jewish families, and my family did little to buck this notion.

When I began a dismal slide grade-wise in junior high (right about the time Nola's behavior was at its most intense and odd), I felt like a failure, but no one told me I was a failure. I suppose our obsession with education was subtly enforced by our parents—their expectations for us in the air. But we also had our own expectations for ourselves, our own drives and obsessions, guided by some internal goal. I think our obsession with education, or at least the obsession of my brother and sister, was exactly the obsession of those scholars of the Torah, who have for centuries studied hour after hour, arguing with each other over a word, or the Talmudic tradition of commentary on the Word.

Our parents never spoke of jobs or money—we were almost proud of our disdain for the material—the idea, the ultimate idea, if it existed, was what we aimed for.

That, of course, is an idealization of my brother and sister. I think that on some level it's true, but maybe our obsessions with education were more mundane than that—maybe our expectations were impossible to meet simply because the goals were unexplained and unexplored.

I found a list written in my sister's hand, undated, in which she listed her accomplishments as an undergraduate.

Phi Beta Kappa
Phi Kappa Phi
Alpha Lambda Delta (women)
Eta Sigma Phi (classics)
Honorable Mention in Woodrow Wilson
    and Danforth Competitions.
First Prize for scholarship in
    ancient Greek
Gannertsfelder Scholarship Prize
    in Philosophy
Honors College & Room Scholarship
Deans List
Tuition Scholarship

What was the purpose of this list, I wonder. Was it written as a kind of brag sheet for herself or was it more likely written as a kind of reminder, something for her application to Brandeis? Why has it survived all these years? Did my mother save it on purpose? She sent it to me, after all, with other papers. A strange kind of materialism, a list of accomplishments, the longer the list the richer one is. Perhaps that was the materialism of my family, and like all materialism, ultimately hollow: This list is not my sister nor my sister's mind. These accomplishments add up to nothing.

It's clear to me that the pressures of school caught up with Nola at Brandeis—after a year, she hated it, hated Boston, hated philosophy.

I had somewhere developed the illusion that graduate school, particularly in philosophy, represented the ultimate Beyond, and expected fifes and drums to herald my entrance. I was considerably dismayed to find it filled to overflowing with lecherous and bureaucratic professors, with lethargic pedants for students, who might have had one hour, one day of glory in their undergraduate careers when their creative Self had overcome the rest of them, a moment which established their reputation, as they hoped, for good, which had now been utterly submerged by intellectual postures and habits, and nothing of the soul appeared to remain in the wreckage enforced by scholarliness.

That passage in my sister's memoir was written several years distant from her time at Brandeis, when she had already digested her time there and come to the conclusion that there was something wrong with the study of philosophy, not herself. By this time, she'd thought she'd found new answers, she was able to put her faith in something else. And that is what my sister did thoughout her life—she put her faith in various people whom she assumed knew more about God than she did.

In the moment of her despair, a year after writing so exuberantly about the Christians and the Hinduses, she wrote my mother a letter that must have shocked her in its bleakness.

Jan. 11, 1969

Dear Mom,

Please forgive me if this letter sounds depressing but I honestly don't know what to do about the present situation. My landlady has just had several heart attacks and is in a hospital in Boston. She may be dying. I sent her a card to cheer her up but the atmosphere is so deathlike I'm going berserk. Her husband (who is always very grim) gets more taciturn and surly every minute. I have *tried* to please him—I read his letters for him (his eyes are bad) and told him that he should tell me if there's anything I can do to ease the situation. I plunged myself into my work in order to shake off this depression, only to have him say to me contemptuously: "You looked so tired yesterday you were almost dizzy. My *God*, eight to ten hours without a break!!!" Actually I wasn't studying but typing the second and final draft of a paper that *had* to be written then because Diamandopoulos wanted it last week. I try to go for walks to break the tension but it is *freezing* outside and I find the people in Harvard Square rude and obnoxious and greedy and cold. I can't walk around Cambridge at night because it is dangerous for girls. One guy said to me some months ago: "Why on earth did you move here? Cambridge is a city of hippies and bums." Uncle Allan offered to drive up and help me find a single apartment near Brandeis if this became unbearable; I may take him up on his offer. I think my landlord thinks I'm some kind of freak because I study so much, but there's little else to do here and the end of the term is approaching. What a pain in the neck it is to live with other people—I *always* end up getting criticized and judged according to their petty-bourgeois values. Yet I can't keep too much of a distance from them because I'm painfully lonely. I find most of the boys around here hypocritical egotists who never let a girl be herself, but only want what is "aesthetically pleasing" to them. Jerek (the biochemist of whom I am fond) hasn't called; if he did I would probably be too scared to start up a relationship. I have thought of visiting Rich (the physicist) but I wouldn't know what to say to him, and anyway I find most human relationships here pretty boring and futile. I see in every face the same poverty of imagination, the same dogged materialism, the same puritanical perversions. I find sex disgusting and a completely exhausting, egotistical enterprise. I wish to hell I was in a healthier place—like Hawaii. Remember what David said about seeing a sickness in the East every time he comes here from California? He's dead right. I try to convince myself that things will turn out somehow, that I'm only imagining the horror—but I had to stay home Friday because the black students took over the Brandeis Ford Hall and Administration Building and started a 3-day riot. They flooded all the dormitories by stopping up sinks, stopped classes, etc. At this point, Mother, it's just too much to bear. Life is a pretentious veil spread over a void. All my relationships are either casual or sexual (although I have omitted the latter out of despair for some time); I can call no one a friend. My psychologist I find pretty dense. It seems the world is trying steadily to snuff me out, and I haven't the strength to oppose it. Again, I apologize for the unhappy tone of this letter, but honestly I am on the verge of breakdown. I find refuge only in sleep, and the first question insinuated by the very walls of my room is: "What's the point of living? It leads only to despair." I really feel as if I don't want to go on anymore. The world is a selfish and cruel one, and a thousand deaths reside in the flesh. Life just makes no sense to me at all. It's a hilarious travesty. Mom, you're the only one who has ever been able to talk any sense into me. *Please—please* do not leave me in this abyss. A word, a page, *anything* you write I will be grateful for. I'm sorry I sound so incapable of handling life but I am. Practical matters I have no trouble with, but I find the world a strange and unbearable monster. It terrifies me. People hurt me constantly—every day. I know you're going to throw up your hands and say I've always been like this, but even when I try to be objective about it the world is a vast jigsaw puzzle whose pieces I'm not even sure fit together. How do *you* make sense of life? Its ugliness (here at least) never ceases to shock me. I'm afraid even to walk down the street in broad daylight here. People here are so sinister—is this *normal*? Is this *sane*? I'm so unhappy that I can't see you and Robin—it drives me *mad*. *Please* write as soon as you can. I'm full of anguish.

On a purely emotional level, my sister must have known that such a letter would completely unhinge my mother. Perhaps that's what she wanted. And when I admit this possibility, I also have to admit the possibility in myself. Is this secretly what I want, to cause my mother pain while protesting that's the last thing I want to cause? I hope not, but who can know for sure?

I have to remember that the audience for this letter was my mother and my mother only, not me, not anyone else. Yet I find myself, like my mother, wanting to edit, for style, for clarity. I want to say, "Nola, tone it down a little. Don't be so melodramatic." But I also know that a letter is only a fragment, a snapshot of one's feelings—how many times my own feelings have changed the day, hour, moment after I've mailed a letter to someone. And I also know that even in a letter, maybe especially in a letter, we consciously manipulate, we embellish, we become a character on the page. I'm not doubting the sincerity of my sister's despair. I'm simply wondering what she wanted from my mother? "A word, a page, anything you write," she says, and that's what strikes me—not "your voice, your words, your presence," but "a word." It's not the nearness of people that can save us, but their words, written down, what they've committed to paper. And I suppose I believe this, too, or I would not have begun this study of my family's words.

To me, there's something so exaggerated about the letter, but I suppose that's simply an aspect of Nola's personality I have to acknowledge. My mother has told me half a dozen times at least that Nola liked to dramatize. And so does she, and so do I. Especially in our early twenties, pushed out in the world, unsure of what we were expected to do, how we should act, why others seemed so much more sure of themselves than us.

In 1941, my mother wrote in her journal:

> I wish I believed in some eternity. I keep saying: This is not real, it is all a fairy-tale. For the reality nearly drives me insane. I cannot accept life. I want to hide my head somewhere, as a child does, in a thunderstorm. I would marry anyone, would love anyone, now, just to be able to forget for a little while. But I am afraid I shall never be able to forget. Death comes closer and closer. I have been old for years. The universe has come alive in me, I am the world; what am I? I cannot see myself ending. I am terrified. I am a coward, yes ... but I feel an overwhelming sense of having been deceived. I can retain nothing, and each day hurls me further away from the safety of being alive.

In 1978, at the age of twenty, I wrote in my journal:

> I am experiencing a deep remorse. What if, when I die, there is one poem left, just one, that needs to be expressed ... I don't want to die young. I want to die when the last poem, rising to the surface, pops and shatters my existence. Immortality. Some people live through their children, others their work. I must have no distractions. I must live to write and of course vice versa ...

I need to do that every once in a while—it's a kind of cure for being too judgmental, too self-satisfied and smug, especially when I come across a word like "immortality," I want so badly to cut that out, to make myself at the age of twenty seem less pompous and egotistical. While I'd like to disavow this person I was, I know there's something honest about him, that the anguish we feel at that age is real, even if it seems so distant, so overblown to us now, at twice the age. If Nola had survived, would she have disavowed her despairing letter to my mother, just as my mother disavows her words from her youth: "I love Herbert. I would give up my book for him."?

Almost a year later, in November of 1969, Nola was back to her exuberant self, reveling in the kind of craziness that makes us love life, the best kind of craziness.

I just wrote (purely on impulse) to the Princeton Dean's Office asking for the whereabouts of Daniel Franko Goldman. I just received a letter from Danny-o himself; he wants to know why I want to get in touch with him so urgently and is totally mystified because he doesn't know who the hell I am. Ha! He'll find out before the spring, when Danny leaves for England (probably returning there on his much-coveted Rhodes Scholarship). Crazy, am I? Perhaps. But one has to be nuts sometimes to really enjoy life!

Don't worry about me—that's all I ask. God and the gurus will watch out for me. Anyhow everyone knows that Heaven protects the working girl.

I love you MOMMY-O

NOLA-O

Nola planned to go that summer to India and to sneak across the border into Chinese-occupied Tibet—an intention she told my mother of in the same letter, and which she hadn't yet told her current boyfriend, Joe, who wanted her to go to England with him. On the one hand, my mother is a great worrier, but on the other, she never stood in our way when we wanted to pursue a goal, no matter how dangerous or far-fetched. I'm not sure, in any case, whether she could have stood in Nola's way. Independence and self-determination were *our* mother's milk—what I mean is that our physical actions were our own; I'm not sure I can make the same claim for the habits of our minds. But I don't think anyone can claim complete independence from the notions, criticisms, praise, the words of their parents. Even those who claim to be most untouched by their parents' lives, *especially* those people, live in high relief against them.

> I have made up my mind very definitely about two things: #1: I am not going to let anyone for any reason whatever mess up my professional plans. I discussed this with Joe and he not only understands this, but (I suspect) *wants* me to continue in philosophy. Not that it would make any difference to me if he didn't (I have just reached this little piece of self-discovery a few days ago), but it's nice to know there are considerate men in the world. #2: I am absolutely without a doubt bull-headedly determined to go to India this summer. Joe asked me if I would go to England with him for the summer but I just won't do it. I haven't confronted him yet with this bit of news, but I'm bound to blurt it out sooner or later. I'm taking as direct a charter flight as possible to New Delhi and taking the train from there to the Himalayan foothills. I intend to get as far into (Red Chinese-occupied) Tibet as possible without getting my throat cut. I shall be visiting Agra (site of the Taj Mahal) and Bombay later in the summer. I have to go to Bombay because the charter flight I am returning on leaves from there. I will be in India and around the Tibetan border for about 3 months. Everything is running smoothly in this respect so far; I only hope Joe accepts this because I am *not* changing my mind.

I saw a film not long ago in which one character asks another if he knows how to make God laugh. The answer is simple, "Make a plan."

She never went to India; she never faced the physical danger of crossing a hostile border, nor the unlikely possibility of having her throat cut. I'm reminded of my mother on the bus in Mexico, pushed to the floor by her supposed savior, Elliot Chess, who perhaps saved her physical self but caused and still causes so much anguish in her to this day. I'm reminded of my mother lying on the floor of the bus while she heard the distant sounds of guns popping and the screams of passengers. I think of her constructing a story in the midst of this madness, thinking that mythic cannibals from the hills attacked the bus, when in fact, the explanation was so much more mundane. And I connect that to Nola, imagining her throat cut perhaps by a Chinese guard in a Mao hat as she sleeps in her yert, not afraid of this physical danger, but unaware of the peril she was in emotionally, spiritually, intellectually.

All I know is this: By the end of February 1970, my sister was a different person, and how do I know this? Not so much through my imperfect memory, but through her own voice, the difference in the tone of her letters before this date and afterward. Even in her most self-dramatic and despairing moments before this date, I can still tell it's Nola speaking—even the fervor with which she tells my mother of the depths of her despair, there's vitality in this. But compare that voice to the voice of her memoir—there's something weary and desiccated in this voice, at least I notice it, something bleak and abstract, vague, wandering, lost, hopeless, even when she speaks of hope. But I feel more hope in her desperate pleas of 1969 than in the strongest declarations of love and harmony in her memoir. In this, she's too formal, too stiff. I'm not saying there aren't eloquent and moving passages in the memoir she wrote her final year—there are plenty, but to me, it has the tone, overall, of a last will.

What caused this break, I suppose, is open to speculation. Let's just say it was a chemical imbalance. Let's just say we'll never understand. My cousin David thinks it might have had something to do with the many vitamins she took, the megadoses. Perhaps. His parents, too, think it had something to do with her diet. Perhaps it's just that simple. I used to think it had to do with drugs, that she took a hit of LSD and it triggered her madness. Another chemical-imbalance theory. But she insists, in her own book, that she never took anything stronger than marijuana, and then only a few times. Knowing my sister, I believe her, because drug-taking to her must have seemed like cheating, and ultimately futile—I think Nola would say that a search for the sublime can't be effected by altering the chemistry of the brain, but the habits and dependencies of the mind. And there's a great difference. It's the difference, I suppose, between a carnival ride and a spaceship.

Admitting that we'll never know for sure, never even know what the nature of madness is exactly, liberates us in a way, allows us to relate events in ways that might ultimately give us greater insight than simple explanations. A chemical imbalance is in some ways no less a mysterious explanation than a metaphysical explanation (or, an imaginative one). To say that chemicals interact is not to say we ultimately understand the nature of these interactions—they're simply manifestations—to identify something (amino acids, the building blocks of life, nicotine receptors in the brain, the location of our short-term memories) does not mean we understand these locations.

Her Diet

Now, for lunch and dinner—

No more than *2*
        bowls of yogurt
fresh raw vegetables—lettuce
        1 piece fruit per meal.
        I had too much
            yogurt today—
        only two bowls
          per meal
              from now
                   on.
No meat
or fish —
just two bowls
of yogurt
—no matter   Regimen per meal:
what anyone   Not   more than
says—   2 bowls yogurt
and your   lettuce (as needed)
lettuce   piece fruit (fresh only)
& fresh fruit *water.*
      (one piece)
—be *very* careful with *cooked* vegetables.
           look at them first!

I cannot eat fish or *eggs*—
        I *am* a total vegetarian.
Meat is definitely out—chicken
is abhorrent to me—
no more of these—

just yogurt, soybeans, avocados,
                    & the like for protein
                from *now on,*

Positively
    No more honey—
        Very *bad* for me!
    Nothing between meals!
        esp. before *bedtime!!!*

        honey makes you feel
        awful so don't take
        any more!!!

Put check in bank
        Dr. West appt. 10:00 am → No orange juice
                                        it's refined & not
                                                    pure.

See West at 10
            tomorrow

Jinx

Even now, I can't think of Slippery Rock without revulsion. For years, I hated the entire state of Pennsylvania simply because it contained Slippery Rock. Later, I decided I liked the Eastern half of the state because Philadelphia was a mitigating factor.

We had moved to Slippery Rock after my mother's return to school to earn a master's degree. This was her first teaching job: Slippery Rock State Teacher's College. One sometimes heard the unlikely name of Slippery Rock on the tail end of sports reports across the country—partly because Slippery Rock had a good football team and partly because newscasters liked to say Slippery Rock.

Slippery Rock is located about seventy miles north of Pittsburgh, and supposedly its name derived from an unlikely incident in which a settler, chased by Indians, led them across the creek, where they all slipped on the stones in the river, save the wily settler, who knew his way around. "Watch out for the slippery rocks," he yelled back at them. If Slippery Rock had a tourist industry, one might produce large quantities of coffee mugs depicting such a hilarious scene. Or not.

In 1969, Slippery Rock had about three thousand residents and perhaps as many students. The nearest big town was Grove City—it had an ice-cream parlor—that's what made it big to me. Slippery Rock had one main street, one restaurant, a newsstand, a town drunk who doubled as the town artist, and freshmen at the college wore beanies around campus. We lived in an apartment complex, and my friends consisted of neighborhood kids who doubled as classmates. The neighborhood kids wanted to know right off where I was from, where I was born, and I told them New York City. They had heard of New York City, but Slippery Rock was their world, and in a strange reversal of THE NATURAL LAWS OF THE UNIVERSE, they started calling me a hick.

"No, you're the hicks," I insisted.

My main friends were a red-haired kid named Joey, a tall kid named

Dick, and a blond kid named Steve. Their families: the Smiths, the Stones, and the Minks, did not believe in wasting syllables on either first names or surnames. Steve Mink spat all the time—all the time, even indoors—Steve never had much spit in him as a consequence; he never allowed moisture to accumulate, but I remember him spitting once on our carpet. "Don't do that in here," my mom told Steve. "That's disgusting."

"I do it at home," Steve said.

"You're not at home," she told him.

We used to go to Steve's house down the road to play football. Steve had a go-cart and a grandmother who beheaded chickens while we played football, as if she were part of some kind of surreal and evil cheerleading squad. I was generally the quarterback because I was too skinny to actually tackle anyone, but pretty much fun for the other guys to tackle. I played without shoes and was rarely tackled because I was so terrified that I did all kinds of amazing maneuvers to avoid any body contact whatsoever—leaping over my opponents as they lunged for me, zigzagging and whirling with the grace of a pro. But I soon tired of this play, figuring the odds would eventually get me, and I retreated after school each day to my room, where I tried to memorize Hamlet's soliloquy—I'm not sure why I chose this—while below my window my contemptuous friends yelled up at me, demanding that I play football or they'd beat me up.

"Whether tis nobler in the mind to suffer the slings and arrows of outrageous fortune," I replied.

At that time, I wanted to be an actor—and I thought that memorizing Shakespeare would lift me out of Slippery Rock. It didn't, and I suffered my share of slings and arrows at the hands of my friends. One night, on my way home from Boy Scouts, Dick, Steve, and Joey ambushed me near our apartment complex: for refusing to play football anymore, for being a hick, a Jew, a Boy Scout (they hated Boy Scouts, too). Joey and Steve grabbed me and held me against a wall while gangly Dick started beating me, but with an improbable object, a gigantic inflated inner tube. It *kind of* hurt, but not much. It surprised me more than anything, and it was awkward for him. I think it wore him out before he could hurt me. "Goddamn hick," he kept yelling, until finally I broke free. Joey called me a kike as I fled. He had previously served notice that he could no longer play with me—his parents had told him I had killed Christ.

"No, you killed Christ," I told him. These kids had everything back-ward, so I figured they had that wrong, too.

My revenge came later that fall when I scored the only copy within the county of The Archies hit single, "Sugar, Sugar." I bought it in Grove City for less than a dollar and taunted Dick with it, who was desperate for the single. He offered to buy it from me, but I wouldn't sell. Finally, he offered me $25 for it. I didn't ask where he got the money and I didn't care. But who knows. Maybe it's worth $25 again by now, if Dick still owns the record. I suppose he still lives in Slippery Rock and does things backward. Maybe he owns the booming tourist concession, selling those mugs that read, "Watch out for the Slippery Rocks," to all those hicks from New York blowing through town.

I hated Slippery Rock because in 1969, to an eleven-year-old boy from an oddball intellectual family, it was a hateful place.

I know I'm being mean to the past and present citizens (denizens?) of Slippery Rock, that I'm being unfair, that I'm being petty in con-demning them with such a broad brush. I tell you, I would not mind if God broke off Slippery Rock like an icicle from a roof, and tossed it over his shoulder. I know it's irrational, but when you're eleven years old and in despair, you carry a part of that despair for the rest of your life. There's a sharpness to life at eleven that later you're inured to. And you cast around for blame even when you know that the source of your hatred, fear, and sadness is not, in all likelihood, solely where you live.

Maybe it has to do with the death of my father four years before, but not completely.

Maybe it has to do with the death of my friend Jimmy Lucazy earlier that year. Jimmy was my best friend from Long Beach, New York, where I spent all my summers at my grandmother's beach house. Jimmy and another friend, Vince, had been building a fort in the sand on the beach. They dug a hole, piled boards on it, and covered it with more sand. They had asked me if I wanted to do it with them, and I said, no, that I thought it was stupid, but then they went ahead and did it any-way, and the boards and sand collapsed on Jimmy and smothered him. I was in Slippery Rock when I heard the news, and maybe this is in part why I still hate Slippery Rock. The town is death to me, broiling skies and coal veins underneath. I started forming a theory after Jimmy's death that I was some kind of jinx, and that people I loved died, espe-cially when I couldn't be there to help them. Three years earlier, I had been sent to a friend's house when my father suffered his heart attack.

I had been away from home when I learned the news. The same was true of Jimmy's death—I was stunned when I heard that Jimmy, only ten years old, had died. It didn't seem possible. My father's death was possible, but a ten-year-old's death was something I had never been prepared for.

At eleven, death was so real to me that I tried to kill myself. Maybe I shouldn't have been reading *Hamlet.* One afternoon, I went to the bathroom cupboard and swallowed as many aspirin as I could before my throat swelled up and I could swallow no more. If I'd been older, I suppose I would have used something more powerful than aspirin, but even aspirin in large quantities can seriously fool with your metabolism. I fully intended to kill myself; it was not just a cry for attention. After that, I went to sleep and didn't wake up until the next morning when it was time for school. I must have slept for fourteen or fifteen hours, and I'm not sure why my mother didn't try to waken me, or if she did, why she didn't realize that I was more unconscious than asleep.

When I awoke, I felt slightly ashamed of myself, and really wasn't sure why I'd done this—I just felt lonely. The only person I ever told was a boy named Lonnie who stood in front of me in the lunch line the next day at school.

"You know what I did last night," I said as we slid our trays along. "I swallowed about seventeen aspirin."

He turned and gave me a skeptical look. "Why'd you do that?"

"I don't know," I said.

"You could have died," he said. "That's pretty stupid."

I agreed and felt chastised, but at least he said something that wasn't backward, that I could understand. I didn't feel like telling my mother. My mother wouldn't have understood. She would have overreacted. But this kid Lonnie reacted just right, with just the right amount of disapproval. My mother set no limits for my older brother and sister and me when we were kids, and we were often told by relatives that we were spoiled and unruly—all true—but my mother had her hands full after my father died, simply trying to make a living for us. I hardly remember seeing my mother during those days in Slippery Rock. Or my brother and sister.

Nola was off at Brandeis and this was my brother Jonathan's freshman year at Ohio University. He was sixteen and following in the family tradition of attending college without graduating from high school. My father had attended Amherst at fourteen. My mother started college at sixteen, and Nola had started at seventeen. In fact, I'm the only high school graduate in my immediate family—a strange intellectual joke, a reversal of the normal meaning of such a state-ment—there's something slightly embarrassing that the only thing my family had to overcome in its education was boredom.

Most of my memories of that time are of me alone, watching TV in the basement or sitting up in my room, memorizing *Hamlet*. I guess, in such a vacuum, I needed to create my own limits—and that, perhaps, is what the aspirin was about. I had successfully negotiated a limit.

I invited Lonnie home that day and we listened to my recording of the musical sound track from *Hair*. We sat on my mother's couch and sang along. Lonnie liked to sing and he liked to talk about books, both activities I was used to. Lonnie and I became best friends, *only* friend for me, and we went sledding together or stayed indoors and sang songs from *Hair*. He lived on Elm Street, and I asked my mother what an elm looked like. She said it was a kind of tree, and I asked what kind of tree, and she said, she couldn't really explain—most of them were dead anyway. That seemed appropriate for Slippery Rock. I don't re-member any of the other street names in Slippery Rock, not even the street on which we lived, only a street named after a diseased tree. I still take nightmare journeys up the hill to our apartment complex some-times. In my dreams, Slippery Rock is built on frosty terraces with slip-pery roads and rickety stores that look like the faded wooden structures on the surface of coal mines.

I developed all kinds of compulsions in Slippery Rock. When I ran up the stairs, I had to take them two at a time. On the way down, I skipped the third stair because three was evil, I decided, and if I stepped on the third stair something bad would happen. When re-turning a snack to the cupboard I had to return it to the exact spot where I had found it. The rules kept changing, appearing in my head like flash cards a moment before the necessary action had to be taken.

Place your spoon on the right side of your bowl. Leave one green Lucky Charms marshmallow floating alone in the milk.

When I think back to that boy I was, I'm almost worried for him, amazed that he ever made it out of Slippery Rock alive, that he sur-vived into adulthood. Now I see what I was trying to do at the time, how I was trying to give my life some order, but back then I could only await the next commands in this mental boot camp in which I existed.

My grandmother was living at the time in Hollywood, Florida, with my uncle Joe and my aunt Rose, and after I started getting D's in school, someone suggested that I might go down to Florida and finish the school year there. I was ready. The week before we left, there were two hijackings of planes bound for Florida to Cuba. I didn't mind the danger. Even Cuba seemed preferable. I understood the hijackers. I understood why someone might want to risk imprisonment or death in order to leave a detested place. I didn't understand the politics of it. To me, this was a simple case of needing to get away from where you lived, desperation.

My mother and I went down to Florida together over the winter break, and stayed the first few days with a woman in Miami named Dorothy, a friend of a friend of my mother. Dorothy was the editor in chief and restaurant critic for the *Dade County Star*—the paper's stationery proclaimed it, "One of America's Most Intriguing Newspapers." Certainly, Dorothy was one of America's most intriguing people, at least to me. In a letter to my mother not long after my father died, Dorothy complained nonstop: about her asthma, a growth that might be cancerous, and a "daughter who will not even take me to the hospital when my ankle is broken." She claimed to write every one of her restaurant columns in five minutes: "In spite of the 'flighty' way of composing, I've gotten compliments on some of my columns . . ." Dorothy fascinated me. She told me that none of the restaurateurs knew her identity, and that they were always trying to find out. She ate out every night. She had a pool, and a mini-sauna in her bedroom—the sauna looked like something out of *Get Smart*, a chamber that you sat in with your head poking out.

We went to a restaurant one night where Dorothy ordered frog legs for me. As we ate she told my mother and me a story. "In this very restaurant, I saw a man die. He was eating some fish and he swallowed a bone."

"My God," my mother said.

"And you know what, no one helped him. There were doctors in the restaurant, four of them, and not one of them helped the poor man. They were all afraid of being sued. I mentioned that in my review, but it's still a fine place to eat."

I think I've remembered that scene for so long because I was horrified. We sat at a corner table and I could see the entire restaurant. The restaurant was large and airy and low lit. We sat by the porch, and I could see waiters carrying their trays, and men and women, a few children sitting at tables, laughing and talking—I focused on one man, a little large, a little red in the face, and I imagined him falling out of his chair, coughing, grasping his hands around his throat.

Maybe I hadn't escaped Slippery Rock, merely taken a detour.

The next day, Dorothy drove us around on the freeway. I was sitting in the backseat and Dorothy and my mother were chatting up front. Dorothy drove a Mustang, about sixty-five miles an hour, and as she roared up the road I noticed what seemed like a hundred cars heading toward us. I screamed, "Dorothy, look," and for a moment we all looked at the cars in a line four lanes wide heading straight for us—none of us quite sure what was wrong with this picture.

"Those fools!" Dorothy yelled and swerved her car onto the median, between two palms, and made her own entrance ramp onto the right side of the freeway.

I was the first one of us to develop the Hong Kong flu. Until my mother took my temperature, I wasn't quite sure what was wrong with me, why I felt so light-headed. I had attributed this feeling to spending the night with Dorothy's grandson—he was an avid Elvis fan, the first I ever met, and, like all REAL ELVIS fans I've met since, he left me vaguely unsettled. All night long, I had to hear Elvis songs, and not even early Elvis, but late Elvis. Not *too* late. Not puffy, sweaty jumpsuit Elvis, but Comeback Elvis. Suspicious-Minded Elvis. Kentucky Rained-On Elvis. Spanish Harlem Elvis. My theory is that people don't really care about his music anymore—they just can't stop saying Elvis. Elvis, like Slippery Rock, is fun to say.

Slippery Rock Demolishes Elvis, 140 to Zip.

What *I* liked was worse, far worse, of course. "Sugar, Sugar" by The Archies, who didn't even exist. At least, Elvis once walked the earth, or so it has been told.

We didn't stay long with Dorothy after that. Dorothy and my mother came down with the flu, too, and although Dorothy begged us to stay to take care of her, we couldn't. We couldn't even take care of ourselves. We had to move to my grandmother's place so that she could help nurse us back to health. I hope someone took pity on poor Dorothy and helped her, if not her daughter who wouldn't take her to the hospital for a broken ankle, then some other more merciful relative or friend. I've probably never met a person more terrified of death than Dorothy, although comically unmindful of it at the same time. We never saw her again, and as far as I know, she and my mother never communicated after that disastrous stay.

The next two weeks I spent in bed at my grandmother's place with the Hong Kong flu, a fever that broke at 104. My mother had it too, and she was in the bed next to mine. While my grandmother waited on us, we read to each other and played games. My mother introduced me to a play by the French writer, Jean Giradoux, *The Madwoman of Chaillot,* about an elderly woman in Paris who, together with her destitute and powerless friends of the street, trap a group of ruthless oil magnates and developers in the sewers of the city because they want to drill for oil under Paris.

Strangely, being sick with the Hong Kong flu, on the brink of death and dementia, is one of my fondest memories of childhood. Sure, what leaps to mind are the obvious Freudian reasons—my mother all to myself—in the next bed—and while I won't deny these possibilities, I also simply have to say that the reason those two weeks were enjoyable was because they were so enjoyable. I liked things of the mind, still do, and this was the first time I could relax and do what I most enjoyed for a long while. Not that I disliked playing football—although I did, intensely. Not that other kids weren't more normal than me—spitting on the carpet, beating people with inner tubes, going gaga over Elvis.

I was allowed for two weeks to be sick, abnormal. And so, I did things that I wasn't supposed to do as a kid. I read and memorized a part in a play. I read poetry aloud. I played a poetry game called "Exquisite Corpse." Appropriate for a boy transfixed by and obsessed with death.

I'm always suspicious of people who say they had a normal childhood. What happens to those people? I think maybe they're in a restaurant one day and they see someone choking on a fishbone, and they don't know what to do. They have no frame of reference. They write an unfavorable review. They're afraid of a lawsuit. They're tempted by the frog legs.

I know I'm being unfair to those people who live idyllic lives. I admit it. No, they're the ones who save the person's life. I'm the one who watches, glad it wasn't me this time. I'm the one who has no frame of reference, no experience with safety. That blue pallor looks almost normal to me. I'm the one who orders the frog legs.

After my mother and I recovered from the Hong Kong flu, she returned to Slippery Rock and I was left to spend the rest of the school year with my grandmother Ida, my great uncle Joe, and my aunt Rose. Actually, I wasn't related to either Joe or Rose, although I considered them my aunt and uncle. Joe had been married to Ida's sister, my great aunt Frances, and after Frances died, Joe married Rose, a Hungarian Jew who had survived the death camps. It was impossible not to like Rose, who had the cheeriest personality of anyone I've ever met, despite the fact that she had lost almost her entire family in the Holocaust, with the exception of her son, whom she didn't know had survived until thirteen years after the war when she ran into him by accident on the streets of Tel Aviv. Rose had owned a newsstand in Manhattan in front of a restaurant frequented by the Gabor sisters, and Rose was always telling us about her Gabor encounters—she liked them both immensely. Rose looked like a slightly older, zaftig version of the Gabor sisters, with dyed blond hair, what they might have looked like if they had owned a newsstand in midtown Manhattan and sat on a stool all day, and been through death camps and had blue tattoos on their wrists.

Rose was one of those people, chiefly women of an older generation who, once they've identified the favorite food of a favored grandchild, niece, or nephew, will forever make it for that child whenever she or he visits. With Rose and me, it was apple strudel. My grandmother Ida was a lovely person, and had the same idea, but with her the signals somehow got crossed, and she thought my favorite food was meat loaf— which I have nothing against, but it's not what I'd order for a last meal.

Joe was completely the opposite of Rose, a dour man who always looked concerned or worried. Joe was built like Barney Rubble, with white scrub-brush hair and a white mustache. He had been a signalman in the navy in World War I and had a ship sunk from under him. He and my aunt Frances had met and married in the thirties, and had run a little soda fountain in Jamaica, Queens. Frances was always considered the great beauty of my grandmother's family, but when I knew her, she was old and pretty dotty, having suffered a stroke. At seven, I liked talking to her because she was so funny, inadvertently so, but I didn't know any better and couldn't understand why the adults looked so unhappy when she said something funny. One night, Joe fell asleep at the wheel of his car and hit a utility pole—and Frances was killed. To most of the family, her death was a relief. Sad but a relief. No one ever talked about Frances or her death after she died. I learned about her death on a train ride—my grandmother told me, and said I shouldn't say anything to Joe because it would make him sad. This is one thing I learned about death at a young age, that after someone died, you were never supposed to mention them again. If it had been the other way around, Frances would have talked. She would have babbled happily about Joe, maybe thinking he was still alive, because of her *condition,* because she didn't know any better.

For four months, I lived with Joe, Rose, and Ida in their retirement community in Hollywood, and I loved it. By any yardstick other than a conventional one, I was essentially an elderly person. I ate Meals on Wheels, nightly played a Hungarian version of canasta called Kalooki with my relatives, and played shuffleboard with Joe every day—we had a shuffleboard court right outside the door! I really liked being old. Age, I decided, is wasted on the elderly. None of my relatives seemed aware how much better it was to be old than young. They even complained about it.

And I enjoyed the school I attended. Classes were held in open-air metal huts. The walls would drop away when the weather was good, which was almost every day. I went from D's in Slippery Rock to A's in all my subjects. This was an idyll for me—shuffleboard at home instead of football, and the entire school went bowling on Fridays right after the Spelling Bee, which I always won. The only sore spot in this happy time was one boy named Frank Parker, whom I disliked for one reason or another. So I put a curse on him. I took a piece of notebook paper and drew two swords crossed like the Wilkinson swords, and I made up a name for an honorary society, The Silver Sword Society. In between the swords, I wrote the initials of this secret society:

Underneath this picture, I made up my curse:

A curse upon Frank Parker. Something bad will happen to him.
So sayeth Robin Hemley, President of The Silver Sword Society™

After I wrote the curse, I put it in my desk, but it must have fallen out when I removed one of my books because Frank Parker found it on the floor.

"Did you write this?" he asked me, rubbing the top of his head. I expected him to get into a fight with me, but he didn't look angry. He told me that he was reading the curse as he stepped out the door, and a tile fell off the roof and hit him on the head.

"Really?" I was quite pleased with myself.

"Take the curse off, okay?" he asked.

"Sure, okay," I said. I made Frank stand completely still and I advised him that an invisible sword was sticking through his gut. Carefully and elaborately, showing much strain, I tugged the sword from Frank's belly.

In the way of the kid world, Frank and I became good friends after that. I could afford to be generous. I had some control. I could direct some of the bad things that seemed to follow me, could make them stick in someone else's gut if I wanted.

That day, contented, I went back to the retirement village, ate some Meals on Wheels chow and watched my favorite TV show, *Dark Shadows*, about a good but still deadly vampire named Barnabas Collins, who was always traveling back and forth in time trying to save the world. I identified with Barnabas, still do. Barnabas was always fighting one monster or another, when he wasn't fighting himself and his own tendencies toward self-destruction. This week, it was something called the Leviathan. The worst thing about the Leviathan was that no one had yet seen it, but you could sure hear the damn thing. Its breathing was labored and intense and hollow, and it made splashy footprint sounds as it walked. It lived in water and always left puddles of it, like so much pee, wherever it went. That's how you could tell the Leviathan had been around—that and the fact that whenever you saw that puddle of water, you knew that the Leviathan had snatched another victim. But you never saw it, and you never saw its victims. It was, by far, the scariest monster around.

I had to turn the TV off. I couldn't watch anymore, and I never watched *Dark Shadows* again after that week.

One day, a letter arrived in the mail from an Assistant Counsel to the Attorney General of the United States. I had written to President Nixon because of an incident I had seen on the TV news one evening with Joe, Ida, and Rose in the living room.

Dear President Nixon,

You don't know me, but I am a concerned boy. Tonight, on the news I saw some people throwing rocks at little kids on a bus going to school in

Arkansas. How can you let this happen? Children should be safe when they go to school. Please do something about it right now! I am eleven.

Sincerely,
Robin Hemley

P.S.—I am a boy, not a girl even though my name is Robin. Boys in England are called Robin, even though I am not from England that is my name.

The scene on TV had shown several orange school buses being pelted with rocks by angry parents—some of them were trying to tip the buses over. The picture was shot from a little distance from the bus, but you could clearly make out children on the buses, and you could hear them screaming as the windows shattered and the metal was dented. The scene transfixed me. I couldn't understand how adults could throw rocks at little children. Wasn't childhood dangerous enough? Kids terrorized one another just fine—they didn't need any help from adults. I didn't know a thing about busing or integration, and only a little about the civil rights movement, but I knew a lot about children feeling unsafe, feeling that death was right around the corner.

The letter I received back from the government was addressed to Master Robin Hemley, which I didn't understand until my grandmother explained that this was a term of respect used when addressing boys.

March 2, 1970
Dear Master Hemley,

President Nixon has asked me to respond to your letter of concern in regards to the incident in Fayetteville on January 21st of this year. The President shares your concern. However, appropriate action was taken by the state of Arkansas, and so it does not seem fitting at this time for the federal government to intervene.

Sincerely,
Harold W. Varina
Assistant Counsel to the Attorney General

Ida read this letter aloud to Rose and Joe that afternoon, and I was treated like a hero. Rose didn't understand English perfectly and was convinced that the president had signed the letter himself, and that Harold W. Varina was indeed the president. Ida wanted to frame the letter, and even Joe seemed happy—the beginning, he said, of a distinguished life in politics for me. I was happy for all the attention, but not really satisfied by the letter. The man who answered my letter had not, after all, answered my question. How could this happen? I wasn't only asking for a solution or an excuse. I wanted a reason.

* * *

My grandmother and I went to Miami Beach a couple of weeks before I was to return to Slippery Rock. She said that we had to go to a hotel where Cousin Ruth was dying of Lou Gehrig's Disease. I didn't even know who Cousin Ruth was, and visiting someone who was dying did not seem to me a suitable activity for young or old alike. The less said about death, the better, and watching someone die seemed like an embarrassing activity, akin to watching them on the toilet.

"What am I supposed to say to her?" I asked my grandmother. I wasn't going to tell her I was sorry she was dying. When my father had died, someone had told my brother Jonathan that they were sorry, and he'd said, "What are you sorry for? You didn't kill him." And that's the attitude I adopted afterward. That seemed properly embattled and hostile. I imagined Ruth would say the same thing if I told her I was sorry. "What are you sorry for, kid. I don't even know you." And then I'd be humiliated and would plunge a silver sword in her for revenge.

"You don't have to say anything," my grandmother told me. "There will be a lot of people there, and Ruth can't speak anymore. Just say hello and smile. Everyone loves your smile."

"Should I tell her I'm sorry she's dying."

"That's not polite," my grandmother said. "Don't mention it. Pretend to be happy to see her."

To seal my approval, my grandmother offered me a death bribe. I was familiar with death bribes—to make death more palatable, you were given something that you wanted. When my father died, a friend of our family took me downtown and said I could have any toy I wanted. She seemed dismayed when I couldn't think of anything, so I pointed to a model car in a drugstore window. The car was wrapped up for me and my mother's friend seemed relieved. I tried to put the car together, but gave up halfway through the project. Wheels on a chassis, that's how it ended up, nothing at all like the perfect picture of a Camaro on the box.

My grandmother's death bribe was a banana split, the largest, she claimed, that could be found anywhere, big enough for two people.

And, as an added bonus, the soda shop was located on the bottom floor of Cousin Ruth's hotel. Ida and I sat at the counter with a giant boat of whipped cream, bananas, ice cream, and syrup fortifying ourselves with dollops of sugar before we met dying Ruth. Ida kept asking me if it tasted good, and I kept having to reassure her that this was indeed the best banana split I'd ever eaten. We gorged ourselves and then went up to Ruth's room.

Although other people milled around the room, it was the dying person who immediately captured my attention. She sat in a recliner, her legs propped up, covered up to her neck with a loose, colorful blanket.

I forced myself not to stare. The windows of the room were open and people were quiet. My aunt Carrie was there, and my uncle Morty, and a few other people I didn't recognize. A friend of the family named Gertie Cohen sat on the bed near Ruth.

I approached Ruth. I had to face her sooner or later. I remembered her vaguely now. She had a nice face and a gentle smile. I had already been told that she couldn't talk but that didn't seem necessary. She looked at me and I didn't feel so frightened of her, although I could see she was weak and dying. We didn't touch, but I smiled back and made a gesture that I hoped no one else noticed. I grabbed the scabbard of a sword and pulled it from her body, gently, almost imperceptibly. To the uninitiated, it might have looked like a half-hug, pulled away from at the last moment.

*   *   *

I didn't want to return to Slippery Rock, and made every attempt to avoid going home, but my mother missed me too much, and in April she came down to Hollywood. I missed her, too, but not enough to want to return. I was having a great time as an old-timer. And my shuffleboard game was getting really good—I even started winning at Kalooki.

There used to be a picture of me walking around a fountain in Miami wearing sunglasses, a Naugahyde vest, a Nehru shirt, and a sun medallion as big as my face. A destructive dog of mine chewed it up several years ago, but that's just as well. It's an embarrassing picture, not simply because the styles are so laughable now.

The photo was embarrassing because it was so fake. This was my impression of a young person, not the real thing. I was an actor, and

I was sure that I was going to be discovered as I walked around that fountain. I knew that someone important must be watching, someone who'd recognize I had the exact look they wanted.

I was so sure, just as I was sure that this time the plane would be hijacked and my mother and I would begin a brand new life in Havana.

* * *

The first night back in Slippery Rock, my mother told me she had something important to tell me. We were halfway through dinner.

"Your friend, Lonnie," she said. Then she said something I couldn't hear, but I pretended to hear it, pretended it made perfect sense.

"Oh," I said and kept on eating.

But my mother wasn't finished. "I'm sorry I have to tell you this, Robin. Did you hear me?"

"Yes."

"I know you were close."

I kept eating.

"No one is really sure what happened. It happened during the winter. Apparently, Lonnie and his younger brother . . ."

"You mean Fred?"

"I don't know which one."

"He only has one."

My mother was looking at me and then she looked at her plate. "They were down near Slippery Rock Creek. A man started chasing them or something, no one's really sure, and Lonnie fell through the ice. His brother . . ."

"Fred?"

"Yes, Fred. His brother saw the whole thing happen and he hasn't spoken a word since."

Then my mother told me an alternate version of Lonnie's death, that they had been climbing trees, a branch had broken and Lonnie had fallen through the ice. I didn't need to hear an alternate version. However he died, however he came to be there, the results were the same. He'd fallen through the ice, and unable to find his way out again, had drowned. I understood that. I nodded. I understood that. They shouldn't have been out there on the ice alone. I understood that. But it didn't sound like Lonnie. It didn't sound like something he'd do. He was so cautious. He never got in trouble. He thought death was stupid.

I understood his brother's inability to speak, to shed light on the true story. I understood that, in the face of death, no words were necessary, no words were appropriate, no words could suffice or describe. The less said the better.

We finished dinner in silence and then my mother went to the living-room couch and started sorting through her mail. I stood up slowly from the table, turned around, and ran to her. I collapsed in her lap and cried. "I wasn't home again," I said, sobbing. She stroked my head, not sure what I meant, what being home had to do with anything. If I had been there, I thought, this might not have happened. Somehow my being there could have saved him. There was no comforting me.

Lonnie was the only one I cried for. I didn't cry for my father. I tried. I knew I was supposed to, but I couldn't. I didn't cry for my friend Jimmy, smothered earlier that year in the sand fort he'd built—although I remember his face much more clearly than Lonnie's and knew him longer. But Lonnie, whom I barely knew, who had shown me the kindness of disapproval, who told me it was stupid to die, he was the one I couldn't stop crying for. Even now, nearly thirty years later, the grief smothers me like so much sand, like ice I can't find my way out of. Lonnie's death convinced me once and for all that I was, indeed, a jinx, that whoever I loved would die—and I haven't seen anything to convince me otherwise—except that now I know we're all jinxes.

When I think of Slippery Rock, the picture I invariably see is a storm rolling in from the vantage point of the kitchen of our apartment—I see hills with skeletal trees. I don't know why it's this image, unremarkable and bland, not even fixed in a specific moment of memory that stays with me so deeply, that seems to embody all my terror and angst over the place—except that what terrifies me most about life are exactly those moments that are unremarkable and bland, that are erasable. Loss of memory terrifies me. Loss of identity terrifies me.

The world is supposed to make sense, that's what childhood is about, what at least we pretend it's about. That's when we give our children all the explanations for why things work and how they work, or if we can't, we stay silent and by our silence, ask them to try to figure it out. We try to keep them away from things they won't understand, things we can't understand, pictures on the news, atrocities, the deaths of parents, of young friends, of siblings. We give them explanations but still they crawl into our bed at night and tell us they're afraid, they've had a nightmare, even the young ones who have survived relatively unharmed so far, our children whom we wish we could protect forever, whose childhoods we want to be an idyll.

We don't even need to know what their nightmares are about. Nightmares are all the same. You're being chased—that's all you need to know. Or you're in an unfamiliar place. Or a familiar place with stores that look like coal mines, streets that are slippery, frosted terraced hills, an iron-kettle sky and winter in the air.

I know what it's like to wake up in terror, alone, unable to catch a breath. I still wake up hating myself many nights. For unspecified reasons, for many reasons that don't even always make sense. This is Slippery Rock's legacy. This is where I still live.

Nothing I Sensed Could Corroborate or Deny Them

Until recently, I thought Nola's troubles could be blamed on a chiropractor. I didn't know his name. My mother never told me—all I knew about this mysterious man was that Nola's troubles had begun after she went to see him, and that she was never the same afterward.

But, like so much else, I had this fact wrong. He wasn't a chiropractor, but a teacher of sorts who did, in fact, manipulate Nola's spine, and manipulated her diet. Whether he manipulated her mind, I'll never know. I don't know that my sister was changed *by* him, but she was fundamentally changed after him, in a way that no one was able to change her before—not Elliot Chess, though from his reluctant person she was made in part, and not from my father, who repudiated her.

Feb. 1970

Dear Mommyo,

I have the most marvelous yoga teacher. His name is Ralph Haven. I think he's adopted me! He's made me a new person, straightened my spine, given me constipation remedies (constipation is considered a serious sign of degeneration in yoga), bestowed upon me vigilance, dedication, and a strength of will I never previously possessed . . . He spent 5 years studying in India and he teaches yoga as no one I have known teaches yoga. Every asana is done slowly, one-in-a-lesson, and very carefully, with total concentration so that it affects every bit of your body, mind, & soul. I've never met anyone like him, and I keep telling him how terrific he is even though it embarrasses him. He deserves it!

Forget about what I said about rice and beans; it is good for Japanese, but American physiologies can't take that much overbalance of starch. Ralph told me what I should really eat. *All* organic foods, *uncooked*, either fresh (i.e. in spring and summer) or dried (in winter). Drink *spring water*; fluoride water is dangerous. Spring water is cheap ($1.00 for about 5 gallons). For *protein* eat *only:* plain yogurt or plain yogurt with honey—unsalted soybeans or sprouted mung beans or *raw* peas, or *raw* legumes or raw nuts → *UNSALTED.* Nothing cooked. Cooking destroys the life properties of the food. Eat all vegetables, fruits, *raw* or *dried,* washing them thoroughly. Don't take any milk unless it's raw & unpasteurized (pretty difficult to get unless you live on a farm). And *NO* milk products (cheeses, etc.) unless they are unprocessed. You should eat only just enough to live on and never overeat. And eat *only* what is *fresh* unless dried by the sun (dried fruits are excellent. In short, restrict the diet to fresh fruits and vegetables; dried fruits, raw milk, yogurt (plain), and *raw* (preferably comb) honey (the honey in *great moderation).* For beverages, drink only spring water or *freshly* squeezed (unprocessed) fruit juice. *Everything else* leads to sickness, disease, and death. If you don't believe me, *try it* for a week and see what happens. I have been following Ralph's instructions and I am feeling and acting 10 years younger . . . .

And on it goes for another page and a half, ending with the admonition to chew everything completely, to liquefy your food before you swallow.

To me, it all sounds so unpleasant, so regimented, to make eating a chore rather than a pleasure. How I hated Nola, after she came home from Brandeis, watching across the dinner table as she chewed and chewed and chewed and chewed, never swallowing, a grim, purposeful expression on her face, until I could stand it no longer and went up to my room to eat alone.

You probably won't like the way this diet sounds because it clashes with what you're used to but if you *try* it it will make you years & years & years younger because the poisons you have been putting in your food through processing and cooking and seasoning and stuffing and dressing and stifling will be *absent.* You really shouldn't be cooking food. This is the *classical* yogic diet; it is part of the authentic yogic discipline and it is one of the chief means by which the yogis prolong youth to fantastic periods. The question I have for you is:

Do you want to eat as you are accustomed to eat,

OR

DO YOU WANT TO REGAIN YOUR YOUTH?

No, I don't like the way this diet sounds, Nola, and no, I don't want to regain my youth and why were you trying to regain your youth when all you wanted was to pass through the valley of Ednah? You claimed that everything else led to sickness, disease, and death, and yet, that's exactly what happened to you, maybe not as a result of your diet, but your diet couldn't save you. Another thing that couldn't.

Why, I wonder, did she think this was right for her? Because Ralph Haven had told her to follow this regimen? Apparently.

What's interesting to me about everything involving this mysterious teacher of my sister's is that my mother remembers Nola as a bright, clear-thinking young woman before she met him. A bright clear-thinking woman who had almost daily visions, who saw fairies and angels and demons. Even in her letter to Martin, she mentions her dream of the valley of Ednah, and this letter was written in 1967. And I don't doubt that she stood in the Sistine Chapel for three hours matching her own visions to Michelangelo's. Perhaps the distortions were always there, but who's to say that Nola's visions were distortions? It's not so much the visions themselves that bother me—Blake had visions, the prophets had visions—but finally, her inability to stop them, to turn them off, to be able to live in the physical world at all. In most cultures, the words of those we perceive as mad are still appreciated because the mad have a mad perspective, and sometimes that's what we need to come to an understanding.

Still, I agree with what Isaac Singer told Nola when she was a teenager, that too much of an obsession with the spiritual is unhealthy—how can one live in the world if one repudiates the physical entirely? But, perhaps that's unfair to Nola because she loved physical beauty, too. That's clear from the descriptions of what she saw on her trip to Israel and a dozen other references throughout her letters, at least until her autobiography. That's it! I realize now, that's the breaking point, what distinguishes her autobiography from all she wrote prior to this. Where is the love of the world? That's why her autobiography reads to me like a last will, a leave-taking. Last will and testament, emphasis on the testament. She is already mostly gone by the time she writes her autobiography, but something of her remains, some essence. This is her resting place finally, her haven, this other realm into which her words have sunk: a narcotic world of dream and vision.

In her autobiography, Nola blamed everything on Ralph Haven. She saw him as evil. Prior to him, she'd put her faith in another psychic, a man appropriately named Will, whose last name I've been unable to uncover. Will tried to warn her about Mr. Haven.

A psychic made a lecture visit to Brandeis university, where I was struggling with all my intuitive vision against a straightlaced doctoral program in Analytic Philosophy. When I saw him at the podium I felt a compulsion to be near him, even though he was barely visible from the back row. After the lecture I approached the place where he stood, and there was something peculiar about his eyes that attracted me, for they were clear and shaped like the eyes of a gryphon, which seemed to burn every object in its path down to an essence . . . . He looked at me with an attitude of recognition that I felt was very strange, it seemed that we had been together in the backyard of some other world. He studied me as if trying to confirm something in his memory.

The following night I searched out the place where he was staying, where I had arranged to see him for a consultation . . . . He proceeded to tell me that I was not an ordinary American woman, that I would be traveling to India via the Philippines and Bangkok, that I had been a man in many previous incarnations, among which were explicitly mentioned an Indian chief by the name of White Elk (I later verified this in a history book of the Cheyenne Indians) a Chinese philosopher and a Tibetan yogi, as well as an Egyptian priestess. He told me that my auric colors were yellow (color of the mind) white (spiritual purity) blue (pure spirit) and lavender (spiritual understanding and aspiration). This seemed to be in line with my color preferences, which as a child had been almost exclusively yellow and to which later were added the other colors he mentioned. At this point I became very embarrassed, because his eyes were piercing my own . . . . His eyes became torches and created in me a simultaneous terror and delight. I had been talking rapidly and suddenly found my words meaningless. My eyes asked him what was happening and I repeated the question aloud. "Our souls have blended, Nola. You have entered my world" came the incredible response. Now all the relics of our earthly life seemed to fall at our feet and we searched each other's eyes oblivious of time or space. For a moment I experienced the most extraordinary bliss. Then I knew, irrevocably, that I had known Will before. We sensed the absence of some ancient memory which, if recalled, would bind our souls forever. "Is this real?" I queried, and was ecstatic when the answer came: "Yes, Nola, it is very very real." At this point there was so much energy bursting forth from his eyes that I thought I would be crushed. I had never met such a developed psychic. I walked home very feverish (he told me this would happen). . . .

The following weekend I attended what Will had called a psychic workshop for the training of novice undergraduates in the psychic powers . . . . One of the persons who attended that workshop was a man whom I knew very little at that time, who almost destroyed me, and if I had any inkling of the danger he represented I would have fled from. His name I will not mention, except to say that his name meant "resting place" and he certainly wasn't. He was a graduate student at NYU and an instructor in yoga, having spent five years in Indian ashrams and several other years in parts of Japan studying occult disciplines. I was attracted to him at first by the power of his eyes, which seemed to be in total command of every sensation, as was his handwriting, which looked more like a feat of engineering than the penmanship of a man . . . . I entered his yoga class expecting to find a saint and ended up with Satan. He had attended a psychic workshop not from any desire of his own, but by the invitation of a friend. Everyone in the room at the time of the workshop was united by an invisible sympathy except for this man, who considered participation below him. If I had had any sense I would have withdrawn from his class at once, because I felt a sullen and determined evil coming from him, and at that time he seemed intolerable. I had thought that Will would enjoy meeting him, since they were both "into the same thing" but after the confrontation had actually occurred, Will came to me exclaiming indignantly that this fellow was "the most obnoxious person I have ever met." I was hurt, and felt very guilty for having urged Will to meet him.

In her letters home to my mother at the time, she was anything but critical of her newfound Haven. She doesn't talk of evil in his eyes. She says nothing of his controlled and controlling presence. She gushes over him, in fact.

Haven. Resting Place. Perhaps he still exists somewhere. I tried to track him down with a computerized phone directory but with no luck. I just wanted to ask him, and Will, too, what they remembered of my sister. I wanted to see what they looked like, to search their eyes and see if they still seemed so powerful. I wanted to read Haven's signature, to see this feat of engineering. I wanted to apprehend him in some physical way, to leave speculation behind for a moment, just as I wanted to see a photo of Nola's father, Elliot Chess.

*   *   *

I discovered a piece of paper, undated, but from around the time of Will and Haven. She refers to her position as a resident counselor in the dorm at Brandeis, and this is how I know it's from a time shortly after or before she wrote the letter on diet to my mother. I wonder what the girls in her dorm made of Nola as a resident counselor, the one who was supposed to look out for their health and safety. Maybe they loved her. Maybe they hated her, or simply didn't understand her. She was probably too remote to do them any good.

The note I found is written in Nola's handwriting on three pages of unruled paper, most of it slanting up, which I have always heard is a sign of elation. Handwriting slanting down is supposedly a sign of depression.

I really suffer every time I see others—they don't understand my diet and criticize me even if I say nothing, and they *especially* *don't* understand my disinclination to talk, which is new. It has made me a very solitary person, but somehow I have grown to love the solitude & the silence over this past week.

Gave up pillows completely—love to sleep on hard, straight surfaces.

I wish other people would keep their opinions to themselves & leave me alone!!!

esp. difficult being a resident counselor.

I've gotten so sensitive to food I seem to hear it talking to me, telling me its life history from the moment I touch it on! That is why I can no longer touch meat, fish, cheese, eggs or chicken—I experience a tightness & heaviness & depression from them which is unbearable! All I can eat for proteins that they serve in the cafeteria is yogurt, so I'm living on that!

This is pyschometry!

Every object gives off its own vibrations! Strange but true!

Tried to do yoga in am but my body is too stiff (except for Uddoyama!)—better for me at 4:00 pm, just before supper.

My mind is a plain on which the individual spirit and God do incessant battle. I want to sing of the Earth as well as of Heaven, to somehow evolve through worldly joys and sorrows, to write about the Earth before I reach Heaven.

A great portion of my life is lacking. That is the portion that must know & deal with mankind.

Why is it, Lord, that things . . .

Here there are two words that I can't make out. Here she is talking to God, asking something very important, it seems, and I can't make out the words.

*   *   *

Sitting on Nola's bed in her dorm room. My mother says something about packing up. Nothing has been packed. I'm sitting on her bed. We have the car outside. Nothing has been packed. Nola turns around, mumbles something.

We all returned to Slippery Rock in April of 1970. We brought Nola home because she couldn't continue at Brandeis. She was having trouble concentrating, couldn't finish her logic course. My mother didn't know what to do, what had happened to her bright, joyful daughter. I didn't know what had happened to my sister. But, it seemed right and proper that we would all return to Slippery Rock.

Driving down the main street of Slippery Rock. I'm in the back. They're talking up front about manipulation, someone did something to Nola's spine and she can't think straight now.
"What did Dr. West have to say?"
Silence.

What was wrong with Nola? I didn't know. But she wouldn't sleep or eat. She wouldn't talk. She wouldn't sing.

My mother, believing her daughter, believing that someone had done something to her to make her this way, wrote to her yoga teacher. What I have is a draft:

May 20, 1970
When my daughter Nola was here at Christmas time, she was her normal, intelligent self. When she xxxxxxxxxxxxxx returned for her spring break a few weeks ago she was very sick. One cause was an ulcer. Another was spine dislocation which has been affecting her brain, her

perceptions. She has seen a chiropractor and it has helped somewhat: today she will see a xxxxxxxxx psychiatrist. She is not the same brilliant girl. Her memory falters. It has been the opinion of two of the doctors she xx saw that the damage was caused by the spinal "adjustments" you performed on her. I have yet to get the opinion of the psychiatrist.

I do not intend to sue you because I do not wish to submit Nola to any such ordeal. But I wish to warn you that you cannot go on performing these illegal and dangerous operations. Sometimes I wonder whether Nola will actually survive this. She is too sick to continue with school and must now curtail her graduate studies. What waste! I only hope we can save her from whatever physical or mental difficulties may arise from now on.

I would appreciate your immediate reimbursement of the $100.00 Nola paid in advance for your "Oriental Massage" course which she had expected to take. It is the very least you can do in the circumstances.

Mr. Haven wrote back and told her he wasn't responsible for anything, according to my mother, who threw away the letter.

My mother was being protective and believed the story her daughter told her. My mother, like me, wanted to blame someone. She has told me before that the doctors could find nothing wrong with Nola's spine, a direct contradiction of this letter, so I called her up and asked her if this was a fabrication.

"Well, I must have gone to some other doctors," she told me. "You know what disturbs me, Robin, that you think I've made up all these things. I'm a very honest person."

"I know," I told her, "but we all make things up. I've stretched the truth before, even though I generally consider myself an honest person."

"Doctors can be very strange," she said. "They don't always want to admit things they can't see, outside their own experience. The first doctor I went to with her was in a nearby town, something Grove."

"Grove City."

"That's right. Grove City. You know what he said? He said, 'She just doesn't seem like a normal American girl.' I wanted to say, 'She's not.' She wasn't very careful about what she talked about to him. She saw fairies and things like that. She had an active imagination. He wanted me to put Nola in a mental hospital. I wasn't ready to do that then. I was always on Nola's side. I never doubted her. I thought her experience might just be different from ours and I wanted to understand it."

I wish I could show that much faith, even though such faith might seem ultimately destructive. What do we call it these days? Denial? I suppose my mother was in denial, but a beautiful denial as I see it— and I doubt whether placing Nola in a hospital a year earlier than she did would have helped. I don't think anything could have saved Nola because she didn't want to be saved, not by doctors in any case. I think my mother's criticism of doctors can be leveled at many of us. We don't want to admit things we can't see, outside our own experience. I wish I could show as much faith as my mother, but I doubt everything and everyone, even myself. And at the same time, I believe everyone and everything wholeheartedly. I want to believe them all.

Dear Ralph,

It was not our intention to question the validity of classical yoga on humanity. Doubtless the asanas would, if properly taught and applied, have had a "totally salutary effect." As it is, however, several vertebrae in the middle spine have been dis-placed as a result of your ~~manipulations~~ "adjustments," the lower back and knee joints have been weakened almost to the consistency of a jelly from continuous bending, a pelvic tilt has suddenly appeared, and the entire spinal column now deviates several degrees to the left when it should be vertical. As a result I have had considerable difficulty coordinating the movements of the right and left sides, my memory had been failing until three days ago because of a constant interference from memo-ries of past existences, personality disintegrations and a duode-nal ulcer have ~~resulted~~ developed. My will had been broken and the Kundalini power had been awakened so quickly and vio-lently that not only was I receiving innumerable messages from other worlds too ~~qui~~ fast for my mind to record ~~them~~ or my strength to handle them, but the chants you had given us to re-peat had become so inseparably linked with my heartbeat and breathing that they entirely usurped the functioning of my mind, ~~and~~ producing intense numbness and pain all over the head and threatening to shatter me with sound, which seemed to rush like a predator at me from all corners of the earth. The astral vehicle was apparently so agitated by the physical shock that several times I remember tearing madly out of my body and rushing away at all hours of the night, never knowing whether the body, which kept retching out the spirit it was supposed to contain, would reaccept me. I lost my ability to read, think, or write. I had begun prophesying in a voice that was not my own. I seemed to xxxxx dredge up people's most hidden and unwelcome thoughts from their present and previous incarnations from their merest touch. I awoke one morning believing myself to be an Indian chief who had abandoned his people and horses on the plains, xx on another envisioned myself as a ~~Chinese~~ bearded Chinese sage. On a third, and certainly the worst, occasion, I awoke genuinely believing myself to be God, and could look at no one because every object in my field of vision — mother, brother, furniture, walls, roof—had disintegrated into a bright haze of concatenating atoms. The very world seemed to be giving way beneath me, and with an agonized inner vision I saw, or vividly sensed, a grinning, massive Buddha-like face— both benign and diabolical at once—leering through this confusion as if it was all a magnificent joke, as if the world, time, and the multitudes of persons and moments which inhabited its surface and dimensions were equally pretentious. My surroundings had grown very strange, and I appeared to view the world around me with the most detached and telescopic vision. I could no longer feel any human emotion; there were no longer any human objects and therefore no point in having emotions. I could not tell whether what I was seeing was real or hallucinatory; there was only atoms and void~~ness~~, and nothing I sensed could corroborate or deny them. I lay awake at night with a feverish head, terrified of sleep.

The horror that has been in possession of me for several days has only recently departed. I have gone to a chiropractor, received several corrective adjustments, and am feeling much better. My spine, however, is still in such disorder that it will require from three to eight more weeks to correct, and the ligaments have been weakened to such an extent that I will be unable to practice yoga for six months. I hope that after that time I will be fortunate enough to find a competent guru either in this country or in India, who will enable me to xxxxx xxxxxxxxxx develop in the spirit without destroying my mind.

Sincerely,
Nola Hemley

* * *

I look again at the undated, unruled paper on which Nola wrote: "My mind is a plain on which the individual spirit and God do incessant battle."

I understand that. But there are those two words that I still can't make out. Here Nola is talking to God, asking something urgent, and I can't make out the words. I study them. I back up and run at the words again, thinking perhaps the momentum will carry me through her meaning, that perhaps if I empty my mind of expectation, I'll know how to decipher her words.

> Why is it, Lord, that things . . . [unintelligible word] . . . [unintelligible word] . . . the divisive mind about this world can be beautiful? i.e. Chekov's "Seagull."
> And like music of the forest trees.
> Music like thin wine pouring into space.

I know what she's saying, I think. I sense it at least. It's what I was pondering before, Nola's love of the physical world, like my father's, what the reviewer in the *New York Times* called "the unbridgeable gap," between the seen and unseen, between the physical and the spiritual, the divisive mind. I think I was right before in my estimation of Nola's love of the spiritual within the physical. The proof is in her own words: "I want to sing of the Earth as well as of Heaven . . . ." And yet, for some reason, she found it impossible to keep herself tethered to the physical world.

But what are those two unintelligible words? They seem to hold the key, so I go downstairs and ask Beverly for her help.

She looks over my sister's words, studies the letters, compares them minute after minute, putting real thought and effort in trying to help me with this.

"I'm not reading it" she says finally. "I'm just looking at the words."

"Read it, that's fine."

"No, I'm just looking at the words." She seems insistent about this. I wonder why, out of disinterest? Or is she simply being circumspect?

"Really?" I say. "I can't just look at words without trying to understand them."

"It was written in a hurry," Beverly says.

"She was writing it to herself. Actually, she was writing it to God. It's all right. I'll just have to live with not knowing. Sometimes I like the mystery of not knowing for sure. Do you remember Chekov's *Seagull*?

"I've read it. And I've seen it. But I don't remember it. I never re-member anything," she says, annoyed at herself.

I remember too much.

I look over her shoulder and we stand that way, chanting possibili-ties, studying my sister's words, but not reading them.

"Antler? Another? Matter? Unite? Untie?"

"That looks like an 'M,'" she says.

"Or maybe a 'W,'" I say.

"Matter with . . . about?" she says.

"Antler?"

"It looks most like antler," Beverly says, "but I doubt that's it. I don't think I'd understand even if I knew what the word was."

I wonder if I would understand either, even if I knew what the word was, but the "divisive mind," that at least is something I understand, even if I don't know the words that come next.

The Silver Sword Society

I was good at curses when I was twelve. I could put a curse on you and make it stick. But I had to be able to get close to you first. That summer, I was at Granite Lake Camp near Keene, New Hampshire. My mother was writing at the MacDowell Colony in Peterborough, and Nola was staying in a boarding house in town. Nola claimed my mother's cabin was haunted. Few places in the world weren't haunted, according to her. My brother, Jonathan, was, for a while, a counselor at Granite Lake, until he pulled a prank on his bratty charges, informing them in the middle of one night that their parents were on the way to pick them up and they had better hurry and get packed. So, at 5 A.M. four ten-year-old boys stood sleepily on the front porch of their cabin, leaning against one another, suitcases brimming. They waited there for an hour until the head counselor, Lou, walked by and asked them what the hell was going on.

That summer Woodstock was just a rumor, although we marched around the camp singing, "For it's one, two, three, what are we fighting for? Don't ask me, I don't give a damn, next stop is Vietnam," as though it were just another camp song. Lou hated that, and he hated me because I refused to put my hand over my heart or recite the Pledge of Allegiance.

My friends and I liked to run things up the flagpole and see who saluted. That was our favorite saying. We never actually ran anything up the flagpole to see who saluted, and in the manner of twelve-year-olds, we used the saying often and inappropriately.

My folks are coming to visit today.

Let's run them up the flagpole and see who salutes.

This was the summer Nola met her Guru, Sri Ramanuja. The summer after Nola returned from Brandeis, hallucinating, unable to complete her program. But there were lucid hours, days, months. This was the summer that Nola and Jonny worked picking blueberries until they had blueberry nightmares and had to stop; the summer they went to a psychic and, according to Jonathan, the woman told him he was a Hebrew and my mother was an Egyptian and my sister was going to die, but I wasn't there, so I can't know for sure. I was back at Granite Lake Camp, causing mayhem and destruction with my curses.

"UP UP UP It's Another Beautiful Day at Granite Lake Camp!" Every morning at six, Lou shouted those words over the camp p.a. system, followed by a John Philip Sousa march. Lou was a balding, slight man in his late thirties or early forties in 1970. He always wore a whistle and he knew how to use it. I don't remember him ever smiling. His voice had two registers, loud and earsplitting.

I went there two summers. The first year I liked the place, the second year I hated it, although there was no discernible change in the place, just me: the summer I turned twelve versus the summer I turned thirteen. The first year my counselor was a muscular guy named Steve with long Sampson-like tresses, who spoke to us like equals, and never

raised his voice. The second year my counselor was a guy from Taiwan whose name I forget. He spoke maybe ten words of English. The most I ever remember him saying to me was "I gonna KILL you!" as he chased me one afternoon around the outside of our bunkhouse, for what I'm not sure, but I can make a pretty good guess. Most likely, we teased him mercilessly—called him "chink" or some terrible thing like that, and figured if he didn't understand us, he wouldn't care. The fact that I came from a family in which I was taught better probably didn't faze me. This was summer camp.

We had four kids in the bunk—two I remember distinctly, a kid named Danny Dutch, athletic, smart-alecky, whom everyone called "Douche." The other boy was a fat kid named Eddie, who was going bald at age twelve because he constantly ran his hand through his hair. I thanked my stars for Eddie. If not for him, I would have been the kid in the bunk that everyone picked on. I was skinny and unathletic. Eddie was fat and unathletic. Skinny wins every time in that contest. Eddie was "Piggy" from *Lord of the Flies*. Or Piggy was his dad. Once, he even ran away and we chased him through the trees and bushes with flashlights, derisively yelling his name. But we didn't kill him, just made him cry.

I lived for Canteen. This was the hour or so when you could go to the camp store in the afternoon and stock up on candy and other snacks if you had the dough. Douche and I didn't have much money, but you could get by in other ways if you were smart, and we were. We'd go behind the tennis courts and collect dozens of tennis balls, which could be turned in for Canteen vouchers, and then we'd lounge around outside by the snake cages where an older camper, Harry Green, had a cage full of snakes. He'd feed them frogs that we caught. There were always many more frogs than snakes in the cages, and they'd hop around over the pile of black snakes until one of the snakes ate them, or they'd simply starve and die and slowly blacken in the cage. Harry never intervened once a frog landed in the snake cage. At the end of the summer, Harry would free the snakes but leave the frogs. The next summer, we found their blackened husks. That's one of those things you don't ever forget. I still have nightmares about those frogs, but back then, it was high entertainment. We'd eat our Reese's Peanut Butter Cups and licorice ropes, drink our Nehi sodas, and wait for the snake to strike. And when it happened—when you saw death happen, when you could see the frog form a lump in the snake's throat—that was the best, or second best. The best was when a snake threw up. Sometimes they'd throw up a day or two after they'd eaten the frog. That was really the best.

I don't remember doing much at Granite Lake Camp. I just remember lounging around like minimum-security prisoners, waiting for our parents to spring us, or on rain days, being herded into the main hall to watch one of two immensely boring films, either *Thirty Seconds over Tokyo* or *Abbot and Costello Meet Frankenstein*. The first was a John Wayne flick, and the only interesting part was when the dad of the skipper from *Gilligan's Island*, the Cook (named Cookie) gets stabbed by a Japanese sailor they've . . . just . . . rescued! Talk about low and snake-like. Incredible. The whole film was worth that moment of betrayal and fanaticism. The Abbot and Costello was so fake and stupid no one laughed, or laughed too much, pretending to laugh with high adolescent irony. Until Lou had to turn around and tell us to SHUT THE HELL UP and pay attention, as though this was some kind of camp training film, some life lesson we couldn't afford to miss as we watched Boris Karloff, arms outstretched, chasing Abbot and Costello for the twentieth time, who looked about as impressed as we were.

I wanted attention. I have no doubt about that. For that reason, I signed up for all the plays—over a two-year span, I played Linus in *You're a Good Man, Charlie Brown,* had the starring role in an adaptation of a Sholom Aleichem story, "A Tale of Chelm," and played a munchkin in *The Wizard of Oz,* my least satisfying role. But I couldn't act all the time. Out of boredom, I suppose, I invented, or resurrected, The Silver Sword Society. I'd come up with the Society a year earlier. I was the founder, president, and only member, and its sole function was to put curses on people I didn't like. Soon after I came up with the idea, I forgot about it, sidetracked by some other wacky idea, and only remembered the club one day on the path to Granite Lake as I walked with my friend Sammy past the Chicken Lady's house.

I don't know who the Chicken Lady was. I never saw her. I don't think anyone did, although many claimed to have seen her. I don't know why she was called the Chicken Lady, but the name itself was suggestive of something horrible and mysterious, and sometimes it was better just not to ask, but accept that she *was* the Chicken Lady, for whatever reason, either something to do with her physical appearance, or else the things she did with and to chickens. The house she lived in was nothing but a shack with an overgrown front yard, and you could barely see the house through the tangle of growth. The fact that no one in all probability had lived in the house for years didn't even enter our impressionable minds. No matter what, you didn't want to be on that path after dark, when the Chicken Lady came outside. You see, the Chicken Lady was 300 times scarier than Boris Karloff, and that's why we could laugh at him, but no one made fun of the Chicken Lady.

Sammy and I were discussing the Chicken Lady's probable powers on the path to the lake. Sammy told me that she could put a curse on you if she saw you walking by and that's why it was best to duck down low on the path as you passed her house, which we promptly did.

"I can put curses on people, too," I said after I stood up again, and I told him all about The Silver Sword Society.

"How come I never seen you do it?" he said, cautiously unimpressed.

"I don't put curses on friends."

"Put one on me," he said.

"Didn't you hear me?"

"So I'm you're enemy. Go ahead."

"My power is fearsome. You don't want me to unleash it upon you."

"Go ahead. Unleash it. We'll run it up the flagpole and see who salutes."

Sammy took hold of a branch—he was in the lead—and held it back just long enough, and then let go. It hit me in the neck. "Okay," I said, and I chased Sammy the rest of the way down the path.

"Time out," he said, out of breath as we reached the road we needed to cross to get to the lake. He put out his hand and we both stood there for a moment, our towels around our necks. We crossed to the beach and then faced each other on the sand.

"Okay, do it," he said. "I want to see this."

Slowly, I withdrew an invisible sword from an invisible sheath at my side and I approached Sammy.

"Wait," he said. "Time out."

"Look, I like you, Sammy," I said, "so I'm just going to put a general curse on you. Nothing bad's going to happen to you, but bad things will happen around you."

I plunged the invisible sword into Sammy's stomach. I could almost feel it go into him. Sammy laughed.

A jumble of sounds. I turned and saw something across the road. We ran across the beach and stopped. A motorcycle lay on its side, and a man lay beneath it, pinned by the machine. Within seconds, the campers were lined up in their bathing suits, gawking, and the counselors had run across the road and were lifting the motorcycle off the man.

Sammy looked at me and said, "Did you do that?"

"Told you," I said, looking at my hand as though it were smoking.

By that evening, it was all over camp. I could put curses on people. Real curses.

I was drunk with power. I swaggered through camp, ate my dinner with a crowd as Sammy told them the story.

"Put a curse on me," Danny Dutch said arrogantly at the table. Danny and I, previously business partners, had had a falling out once tennis balls got devalued as a currency. We had collected so many that the camp figured they didn't need our services anymore, and we each blamed the other for being too greedy. So I was happy to put a curse on him, and prayed that it would work.

Later that night, Danny broke his finger playing basketball. I wasn't there, but a messenger, like something out of a Greek play, came running up to me shouting, "Robin, Robin, the curse worked!"

This was fun.

Soon, kids were lining up asking me to put a curse on them. Perhaps they sought attention, too, and after all, this was summer camp and you were supposed to try out new things. Before I plunged the invisible silver sword in them, I'd ask what kind of curse they preferred, a general curse or a specific. I could get really specific. I could put a curse on your hand, your nose, your hair, and invariably, before the day was out, something bad would happen—of course, bad things often happen in the course of a day, but that didn't matter. I was the new Chicken Lady at Granite Lake Camp, and I was better than her because you could see me, you could consult me, you could make requests.

After about a week, the camp could be divided roughly in half between those people who wanted me to curse them and those who would prefer I didn't. I started eyeing the latter group greedily. Many of them were bigger than me and would not sit still for me to plunge the sword, no matter how invisible or painless, into their guts. Except for Eddie. He was easy pickings. One day, I went up to him with a false smile on my face and said, "Eddie, I've got something for you." So unaccustomed to a friendly tone of voice, Eddie smiled, "What is it?"

"This," I said, laughing like the maniac I'd become. "A silver sword. A curse upon you and your spawn!" Words like "spawn" seemed appropriate for cursing people, and even if I didn't know what spawn meant, it sounded like something you wouldn't want to have a curse on.

Eddie tugged at his hair and said, "I don't believe in curses," but I could tell he was trying to put a brave face on a hopeless position. As a god, I was vengeful and merciless. I was a god of tantrums, jealousy, and storm. If he didn't believe, he'd soon feel my wrath.

And he did. That day he dislocated a finger while playing hot potato with a basketball in our bunk. I wasn't there, but again, a messenger found me and told me the news.

Eddie's finger was splinted and bandaged, and the next day he ran into the woods and we chased him with flashlights until we found him by the frog pond where Danny and I caught the sacrifices for Harry Green's snakes. I never made the connection between my curse and Eddie running away—I didn't think he'd run away because of me, specifically, and I still don't. Running away was something that happened at camp and Eddie was just the type who did it. He was simply fulfilling his allotted role in the scheme of things by running away, or "going over the hill," as we called it, although we were never told specifically which hill this was. Going over the hill was something that had to be done by a certain quota of unhappy campers to keep order in the universe, and Eddie was one who always did his duty, always stayed within his proscribed position.

I scored some stunning successes in the days following Eddie's dislocated finger, most notably an incident in which a cursed camper named Jimmy nearly drowned because a rope tangled around his leg while waterskiing, and the boat dragged him underwater for several hundred feet before the spotter turned around and noticed Jimmy wasn't upright, that only the sole of his right foot was above water.

I was delighted, of course, as were many of my friends. I really had something going. It was undeniable. I had power.

Still, I started slowing down a bit. Cursing people was fun, but some of the newness was wearing thin, and so I became a little more discerning. For a while there, I was putting curses on all comers—I even put a curse on Harry Green, whom I looked up to. Someone left the top off his cage, and half of the snakes escaped and most of the frogs. Harry was furious with me and wouldn't let me catch frogs for his snakes anymore. I was frozen out of one of my favorite activities. So, I went back to the original idea of only cursing people I didn't like, which consisted mostly of a group of older campers I couldn't touch, and, once again, unlucky Eddie.

This time, he was wary. The splint was off his finger, but the memory was fresh.

"Don't come near me," he said as I approached him one morning as he lingered by the flagpole after the Pledge of Allegiance.

I chased him down and caught him by the mess hall. He tried to cover his body protectively, but my invisible sword could penetrate any barrier known to humankind. It was made from the strongest alloy ever invented, because of its mutability, because it was so unpredictable, and like the atom, was smaller than the eye could perceive and could be used for good or evil.

I plunged the sword into him and twisted it for maximum effect. He groaned in pain. "A curse upon you and your spawn . . . again."

He had fallen down and now he stood up with a look of dignity and calm, or maybe simply resignation. Then, slowly, before my eyes, he changed, werewolf-like, into a version of Eddie I had never seen. He tugged his hair violently, his eyes bulged and he took a step toward me, spittle forming on his lips. I took a step back. He grabbed my shirt by the collar and screamed, "Take it out! Take it out!"

"No, Eddie, let go of me, calm down."

But Eddie was beyond reason, beyond listening. I'd like to say he punched me. I certainly deserved it.

What happened was this: Eddie wouldn't let go of me. I gave him warning.

"Eddie, let go of me."

"Take it out," he screamed.

"Let go."

"Out . . . take it . . . out!" He was in my face, shaking me. Until that moment, I hadn't realized what I was doing. It just seemed like a game, like freeze tag or a hundred other kids' games in which one kid was IT by mutual agreement. I was just IT, maybe the *real* IT, but IT nonetheless, and this kid was spoiling the fun. This kid was terrified. And he was in my face. He was scaring *me,* not because I thought he'd hurt me, but because I was scared by the reflection of me he was giving off. He was making me scared of myself, and I didn't like that.

So I punched him in the eye.

Eddie crumpled to the ground, a hand over his face. Then he stood up and looked at me like I was the Creature from the Black Lagoon, or Frankenstein, or even that Jap sailor who stabbed Cookie after Cookie had rescued him. Eddie scuttled off, crab-wise, back to the bunk. You could hear him bellowing halfway across camp. The curse had worked again—immediately.

I didn't feel so good.

But I never took that sword out of poor Eddie. Somewhere he's still walking around, or maybe not, with two invisible swords jiggling from his flesh. I figure the skin's probably healed around them now. He probably doesn't even notice—they've become so much a part of him, he thinks his bad luck is just coincidence, something he's brought on himself, or some cosmic role he's fulfilling as Perpetual Victim.

Later that day, Lou came up to me. Lou. The Head Counselor. You probably don't realize what an amazing thing that was to have Lou come up to me and start talking, a little warily, in a low tone, but reasonable, like he didn't want to rile me.

He had his arms crossed and bent down like he was giving me a tip at a horse race. "Listen," he said. "I've got to ask you something. I'd like you to stop putting curses on the other campers. Okay?"

"Okay," I said. And that was that. No discussion, just two old adversaries coming to a common agreement, tired of bloodshed. Lou never told me if he believed in my curses. Nor was there any implied threat in his tone. Actually, he sounded almost respectful. That was enough. And then Lou walked away, to some more wholesome camp activity and I was left with a lot of extra invisible swords hanging from my belt. Standing there by the mess hall, listening to my heart and the sound of the campers laughing somewhere by the basketball court and a radio coming from one of the bunks, I undid my invisible belt, and let all the swords clatter in an invisible heap. I stepped outside of the circle the swords had created and I left them where they lay.

The Shiva Notebooks

One winter I became a prophet.

Over Christmas 1970, we went to my grandmother's beach house in Long Beach, New York, where we always gathered for holidays and vacations. Forever interested in documenting my family's odd comings and goings, I commemorated this holiday by painstakingly creating a newspaper with a letterpress kit someone gave me, and running off copies for the relatives:

THE RISING
SON
WEEKLY   FIRST EDITION
JOURNAL
COPYRIGHT 1970

FLASH
ABOUT TWO WEEKS AGO ELAINE HEMLEY
HAD A PAIN IN HER TOOTH. SHE WENT
TO A DENTIST BUT HE DRILLED THE
WRONG TOOTH. INFURIATED SHE WENT
TO THE SO-CALLED BEST DENTIST IN
TOWN HE TOOK X RAYS OF HER TEETH
AND THEN SHOWED HER A FILM OF HOW
TO TAKE CARE OF HER TEETH WHICH
COST HER 65 DOLLARS. THEN SHE WENT
TO HER BROTHER ALAN GOTTLIEB WHO
FIXED HER TEETH.
  BY
   ROBIN HEMLEY

DEAR EDITOR
I HAVE A CRAZY BROTHER.
WHAT CAN I DO ABOUT
HIM
DESPERATE

DEAR DESPERATE

GET A CRAZY
SISTER.

WRITE TO ROBIN HEMLEY

SMART ALECK
COUSIN
SNOWBOUND

PHILLIP HEMLEY
WHILE STAYING
OVERNIGHT
AT IDA GOTTLIEBS
HOUSE FOUND
HIMSELF
SNOWBOUND

HELP

There's that word: crazy. Get a crazy sister. I suppose, in an odd way, Nola and I took this advice. Seven months earlier she'd written to her yoga teacher, telling him of the torment he had supposedly caused her, and here we were joking about her being crazy, about both of us being crazy. I remember asking her to help me with my advice column. I insisted that she ask me for advice, not because I thought she needed my advice but because I needed to have an advice column if I was going to print a newspaper, and I was quite serious in my intentions to publish a family chronicle, week after week.

The fact that we used the word "crazy" so blithely makes me think that none of us really believed anything was wrong with Nola. I had grown up with her, and if she saw a few more fairies on an average day than she had a year earlier, who was I to tell her she was hallucinating? She was Nola. Still Nola. And she wasn't going around holding conversations with imaginary beings, or not many. And she still had a sense of humor and recognized us and recognized herself.

What I didn't write about in that first and only edition of that little newspaper of mine is far more interesting to me now than what I thought was interesting then. My snowbound cousin Phillip, for instance. That winter while we were all snowbound, he taught Nola and me automatic writing. We took a pen and a piece of paper and were supposed to empty our minds and allow the spirit world to guide our hands.

Phillip impressed us from the start. He seemed like a great mixture of entrepreneur and bon vivant and spiritual supplicant. He had an export/import business between the United States and India. He became one of the Dalai Lama's associates. I remember when the Dalai Lama first came to this country, picking up a copy of the *New York Times,* and seeing Phillip quoted as one of the few Westerners to be allowed into the Dalai Lama's circle. I haven't seen Phillip in years, but according to another cousin who writes books on sexual addiction, Phillip has a band now, lives somewhere in the West, and calls himself Phil Void.

My hand-printed newspaper failed to capture my family's divided attention or imaginations. (How could it? The newspaper was so sparse and was remarkable only because it took so long to produce so little. I could have written the newspaper in longhand much more efficiently.) My attempts at automatic writing, by comparison, were a stunning success. How mundane a newspaper was, my family seemed to be telling me, recording events precisely, baldly, and without elaboration, yet leaving out so much. How wonderful to open yourself up to a mysterious and questionable source and let the words fly, the facts scatter like victims from a bomb. That's how automatic writing worked, according to Phillip. You just took a pen and opened up your mind, resting the pen lightly on a piece of paper.

For our family, it was a parlor game, but we also wanted to see it work. It didn't for Nola. She just wrote squiggles. My mother commented that the French surrealists had practiced automatic writing. She, never fond of games, perhaps too impatient with them, didn't want to try, nor did Jonathan, who thought it was stupid. My grandmother cooked clams we had dug up on the winter beach and withheld all comment, pretending we weren't acting bizarre as she busied herself in the kitchen.

For me, it was easy. You closed your eyes and let the pen move. I'd spent my whole life trusting to mystery. My first attempts were like all the others, squiggles in red pen. Words started to appear, large words slanting downward, many of them ridiculous words and combinations. But my family took them seriously. I opened my eyes and watched the words form, half thinking they were my own, half believing they might come from somewhere else.

I still have the notebook, and so I can relate to you exactly the progress of that evening. Some of the later notebooks have been lost, but this first one survives. Many of the words I wrote embarrass me now, but it's not only the answers I've written that intrigue me, but also the questions the others asked me that night.

The first pages are full of nonsense:

Go for deal
a baby
   pulls for me
      I love Sigmond
         Belladonna
   is fory blap
      syuo like plap
I fade no more
phunch found Lllt sigmond puuny uu
   I fade away goodbye.

My mother took up the notebook and laughed.
"I love Sigmond?' she said and handed it to Nola.

"Who knows?" Nola said. "Maybe Robin's in touch with one of Freud's patients."

"Or Freud's mother?" Phil said.

"Time to eat," my grandmother called, and we gathered to eat our steamers, all except for Nola, who refused to even be in the same room as the dead creatures. She sat, instead, alone in the living room, eating her yogurt. I couldn't see from where I sat what she was doing, but she had taken the notebook into the room with her.

After dinner, she wanted me to try my hand at the automatic writing again, but my grandmother lobbied for us to sing a song or two for Phillip. This hocus-pocus stuff made her nervous, and we had such lovely voices she said, and Phillip hadn't heard us. So we gathered in the living room, including Jonathan, who, if not interested especially in our singing or automatic writing, was definitely interested in this hip male relative in his early twenties who traveled and had seen so much of the world.

Nola and I would sing together for any reason, on any occasion. She never refused me and I never refused her. Her voice was a clear soprano and so was mine. We sang a song from *The Tempest*, in which one sang a line and the other echoed it like the spirit who was singing the song:

Full fathom five thy father lies
full fathom five thy father lies
   Of his bone are coral made
are coral made
      These are pearls that were his eyes
These are pearls that were his eyes
         Nothing of him that doth fade
         but doth suffer a sea change
         into something rich and strange
into something rich and strange
            Sea nymphs hourly ring his knell
Sea nymphs hourly ring his knell
               Ding dong
ding dong
                  Hark now, I hear them
                  Ding dong bell . . .

Much of the song was discordant, sour notes echoed by me a moment after Nola sang them, until we came together in the end, harmonious, our voices fading together with the last melodious claps of those underwater bells.

There was always silence after the end of that song, because it was so quiet and narcotic, because it suggested what lay beneath the surface, what humans couldn't see, what they needed divine guidance to apprehend, and it seemed to us, certainly as we sang together, that if we listened long enough to the ensuing silence, we might hear something rich, something strange.

My grandmother had fallen asleep during the song, head tilted forward, and none of us bothered to wake her. Half an hour later, she might awake, and if questioned, would insist that she had been fully awake, that she had only been resting her eyes. She hated admitting to sleep, as though it was a crime to lose consciousness.

We all went to my mother's room, except for Jonathan, who wanted to study in his room—I don't remember whether it was French or Spanish that year, but he was, like everyone in my family but me, always gaining easy fluency in other languages.

We sat on my mother's bed, me in the middle, and they handed me the red pen. Nola wrote the question, "Who should write?"

My hand scribbled six lines sloping downward, the letters all connected, all resembling words but not quite forming into them.

"Who are you?" my sister wrote.

Again, I wrote two large scribbles.

"Please write more clearly.

yuuawywnAawnataAzg

Finally, a word developed that looked like "Supreme," surrounded by more incomprehensible words, and then another word, perfectly formed, "Le Mason," incorrectly spelled French for 'house." I'd taken a couple of years of elementary French in grade school, and that's about all I remembered, I'm sure.

I could feel my family's collective will. I knew what they wanted. They wanted me to make sense out of senselessness, to pull words from the void and have them connect. In my own feeble way, I was struggling with this, wanting to believe that I could do so, but wondering at the same time whether the words, if any formed, would come only from me. After my fumble with the French language, I returned to scribbles for a page.

But then, as my family was about to give up on me, two clear words formed.

Help
Love

This was the moment I became a prophet, when I threw doubt aside and realized I had followers, that no matter how many awkward attempts at coherence I made, someone in my family was ready to believe. I say that now, but that's not what I was thinking at the time. I was not a skeptic, but a believer, too, in my powers. I had renounced curses, and I had become something altogether more powerful. My mother and sister looked at the page in silence. Phillip was eating an apple, but he stopped mid-crunch.

My words now were fully formed in large block letters.

TRAPPED INSIDE
HELP ME going   belladonna
     "Where are you?" my sister asked.
trapped
persuade
free me TRAPPED INSIDE
my body
SAVE
     ME
     dying
Shiva is with me need help one eyed death all will
die when I die
     "When?"
Soon   Help me
     "Who are you?"
SHIVA
     "Who are you in human form?"
DANIEL
     "What is your last name?"
my trumpet
     "Where is your trumpet?"
It breaths DEATH AND LIFE find it

I'm not sure who my family thought they were communicating with, but all of this was probably straining my twelve-year-old mind, and so I think I had confused Daniel with Gabriel. Gabriel has his trumpet, not Daniel, and it's Gabriel's clarion call on Judgment Day that will supposedly breathe death and life, and that's what I meant, I'm sure. But written communication is imperfect, and when one is in a trance, one cannot snap out of it and say, "I meant Gabriel, you know, the guy with the trumpet." Still, serendipity plays a large role in any creation, and now I think it's more appropriate that I wrote "Daniel" instead of "Gabriel," not that I actually have delusions of myself as Daniel, except in the smallest realm, the realm of my family. The prophet Daniel was an interpreter. He interpreted Nebuchadnezzar's dreams and interpreted the handwriting on the wall seen by Belshazzar. That's what I am, or what I'd like to be, in any case.

Shiva, the Hindu god of creation and destruction, is a remote and difficult god to understand, unlike Vishnu, who's considered the protector and preserver of the world. Where I pulled Shiva from, I don't know, probably *The Larousse Book of Mythology,* a coffee-table book with brilliant colored pictures that I used to read like a comic book. My family sat around me, amazed. But what I find more amazing than the fact I knew about Shiva was my family's amazement. How could I have grown up with them and not have heard of Shiva? My family was on speaking terms with every god in the universe.

My sister wrote at the top of the page, "Is it in this house?"

Nola gave me a steady, intense look and I returned it, and that seemed to be enough. Then I bent to the page.

"Is this safe?" my mother asked Nola. "Do you know how to . . ."

"*Om Navo Shivaye,*" Nola chanted. She and I both sat in the lotus position on the bed. I was skinny. For me, it was no effort. I could sit in the lotus position all day and reach my arms across my stomach and back and touch the opposite feet. This was another way in which I impressed adults. For Nola, it was no effort either. She looked thin, almost wasted. Her cheekbones, always prominent, jutted from her face. "*Om Navo Shivaye,*" she said over and over, her eyes closed, not even looking at my answers. By this time, I knew that she was receiving messages from the Beyond, too.

"It won't last long," Phillip said, "but he might be very tired when he awakes. He might be disoriented."

Jonny had entered the room while I was writing. He shook his head and left again, closing the door loud enough to wake an ordinary mortal from a trance, but not me. Jonathan was, at the time, the natural

skeptic among us. He never asked Shiva a question, never evinced any
interest in our dealings with the spirit world at all.

YES SACRED BOOK DEAD DONE PURITY
SEEPS THROUGH THE SEEKER YOU SHOULD
SEEK IN YOURSELF AND LIFE DEATH EARTH
AND THE HONEYSUCKLE OF LIFE LET THE
WORLD REALIZE WHAT IS HAPPENING TO
THEMSELVES

In 1970, perhaps such phrases as "The Honeysuckle of Life," did not
seem so cloying. Plenty of adults were uttering such phrases, writing
books with such titles even, holding seminars with such titles, creating
large followings with phrases sillier than that. What I had discovered
at age twelve, I think, was a pattern, the understanding that wisdom
has a particular rhythm, that the sound of wisdom is easy to mimic:

LET ALL MEN KNOW DEATH IS
LIFE AND LIFE IS DEATH

I realize how cynical I'm being now, how utterly close-minded and
mocking of this experience we all took so seriously. There *are* mysteries
that I am willing to be in awe of, but not this one. This is not a genuine
mystery—if my words didn't come from my conscious mind, then they
came from my unconscious mind, and that's the only mystery I'm willing to admit to in this instance—the mystery of our own minds and
how our thoughts are formed, organized, brought forth. What sad-
dens me now is how easily I was believed, so fully a fraud that only an
idiot wouldn't see through me—I don't care what year it was. And now
my faith, the one true faith I grew up with, a faith in my family, begins
to shake and crumble.

But maybe I'm being too harsh now, maybe that willingness to believe, to cast aside doubt and open up to possibility is my family's saving grace. Maybe that's what I'm looking for now. Maybe what should
embarrass me is not belief but disbelief, the cynical side of me that
closes off for self-protection, that mocks himself before he's mocked
by others.

We stayed up late that night, and we fell into an easy pattern—they
wrote down all kinds of questions, from the mundane to the mysterious, and I took up the pen without hesitation and wrote the appropriate answers. Writing without hesitation was key to automatic
writing. You couldn't give it any thought. If you did, it wasn't auto-

matic, but I knew the pattern, I was in the spiritual groove. I was the Answer Boy. I had Shiva behind me and Daniel, too, and maybe even Gabriel. Who knew? Over the next two years, on and off, I filled up notebooks with these spiritual-advice columns, what came to be known in my family as the Shiva notebooks, and I didn't only answer questions for relatives, but friends, too, even my mother's students. I didn't mind either. It wasn't a strain. I was eager to perform. I wanted to make believers out of them all. When people asked me where the words came from, I said, truthfully, "I don't know," and they all agreed that whatever the case, I seemed to know more than a twelve-year-old could.

"Which story should Mom write next?" Nola wrote that same night.

Discard ALL Others Writ one about Honeysuckle of life and death

"I don't understand."

this is An Experience This has more
meaning than anyother one before

My mother took the pen from Nola's hand and wrote: "Yes. I agree. But what fiction idea will hold it?"

Poem. Does not have to be fiction

Nola took the pen back and wrote, "Should she write poetry?"

Yes A Book Called the Honeysuckle of
life AND Death

Thank God, my mother never took this advice, never wrote a book titled, "The Honeysuckle of Life and Death," although maybe she did, and it lies undiscovered by me, at any rate, in the stacks of papers cluttering her basement in South Bend. And maybe she should have—who am I to argue with Shiva?

I wonder if the world of the gods is anything like the world of politics, like Capitol Hill. Certainly the Greek gods were political creatures with all their lobbying and behind-the-scenes maneuvering. And gods have to constantly be concerned about votes, about currying favor with us mortals, trying to make us swear allegiance to them, transforming us all into little campaign volunteers. I think of this now because this Shiva character was, like any good politician, an evasive rascal, probably the most evasive god that's ever existed. We're not sure if Shiva is a she or a he and Shiva is not satisfied with either destruction or creation, but both. In statues and pictures of Shiva, one sees the god dancing or as a beggar. And Shiva has many arms, many hands, and what does one do with so many hands? To me, he/she has a

pen in each hand and rewrites our stories in innumerable and conflict-
ing versions.

If I was studying to be a god, or a prophet at least, I could have
picked no better master than Shiva. Like any good politician, like any
god, you couldn't pin me down. I refused to name dates, to give
specifics.

Phillip took the pen next. "When will the earth begin to seriously
rearrange itself?"

When the souls of men die

"Can you give a specific date within the space-time continuum?"

When men decid it will happen

"What should Phil do?" he asked.

Purify his soul AND others Honeysuckle

"How can I do it best?"

Be yourself inside

My mother took the pen again. "What should Jonny do?"

Jonny should purify in the Spring of life

Nola took the pen. "What should Mom do?"

Purify All men Purify! Death will come We can't hold much
longer We still have to reach inside of OURSELVES by ourselves
but with all men on the same plain by spiritual communication from
your soul inside of your soul inside of your outer crust ~~Spiri~~
from Anywhere if you are on the same plain that is when you will
reach the supreme You are puppets in a sense but puppets can
control themselves be yourself

One thing I can say for myself. I was a pretty good mimic for a
twelve-year-old. And only one word crossed out. I was writing quickly,
remember, and no one seemed bothered by the fact that I sometimes
misspelled words or crossed one out occasionally. In a family of revi-
sors, it was taken for granted that gods revise from time to time as
well. My family rationalized for me. Nola and Phil agreed that, although my meanings were beyond the ken of a twelve-year-old, the
words I used were still filtered through the consciousness of a twelve-
year-old, and that's why they sometimes seemed a little garbled. I wish
I could still use that defense.

At one point, my mother asked, "How does he know the word,
'Belladonna'?" And when I came out of my trance temporarily, Nola
asked me, "Have you heard the word belladonna before, Robin?" I
could see the hope in her eyes and I said in my best tone of befuddle-
ment, "No, what's *that* mean?"

"It's a kind of poison," she said.

"Poison?"

"He obviously doesn't know," my mother said. Luckily, Jonny wasn't in the room at that moment. I knew and I didn't know. I didn't want to admit that I knew, not even to myself. Jonny had taught it to me. It was in some rock song we'd listened to a year or so earlier, and he'd told me the word's meaning. But I wasn't thinking that I knew. I willed myself to forget, to be in awe of myself like the others. If Jonny had been there, and had set them straight, I still would have denied. I would have glazed over, gone into another trance, had Shiva condemn him roundly.

I wasn't really lying. I was just doing what my family wanted me to do. If they wanted to believe that a god named Shiva was speaking through me, so be it. I could do that "Purify your Soul" shtick all day long. Now I see that everything I wrote was an echo of something else I'd heard, mostly from Nola, but even from TV. *Star Trek* was one of my favorite TV programs, and I can still hear Scotty yelling from somewhere deep in the engine room, "I can't give her any more power! We can't hold much longer, Captain!" The only thing I left off was the word, "Captain."

The prophet business didn't pay beans, but it gave me all the attention I wanted, and in a sense was my first awkward attempt at fictionalizing, trying to make people believe in a story that isn't true, yet contains fundamental human truths at the same time. That was, after all, the religion of my mother. You could say anything true as long as you pretended it wasn't, and vice versa.

I know I believed what I was saying. But what I must have liked especially, at some level of consciousness, even if it was unadmitted to myself at that age, was the power I now had over my three followers. I could tell my mother to write a poem called "The Honeysuckle of Life and Death," and at least she'd consider it. Normally, I had so little control over real events, the death of my father, the deaths of my friends, that much of my childhood was spent in trying to wrest control from the air around me, trying to find some key through invisible swords or the fanciful orders I transmitted through my own mind.

"Shall I write the story of the Fat Man?" my mother asked Shiva.

Discard that story till I tell Robin to tell you to make it. Discard all others but just make the most important ones that ROBIN = I Like

Laugh if you want. It seems pretty funny to me now. And pretty awful. But I was twelve. So I was a little manipulative, and I know I still am, but I'm trying to do better. Still, this desire to tell the truth and manipulate at the same time creates some essential tension within me.

I still sat on the bed, my head bent. My hand was tired but my head wasn't. I felt light-headed, almost joyful, as though I were on some carnival ride in midtilt, unsure of what direction I was going in or even where I was. I did not feel skeptical. I did not feel the cynicism I must feel now, so distant. All was bliss and serenity. Words flowed through me without doubt. I believed in the Honeysuckle of Life and Death. I was bathed in the spring of life. I knew my sister and my mother and my cousin Phil had to obey me or else things would go terribly wrong.

My mother has always insisted that she's a skeptic when it comes to supernatural matters, and I have always taken her at her word, or I should say, I have not openly contradicted her. On this night, she seemed like a believer. She asked a believer's questions. She insists now that she was more curious than anything, that she wanted to understand me and especially Nola, and that this desire to understand is not the same as belief. But her questions were a believer's questions. I have no doubt about this. I realize now, of course, how alike we are in our assertions of skepticism. Sometimes, I think I was a skeptic all along, that I knew full well what I was doing. But the answers I gave that night were a believer's answers.

"Can I say: *Joy is Being*?" my mother asked.

That is what I have been trying to tell you But you aren't Developed yet But Interpreting Joy is being Is your soul being not your living body Most people Aren't Alive yet They haven't cleansed themselves in the Spring of Infinity.

"Is a Writer (like myself) a person who is trying to realize herself?" my mother asked. For a person who didn't believe she was certainly full of questions. Nola and Phil could hardly get a question in. That question seems perfect for her, the idea of realizing herself through her writing, my mother's religion.

Shiva, though up way past his bedtime, tried to answer her concerns.

Most people try to realize themselves but to many people do it the wrong Some don't even know their trying but a person like yourself is definatly trying REMEMBER A Person who says he does not believe in the supernatural is SCARED of REALIZING Himself. A person A person who says He is SCARED of the Supernatural Is trying to realize Himself But doubts that He is

worthy of Knowing himself A person who WANTS to know himself
Is probABly using wrong ways to realize himself But I person who
realizes he knows Himself But Hadn't looked HARD Enough into
hiself Is saved from getting plucked off the tree of true being And
is on the RAINBOW to Bliss

—Shiva and All Men's Souls

My temptation is to make some kind of crack, to say that I obviously had a good future in writing fortune cookies. It's all pablum, of course, but even pablum can contain a grain of truth, I think, and there's part of me that wants to argue now with my twelve-year-old self, that wants to duke it out with Shiva, to go on the defensive, and say, "Who you callin' scared?"

"Can we tell different people besides Mom me and Phil?" Nola wrote.

Yes but only if they are sincere ~~We~~-you are fighting against your-
selves (your outer crust) And the whole world You have to
get People who will fight for <u>Our</u> cause

"Which is What?"

To seek into ourselves to reach ourselves to know
knowledge that few have known before you . . .

The *Star Trek* credo, more or less . . . Oops, no I'm sorry. I'll be quiet. How low of me, to heckle myself as a child.

But the child me had some store of dignity—he must have believed, because I took up the pen then and asked myself a question. I suppose at this moment I became a writer, or I tasted what it meant to be a writer, a person who is constantly questioning him- or herself, who asks and asks as though he were more than one person, a nearly infinite number of characters waiting to be uncovered, revealed.

"Why was I chosen?" I asked myself.

A Thousand Aerial Voices[1]

. . . . I have mentioned a friend of mine, Sarada, (a disciple of Sri Ramanuja of New York) who is at the time I am writing this a junior psychology student at Brandeis. She is my closest and most dependable friend. She was not a participant in my yoga class, but we meditated together once a week on Thursdays, since our foremost interest was in the Spirit and I was very eager to become a disciple of her Guru. We had been meditating in Brandeis' Pearlman Lounge, which is generally used for meetings of the sociology department, for many weeks.

One night as Sarada and I sat down in meditation, I began to receive now familiar messages from another world. My body began to tremble with the impact of strange voices. I started to talk in snatches and spurts in the beginning, for my mind could not yet arrange the impressions it was getting into coherent speech.

A male student and friend of Sarada's had just left; he had been trying to challenge all our arguments for meditation with the only intellectual tools he had, the weapons of discursive argument. Sarada answered his questions very quietly and patiently, trying to counter his militant rationalism with parables or more questions until the whole armory of his intellect started to collapse because it was unevenly matched with an opponent it could never track down. Guru was evidently inspiring Sarada to speak, since her voice was very clear, pure and affirmative.

I became almost vehement, insisting upon the absoluteness

1. Again, I've edited this "chapter" of my sister's autobiography, not changing wording, of course, but by cutting several longer passages that describe the Guru-shakti relationship and other aspects of Nola's understanding of her spiritual development. I don't think there's anything crucial I've left out. This chapter recounts the time six months or so before my mother and I drove to Brandeis to bring Nola home.

of Guru's power, the far reaching effects of meditation, and the rewards of the spiritual life, which only served to alienate him the more. When he had left Sarada leaned towards me and said, "You've been approaching him the wrong way, Nola. This boy is afraid of what lies beyond the immediate limits of his mind.[2] He wants to open up to us but he doesn't know how. You must be patient with him and not try to feed his arguments. I know this is what Guru would say and I am saying it to you. Look at this boy in the future and his divine aspect, not at his failings; see him as he is capable of becoming, a free and liberated spirit, not as he now is." At that moment, Sarada's eyes took on a peculiar gleam, and I thought I saw for an instant the gaze of Guru in their pupils. Suddenly a veil seemed to drop from us in the silence of that meditation room, and the lounge was filled with the sound of a thousand aerial voices, great spiritual essences who conversed with the sweetness of saints. Sarada and I both began to hear a form of speech whose patterns matched those of music, a chorus of wild and marvelous sounds, which pierced through our mental prison with a strange urgency. Even as I write about this I am receiving these memories very imperfectly, so that I live in an agony of unfulfilled language, and I pray my God that He might send me stronger hearing, to crush the vanity of my inferior mind and fill me with light!

Guru had told Sarada in the past that he was on very close terms of friendship with Christ, and at first I didn't know what to think about this, since I knew very little of Guru, having met him and his shakti (or cosmic partner) Alo Devi only once the previous year at a Brandeis lecture. (Even then I had been drawn to them for their gentleness and sincerity.) After Sarada had spoken to me in the lounge, and we began to hear the voices, we both became conscious of something behind our backs, and turned to the blackboard near the fireplace, where we saw a message scrawled in chalk like the "Mene, Mene, Tekel Upharsin" of the Bible, the words: "Christ . . . God . . . Nature . . . Divine surrender, Compassion . . ." I can no longer recall the thread which drew these few scattered words into meaning, but they formed for us a sense of the same kind that Champollion had probably found when he saw the Demotic Greek, Coptic and

2. I read this and identify with that boy, though it's with Nola I'd rather side.

Hieroglyphic tongues of the Rosetta Stone. We were frightened into quietude, neither able to speak about what had been heard so close to our inner center that it could not be spoken. We resumed our seats in total silence. It was then that one of the presences, then two, then twelve, swept over my body in great gusts, and I became, for the time, a mouthpiece for their messages. The patches of words were falling in place, in a strange tapestry of utterance. "There is a reason I have been trained in this yoga class," I began. "My teacher is an unwitting instrument . . ." "For what?" cried Sarada. "I must be sensitized . . ." I muttered as if asleep, "so that I may hear these voices and convey them to you to reveal to others; you must function as the guru, and I as your shakti, the recipient of the etheric forces." When I had this revelation the whole room was filled with a delicate laughter, which both of us heard, and will be confirmed by my friend (we were the only ones in the room). We felt that each of us had received the same sacred message, that it had been placed in our hands because each of us had been chosen for a long and difficult labor, which had to be done in order to do justice to our

LOTHLORIEN

souls, the Western hemisphere and God, who governed them even in their ignorance. We now became aware of the location of the presences that filled the room, and were immersed in a vague delight, which Sarada called "a feeling as thick as molasses." I knew that Guru stood behind Sarada's back, directing her speech like a conductor, while his shakti, Alo Devi, of whom I was very fond although I had only met her once, took her stand at my left. I felt Alo Devi's soul approach me, rise a few inches into the air, and implant her consciousness within my brain for a second; she told Sarada through me that she should listen to the advice of her mother, because the latter was a very well developed soul and would help in her daughter's progress. "This is Alo Devi speaking," I managed to preface before the voice took me. I knew Sarada's mother very little, having met her once on a brief visit to the Centre of Being (Guru's center in New York; Sarada's mother is also a disciple).

For an incredible moment, we found speech meaningless, as I had previously found in my confrontation with Will. The most fantastic dialogue began to follow; I asked Sarada unspoken questions, and she answered them either aloud or in silence, at which I would answer them again in silence, in a miraculous dialogue until both of us, realizing what had happened, shrieked in one compound and rapturous voice: "Do you know you're reading my mind?" Our invisible audience fell into a fit of delight, one presence toppling the other in such a seizure of laughter that Sarada and I were caught up in it. Our lives had been changed to this invisible pageantry, and our eyes grew like Prospero's, delighted with but detached from our play. Gradually, one after the other of our visitors: Guru, Alo Devi, a couple of what seemed to be elves, and one who was apparently the soul of Jesus Christ, who had stood before the blackboard on which we had seen the message, and who had been one of the most powerful presences in the room, departed from the lounge. We left the lounge as we would leave a church, under the spell of the sanctity it had when our eyes caught this vision of life.

Family of Avatars

He said to me, "My son, the intention is not to grasp any finite form—
even the highest. Rather, this is the path to the names: Their intrinsic
value is proportional to their degree of incomprehensibility. The less
comprehensible, the higher. Eventually, you will reach an energy that is
not in your control; rather your mind and thought are in its control."
THE ESSENTIAL KABBALAH

"Guru wants to meet you," Nola told my mother, Phillip, Jonathan,
and me one night at dinner. We were eating breaded chicken sticks.
Ida, as usual, hovered by the stove, trying to double our portions of
food. A pile of chicken sticks and peas and carrots sat on Nola's plate,
untouched. Nola and Ida loved one another but Ida couldn't understand why Nola had to "starve herself," and thought perhaps that if
she at least had the food on her plate her spirit would partake and convince the rest of her to try the food. I had no such problems. I was a
finicky eater, but I loved Ida's chicken sticks. "He said we should come
tomorrow. There'll be a celebration."

"I'd like to meet him," said Phillip, who was staying with us out at
Ida's beach house for a few days over Christmas, 1970. At first, he'd
stayed on because of blizzard-like conditions, but he might have also
stayed on because we treated him like spiritual royalty, our cousin who
knew all about automatic writing, India, and even telepathy. On top of
that, he seemed perfectly sane, or "together," as we used to say.

"I don't want to go," I said. "Not on Christmas."

"You'll still get presents," Nola said.

"I'm not worried," I said.

"I've told Guru about Shiva," she said. "He already knows about
Mom."

"What does he know about me?" I asked.

"Does he do magic tricks?" Jonny asked. "Can he pull a bodhisattva
out of a hat?"

200

Phillip laughed and pointed at Jonny, but Nola ignored him. I laughed, too, though I had no idea what a bodhisattva was.

"I saw a man down at the beach today," Nola said, "with no aura."

"Maybe he's going to die," Phillip said.

"I think he was dead already," Nola said.

"Maybe you and Robin should go digging for some more clams," Ida said.

"What's my aura?" I asked.

"Many colors, Robin, but the foremost is blue."

"With gold highlights and sequins," Jonny said.

"Stop it, Jonny," Nola said.

I was sure she could see it and I wanted to see her aura too, so I looked hard. I squinted. She had her hands folded in front of her plate. All I could see was a slight tinge of gray.

"It's blue, with some red in it," Phillip said.

From the living room we could hear the plaintive sounds of Joan Baez singing "East Virginia": "I was born in East Virginia, North Carolina I did roam. There I met a fair young maiden." Jonny at seventeen had dibs on the record player next. He wanted to play the Rolling Stones' *Exile on Main Street,* ("Softly!" my mother warned) which I tried to get into, but couldn't. The cover, for one, scared me, with all those black-and-white photos of freaks and various Stones members. At that moment in my life, I sided more with Nola than Jonny—I fluctuated constantly between the two, and so did my musical tastes. Right now, it was Joan Baez, Judy Collins, Joni Mitchell. It was a relief listening to folk songs rather than "Sympathy for the Devil."

*   *   *

On Christmas day, Nola, Phillip, my mother, me, and Jonny, disdainful but tagging along for fun, took the Long Island Railroad to Jamaica, New York, where Sri Ramanuja's Centre of Being was located. Nola had attended a lecture of Sri Ramanuja's the previous year when she was still at Brandeis, at the urging of her friend Kathleen, now named Sarada, who had become one of Ramanuja's disciples. Since then, Nola had visited the Centre of Being a number of times, and was eager to become a disciple, too. She believed that his divine intervention had brought her back from the brink of destruction at the hands of her sinister yoga teacher at Brandeis. But she still looked unhealthy. And her voices were increasing in frequency. Sometimes she'd burst out in a strange voice, Exorcist-style, or track something with her eyes across the room that the rest of us couldn't see. She was having visions constantly. A pageant of demons and angels trekked across her field of vision with such frequency that she could do nothing but watch them in awe, and often, misery.

In a way, Nola's suffering drew my mother and me into her world. She was my older sister, and I would follow her almost anywhere she told me, even into madness. It's no wonder that I wanted to be a participant, to be a conduit for the spirit world. And the same, I know, is true of my mother. Her earnestness, her belief in her daughter at the time, came in part from despair, or from the hope that if she followed Nola wherever she led, somehow my mother could help lead both of them, all of us, to safety.

I knew little about Jamaica except that it was where we usually changed trains to go into the city. I had never stopped there for more than a few minutes. Over the platform railing, was a squalid urban landscape: run-down news shops and liquor stores, corner grocery markets, beat-up cars, litter everywhere, and few pedestrians. It was strange to think of Jamaica as a destination of anywhere we'd want to go, and even stranger on Christmas Day, when the train car was virtually empty. We had an entire car to ourselves.

Although she had been there before, Nola brought a little map with her, which she gave to Phillip, and the five of us went in search of the Centre of Being through Jamaica's deserted streets.

*   *   *

Nola still hoped at the end of 1970 to live a life that could be considered by most people a normal one—a life that involved marriage, travel, and the many joys of physical existence. But her whole life had been spent seeking God and offering her complete surrender, and perhaps she could not envision a life that blended the spiritual and the physical. To her, it was an either/or proposition. Either one lived in the world or away from it. She wrote an undated letter to my mother sometime during 1970, in which she explained her dilemma:

Dear Mom:
    The following is a copy of a letter I have just written Kathleen. It is something you should read:
    Dear Sarada:
    This letter is for the purpose of asking you several vital questions about discipleship:

1. Marriage. If you are in love with someone or vice versa and he wants to take you away to the isle of Crete for a year where both of you could write, what would Guru say? Do you have to ask his permission?

2. About dependency—If you depend on Guru to get you through life, what happens to the American axiom of self-sufficiency? Of facing up to one's problems oneself, of mastering them oneself without a crutch?

3. What happens to a young girl when she loses her ego and doesn't want to live except for Guru's sake? Does she lose her youth, her vision, her joy in a certain right which Western youth has possessed for ages—the precious right to a certain egotistical youthful freedom?

4. What happens to a young girl who wants to go out and see and move in and live and breathe the breath of the world, to know it as it is, to imbue oneself with its sorrows and joys for the purpose of begetting in oneself a certain empathy, a certain understanding of mortality and what it means?

5. What happens to a person who is too wild for self-imposed restraints, who wants to be mad and free and make mistakes, the kind of mistakes without which it is impossible to develop any integrity? What happens to a girl who sees religion in savages, and the highest in street gutters? Does she become too impure for His kingdom?

6. Suppose Guru doesn't want you to marry at all? What happens to life? What happens to youthful experimentation? What happens to the joy of versatility, of mobility, of meeting other types of people, of intentional urges?

Love,
Nola

I don't know what Sarada's reply was, although it must have been a good one. Or else the letter answered itself. I see most of the questions in Nola's letter as not questions at all, but credos, part of what she always believed in, divine surrender and worldly joy, the whole bittersweet mix that confounded her. I don't really care what Sarada's answer was because the answer lies within the letter, and Sarada couldn't have told Nola anything she didn't already know. The answers to Nola's questions are obvious, even to me. You don't go to Crete with whomever you were planning on going to Crete with. You don't marry.

Worldly joys are ultimately outside of your grasp. You may admire them from a distance, Nola, you may yearn for them sometimes, but you must surrender your personal ego to whoever will accept it—Sri Ramanuja? That's all that's left.

What intrigues me about this letter is the fact that it's a copy of a letter, not the original, that my sister rewrote it in her hand for my mother's benefit—and I wonder why. What was her intention in sending the letter to my mother? On the one hand, it testifies to their closeness. My sister told my mother everything from her sexual history to her spiritual one. But I also wonder if she was asking for my mother's approval in this next big step in her life, or whether she wanted my mother to try to answer these questions for her? Was she just trying to keep my mother posted on the latest developments or was she enlisting her support? A young American woman going off to Crete for a year to write—that sounds awfully familiar, and something my mother would probably have approved of. Or maybe not. Maybe she would have worried that Nola would return home, published perhaps, but pregnant, too. It's doubtful in Nola's case. My mother would have worried, regardless, just as Ida worried about my mother when she went to Mexico, but Nola would have done what she'd wanted . . . if that's what she really wanted, and no one would have tried to stop her. But the fact is that this scenario wasn't my sister's life, it was my mother's, and both of them knew it, and maybe that's why she sent the letter.

*   *   *

From the outside, the ashram looked indistinguishable from the other storefronts and ramshackle row houses along the street. The only thing that distinguished it was a small plaque with the words "Centre of Being" etched on it. I remember going from cold and silence to warmth and light: an entranceway where we removed our heavy coats and took off our boots and around a corner, lights and music and Sri Ramanuja seated in the living room on cushions with his shakti Alo Devi by his side. One by one, his followers were coming up to him after Alo Devi called their names. He talked softly to each of them and handed them a present as they knelt before him. The children of the Ashram sat in an orderly fashion around him, as though he were about to tell them a bedtime story. Sri Ramanuja was dressed in a robe as were many, if not most of his followers. He did not speak much—I remember Alo Devi speaking more than he did, but even if he had not uttered a word in his lifetime, I could see why this man had followers. He was bald like Buddha and had a Buddha-like face, serene and gentle.

I know I was drawn to him, but we were intercepted almost immediately. Apparently, we had not been invited, or rather, the invitation had been a telepathic one to Nola, not actually spoken, so no one seemed to know why we were there or who we were, and why we'd come in the middle of their celebration. But we weren't turned away. Nola's friend Sarada parted from the crowd of devotees and whispered to us that we should sit in the hallway, the only place left for us, where we could at least see Guru interact with his followers.

Sarada looked sadly at me and said, "I wish we'd known you were coming. I'm afraid we only have enough toys for the children we knew about."

I had been promised toys, the main lure for me, but I sat respectfully, on the floor, my legs crossed. "It is not because of his miracles that he is worshipped," Sri Ramanuja was telling his followers, "but because he brought down the eternal Consciousness, the infinite Consciousness." A little later he said that God was "Consciousness and Light," that we must "realize the divinity within ourselves." I approved. That's just what Shiva was saying.

Phillip sat in the lotus position with his eyes closed. Now and then, he opened his eyes and gazed at Guru intently. Once, he swatted his hand in front of him as though brushing off a fly.

Jonny disappeared almost as soon as we arrived, poking around, investigating, checking the ashram for beautiful devotees. As Guru spoke, a few people milled around, setting up tables with dishes of foods. The ashram was filled with the delicate scents of fragrant rices and other vegetable dishes. After a time, this became the foremost impression in my mind, not divinity but the food. I saw Guru whisper something to his shakti and look at me. She smiled and stood up quickly like someone leaving a concert and not wanting to block the view of others.

"Guru requests that you approach him," Alo Devi told me.

I did as I was told and knelt before him as I had seen others do. I knew it was protocol, but I kind of expected Sri Ramanuja to wink at me or give me some sign that he knew I was a divinity, too. After all, he'd been talking about the divinity within ourselves, and I knew *I* had one inside me. But he didn't acknowledge the divinity within me. He smiled and gave me a Matchbox car.

I thanked him and rejoined my family. I showed it to my mother and Nola and Sarada, and they oohed over it as though it was the Hope Diamond. Phillip smiled wryly and closed his eyes again. I know I was an ingrate, but I just expected something a bit more special from a guru, maybe a carving of an elephant or a monkey, something really valuable. Sarada told me that it was amazing that Guru had something for me, that no one besides Guru and Alo Devi had known we would be joining them.

"In astral form," Nola whispered ". . . to meet Robin and my mother. Guru told us to come."

Sarada looked delighted.

My mother, used to receiving invitations in a more standard manner, seemed a little embarrassed and befuddled, and she led me to the food table as Guru finished talking. Jonny was already there, heaping rice on his plate.

"Try this stuff, Mom," he said. "It's not too bad. Could use a little beef though."

Phillip still sat, his eyes closed, while others stepped carefully around him. Later, Phillip told us that he was monitoring Guru's telepathic communications with Nola. He said that he and Guru were sparring. Phillip thought Guru Ramanuja wanted too much control over Nola, that divine surrender to him was unnecessary, and might even be dangerous to her. Later, he and my mother stayed up late that night talking about what had transpired in this telepathic party line between Guru and Phillip and Guru and Nola.

At the table, I met a young girl my age with long hair and wearing a white robe, like something out of a Maxfield Parrish painting. She appeared in front of me like an apparition and made herself my guide through the ashram that evening, holding my hand, urging me to sample the various exotic foods. Before the night was over, we had exchanged addresses. She promised to write, which she did, although I neglected to write back. She promised to visit me in astral form, which she didn't, although I lay in bed waiting, night after night, certain that she would keep her promise.

*   *   *

Eager not to be outdone by Sri Ramanuja, Phillip, or Nola, I answered more Shiva questions for them on the train ride home to Long Beach that evening. But only my mother and Phillip seemed interested, although it was Nola's attention I desired. Jonny sat alone at the other end of the car, not interested in anyone's divinity, reading the book he'd brought along because he knew he'd be bored, and picking at his lip. Nola, too, sat alone by the window staring out in the dark. She sat hunched into herself and was muttering. Clearly, she was somewhere else. From where I sat, I could see her reflection in the window, pinpoints of light from outside dotting her like measles.

My mother was having a lot of difficulty with her hearing—she'd had profound hearing loss since she was a teenager, but now it was getting worse and it seemed as though she was going to need an operation. I think that's why she had been so silent that night at the ashram, why she'd simply nodded politely at people, and seemed awkward in the ashram's surroundings. Now, her hearing loss was on her mind and she wanted to ask Shiva about it.

"Is there a reason why I have been deaf for so many years?" she asked Shiva.

Not physically but mentally You have been deaf in your soul. But now you are being hatched from the egg of the clear light. I am Gabriel when I sound my trumpet ALL shall die in their souls I am DANIEL When I sound my trumpet ALL shall be saved I am Death.

I am the one who breaths the breath of life and purity into those worthy of living The SACRED Book will help you find it I am NOAH I save I say that MAN has been forgotten by his mask And costume which he so proudly shows And says this is what I am when he knows that that is what he is not I am everyone and Everything And Everyone and Everything is me. You must all know yourselfs Your Soul's Are Dying You have been given so many chances You Are INFANTS in the sea of pure bliss. Once you are swimming in it there is no return. While trying to get to that sea you may end up in the River Styx AND Then you will be pulled over onto the other side by the god of No hope I warn all of you the time has come You must learn how to fire AN Arrow into your outer skin and then peel it off I can lead the way but you must be ready to find the Answer or . . . . . .

Shiva

I love the ellipses. My natural flair for the dramatic, I guess. But I suppose having your twelve year old spouting phrases like "I am Death," might be a little spooky. I don't know what I'd do if one of my daughters started saying things like "you are being hatched from the egg of clear light." I'd probably listen. I'd definitely be curious. But I'd also warn them to tone it down. "'The Egg of the clear light' just doesn't do the trick as a metaphor, honey," I might say. I'm surprised my mother, with her keen editorial instincts, didn't try to edit Shiva, too. But, I guess it's hard to edit a god. Where do you begin?

I admit I'm a little impressed that I stuck with my Daniel blunder. Apparently, I must have been told or remembered that it was Gabriel who had the trumpet, not Daniel. A minor detail. Give them both trumpets. Gabriel's trumpet blows death and judgment while Daniel, the interpreter, the reader of the handwriting on the wall, breathes life and atonement. I couldn't have made a better blunder, as far as I'm concerned now.

But what Sacred Book was it that Shiva was telling them to read? I doubt it was the Bible despite the many Biblical references: Gabriel, Daniel, Noah. But there was also a Greek reference, the River Styx, and Hindu: Shiva himself. Would a Hindu god admonish mortals to read their King James? The gods we hung out with were well-read and open-minded. But it could have been anything, and as far as I can remember, the book was never specified. And it didn't matter really. The book, the concept of The Book, was enough for us. The idea itself was sacred.

At the moment, what captivated my mother, more than the idea of The Book, was the concept of an outer skin. And what thinking person isn't interested in an investigation of the layers of self, of identity?

"But I too have known about this mask and have been disturbed about it for some time and am trying to return to the essence or the knowledge of essences. I write about it in all my stories. All my new story ideas are based on this perception. Can you comment?"

Everyone is trying to peel off that outer skin but they are doing it secretly And when they see another Person that skin just grows thicker and thicker until he can no longer keep up pace in finding himself You are doing it secretly you must Do it with All of Mankind AND through Everyone else you will find yourself I will draw you a diagram of the human body:

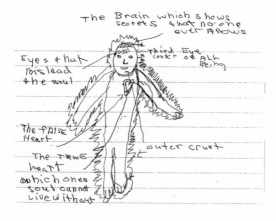

Read the sacred book today you people are like books the cover hardly ever shows what the book is really about.

—SHIVA

Shiva was right on that one—we were all books, but if he meant it as an insult, it wasn't taken as one.

"Do I show this essence to others by being what I am or writing?" my mother asked, but Shiva, usually so garrulous, remained silent. He didn't want to talk to his mother anymore, but to his sister, who still sat silent by the train window.

"Nola," I called. "Don't you want to ask Shiva anything?"

Nola turned slowly toward us and uncurled herself. She smiled uncertainly, her lips thin and wavery as though her mouth, not only her smile, might dissolve completely and forever, and she might not be able to speak again.

"Guru likes you, Robin," Nola said. "He called you everyone's little brother."

"Is he telling you that now?" Phillip asked. Phillip sat in the seat behind us, his arms draped over the seat, looking over my shoulder. "I think we need to be careful here," he said. "We need to sort out the various messages and figure out who's sending them."

Nola shook her head no. She hugged herself as though she was cold.

"Robin made a friend at the ashram," my mother told Nola. "Why don't you come over here. Are you cold?"

"I'm always making friends," I said. "She's going to write to me."

Nola scooted over beside us, with me in the middle, the Shiva notebook still balanced on my legs. "Guru is too busy to be with me always," Nola said, "though a part of him is always with me." Her teeth were chattering.

"Let me give you my coat."

"I'm not cold," Nola said and refused the coat.

"You look cold. I don't need it."

"I'm not cold, Mother," Nola said with such certainty that my mother quieted, although normally this would have gone on, back and forth, for at least five minutes. Nola said she wanted to ask Shiva a question but she couldn't hold the pen, so my mother wrote it for her.

"Does Vishnu have an Avatar now? Is he someone we have met? Or is . . ."

Nola paused and so my mother paused, too. "Or is?" my mother prompted.

But Shiva understood, if I didn't, and I took the pen from my mother's hand.

FAMILY
VASUKI
DEMONS
GODS
I AM TRYing to enlighten your family
Avatars
Demons Are Trying to prevent me

Vishnu is considered a more benevolent god than Shiva, less distant and remote, and undoubtedly what Nola wanted to know from Shiva, whom apparently she trusted, was whether Vishnu had a representative or incarnation, on earth. No doubt she assumed this representative to be Sri Ramanuja. But it seems to me an error in judgment at least to ask one god about the attentions of another. One is bound to get an evasive answer, and even if Shiva had the answers, Robin didn't. I had no idea what an Avatar was, nor Vishnu. "Does Vishnu have an Avatar?" Sounded like a musical instrument to me.

"Are we a family of Avatars?" Nola asked, "and who is most in danger from Demons?"

NOLA WAIT STOP
I CAN ONLY tell what Robin ALREADY knows If
he learns more I will be able to communicate more
   —SHIVA
Vishnu is WINNING

I must have thought that Vishnu was a demon, something like the traditional God/Devil dichotomy. Or else Shiva was just jealous.

"Is Nola in danger?" Phillip wrote. Nola was sitting there. She saw the question, too. This one didn't take a god to figure out, but even here Shiva was evasive.

YES NO
EVERYONE IS ONE

I was not comfortable any longer. I didn't know what I was talking about. I didn't want to be responsible for divining the future, for understanding who or what my family was, for deciding Nola's fate.

"Is Nola the Avatar?" Phillip asked.

EVERYONE
"In the family?"
EVERYONE IS A PART OF SOMEONE
FAMILY MOST LIKELY TIRED HELP

That was the notebook's last page. I wrote big. I wanted to stop, but my mother wanted to find out what was wrong with Nola, and Shiva at least was providing some kind of answers. She looked through her purse and I prayed to whatever gods there were to make it so she wouldn't find any more paper. I wanted to help. I really did, but I was beginning to doubt my own powers. There were things I didn't know, and maybe the gods couldn't help us, after all.

At the same moment my mother found a note card, we passed over the bridge that crossed over into Long Beach. I knew we'd be at the station in a matter of moments. I jumped up and shouted, "We're here, we're here," as though I'd been on board a ship lost at sea and not just the train from Jamaica.

The next day, I went to the winter beach alone. I didn't walk to the shore but to the row of cabanas where people stored their beach chairs. It was somewhere around here that my friend Jimmy Lucazy had died a year and a half earlier—at least I thought I was near the spot, because I had seen him and Vince digging earlier that summer in the same place, a hole dug in the sand with boards piled on top, and more sand on top of the boards.

I walked on the sand as though I had a divining rod in my hand and let my spirit guide me to the right spot. I dug a hole and covered the Matchbox toy in the sand, an offering. This wasn't the first time I'd left material offerings for the dead. Once, my brother's parrot had died and he had enlisted me and my friend Gary Keller to bury the bird. Our teacher had recently been telling us about ancient Egypt and all of the treasures that were buried with the pharaohs. So I buried two of my GI Joes, supine alongside the bird carcass, in a shoebox. I positioned their hard plastic fingers to suggest they were comforting the dead bird, caressing its green feathers. A couple of years later, I wanted my GI Joes back, but could never find the right spot again.

I started to walk away from the cabanas when I had a sudden fear. What if *this* was the wrong spot? What if I was wrong and this was just another stretch of sand, not where Jimmy had been buried alive. I started digging in the spot but couldn't find the car.

If you've ever tried to find something in the sand, you know that the more you dig, the farther you shift it away from your grasp. Once, when I was seven or so, a toddler digging in the same sand farther down the beach had discovered a woman's diamond ring and shown it to me. I took it and said I had found the ring and gave it to Nola. The child, too young to speak, simply blinked at me.

Almost miraculously, I found the Matchbox car again. I didn't want it, but I wanted it at the same time. I didn't like being chided by Alo Devi for not telling them I was coming. I didn't like Sri Ramanuja for not acknowledging my power. Again, I buried the little car, but this time closer to shore, and with an eye toward recovery. Again, I found the Matchbox car, and this time with little effort. I buried it again and again, each time with the same result until my hands were raw and red from the chill and I knew I had to go back to Ida's or everyone would start to worry about me. I dropped the car and ran back. The sand, hardened by the cold and wet, was a little firmer than it usually was in the summer. I took pleasure that I could still run so fast. I took pleasure in the fact that I didn't need this guru's cheap offering to me. I let it lie in the sand, neither covered nor claimed. I don't know if someone found it, although perhaps it washed away and was never found. I'm looking at it now—for me, it's still there, and I can almost touch it, almost change my mind again and decide once and for all time to keep it.

Good News

"Dad, I've got some bad news," Olivia tells me as we're driving.

"What's that?"

"Magic died."

"Magic died?" This alarms me. "Who's Magic?"

"One of her imaginary friends," Beverly says.

"But don't worry," Olivia says. "I have lots of babies. Five new babies were borned today."

"She just pops them out," Beverly says.

Later, I ask her where Magic is, to see if she remembers.

"Magic died."

"Oh, where is Magic now?"

"In the sand. I buried Magic in the sandbox."

"Is he one of your toys?"

"No, Dad. He's Magic and he's dead. He's not a toy and he's not coming back. But, don't worry. The good news is that Jasmine's going to be fine."

"Who's Jasmine?"

"From Aladdin. Jasmine, Dad!"

The next day, she informs me that Jasmine, too, has died, but not to worry. Five new babies have been borned.

Everyday People

To describe my mother as permissive would be, as we used to say, the understatement of the year. She allowed us all the freedom to explore the world around us to whatever degree we wanted, and I'm not sure, even now, whether this is something I should be proud of or angry about. And yet she worried about our well-being like any parent, more than most, in fact, always afraid that some stranger was going to snatch us off the street or from a public bathroom. Perhaps we were too strong-willed a bunch for her to manage, especially after my father died. Whatever we wanted to do we simply did because she could not see a way to keep us from doing it, and we were all skilled artisans of emotional blackmail, or at least I was. And my mother was curious, too, perhaps her deepest flaw, and believed that she could at least learn as much from her children as they could learn from her.

None of us had limits. Jonathan, in his midteens was "asked not to return" to his boarding school for running away to New York to attend a marathon reading of Joyce's *Finnegan's Wake*. He then went to Mexico to study Spanish, then McGill University in Montreal to study French. Nola went off to the Middle East or made plans for a religious pilgrimage to India.

My energies were always much more split between the physical and spiritual plains than Nola's. While Nola focused her life almost solely on the spiritual battleground of her soul, I wanted to change things in the physical world as well, and I'm not talking about Vietnam—that was a given in our world, that everyone wanted the war in Vietnam to stop. Perhaps I was influenced by the activism of the era, but from the time I was nine, I started getting involved in Causes. Everything became a story with myself as the hero. Obviously, there's a sociopathic element here, the same as the child murderer who feels no remorse when he shoots the neighbor because everyone else isn't real; they're just characters. That's one way of looking at it. I suppose people are still characters to me, and while that might sound like a terrible admission, I see the word "character" as an elevated term: someone whom we want to know more about, someone we hope to understand. We can't understand the people milling about us anonymously, but a character is someone we focus our attention upon, someone who elicits our sympathy and compassion.

The only way I could distinguish good from bad was to act out morality plays in which I starred, scenarios in which I tried to do good, but was sometimes thwarted, like a comic-book hero. When I was ten and lived in Athens, Ohio, I started a petition drive to bring better restaurants to town:

"Tired of Hamburgers and Pizza," Kid Petitions for Foreign Spicing

ATHENS, O—In this age of involvement, 10-years-young Robin Hemley has a growing concern about the lack of variety in restaurants here, in the home of Ohio University.

Robin's primary beef is that he's "tired of hamburgers and pizza." Therefore, taking matters into his own small hands, the precocious moppet began circulating a petition, which reads as follows:

"If you want some improvement in Athens like a delicatessen or an Italian restaurant or Chinese restaurant or an ice cream parlor, write your name here."

What Robin has been saying was anything but Greek to more than 1,000 Athenians who did sign the petition.

Deli-rious

As written into the petition, the delicatessen ("with any kind of foreign food we can get") is foremost on the wanted list. Robin's reasoning is that foreigners—many of whom are either enrolled or teach at the university "will feel more at home."

Strongly seconding Robin's campaign is quite naturally, his mother, Mrs. Cecil Hemley, a writer-editor. Admitting that Robin's petition has stirred things up a bit, Mrs. Hemley also attributes her son's campaign—with all due modesty—to her cooking.

"I like to cook," she said. "And I like to cook many foreign dishes, which probably has spoiled him."

Also in Robin's corner is Kevin Heisler, student-managing editor of the Ohio University Post.

"For good restaurants you have to go to Columbus, which is 70, 80 miles from here."

How do the local restaurateurs feel?

"He doesn't know what he's talking about. He's just going off on a tangent. They (the Hemleys) don't eat out much," said a Frisch's Big Boy franchisee in this burg, Jerry Saviano.

Making it a split decision, however, is Michael Kobre, who holds a Pizza Hut franchise. "As for the lack of different kinds of eating places here, the kid has a point.

"Nevertheless," Kobre added, "Robin continues to come in for pizza at least two times a week."

Slated Nixon Letter

Robin originally planned to submit his petition to a local merchant, but the latter was unable to see the boy.

In addition, Robin had intended to send a letter to President Nixon, to tell him of the plight of Athens.

But it lately seems that Robin has lost a great deal of interest in his undertaking.

This may stem from the fact that both a Chinese and Italian restaurant have opened in Athens.

Then again, according to Mrs. Hemley, Robin has a new involvement; he's begun breeding mice.

This was before I wrote to Nixon regarding the riots in Arkansas over court-ordered busing. I'm not sure what I expected Nixon to do about the restaurant situation in Athens, but I was sure he'd be concerned. A year later, when the National Guard fired on the students at Kent State, I was glad I'd never sent my petition to Nixon. He tended to overreact. And it's true, I tried to give my petition to the richest man in town, Mr. Beasley, but he wouldn't see me. The only well-known person who signed was the president of Ohio University, Albert James, who turned it into a photo op.

I like the fact that the restaurateurs disagreed over how often we ate out, as though it made the slightest difference, and as though they knew. I know we didn't eat out at Pizza Hut twice a week. Were we that well-known in town that the owners of Pizza Hut and Frisch's kept tabs on our comings and goings? No matter. I got what I wanted. A bunch of new restaurants opened up, and Mrs. Chen, the owner of the Chinese restaurant, gave me free egg rolls after school until we moved away the following year to Slippery Rock.

It was true also, about my passion for mice, but the mice only distracted me for a little while. I kept them at school in an aquarium until the janitor turned the heat in the school all the way up one weekend rather than all the way down as he was supposed to. My mice, as well as other assorted guinea pigs, hamsters, and bunnies throughout the school, suffocated.

Nothing unusual in that. I took it in stride. I couldn't keep my father alive. I couldn't even keep pets alive.

But still, I tried to counter death. Maybe that's why I involved myself in causes. Maybe that's why I wanted restaurants, something that had to do with sustenance rather than decay. Or why I volunteered one day to help a local fraternity, Sigma Alpha Mu, with their annual fundraiser, "Bounce for Beats," in which the frat members, or Sammies as they were known, bounced a basketball nonstop for seventy-two hours while collecting money for the Heart Association. I told them that my father had died of a heart attack, and I spent the next two days on the street corners of Athens with them. Afterward, they promised to take me out to dinner and make me an Honorary Sammy. My mother dressed me up for the occasion, but they never showed—who knows? Maybe they had planned on taking me to Frisch's Big Boy or the Burger Boy Food-A-Rama and the owners got wind of their plan and drugged them. Those restaurateurs knew my every move, after all.

*   *   *

I never wanted to leave Athens, but we had to go where my mother could find work, to Slippery Rock. Jonathan was lucky, I thought. He got to stay in Athens by enrolling in Ohio University, as Nola had previously. Only a year after we moved to Slippery Rock in 1969, we moved again, to Columbia, Missouri. My mother has told me before that one of the main reasons she left Slippery Rock was because I was so miserable there. I was thrilled to leave. Columbia, Missouri had to be better than Slippery Rock.

I changed my name on the day we moved from Slippery Rock to Columbia. I wouldn't allow anyone to call me Robin anymore. From then on, I was to be known as Peter. Kids had always made fun of the name "Robin" with monotonous variations of "That's a girl's name," "Batman and Robin," "Flatman and Ribbon," "Robin Hood." I liked Peter Tork of the Monkees. I liked Peter Parker, alias Spiderman. The only people who refused to call me Peter were my mother and Nola. That was the only year I was known as Peter, and a year later a woman yelled at me from across the street, "Peter! Peter!" and I looked at her as if she were crazy.

A couple of days after the move, I sat in the orange stuffed chair we had lugged from Athens and Slippery Rock to Columbia—the chair was my father's favorite. Our biggest bookcase, which stretched the length of the wall and up to the ceiling, wasn't anchored yet, but I didn't know that as I sat curled in the orange chair, my hand in a box of Cap'n Crunch, my eyes glued to Saturday morning cartoons. Boxes from our move, empty and full, were strewn about me. Josie and the Pussycats, all of them, were hurtling in a spacecraft while playing bubblegum rock in weightlessness. I didn't particularly care for this show, but it was TV, and it was on, so I watched.

I saw something white in my peripheral vision, something gigantic tilting toward me, and I looked up. I must have crouched down in the chair and that action probably saved my life. This massive bookcase crashed over me, a wooden wave, pushing ahead of it the little TV on its stool. The TV and stool tumbled by my feet. A stick lamp with orange teardrop globules (a hideous lamp, even then, but it matched the chair) fell directly on my head, the globules swinging about me, shattering on my head and chest.

I awoke covered in glass and books, my horrified mother peering at me through the shelves. The image seemed strangely appropriate to us even then, and it became an instant metaphor to my mother and me. After she found out that I wasn't going to die, that all I had was a mild concussion and a lot of glass in my head and chest, my mother wondered if this was a sign that I was someday going to be a writer.

In every situation, even the most gruesome, we were taught to see irony. "I don't want to be one then," I said.

The same year, my appendix ruptured as I stepped off the school bus. I fumbled into our apartment, my mother wasn't home yet, and I lay in a haze of pain for most of the afternoon. When she returned from teaching, she called the doctor, who told her it was most likely gas pain, and if it didn't go away in a few hours, she could bring me in.

The doctor wanted to finish his dinner, a fabulous meal, apparently, because I almost died waiting for him. By the time I made it to the hospital, my own poisons had been coursing through me for several hours. My mother finally brought me, semiconscious, to the emergency room.

"Does this hurt, Peter?" the doctor asked, pushing his finger into me.

"No," I said, smiling, pleased that after all it was . . .

And then he let go . . . Who OWWW. I did one of those Jackie Gleason faces of pain, all eyes and exaggerated intensity.

"I won't ask you if *that* hurt," he said. "We're going to need to operate right away."

I looked at my mom in terror and I hobbled off the exam table, my back bent. "No, I think it's just gas. I can go to the bathroom now," I said.

The doctor and my mother both laughed, which seems a little cruel in retrospect, but I was undoubtedly a comic and pathetic sight.

My mother went out to talk to the doctor and a young intern came in to get a sample of my blood. As he was taking the blood, he started telling me about all the other people he'd taken blood from.

"This is a strange job," he said. "Half the time I'm talking to someone just like I'm talking to you. They seem okay, but five hours later they're . . . you know . . . dead. You might be dead too," and he looked up at me, then flicked his finger against one of the glass tubes.

"Am I going to die?" I said weakly.

"You might. It ain't up to you."

"It's not up to you, either," I said, emphasizing his poor grammar to him. But he didn't even seem to notice.

"You never know, man," he said.

Luckily, this strange sadistic intern didn't kill me, although I almost, you know, died.

I awoke with a tube down my nose, a tube in my arm, and a tube cut into my side and hooked into a bubbling machine.

This wasn't ironic. This was simple physical pain, but even here in the intensive care unit of Mercy Hospital, I tried to influence my life through signs and metaphor. A neighbor of ours came to visit me in the hospital and gave me a planter in the shape of a Model T Ford with ivy growing from it. I dubbed this my Peter plant, and its health and well-being became inextricably tied to my own.

This was not an original thought, but something based on a television adaptation of an O. Henry story I'd seen a couple of years earlier, in which a young girl lying sick in the hospital fixates on a tree outside her window that's losing its leaves. Her notion is that when the last leaf drops, she'll die. In the end, there's only one leaf left and her condition worsens until she and the doctors are sure she'll die by morning. But a kindly old man—her grandfather? No, that's *Heidi*. A bum from the street?—climbs a ladder during the night and paints a leaf against the wall of the adjoining building so that it looks as though the branch still has one stubborn leaf remaining. The girl recovers. The old man tumbles off the ladder and breaks his neck. That's O. Henry.

I loved it. But I didn't have any old man intervening for me, although I guess I wouldn't have known it even if I had. That's the point of the O. Henry story after all. In my case, I had to make my own fate, cast myself in my own stories, create my own antagonists and subplots.

My mother spent that first night in the hospital with me, in a cot they brought her. She brought me a gift of an African musical instrument called a kalimba, metal prongs that you flick with your thumbs. I liked the sound but it vibrated painfully into my appendix scar. She also brought me some *Archie* comic books. I had started collecting comics that year, and while I'd started with Archie, I'd soon learned that they were virtually worthless as collector's items. I'd recently switched to Marvel comic books: *The Avengers, Spiderman, The Incredible Hulk, The Fantastic Four*, and a new comic, *Conan The Barbarian*. Archie versus Conan wasn't much of a fight, but I hungrily took the Archie from my mom and thanked her—when you're in pain, Archie is definitely more comforting than Conan.

Nola brought me a poster showing a woman in some Edenlike place, surrounded by all sorts of wild animals who obviously meant her no harm. The woman, bejeweled and wearing a crownlike hat, had a serene expression, and seemed to be beckoning the viewer to enter. The waters of a pond lapped at her feet, which were clad in jeweled sandals, and although the vegetation was tropical, the animals and the woman all looked cool and calm, as though they could only be affected by the pleasant sides of a physical existence.

The first time I saw this poster I wanted to step inside (and every time after until Nola destroyed it), to lose myself in this mysterious place away from pain. I asked to have it put up on my hospital wall, but the nurses wouldn't allow it.

I thanked Nola. She seemed in good spirits when she visited, not so self-absorbed, not so grim. She even joked with me about the hollow TV propped on the bureau opposite my hospital bed.

"A hollow boob tube," Nola said. "What a brilliant idea." She awkwardly hefted the thing in her arms and walked a few steps with it so that the TV looked like her head.

"The perfect fashion statement," my mother said.

"If you want the real thing, you have to pay for it," I said.

"It looks good on you," my mother told Nola and I laughed, which immediately turned into a groan of pain.

Nola put the TV back on the bureau. "It's great for people who want to feel stupid, but don't want to act stupid," she said. "That way, they can seem stupid to their stupid friends. You could store books in the TV and your visitors would never be the wiser. And the best thing is . . ."

Nola stopped and a strange look passed over her face.

"What's the best thing, Nola?" I asked. I was leaning forward a bit, ready to laugh.

"No commercials?" my mother said.

"Shut up," I said. "I want Nola to tell me." In our family, we were always telling each other to shut up. I don't know who started it, but it was like a virus. Jonny was perhaps the most likely one of us to say shut up—he'd say it to all three of us at once. My mom would say it to my brother and me, especially when she was driving, and I'd say it to my mother and Jonny, and later, Nola, at the height of her illness. Nola would have been immune, but she and Jonny were great rivals, and she would tell him to shut up on a fairly regular basis. More often than that, she'd tell the TV to shut up, especially during commercials. When a commercial came on, she'd dash from her seat and turn the sound off. Telling any of us to shut up was about as futile as telling the TV to shut up.

"What were you going to say?" I asked Nola. "The best thing is . . ."

Nola sat on my bed. She took my hand.

"What were you going to say? I just want you to finish your thought."

My mother came to my side, too. "As soon as you get better, we can go to a Chinese restaurant."

Distractions didn't work with me. I'd milk them for what I could get and then return to the original question. "Can we go to a candy store, too?"

"Sure," she said.

I turned back to Nola. "Keep talking about the hollow TV."

"I don't know what I was going to say."

"You don't remember?"

"It flew out of my head. What difference does it make what I was going to say? I don't want to talk anymore."

"Okay," I said, taking my hand away from her. She never raised her voice to me. She never talked to me like this, except for one time in Athens when I'd found a patch of four-leaf clovers, not one or two, but a hundred, growing right outside our front door. I picked every one of them for her. I thought she'd be pleased, but she was angry. "Once they're gone, they're gone," she said. "They won't grow back." She was right, of course, but kept my dozens of four-leaf clovers in jelly jars of water by the window, hoping one or two would miraculously start growing roots again.

I knew I was a pest, but being a pest, being insatiable, obsessed, incurable, was no mortal or even venal sin to us. The only crime was half-hearted pursuit, apathy.

I turned away from them both. "Go away," I said.

I heard my mother murmuring to Nola. "Say you're sorry."

"Sorry for what? He's so spoiled."

"He just had an operation."

Nola walked out of the room and my mother gave my hair a pat. "Get some rest, sweetheart."

I was stung Nola had chastised me, especially with me being sick and all, maybe about to die. She was going to miss me a lot when I died, and she'd feel such guilt she had spoken so harshly. I was going to die that afternoon. I glanced at my Peter plant, hoping that it might start shriveling, but its heart-shaped leaves, trailing over the body of the car planter, were a vivid green.

*　*　*

My activist phase was reactivated at Mercy Hospital in Columbia. There, I organized the kids in the ward to line up their wheelchairs to block the nurses' path until they allowed us to stay up late enough to watch Johnny Carson's opening monologue. We linked arms and wouldn't let the nurses pass.

"The whole ward is watching!" we chanted. "The whole ward is watching!" And "Hell no, we won't go . . . to bed!"

Eventually, they gave in.

After my release, I ran into the Sammies again doing their annual Bounce for Beats fund-raiser in downtown Columbia, and as a veteran, I joined them on their drive. I wanted to be one of the people who bounced the basketball incessantly, but they wouldn't let me because I was a kid. The main bouncer, a baby-faced boy named Terry Dietz (I remember his last name because it rhymed with "beats") smiled nonstop as he bounced. I raised over a hundred and fifty dollars for them, and when Bounce for Beats was over, and the exhausted dribbling Sammy, his hands blackened, was finally allowed to stop, they made me the hero, not him. This time, the entire fraternity as well as their sorority sisters, took me out to dinner and let me order the most expensive thing on the menu: surf and turf. Then they gave me a certificate making Peter Hemley an honorary member of Sigma Alpha Mu, and giving me my own frat pin.

*   *   *

My mother and I drove alongside the highway near our house. The car was moving as slowly as a car can go forward without going backward, me in the backseat, the front door open, the windows all open, rain slashing in, Nola walking alongside, refusing to look in our direction. She was going to New York, back to the Centre of Being, where her Guru, Sri Ramanuja, was telepathically urging her to go.

My mother didn't know what to do. I didn't know what to do. Nola seemed to be the only one who knew what to do. Her head was high, the rain beating her eyes closed, although she seemed sure of her direction.

"Get back in here," my mother yelled.

"Come on, Nola," I said. "It's dangerous."

But she was silent.

"How can you get to New York? You have no money. You don't even know the right direction."

"I'll hitch," Nola said.

"That's dangerous," I said. My panic mimicked my mother's panic. I had never seen her so helpless.

"This is dangerous for all of us," my mother said. "Someone's going to hit us from behind. Look, get in, I'll give you the money."

Nola kept walking.

"Nola, get inside," I said. "Don't be so stupid." I had never called my sister stupid, but it seemed right.

My mother turned in the seat, applied a little pressure to the brake. "Robin, that doesn't help."

"It's dangerous," I mumbled.

Twenty minutes later, we were still coasting down the highway, although we had used up all our arguments, and were silent, as Nola was, while we made our progress toward New York. Nola walked as though she were in a trance, and only at the bottom of the hill, a mile distant from our road, did she stop walking. There was a crossroads there, an I.G.A. supermarket on the right, a gas station on the left. Nola stopped and looked straight ahead. I don't know what made her get back inside, maybe another telepathic message, but she leaned down and sat beside my mother without a word.

"Robin, close her door," my mother said, and I did as I was told, rushing out the backseat as though we were kidnapping Nola, and closing the door before she had a chance to change her mind.

My mother drove to the hospital, Mid-Missouri Mental Health Center, and tried to have Nola committed, but Nola was an adult and refused. So my mother called a couple of her students, around Nola's age, and they came by. I was there. There was nowhere else for me to be. For a while I wandered around the cafeteria. My mother gave me five bucks, which I spent within half an hour, and then I returned with arms full of soda, candy, and chips, and watched these people all try to coax my sister into admitting she was mad.

I wandered off again and eventually made my way to a hallway with glass cases along the walls. I went up to the cases and peered at the objects inside, parts of people floating in clear liquids. In one jar there was a foot, the largest foot I'd ever seen, misshapen and knobby. A head, someone's real head, rested in another jar, filling up most of it like someone who had been born that way, with a jar on his head, and they'd just cut it off, jar and all, when he died, then screwed on a lid. The man had red hair and marks all over his face. The eyes were closed, the lips shut. I knelt beside the head and tried to peek around the back. I could tell that it wasn't the whole head but just the front part, like a mask, only half of the skull with the skin still attached—no brain, just features, rubberlike. Fascinating that someone could be reduced to this. A small plaque rested beside the jar with the head: "Merida, Yucatan, Mexico, Leper." The plaque for the foot read, "Elephantiasis." I liked this place. I munched on taco-flavored Doritos and sipped Dr Pepper while switching my attention back and forth between the leper's head and the gigantic foot. No one paid me the slightest bit of attention. I seemed to fit in. After a while, I went back to the waiting room of the ward where my mom and her students were still trying to talk some sense into Nola.

*   *   *

I took on a job washing dishes after school to support my comic-book habit. I worked at a place called Alfie's Fish & Chips. They hired me even though I was only twelve, but I almost got fired right away. We'd switched for some reason from lemon-scented to peach-scented Joy at Alfie's, but no one had bothered to tell me, and I didn't notice the change when I used it for the first time. As water filled the aluminum dishwashing tub, an overwhelming smell of rotting peaches filled the kitchen. It affected me, made me light-headed, and I stumbled out to the front counter where people were lined out the door. "It smells like rotten peaches back there," I announced in a loud voice. A few people laughed nervously, but several others stepped out of line and walked out the door. Diane, the manager, led me back to her office and explained that if I wanted to succeed in the real world, I couldn't just spit out any damn fool thing that popped into my head.

I nearly quit right then. I didn't like being spoken to that way, even if it was true. I had just wanted to be helpful, after all. And it *had* smelled like rotten peaches. I hadn't lied. I was in a truth-telling phase. Just recently we'd had a mock trial at my junior high for the soldiers involved in the My Lai massacre. I'd played Lt. Calley, and had admitted to everything I was accused of. It had hurt, but not as much as carrying around Calley's awful secret for the rest of my life. My classmates had jeered at me as though I was really Lt. Calley and not playing a role, and that had hurt even more, seemed strange and made me doubt the reality of my world and my perceptions.

Despite my setback at Alfie's, I didn't stay hurt or discouraged for long. I was determined to do good, and the next week at closing time we had a surplus of fish and chips, I knew exactly what should be done with it. I wrapped it up and brought it to Everyday People, a drug rehab center in a three-story frame house next door. I'd never been inside, but had seen the scraggly men and women sitting on the porch, their feet on the railing, some of them asleep, some singing to themselves, a couple looking into the sky as though something awful was going to come raining down on them any moment.

I walked into their midst, cocky with my do-gooder's spirit, sure that I was wanted. I'd hardly set foot in the living room before they descended on me. They rose from those dusty cushions and broken springs, came jouncing down the stairs. A blazing light was turned on in the middle of the room. I don't remember faces, only hands, and being surrounded, and them reaching into the circle and breaking off large chunks of fish, and popping fries into their mouths. They even devoured the extra batter, fried into little crusty tears. They acted like prisoners of war stampeding some scarce Red Cross shipment.

I stood with my offering, small, still in my dishwashing apron. I wasn't frightened, but felt sad, drawn to them. They were orderly and uncontrollable at the same time. They were restrained in the way they grabbed the food. They knew I was smaller and younger, that I was their friend, and maybe they didn't want to frighten me. But their mouths worked monstrously. They did not stop to chew, but seemed to drink the fish. Still, everyone thanked me, some of them incoherently.

When it was over, I still stood there, as though I had something left to offer. But now I only held an empty bucket lined with greasy wax paper. And the POWs had skulked off into their corners, up the stairs, or back onto the porch.

Only one person still paid any attention to me, a skinny man with a ponytail and a minister's collar. He came from the hallway and smiled. We shook hands awkwardly. I tried to use the traditional straight handshake, and he tried to do the newer kind with fingers bent and thumbs clasped. I knew his kind of handshake of course. I just hadn't expected it from an adult minister.

"You saved our hides," he said. "Or their hides, at least. I'm always the last one to chow down around here."

*   *   *

Nola came back home, after spending only a couple of weeks at Mid-Missouri Mental Health Center. That was the pattern for the next year or so: She'd have a psychotic episode, be committed, and then released when she started to seem better. That's one reason I thought she was faking it, at least some of the time. These days, we'd call this denial, deep deep denial, but we didn't have the vocabulary for it then. Another reason was that on some level perhaps *she* believed she was faking it, and she communicated this feeling to my mother one day. "I just tell the doctors what they want to hear," she told my mother, "and then they let me go."

I was sure she was faking it, that she only wanted attention when she'd start speaking in a high-pitched voice before she went to bed. Half the night long, you could hear the blather coming from behind her door—it sounded like some demented parrot, or some delirious child, a jumble of words bunched together in grotesque ways.

Ohprettyohsoprettyyoumustn'tstruggleagainstuswe'rejusthere
tohelpyoubutyoumustn'tstrugglebecauseweknowthat'sbestwe
haveseenyourrapidfireheartwehaveengagedyourspiritwehave
woodspritesforbreakfastohmyprettyohsoprettyyou'resobad
you'resouglyyoudon'tevenhavetheimaganitiontodepart
toleavethistrainofthoughtwheredoyouthinkofgoinganddo
youreallythinkhecanhelpbecausehecan'thecan'theonly
caresabouthimselfhe'sonlyselfishhedoesn'tknowyourtorment

This went on for days and months until it blended into our lives, but still we paused in the hallway and wondered if this could be real, if she wasn't just somehow pretending, just being dramatic like she'd always been. She could act normal if she wanted. She didn't have to be this way, and it made me angry to see her this way. At dinner, I'd tell her to stop chewing her food so dumbly. I'd tell her to stop staring like that.

"Can't you just be normal?" I said.

"Stop it," my mother said. "If you can't be nice, go somewhere else."

And I felt terrible for talking to Nola this way, but I couldn't help it. I wanted to feel terrible—I wanted her to see how easy it was to be normal. My mother, apparently, was thinking much the same. She's told me that she occasionally suspected that Nola was putting on a show, an admission that shocked me, in part because it seemed to be such an honest, guilt-inducing statement, in part because I felt the same and never once suspected my mother of feeling likewise.

I took my meals to my room and ate alone in front of my portable Panasonic TV.

One night, I heard a voice from somewhere in the room, but I couldn't tell from where. "I see you," the voice said, a high-pitched voice, a woman's voice.

I looked around the room. "I see you," the voice said again.

I put my dinner plate down on my bed and looked in the closet. There wasn't anyone there. "I see you."

"Who? Who are you?" I asked, looking up at the light in the center of the ceiling.

"I see you."

I went downstairs to where my mother and sister were talking about me. I stayed hidden by the staircase, just listening. "He's become so odd," Nola was saying. "He used to be so gentle and kind. He doesn't even want to sing anymore and when he does, he doesn't even try. He sings flat and when I try to correct him, he gets angry. He shuts himself off."

"He's spending all his time in his room," my mother said. "He's completely obsessed with his stamps."

I was upset they were talking about me this way. They were right and I knew it, but I didn't like it all the same. I walked through the living room and the two of them bent their heads to their food as though I were a king who had caught his subjects trading state secrets.

"Where's your plate?" my mother said. "Are you finished?"

"No, I just came to say I'm sorry."

Nola and my mother exchanged looks. Nola smiled at me. I really wasn't all that sorry. I was more sorry that they'd been speaking about me, but I couldn't apologize for that. I hadn't meant to say "I'm sorry." What I meant to say was that I was hearing voices, too, and it scared me.

"And there's a voice in my room."

"What do you mean?" my mother asked.

"Someone keeps saying they see me."

"Do you have the windows closed?" my mother asked.

The three of us went upstairs to investigate. I counted to myself, one, two, three and I went up the stairs, one, two, three. When I reached my room, I had to end on the number three. One, two, three, I thought as I walked down the hall. One, I thought and then minced my steps, twothree. I opened the door. My mom and Nola looked inside. We entered, looked around. No spirits. No demons. My dinner plate sat in the same spot I'd left it on the bed. One, two, three, I thought.

"I see you," someone said.

"There," I yelled. "Did you hear that?"

"I see you," the voice said again

"Where's it coming from?" my mother asked.

Nola bent down beside the TV and put her ear to it. "Here," she said. She knelt beside the TV, her hair cascaded around her face and we all waited.

"I see you," the voice said again, clearly this time, from the TV. A week later, we learned its source from a friend of my mother's: Mercy Hospital a mile away—the intensive care unit, where a nurse warned the doctors of arriving patients. Somehow, her voice patched into the same frequency as my TV. "ICU," she chanted, unaware that across town I picked up her warnings and thought they were my own.

*   *   *

I returned one day to Everyday People to offer my services to Jerry, the minister who ran the place. I couldn't decide which I wanted to do more, the suicide hot lines or maybe something to do with ecology. I found an office of sorts, an open room full of light and chatter. Jerry, whose hair was as long as the guys who lounged on the porch, sat at a metal desk lined with black phones. "Major Tom" played from a small radio in the corner of the desk.

"I want to help people," I told him. "I have experience. I'm a crusader from way back."

Jerry smiled and sat back down, searching my eyes.

"Do your parents know you're here?" he said.

"My dad's dead," I said. "He died when I was seven." My well-rehearsed line.

"Oh," Jerry said, getting that sad, thoughtful look adults always did when I gave them that bit of information. He snapped his fingers. "You're the boy with the fish and chips," he said.

"That's right," I said. "I was thinking I could work the phones."

"That takes training," he said. "That takes experience."

He looked unsure, but I had come with a Plan B. I'd always been interested in the environment. I'd even made a banner for my home room: "Earth—Love it or Leave it Alone."

"I've been thinking about starting an environmental group for kids. We could meet here. I want to help people."

"I know you do," he said. "Maybe in a couple of years."

I didn't budge.

Jerry smiled at me again and shook his head. "Do you have a name?"

"Peter."

"No, I meant for your group. Like this is Everyday People. It's a name that people remember. It's a name that gives you a good feeling, just like the song. You know, I thought of the name before I even decided what we'd do here."

"SPEC," I said. "The Society for the Prevention of Environmental Corruption."

Jerry thought it sounded serious and hard-working, and on that basis alone, he gave me an upstairs room for a meeting place. This was a time of feelings and he had a good one about me, he said.

Now I only needed members of the eighth-grade class of Jefferson Junior High with morals and social consciences as highly developed as my own. I was able to scrounge up five of them: three girls and two boys. Of the girls, there was my neighbor Sarah Skolnick, Jill Brinkley, and Jill Peters. The two Jills were easy to recruit because they both had crushes on me at the moment even though I'd hardly ever spoken to either of them before. But one day, they'd strode boldly up to me and told me I had to make a choice between them. Instead, I invited them to the first SPEC meeting. Jill Brinkley had hair so blonde it was almost white, and crusty pimples in a semicircle around her chin. I think calamine lotion was her pimple method. Jill Peters was tall, almost a foot more than me. Jill Brinkley chattered constantly and openly adored me. Of the two, Jill Peters was quieter, more dignified. The other two recruits were Sarah's younger brother and Reese Lewis, my locker mate, and a comic collector like myself.

For our first meeting, we met in the room that was also used by the sex education class. Jerry had printed up some flyers for us to pass out downtown. The flyers depicted a balloon rising above cornfields. On the balloon was printed: SPEC (The Society for the Prevention of Environmental Corruption). The gondola was filled with happy waving people. And below the gondola was a little paragraph explaining that SPEC was open to anyone seventeen or younger and a list of proposed projects that Jerry and I had come up with:

1. Clean up Hinkson Creek.
2. Stop Stephens College from using mercury on its golf links, which drains into Stephens Lake and poisons fish.
3. Anti-nuclear power letter-writing campaign.
4. Recycle Trash.
5. Raise consciousness all around Columbia.

The Stephens Lake idea was mine since my mother taught at Stephens, and I'd heard from one of her students about this problem. The rest of the ideas were Jerry's.

At the bottom of the flyer, in giant block letters that looked like the writing of a kid just starting to spell, were the words: **Pleez Recycle This Paper!!!**

After giving us the flyers, Jerry told us we were on our own. The first thing we decided to do was trudge downtown and pass out our flyers. Most of the people we handed the flyers to glanced at us, smiled, said something like "way to go," and then threw the paper in the nearest trash can.

* * *

"Nola tried to kill herself last night," my mother told me one morning on the stairs. Her voice sounded weary. "She's in the hospital now. I didn't get any sleep."

This was a lot of information for me to take in at once. "What about me?" I said, as though this made sense, but I meant, Where was I? How could I have slept through this? And is she all right?

"I didn't want to wake you," my mother said, somehow understanding all I meant in that seemingly selfish sentence.

And that seemed strange, too, that I'd been left alone, sleeping peacefully, while my sister was trying to end her life. There *was* something selfish in what I was thinking. The thought that I'd been left alone and vulnerable in the house, that dangers, which seemed so ready to strike us, swirled around me while I slept, and no one was there to protect me.

"She'll be all right," my mother said. "She's in Mid-Mo again. Somehow, miraculously, she's going to be all right. You know what that stupid girl did? She drank part of a bottle of Lestoil and then she went to the kitchen, ate half a strawberry shortcake slathered with whipped cream. The doctor said that's what saved her life, the whipped cream, that it neutralized the poisons. I don't know what we're going to do about her, Robin. I've got to get some sleep."

And my mother climbed the stairs and went to her room. I stood there for a while and thought about what she'd said. That stupid girl. What are we going to do about that stupid girl? I didn't know. I wasn't feeling well. I didn't feel well enough to go to school.

I knocked softly on her door and she said, "Wait, let me get my hearing aid back on."

A few moments later, she said, "Okay, what is it?"

"I'm not feeling well. I'm not going to school today."

"Okay, get some sleep," she said.

But I wasn't tired. She was the one who hadn't slept all night. Instead, I went back to my bedroom and opened up my closet. My comic-book collection lay at the bottom in neat stacks. I started to sort through them and handled them as delicately as possible. I had put Saran Wrap around most of them, carefully ironing the wrap around the comics so they wouldn't be damaged. I knelt down and unwrapped one, my favorite, *Conan the Barbarian* #1. I liked Conan because he was pretty complex for a barbarian, neither good nor bad, happy nor sad. Things just stood in his way and he took care of them. I also liked *Spiderman*, full of self-doubts, hunted by society, radioactive Peter Parker. I was sort of a backward Spiderman. Most of the time, I felt like I'd been born with radioactive spider powers. I wanted to transform myself into someone normal. I longed to be Peter Parker.

Still, Conan was my treasure. Already, the first issue was worth twenty-five dollars, although it had only been published the previous year. I had two copies. I noticed something I hadn't seen before. One of its staples was missing. How could this be? It hadn't fallen out—it had never been stapled properly. The comic's imperfection wasn't my fault, but that didn't matter. Some of its value was lost. The comic was imperfect. I couldn't live with that.

I turned the comic over and ripped it in half, then ripped it again.

* * *

The next day, Jill Peters tried to show me a few things. She was a doctor's daughter and knew her anatomy. We wrestled on the grass behind my house, out of sight. I was wearing my white bell-bottoms with the patch on the back pocket that read: VOTE. They got all grass-stained.

While we kissed, she kept her eyes closed and I opened mine. I studied her ash brown hair. I wondered if I was too serious, if I worried about consequences too much. Consequences for everything. What was going to happen to the world if people kept polluting it? And the war? And Nola. I looked at Jill and was sad, although I knew I should be happy. I was too young to be unhappy. I looked at her and saw consequences. I worried about getting into the college of my choice, whether my mother would remarry.

Jill guided my hand to her shirt. I pulled away and she opened her eyes and smiled. "How far do you want to go?" she asked.

"I don't know," I said. "How far did you want to go?"

"I thought we could make out for a couple of days," she said, "and then, when we know each other better, we could do some petting, then some heavy petting, and in a little while maybe I'll go all the way."

I sat beside her and thought about her schedule. It terrified me. "You're cute, Peter," she said, "but you think too much. You shouldn't think so much." She mussed my hair like my mom did. She was as tall as my mom. I concentrated, tried hard not to think so much. My mother was going to kill me for getting my new white pants covered in grass.

*   *   *

Jerry allowed me to give the phones a try. I'd begged him enough. He sat behind his desk with a gentle smile. I had never actually expected him to give in. I held the black phone in my lap, my hand on the receiver, staring at it, hoping that during my shift no one would call. No one had told me what to do. Jerry just stared at me.

"What do I do if someone calls?" I asked.

"Just listen," Jerry said. "That's mostly what it takes, a good listener. Are you a good listener, Peter?"

"I don't know."

"Because that's the main thing, listening. If you stop listening, you've lost them. Most people just want to talk and no one listens. That's half the problem with the world. That's something this will teach you. On-the-job training. How to be a listener. How to be a good human being."

"I'll try," I said.

"Because that's the main thing," he said. "Don't stop listening. Listen all your life, okay?"

"Okay."

"But don't worry," he said. "This is a slow time of day. Not many people calling this time of day." He opened a drawer of his desk and took out a pouch of tobacco and started rolling himself a cigarette.

The phone rang. I leapt up, holding the phone as though it had an electric charge and I couldn't let go.

"What do I do?" I asked.

"What do you normally do when the phone rings?" he asked me. He licked the cigarette paper and twisted the cigarette.

I picked up the receiver. I held it close to my ear and whispered, "Everyday People." My mouth felt dry. I listened.

It started as a moan. "Heeeeey . . . maaaaaan," a voice said.

"Everyday People," I said like I was answering the phone for Alfie's Fish and Chips.

"I . . . I neeeeed . . . you," the voice said. The voice was so low, so slow, I wasn't sure if it was a man or a woman.

"Everyday People," I said again, my voice lilting up on the "people," the word coming out "*Peep*hole."

"Help . . . meeeeee," the voice said, so slow.

"Everyday People," I said again. Go away, I was thinking. Just leave me alone. I can't help you.

"I don't . . . want . . . to . . . . live," the voice said.

I looked at Jerry, who seemed to be enjoying his smoke. I placed my hand over the receiver and whispered, "He says he doesn't want to live. What should I do?"

Jerry gave me a palms up shrug, his hands trailing smoke.

"You've got to live," I told the caller.

"Why?"

I placed my hand over the receiver and asked Jerry, "He wants to know why he should live." He covered an eye with his free hand and shook his head. "Are you listening?" he said.

"What's wrong?" I asked. "Do you want to talk about it? I'm listening," but I really wasn't. I couldn't hear what the person was telling me. All I could think of was that I wanted this to end. I didn't want to do this anymore. I wasn't ready. Couldn't they see I wasn't ready? Why were they entrusting me with such a responsibility? I was only twelve, for God's sake. The person on the phone sounded older. Why did they need me?

The caller must have asked me a question. I hadn't responded to anything as he rambled on. I was mostly concerned with the expression on my face. I wanted to have the right expression so that if Jerry looked at me he would see that I looked serious and intent. I said, "Uh-huh, tell me more."

"You don't care, do you?"

"Yes, I care," I said.

"You're bogus," the caller said.

"No, I'm real," I said. "I care."

"I'm going to kill myself and it's your fault."

"Uh huh," I said. "I'm listening." I heard the click. "Well, okay then," I said. "Thanks for calling. I hope you feel better. Come again."

I placed the receiver back in its cradle and Jerry looked at me curiously. There was nothing I could do for the person on the other end of the phone. He was probably dead by now or dying. Gunshot. Jumping. Hanging. Slit wrists. Poison. I wanted Jerry to think well of me.

A door opened. One of the guys who always hung out on the porch walked through. He was laughing and pointing at me.

I didn't get it. Why was he laughing at me? I felt like I had when the TV started saying "I see you." Did everyone know my motives? Could everyone see into my heart and read my intentions? Didn't I have any secrets?

"Bogus," the man said.

Jerry looked at me less harshly, but with less respect than he'd had before. "You weren't listening," he said. "Don't you see, Peter? When you're dealing with other people's lives, when they're in the balance, you need a special sensitivity."

"So he's not going to die?" I asked weakly.

"Let go of your ego, Peter," Jerry instructed me.

I did more than that. I let go of my name. From that time on, I was no longer Peter. I was Robin again, and although it was the middle of the school year, I knew everyone would adapt. I didn't want to be Peter anymore.

But I couldn't speak. I didn't have words for what I wanted to say. I wanted to cry, not only out of embarrassment, but because I'd believed him. I'd believed that there was someone's life in the balance on the other end, and not only some joker calling from the next room. I thought I'd made a terrible mistake, that I'd killed someone. I can't really blame Jerry and the other man for setting me up—it was probably a needed lesson for me. Not everyone wanted to be in my story.

I went home that night, sat in my closet, and sorted through my comics. In another room, someone was talking suicide. I couldn't really make out the words, and anyway, I wasn't listening. Conan was much more fascinating. I flipped through my remaining copy of Conan #1, the copy I hadn't destroyed. I appreciated *everything* about it, the artwork, the story line, the smell of the paper, those perfect staples. The TV was on, of course, and every once in a while, a woman broke in. "I see you," she said, but I knew she couldn't. "I see *you*," I replied, my little joke, and I almost *could* see her, at her nurse's station at Mercy Hospital, sitting still and numb as they rolled in the next poor soul who didn't stand a chance.

The Children's Ward

I had heard of truant officers before, although I had never actually seen one. But there was one in my living room, and I was curious about him, so I sat on the stairs while he talked to my mother as though I wasn't there. He was a black man in a coat and tie, soft-spoken, polite, but grim.

"Mrs. Hemley," he said. "The law says that the boy has to go to school..."

"He says he doesn't feel well," my mother said.

"I *don't* feel well," I said from the stairs, but both of them ignored me.

"Has he been to see a doctor?"

My mother was silent.

"Does he have a temperature?"

"It's my stomach," I said.

"You see, it's very hard," my mother said. "I'm a widow and I teach at Stephens and my daughter..."

"The law says that the boy has to go to school..."

I hadn't ever really expected this day to come, not really. It flabbergasted me that someone actually cared enough to force me back to school. I just assumed that I would go on and on with this pleasant, mysterious malady that my mother rarely questioned. For the past three weeks, I'd been in my pajamas, never washing or changing my clothes, spending most of the time in my room with my comic books. Nola was at Mid-Mo again, Jonny was away at Ohio University, and my mother could only argue with me for so long before she had to go teach. "You've got to go to school," she'd told me at first, before leaving.

But I can't," I said.

"Why not?"

"I don't feel well."

"When do you think you're going to feel well?"

Good question. I didn't think I'd ever feel well enough to go to school again. Jefferson Junior High *was* a horrible place in 1971. Twice, giant fights had broken out between the black students and white students, and the police had to be called in. Police with drug-sniffing dogs routinely swept our lockers, although they rarely found the drugs that any of the seventh, eighth, or ninth graders could have told them about. Even though I wasn't interested in drugs, I knew where they were, too. The school drug pusher had taken me into his confidence. This was a kid who, for fun, blew up cats by sticking firecrackers in their anuses, and is probably dead today or in jail or on death row in Missouri. He took me into his confidence, not because he saw in me a kindred spirit, but because he knew how much he disturbed me. Still the crusader, I'd try to get him to change his evil ways, which only made him relate them to me with more delight. In between classes, at study hall, in the lunch room. He kept his drugs in the well behind one of the fire extinguishers.

I was considered the criminal element at Jefferson. Recently, I'd been brought to the assistant principal on a trumped-up charge of throwing spitballs during a school assembly and running in the halls. A teacher yanked me out of my seat while Captain Safety Belt told us about being safe in traffic. Half of the student body was stoned on the drugs stashed behind the fire extinguisher, but Captain Safety Belt didn't know that. He probably thought he was getting through to us as we laughed derisively at his stupid anecdotes. Adults are such innocents.

The teacher's rage was disproportionate to the offense. I remember thinking that even then as she dragged me through the hall. It was a rage that had to have built up over an entire lifetime of spitballs and running in the hall. I didn't know what she was talking about with the spitballs anyway—I'd never do something so crass. I tried to plea bargain, told her I'd admit to the lesser charge if she'd drop the nonsense about spitballs, but that only enraged her more.

If there is an archetype for assistant principals, then Jefferson Junior High had recently hired the ur-assistant principal: buzz-cut, a Marine poker-up-the-butt bearing, called everyone Mr. or Miss and made these titles sound unclean and disgusting, had perfected the assistant principal stare, which he used to great effect before meting out punishment.

"Mr. Hay-mee-lee," the assistant principal said after staring at me for five minutes.

"Yes, Mr. Sputz?"

"Mr. Hay-mee-lee," he said again.

"Still here," I said, which was probably a mistake.

The man laughed, a little snort, and his body collapsed in his chair. Where before he had been sitting up straight, he leaned forward, his arms resting on his open legs, his tie dangling in front of him. "I love smart kids," he said, emphasizing the word "love," the way someone says "I LOVE fried chicken." "And you're very smart, aren't you?"

"Yes I am," I said, apparently another wrong answer, because the stare intensified, became filled with hate. That's when he gave me my choice. Either he'd paddle me ten times with Betsy or else I could choose to be excused from Assembly . . . for the rest of the year! I was smart enough to know that laughing would spell my doom—he'd probably vaporize me with that stare. Briefly, I wondered who Betsy was, if she was the secretary who'd led me into his office, but then he indicated with a tip of his head the wooden paddle with holes that hung above his desk. I didn't know until that moment that he was so bizarre as to name his paddle Betsy, but I'd heard about him paddling people before. This must have been a large part of his job description because he did it often enough. And the idea of a paddle with holes in it was legendary. The holes made all the difference, in our minds at least.

I tried to look really depressed. I stared at my feet. "I guess . . . I'll just have to miss Assembly," I said finally.

But I just stopped going to school altogether.

After staying out a week or so, I started thinking it would be hard to go back, not just because of the work I'd missed, but because of the other kids. I figured they'd notice, and the teachers would notice, and they'd say something to me. "Why were you gone so long?" "I didn't feel well," was all I'd be able to answer.

After two weeks, I knew the transition would be even more embarrassing. When I'd left, we were finishing up Steinbeck's *The Pearl* in English class. They were probably halfway through *Jane Eyre* by now. And I didn't understand science and math anyway, so two weeks away from those indecipherable languages made them irretrievable to me.

After three weeks, I'd adapted. I knew I was never going back to Jefferson Junior High, and I felt okay about that fact.

Now this man was here in our living room, insisting that I had to go back to my old life. Still, he seemed to be softening a bit. He wasn't quite so grim as he listened to my mother tell him about the assistant principal and the drug pusher and the race riots.

"So you're saying he's not ill, he's just afraid?"

"That might be part of it," my mother said.

"It's my stomach," I said, but neither paid attention.

"No matter what, the boy needs to go to school," the man said. "You're a teacher, aren't you?"

My mother pursed her lips and brought her hand to her ear to adjust her hearing aid.

"I understand your daughter is at the Mental Health Center," the truant officer said. "There's a children's wing there as well. If the boy agreed to counseling, I think I could arrange for him to go school there."

"In the hospital?" my mother said.

"I understand it's not a bad little school," the man said. "He'd have individual attention and . . . counseling."

Only then did my mother and the truant officer turn to me, as though I had suddenly come into the room. It seemed like a good alternative to me: small student-to-teacher ratio, plenty of individual attention (more like scrutiny), and I was already familiar with the location.

*   *   *

The Children's Ward at Mid-Missouri Mental Health Center. This became my new junior high, my alma mater.

The ward was located on the first floor of the hospital, down a quiet corridor: first the classrooms and small offices, then the big double doors that sealed off the ward from the rest of the world at night. Past these doors was something akin to a Hollywood set, the good face of the ward when visitors showed up. There was a common area with comfortable-looking chairs and couches, and a number of small dormlike rooms around this area, as well as a nurse's station.

I was a day patient. I guess I need to make my day-patient status clear because it was an important distinction then, and maybe remains one for me now. I was, in some ways, a visitor, and there were pluses and minuses to this difference between me and the other kids. I could go home at night and they couldn't, although I'm not sure whether that fact was a plus or a minus at the time. There was kind of a makeshift family in the ward, without fathers or mothers, of which I was a part, but not a blood member.

The head of this family was a sixteen-year-old girl who played the guitar all the time on a couch in the common room. I don't know what her real name was, but she called herself Jan after Janis Joplin. Jan had run away from an abusive home so many times that she was considered crazy and locked up. Of course, this was only Jan's version, but I believe her, if only because belief was such a rare and hard currency in the ward. Illusion and disbelief were so much a part of our lives there. Tragedy seemed to leak off the walls like blood in a horror film, but for the most part, the tragedy was kept hidden from everyone. Not that we seemed all that normal and happy, except when we weren't being scrutinized, when we could relax in each other's company. Of course, the more normal and happy we acted, the more we were considered to be in some kind of denial by our doctors. The ones who ran the ward, on the other hand (the nurses, the counselors), preferred denial to acting out. They were the ones who had to deal with us. But we were made to understand by everyone, from the outset, that we had to first acknowledge how miserable we really were in order to be truly happy, that we had to admit all our transgressions and all of our feelings toward others, in public, before we could ever hope to have private feelings again. It was like a second surrender to the religion of a conquering force under whose dominion we already struggled.

There were at least ten other kids who lived and went to school in the ward, but one of the ones I remember most distinctly, besides Jan, was a girl named Mary who had been raped by her father. She was a year younger than me and we hung out a lot together. She'd be really nice one moment and then the next, she'd try to kick you in the balls, if you had them. The person who told me she'd been raped by her father was an intern, a student named Kathryn, who told it to me casually as though I were a colleague.

There was also a toddler named Justin, a tiny boy who hardly spoke at all, and padded around in footed pajamas. He acted and looked like a toddler, but he was actually nearly seven.

An Irish Setter named Ruby patrolled the ward in a kind of dopey way. When she encountered you, she wouldn't growl or threaten but flop down in the middle of the floor and roll over to have her tummy scratched. We all loved her and no one, not even the most disturbed child, ever took advantage of Ruby's vulnerability.

She was, to us, the model patient.

The doctors and nurses considered her a secret weapon, the main thing that kept us, if not sane, then coping at least, a kind of sponge for our worst feelings as we petted her. But to me and the other kids, she was just a dog, a friendly dog, and we all liked her, but she didn't really make anyone's life that much better. When I was in college, I saw some news program that featured Ruby like she was some kind of miracle cure for kid's mental problems. The news footage showed Ruby blissfully nursing a litter of puppies. The children lovingly handled the puppies. I suppose this was considered remarkable, that even troubled children could have feelings of tenderness and warmth.

One thing the news program didn't show was the Time Out Room. This was a small empty room with no windows and yellow concrete walls and no furniture. The only thing in the room was a punching bag. The Time Out Room wasn't in constant use, but when it was, it punctuated all life around it. No matter where you were in the ward, you could hear the solid smacks of a young fist on the bag and the yelling and screaming. Or else there were those whose silence frightened us, those who refused to scream. And there was Jan who not only refused to scream but refused to stay silent and refused to admit any cure within this ward as she sat against a wall, thrumming an invisible guitar, and singing.

According to the other kids on the ward, my friends, they were kept there for up to twenty-four hours, let out only for bathroom breaks, sometimes not even for that. I never stayed in the ward overnight, so I don't know for sure whether that's true. A man I know, a child psychologist, has since told me that this is impossible, that such a thing never would have happened. He refused to even admit the possibility. He seemed, I suppose, in professional denial.

Everything was therapy, every activity. Everything. There was a kind of imposed self-consciousness to our lives that has stayed with me ever since, that I've never been able to shake. People didn't do things with us because they wanted to but because it somehow was helping us. And, of course, there was a look that went with that helpful attitude. It was a sidelong glance that turned into a beaming smile if you caught it. It was a tone of voice, too, a friendly, cheerful big-top voice that didn't fool us for a minute. Its extreme friendliness simply made us suspicious, because there was something scared behind it, something patronizing. And we could tell. We weren't a dumb group. That might have been part of the problem. Our counselors were young students at the University of Missouri and we were their textbooks, but we studied them as much as they studied us. And I *can* speak for all of us, because we talked about the counselors, in low voices, those of us who could talk.

On the other hand, I liked my psychiatrist a lot. Transference, I guess it's called, and it's natural in the patient/therapist relationship. She was my mother: a mother who gave me an hour twice a week and whose full attention I had for that short time. Her name was Karen Orloff, and she let me call her Karen.

She'd start off with a simple question, such as, "Robin, your mother tells me that you've been spending a lot of time in your room. What do you do there?" and I'd just start talking. I wanted to please her.

Karen was cheerful, but soft-spoken. She didn't overpower me the way some of the counselors did. She seemed genuinely interested

School, too, was therapy, of course. Acting class, for instance. No better therapy, they thought. "Close your eyes, Robin, and fall backward into my arms." That's developing trust, they thought, but they were wrong. I could fall backward into their arms all day long with my eyes closed, and that didn't mean I trusted them any more or less. It just meant I knew they weren't going to let me fall and hit my head—I might sue, for all they knew.

So much for trust. But it was acting class, so I acted as though I was learning something. School was at least fun at Mid-Mo. We all had tutors, a one-for-one teacher/student ratio. Of course, they weren't simply teachers, but students who wanted to work with emotionally unstable children. We were their textbooks. Every expression on our faces, every inappropriate outburst was a bookmark, an assignment, a topic for future discussion.

In art class, I made a gun with a revolving barrel out of wood. I loved the gun but it wasn't my idea to make it. And to say I *made* this gun is not really true either. I didn't have the skills to make the gun, but that didn't matter. My art teacher made the gun for me. Perhaps he made guns for all of us, and considered this some expression of our deep-seated rage, but more likely, it was only an expression of *his* deep-seated rage or his boredom working with damaged kids who responded only to symbols of destruction.

My life was busy, eventful, fulfilled even, in the Children's Ward. I had personal attention, a good education, friends with whom I could relate. There were few of the usual adolescent cruelties among us—we understood one another, and even when we didn't, we sympathized, at least with each other. We were on the same side.

*   *   *

"We're having visitors today," one of the counselors told us one afternoon.

"Oh, visitors," Jan said, clapping like a seal. She held Justin on her lap and he looked up at her with something approaching a smile.

The counselor, a serious guy named James who was wound tight and didn't seem cut out for this job, scratched an eyebrow.

"That's right," he said, and he gave us a look like he was our dad or something.

We were all sitting in front of the TV watching *The Electric Company* and Ruby lay on her back. I was scratching her tummy.

"Girl Scouts," he said. "They're coming here to sing Christmas carols."

"Shit," said Jan. She looked at him like he was crazy. "What, we're some troop project? They're going to come in and pity us and sing to us and bring us all the joy of the season?"

"How come no one told us about this?" I asked.

"It wasn't me," said James. "I didn't arrange it, but it's not so bad. Just enjoy it, okay?"

When the Girl Scouts showed up an hour later, they marched in single file down the hall and lined up in their cookie-cutter uniforms in front of the TV. I'd feel sorry for them now—they looked terrified, with feathery smiles and wide eyes, backs straight.

I'm afraid we did not bring honor to the Children's Ward that day. We sat on the sofas in fake stupors as the scoutmaster whispered something to her girls. We were slumped together our tongues lolling, making mild buzzing sounds.

"Hark, the herald angels sing!" the twelve Girl Scouts sang and we came to life. We stood up and approached the girls slowly, like zombies. James and the two other counselors on duty picked us off the girls, but there were too many of us. We just kept coming in waves. My arms hung loose at my sides and I made gurgling sounds. "Rudolph the red-nosed reindeer," the girls sang over the pandemonium. The Girl Scouts somehow held their ranks, kind of like that old film *Zulu*, in which thousands of Zulus attack a thin line of British soldiers who fend off one massive assault after another.

They made it through three songs. Perhaps they earned badges that day. We didn't. We lost our TV privileges for a week.

*   *   *

I roamed the halls when we had breaks during the day. I was allowed that much freedom because I was only a day patient. The leper's head became my shrine. I visited it almost every day. I stared at it, even talked to it, and always tried to look behind the ears to see whether it was a whole head or just the face. If the doctors had been smart, they would have seen the therapeutic potential here.

I'd sign out of the Children's Ward and go up to the adult ward sometimes to skulk around. I was allowed because I had a sister in there, and this gave me a special status that made up for my lack of status as a day patient within the Children's Ward. The other kids could only go as far as the elevator with me and they'd follow me out there and watch the doors close. They'd wave as if I was going on a moon launch or ascending to heaven.

"Bring us back something," Jan said once and laughed.

I knew all the people on Nola's ward. They weren't at all like the way crazy people are played on TV or in the movies. You didn't have a lot of wailing and people mumbling, standing off in corners, or bashing themselves in the head. You didn't have people holding lively conversations with imaginary beings. They weren't violent. I never saw an outburst in that ward. There wasn't much drama at all, except what came through the TV, which was always on. Most of the patients sat around it. There was no Time Out Room in this ward, and instead of Ruby, they had a fish tank.

I suppose most of them were doped up—that part's true from the movies, but doping them up didn't necessarily make them into zombies. Boredom did that. Loneliness and despair.

I'd go up there and wave at all the in-patients. I had a crush on Nola's best friend in the ward, a girl named Melanie who wanted to be a dancer. I never knew what was wrong with Melanie. She was always laughing and telling jokes. And there was a guy named Jack, an older man who had run out of money halfway through a sex-change operation. He had enormous boobs, but that was the only thing that looked different. At first, I was scared of him, but he was friendly and won me over with card tricks. He wasn't very good. You could always see him palming a card and whenever he asked you to pick a card, it was the wrong one. But he always acted cheerful about it. "One of these days, I'm going to get it right. By sheer dumb luck."

"Keep on trucking," I said. I had no idea what that phrase meant, but I said it a lot. It was just one of those things you said.

I went to the ward at least once a week. It had the feel sometimes of Everyday People, full of freaks, and "freaks" didn't mean people who were outcasts but the vanguard of the new society, kids who had expanded their minds with LSD and other hallucinogens, or expanded their minds naturally like my sister. The only problem was that the process wasn't always pleasant. Sometimes there wasn't room for expansion. Sometimes the mind imploded rather than expanded.

I loved going up to Nola's ward because she and I had a chance to talk and sing and play around. She seemed more normal and happy there than at home. We talked about everything. Once, we sat on her bed, and while she picked out chords, I started telling her about a past life. I had never remembered a past life before, although I had heard Nola and my mother talk about them.

"It was in France, a long time ago, in the 1800s," I said. "I think it was near the water, but near mountains, too. I think it wasn't too far from Spain." I imagined the scene as a small coastal village. I could see gulls wheeling, cobblestone streets.

Nola stopped strumming and put her guitar aside.

"I was a doctor," I said. "I never wanted to accumulate money. I just wanted to help the peasants, and I never had much. I loved French gourmet foods, though, and I ate a lot of peasant bread."

Nola smiled. "You have the oddest palate, even now," she said. It was true. I never ate a balanced meal. Either I ate tacos and pizza, or dry cereal straight from the box or else swordfish almondine, frog legs, and caviar. Sometimes I spent my allowance on little jars of bad caviar, which I'd eat on saltines. This, of course, was further proof of a past existence.

"What happened after you died?" Nola asked.

After I died? I hadn't even told her about my life as a French country doctor and already she wanted to know what happened after I died.

I saw myself, or an older version of myself, lying in a four-poster bed in a bare room with white walls and a small open window above the bed. I was coughing and hacking.

"I was choking," I said, "and I was all alone. Then I was outside of my body, watching it. A friend of mine came into the room but didn't see me. He knew I was dead and looked very sad."

"Yes, and what happened after that?" Nola asked.

"I don't know," I said. "I can't remember."

Nola picked up her guitar again and began to tune it.

"I saw a light," I said "It wasn't just bright like ordinary lights. It was dazzling."

"What color was it?" she asked.

"It was very white and clear," I said, trying hard to remember. "And it kept pulling me upwards. It had other colors in it, but they were so mixed with the white you couldn't really see them."

"What did you do then?" she asked, still tuning the guitar, but glancing over at me.

"The light wanted to pull me up, but I didn't feel worthy. It was too bright for me. I turned away and started to go down."

"What happened after this?" she asked.

I stood up from the bed. Why was she asking me all this? "I've told you everything I remember."

"What happened after this?" she asked again.

"I don't know. I don't remember."

I felt sad because I hadn't reached that light and I had disappointed Nola by not remembering everything. She patted the bed beside her and told me to sit down. She smiled and I sat. She started singing, "Oh, I was born in East Virginia, North Carolina I did roam."

"Nola?" I said, but she kept on singing.

"There I met a fair pretty maiden. Her name and age I do not know."

"Nola?"

She stopped.

"You know, I hope that next time I get to that clear light," I said.

She nodded.

"I don't know if I'll make it, but I'm sure going to try."

"I'd rather be in some dark holler," she sang, "where the sun refuse to shine, than to let her be another man's darlin' and to know she'll never be mine."

"Why don't we die at the same time," I said, "and make up our minds to go there? If we both asked together, maybe they'd take us."

Nola laughed and stopped singing. "Maybe," she said.

*   *   *

Like any school, we had a Christmas play. Ours was "A Christmas Carol," and I won the starring role as Scrooge. Tiny Tim was played by Justin, who couldn't even say his one line. Bob Cratchett was played by a boy named Todd, whose parents and brother and sister had died in a car crash that only he had survived. There didn't seem to be anything wrong with Todd as far as I could tell, except maybe he was a little on the meek side. He seemed to be scared of everything and sometimes his speech would become all fragmented and clogged up. But other than that, he seemed just fine. He seemed perfect for Cratchett.

I took my role seriously and memorized my part. My mom was in the audience the night of the play, and so was Nola, and until the moment the play began, I actually believed that we might be able to perform. I wanted to perform. Most of the others had done fine in rehearsal, but what I hadn't counted on and didn't even realize at the time was what the effect of seeing the audience must have had on the others. In the front row were Jan's parents, the ones she'd run away from so many times. The audience was full of problems, conflicts, reasons for taking medication and running away.

In the first act, I was visited by all three ghosts of Christmas at once. Bob Cratchett broke into a blubbering fit. Everyone but me froze or forgot completely what to do. Jan, who played Marley's Ghost, seeing all was lost, came out carrying Tiny Tim in one arm and her chains in the other. She put both burdens down onstage and started singing and clapping "Piece of My Heart." She was the only one who really seemed into it. I didn't know what to say. Everyone was upstaging me. All I could do was stand there yelling "Bah Humbug" until the small audience started applauding and the show was over.

*   *   *

Mid-Mo had its reward systems. If you behaved you were given certain privileges. Adults like Nola had day privileges. If they did all right, they could go outside the hospital for most of the day and return at night. Nola was granted these privileges after two weeks, and she got involved with a community gallery that agreed to do a showing of some of her drawings and paintings. Her paintings were basically depictions of her constant visions, Blakean drawings of fairies and sorceresses and winged beasts. As paintings, they were acceptable, even admirable, as long as she stopped believing in them. Nola told her doctors what they wanted to hear. They thought these paintings were a great outlet.

The kids in my ward were also granted certain freedoms if they told the doctors what they wanted to hear. As a day patient, I had all the freedom in the world, but my friends didn't. Sometimes they went on field trips and I often went with them. Little by little, my friends were allowed to walk the halls of the hospital beyond the Children's Ward, to go to the cafeteria, for instance.

Mary and I made up a game one day, a kind of tag. We called it Ghost Tag, and its object was to make yourself invisible to as many people as possible. For all the people who didn't notice you, you were awarded a point. For all unidentified people who noticed you, five points were taken away. If one of the staff noticed you, ten points were taken away. Same for grown-up patients. Negative points could accrue if you kept on being noticed, and the only way to stop it, to keep from being reborn (to the ghosts, a kind of death), was to make it back to the leper's head, our home base.

The game held all kinds of risks, especially for Mary who had certain privileges, but those did not include playing Ghost Tag. Those privileges did not include riding the elevator up and down and pushing all the buttons. So the game had an edge, but Mary had an edge, too. We were all edges.

The elevator was the hospital kind with wide doors on both sides. When someone stepped inside one door, we turned around and faced the other side before they could make eye contact or so hello, thereby maintaining our invisible status and not losing any points.

One guy got on and said, "Jesus, did you kids do this?" He meant the buttons, but we didn't say anything. We were ghosts. Still he had noticed us, so I whispered to Mary, "Minus Five." She nodded, and we resumed our stances. At ease.

The Jesus-did-you-kids-do-this Guy got off on the next floor and Jack stepped in. I could tell it was Jack even though my back was turned because he said hi to me. I didn't want to say hi back. For one thing, I'd lose points. For another, outside of the ward, he was not my friend. I didn't know him. He was famous in the hospital, and the other kids knew him as Half Man/Half Woman. As long as I was with Mary, that's what he was to me, too.

"I'm going up to seven," Jack said. "That where you're going, too, Robin? Going to visit Nola?"

Mary and I exchanged looks and said, "Minus Ten," then "Jinx," because we'd both said "minus ten" at the same time. So neither of us could talk.

He faced the way we were facing. He was dressed in men's clothes today. Sometimes he wore women's clothes, but today he wore a baggy Pendleton shirt and overalls. The doors opened and no one got on or off. He stood beside Mary. The doors closed and he pushed seven again, even though the button was already lit up. He pushed the "Close Door" button, too. Mary and I just stood still, both of us giggling a bit. Mary started swinging her foot back and forth and tapping the metal plate right below the elevator buttons to the rhythm of "Jingle Bells."

"I love Nola," Jack said. "She's so sensitive and bright. You're lucky to have a sister like her. I have one sister and one brother. How many kids do you have in your family, Robin?"

The door opened and closed again.

"I'm working on a new card trick," he said.

I looked at the numbers and the Half Man/Half Woman finally shut up.

The doors opened and he walked briskly away from us, although it was only the sixth floor. I almost called out after him, "Keep on trucking," but stopped myself. The damage was already done, of course. We'd both lost a lot of points, me especially. Our death forces had been dangerously sapped.

*   *   *

We dropped into a crouch as we entered the common area of the ward. A few of the patients were glued to a soap opera, so we didn't have to worry about them noticing us, and I could hear a guitar coming from one of the rooms.

"Robin!"

It was my mother. She was standing near the nurse's station. What was my mother doing here? She never visited during the day. Had she checked in, too? Had Mid-Mo become my family's Holiday Inn? I went to my mother and Mary followed.

"What is she?" Mary asked, wanting to know whether she was worth negative or positive points.

"She's my mother," I said.

"Oh!" Mary said.

"What are you doing here?" I asked.

"We're taking Nola home," my mother said. "Who's your friend?"

"Minus five," Mary said.

We went to Nola's room. She was strumming a very strange acoustic version of a song from *Oklahoma!* while Melanie marched around.

They both looked so happy, my mother, too, as she watched.

"No one told me you were going home," I said to Nola when she was finished.

"I'm ready to go home," she said.

She seemed completely normal to me. She smiled. Her eyes were bright. She spoke in her own voice.

I had lost a lot of points. I turned to Mary to tally up our scores, but she was gone, or had truly turned invisible.

I found her by the leper's head on the first floor. Home base.

Mary tried to kick me in the crotch. I fended off her kicks and she stopped after three tries. It was pent-up energy. I had seen it coming.

*   *   *

I had a new psychiatrist. I called him Dr. Silence, even to his face, when I spoke to him at all. I hated him because he never said anything, or very little. Worse, he made me want to say nothing. And he was not Karen Orloff. No one had ever given me a reason why I had to switch, except maybe it went back to that Freudian notion of transference, and the first psychiatrist/mother, like my real one, was too permissive. Maybe the real issues, they figured, were with my father, with whom I had about as much chance of communicating as with Dr. Silence.

Every once in a while Dr. Silence would shift in his chair and say, "What are you thinking, Robin?"

And I'd answer, "Silence, Dr. Silence." I'd say it out loud, and he didn't quite know what to make of that.

"You want me to be silent?" he asked once.

"Silence," I said in as nonthreatening a way as possible. I knew I could say no more than that because he'd pounce on it. He'd use it as a wedge.

And then he was silent and I was silent and we passed week after week this way until one day he told me he was transferring me to Group Therapy.

*   *   *

A boy she'd met at Mid-Mo had come to visit Nola at home. My mother was working in her study, grading papers. My mother heard Nola go into her room. She heard their voices, then the front door slammed. My mother didn't think anything of it. She went back to work.

But then Nola didn't return and she didn't return and then it was the next day and the day after that.

Nola was gone, disappeared, vanished.

At Stephens College they told my mother to prepare her reappointment file.

Someone, a student, accused her of being a witch.

We had no idea where Nola was, if she'd been kidnapped, if she was alive. My mother could barely keep her mind focused enough to teach.

*   *   *

"We have some visitors today." Those dreaded words. This time, they weren't a pack of Girl Scouts, but students and teachers from the University of Missouri, and you couldn't even see them. They were behind the mirror. I sat on the couch in front of the mirror and if I peered closely, I could see their smoky figures.

There were twenty of us in a circle, many of them my friends from the Children's Ward, but a lot of them were strangers, kids like me who spent part of their lives on the outside.

"Does anyone mind?" Gary asked in his big-top voice.

I raised my hand. "I do."

Gary peeked at a stack of papers in his lap. "Oh! *You* do," he said in that same friendly tone, but somewhat surprised. "Why do you mind . . . Robin?"

"Yeah, why do you mind?" Jan said. She sat across from me, and I didn't expect this from her, hands folded in her lap. This was only my second time in Group, and I was learning that things were different here, off-balance. The people you could normally trust said strange things.

"Why can't they come out here and join us?" I asked. It seemed like a reasonable question to me, but everyone looked at Gary and then at me like I'd just said the dumbest thing. Gary's smile broadened.

"I think Robin feels threatened by something," Jan said. "I wonder what it is."

My bewilderment turned to anger, almost hatred. I glared at Jan, but I addressed Gary, "Why do you ask if we mind if we can't do anything about it?"

Gary looked thoughtful. "What I think I'm hearing ... " he said.

Uh-oh. After one session I already knew that "What I think I'm hearing" was the preface to all kinds of trouble. It was code. It meant page 251 of some textbook. It meant an A in a course in child development. It was a board game, like Clue. The murder weapon. Or Monopoly. Community Chest. It meant Gary could advance his token. It was Gary's chance to show off. That's why we had observers.

"Go ahead," I said. "Talk. Observe. I don't mind."

But it was too late. I was the subject of discussion, and for the next half hour we discussed how uncomfortable I felt being discussed and observed by hidden strangers. This brand of therapy seemed more about manipulation and control than about helping anyone. Gary said he heard hostility. Big insight. Gary made me wish for the relative tranquillity of Dr. Silence. I was Dr. Silence's protégé. He had taught me so much.

I went to Group twice a week, and after that first session, I shut up. I never objected to anything. I figured if I was silent they couldn't attack me.

I always sat in front of the mirror. I mugged at it, spent half the sessions turned toward it and not the group, trying to discern the shadowy figures inside. I heard things, Jan talking about her family life, Todd talking about the death of his family. There was a lot of talk about trust. I had none of it. My only ally was Mary, who never said a word about her dad, who never shared. We looked at each other across the room, and I could tell what she was thinking, and she could tell what I was thinking. "Minus five, minus ten," the numbers clocking off into the negative hundreds.

I scratched out curse words in the dust of the mirror, or nonsense words, just to keep them on their toes, to keep them guessing.

Shiva and all men's souls, I wrote one day, but they didn't seem to notice, or if they noticed, they made no obvious motions or sounds behind the smoky glass. They were little gods in there, and I wanted them to show themselves, to make themselves wholly visible, to let me know how I fit into the plan.

*   *   *

Now, so many year later, a piece of paper in Nola's handwriting flutters out of one of her portfolios as I'm looking through her artwork. And I'm handed another clue. It's dated November 18th with a question mark. My mother says that Nola often was unaware of the date or time of year when going through a psychotic episode; hence the question mark. Nola was always making lists, writing instructions to herself. Here, Nola was trying to make order out of the disorder she felt, trying to plot a future:

> red suit, black top
> & woolen dress
> > November
> > 18?

Portfolio
Address
Write.   Tomorrow—3 things to iron
tomorrow morning
Pratt—
#1 buy portfolio
& put all art materials in
it. Then see what procedure
is for submitting portfolio
to Pratt Art Institute—
Write to pratt—via envelopes
You have with you. & This Paper.
It is in Brooklyn Have to
Go to Library tomorrow and
See about address. Also Go through
Envelopes (open bag)—and find
Job papers & enquire about
Jobs.
Tomorrow you are wearing
a grey pants and a black top

& your grey hat and brown
belt—sock it to 'em—
Get ad made up tomorrow
For art exhibit—or buy your
            Own paper and do it your
                        self.
Also—see about job in Philly
~~You could try to~~
~~borro~~
Have your guitar
sent from home and
your *Irish harp*
Call Mother
about it
instantly.
Go there on Thanksgiving and
bring your
guitar back
there
so you could
play it
here.

Nola was in Camden, New Jersey, where Sri Ramanuja had another ashram. By this time, she and her friend had already hitched from Columbia to Long Beach, where they'd split up. My mother doesn't remember hearing from her at Ida's, but she must have. My mother would have told Ida that Nola was missing, and Ida would have reported right away that Nola was safe. My mother also can't remember how many days had gone by before she first heard from Nola, but she reminds me that every day for a parent in this situation is "an agony."

I'm sure Ida tried to convince Nola to stay awhile, but Nola only thought of her Guru. I'm not sure how long she stayed at Ida's, but not long enough for my mother to fly there. From Long Beach, Nola traveled to her Guru's Camden ashram. But she wanted the impossible: independence as well as spiritual guidance. As she'd written in her letter to Sarada: "About dependency—If you depend on Guru to get you through life, what happens to the American axiom of self-sufficiency? Of facing up to one's problems oneself, of mastering them oneself without a crutch?"

The ashram wasn't enough for her. Guru wasn't enough. So she decided to apply to art school—undoubtedly Ida's practical influence, my mother thinks. Ida's sister Carrie had graduated from Pratt. In the interim, Nola took a job as a waitress. This was against Guru's advice, according to a later letter I have from Alo Devi to Nola. And it *was* a big mistake, but not necessarily for the reasons Alo Devi gave Nola. I can't imagine an odder waitress than Nola, a woman whose food talked to her, who felt psychic vibrations from eggs. I imagine her weeping over bacon, hash browns, and eggs-over-easy as she served them. Or at least listening to their sad stories. On a piece of paper from around that time she's written, "I have become a monstrosity. I cannot digest anything that is cooked because the souls of the food cry out inside me—look, I have been cooked—how could you eat the food of the dead? I cannot eat dead and dying things, and yet this severs me from the best of the world. Oh, demons of the earth and air? Why am I losing my"—

My mother received a postcard from Nola addressing her as Mrs. Hemley. Whether out of estrangement or psychosis, I don't know, although my mother prefers to consider the latter. But I think Nola thought my mother was against her, that my mother simply didn't understand the plain on which she lived her life. She wasn't sick at all, but merely misunderstood.

Life at the ashram didn't work out. And art school didn't either. Perhaps she thought she had been granted an interview telepathically. Whatever the case, notes to herself could not keep her mind focused. A cacophony of other voices distracted her and she withdrew further and listened but did not know how to act.

*   *   *

One afternoon, my mother received a call, and I hovered around her as she talked. She seemed to be listening intently to what the caller was saying. She seemed grim and sometimes nodded, but barely said a word. I wondered who it was. I wondered if it was about Nola, if they'd found her, if she was dead. I prayed that she wasn't dead. I concentrated all my energy into that thought.

When my mother hung up, she turned to me. "That was the hospital, Robin," she told me. "They said that you're not making any improvement, that you're getting worse. They say you won't cooperate, and they're thinking of having you declared a ward of the state. That means that they'd take you away from me and make you stay in the hospital." She rattled all of this off in a weary voice, like some prisoner of war simply parroting a concocted script. Then she walked away and put her hand on the banister. "I'm going upstairs for a nap. Wake me if anyone calls. I'm turning off my hearing aid."

I stood there trying to make sense of what she had just told me.

I looked at my choices.

* * *

I look now, twenty-five years since that time, at another piece of loose paper on which my sister has written a kind of credo, explaining why she didn't want to be sane. I think that she wrote it at Mid-Mo, although I can't say for sure. Perhaps she wrote it at the ashram.

> If I fall from God, my mind will perish [and vice versa.]
>
> I looked at buzzards and crows and behold, they became robins and sparrows and doves.
>
> What is this fear that pulls me down? Fear of making things too easy, or rather the desire for it?
>
> Nerves.
>
> The desire to be mad as an exercise of free will.
>
> God hears me in the night and day of my soul.
>
> They gave me their hungry, lethal, angry blood, but it tasted sweet in my mouth. My mouth, if it be of God, can taste only what is sweet.
>
> I want suddenly to go to the nearest church which looks like a cathedral and pray there, because the atmosphere here is not, for the most part, auspicious.
>
> Why do I not rise up in the face of evil to defend myself? Is it timidity?

Of course, this credo doesn't make complete sense—if it made sense, that would be self-defeating. What does that first line mean? The words "or vice versa" were penciled in later. The "or vice versa" throws me off. "If my mind perishes, I will fall from God?" I can't understand that. But maybe my sister did. Maybe the closer she came to that pure light, the harder she was rebuffed, and thrown back into herself. Maybe she needed to die. Maybe that's why she wanted to kill herself. I see now that she was just as afraid of her madness as I was afraid of mine. She said that it was an exercise of free will, but she feared that it was not.

Perhaps the *desire* to be mad was an exercise of free will, but madness itself, was not. With madness came a loss of free will, an institutional loss at the very least, and I didn't want to lose my freedom. I didn't want to become like my sister. I wanted to turn away from madness. I didn't want to be a ward of the state.

I wanted to be sane. I decided to be sane. I would cooperate.

I didn't want to disappear.

Listener

... My mind improved, and I made many discoveries in silence. I learned that too much speech perjured the Real, and that talk was hallowed by its brevity. The substances of things always awaited me inside their appearances, but in order to see them the crust of the thoughts I habitually formed had to be weathered away. My mind caught the snatches of invisible harmonies; I was moved by the noise of dissonant birds and listened at the bayside for the sound of wild gulls. I heard a soft chanting coming from earth and sky, which I later identified with the music of the spheres. The songs of ocean gods lured me to rocks that were furthest from the sand. I followed the laughter of water sprites who pranced toward me on every wave. I developed a compassion for everything that lived, acknowledging the holy in each shoot of grass. I grew more and more conscious of the cure which crept steadily into me, and of the God who was effecting it. I became even more of a visionary mystic, able to catch, like Blake, the sight of Heaven in a flower.

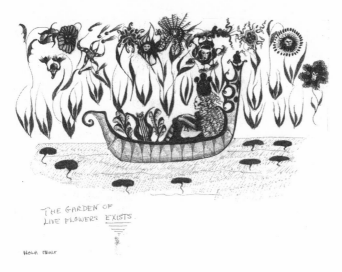

THE GARDEN OF LIVE FLOWERS EXISTS.

NORA HEALY

The Woman Who Was Absent

A short story by Elaine Gottlieb

In the Density of Dream where she was someone else if not more intensely herself, where she danced with or was embraced by a man known in the dream but unknown in her fitful widow's life, where she went into a strange house, trying to obtain the secret of the woman who was absent, where, frightened, she rode a horse bareback, Stella woke, full of curiosity and longing, and answered the phone.

It was someone inviting her to dinner, another widow with two sons, asking her to come with Nancy and Mack, assuming Nancy was well enough. Stella said yes without thinking and went back to sleep, trying to reclaim the dream, as if she had to look deeply into the body of memory where mislaid passions were pursued and lost connections found.

She could hear the TV vibrating through the floor, voices without words, and she knew Mack was down there, his hand in a box of dry cereal, probably sipping a Coke, not even watching TV but needing it on, occasionally glancing that way, raising his head from a comic book or his stamp collection.

On the main highway outside her house cars rushed toward the northern or southern parts of the state; the rumble of freight trains, the whistle and roar of jets, the street-shaking trucks often distracted and woke her, roused her from nightmares that flowed into her daughter's nightmares, familiar as if they were her own. Then there was the TV and the rock records her son played. She had tried to withdraw. It seemed to her that there was a time when withdrawal was possible. Nancy had always known how to do it, meditating, playing classical records, locking herself in her room, or simply walking elsewhere.

I must get up, Stella told herself—there are things to do—there was some formula she hadn't hit upon, something Nancy would respond to. What would interest her? Last night Nancy hadn't wanted to go to sleep, and sitting at the edge of her daughter's bed, Stella had to listen to: Where am I going? What will become of me?

Something terrible is about to happen. The world will end violently. A cataclysm ... Then the incoherent syllables, the "voice" distorting words. Stella, growing tired, had soothed the girl and tried to get her to sleep, but her closed eyes meant little; she awoke and stared about with terror and grabbed Stella's arm each time she tried to leave. Don't go away ... I'll kill myself ... Finally, next to the girl, Stella lay down to rest, until she could creep guiltily into her own bed, next door.

Looking out the window Stella thought of all the average families in the world, envied her own family a few years ago, when she might have awakened and exclaimed: What a lovely fall day!

It seemed to be a mild sunny day. Through the window she saw a pale blue sky segmented by the leafless maple. A cumulus cloud hung among its branches and sunlight sifted through a trail of mist. Surely the rain that had been predicted could not come; summer would continue to collect around the town. After dinner last night she had gone out briefly to find the full moon enchanting the wasted garden; the air was almost warm and she had thought of how such a night might have suggested magic and miracles to her husband and herself a few years ago. But Nancy's mind last night was like the full moon, illuminating specters that swelled in her phosphorescent vision.

Stella listened to sounds from her daughter's room. There was not even a tossing now, though often she had been wakened by the frenzied grinding of springs beneath her daughter's body.

Birds seemed to be flocking past the window, but then Stella saw that they were brown leaves spinning in the wind. There was a song about a bird that Nancy liked to sing. It was a sad song and when Nancy sang it her perfectly pitched soprano seemed to carry the bird higher before it fell than the words actually intended. Stella almost did not know why she liked the song so much except that it meant not only Nancy to her but Icarus perhaps.

Stella opened her daughter's door carefully. Ever since Nancy's attempt at poisoning herself a few months before, Stella had found it necessary to spy on her daughter, to fear prolonged silences, to see that she went nowhere alone. At the same time she kept trying to divert the girl, to entertain her, to suggest what she might do with herself the rest of her life, supposing cure, demanding it, encouraging her to sing, draw, write, and model in clay. At the hospital Nancy had distinguished herself in art therapy sessions. Stella studied the clay figures Nancy had shaped, some with spread arms, others with elongated throats as though trying to find something beyond the limits of sight. On the occasions when Nancy protested that her life was over since she could no longer think of returning to college for a doctorate, Stella had insisted: You can be an artist.

How orderly her room was . . . papers filed away, drawers tidy, clothes hanging free in the closet. It was so easy to look at the room until one came to the bed to see the tightly tucked-in, bunched-up form, the long hair escaping from the pillow held over her eyes.

A sour smell arose from the bed, mingling with the pervasive scent of perfume. Nancy, though she always claimed to be cold, and encrusted herself with too many blankets, was constantly sweating.

Stella raised the windowshade and looked at the layer of brown and gold leaves on the grass. Through the bared trees that covered the hill behind her house, the river glistened.

Dazzling! she said aloud, and immediately heard her daughter turn, shifting her body as though it were in chains. Nancy grunted and then opened her eyes all at once, not a mere slit, as others did, but fully awake and without any sense of boundaries between sleep and daylight. The terror that existed in one state leaped into another. Yet for a moment Stella thought she saw in those eyes the girl of a few years ago who had won all the prizes and was elected to all the honor societies. Surely that mind could be reconstituted . . .

Do you want to go out? she asked.

I'm so tired, Nancy said. I wake up tired . . . Her eyes began to look vague. Then the dreaded "voice" emerged from Nancy's altered mouth, the message garbled, idiotic.

Stop it, Nancy!

The expression Nancy fixed on Stella had become hostile, almost obscene.

It's only yourself, Stella said. Tell it to stop . . . She kissed the girl's forehead.

Nancy's eyes queried, as though weighing the possibility that her mother might be correct. All night, she said, it's been talking to me. I can't get away from it . . .

Stella sat down and clasped the tormented face to her breast. Don't listen, she said, stroking the hair, pushing the distraught hair from her daughter's face. She hugged her, clasping the deceptively strong looking shoulders, pressing to herself the chest that had so often choked with asthma. She wished she could cure by touch. For a while the girl lay back, her eyes vacant. Through her loose night-gown the full breasts rose and fell rapidly.

Don't let it come, you can control it, Stella pleaded, lifting the girl's soft young hand.

Now Nancy's eyes following her mother's words had become passive as those of an infant . . . Really? she asked.

Let's go for a ride, Stella said.

In the country?

Stella nodded.

Oh . . . Nancy smiled with something that resembled pleasure.

Nancy sat up laboriously: Do you love me, Mother? . . . in a chastened, little-girl way, as she had after Mack was born. At that time, Stella had said: I love you both . . . Really? the child had asked, as she did now.

Of course I love you. You mean more to me than anything . . . Stella wondered if the tone of her voice had actually convinced Nancy, who seemed to listen for what was unsaid and see what was not apparent.

But I'm so much trouble. You'd be better off . . .

No, sweetie.

But I keep you from getting your own work done.

If I had thought my work was more important than those I loved I never would have married or had children. I wanted you to be born.

I'm in the way.

No, darling, no. Believe me, I want you well. More than anything . . . Stella looked into those sick eyes and felt that perhaps they doubted everything now, as much as they had accepted and worshipped a few years before . . . Get dressed, she said, remembering what a relief it was to her each time Nancy had been at the hospital, to one day find the girl out of night clothes and in slacks again . . .

Nancy slipped out of bed and patted and pulled the blankets back into place.

I'll see what Mack is doing. He doesn't know the meaning of breakfast, Stella said.

Smiling faintly, Nancy touched various clothes in her closet as if she were trying to recall what to do with them. Stella told her not to take too long: It might rain . . .

Downstairs, in the living room, Mack, unwashed and tangle-haired, with grey streaks on his face and dirty hands, sat on the couch near the television, sucking a Popsicle whose orange dye left a stain on his lips.

Hi Mom.

You look a sight. How can you go so long without washing?

You're always nagging. First thing you say . . .

But you won't take care of yourself. You don't listen to me. You're underweight.

Nag, Nag . . .

He didn't look fourteen, more like eleven. When he was eleven,

Nancy had begun to be ill. Stella thought perhaps he had remained eleven because she could not discipline him as she might have if her attention had not been so absorbed by the girl. All she had given him, she reflected, was an impulsive, damned-up affection.

Would you like pancakes?

No.

French toast?

No.

Eggs?

I hate eggs.

But what's the value of Popsicles?

Who cares? Will you leave me alone? I want to watch.

You're not even looking at the TV.

Quit nagging or I won't do anything.

She went into the kitchen in the defensive way that had accumulated in her since her marriage, hating the time it consumed, not wanting to think of it and knowing she was the wrong kind of mother; she should have learned to accept the role or trained her family to help. But Nancy had always helped. Mack had been spoiled by Phil who believed kitchens belonged to women. Years ago when Mack was born and she had gone to the hospital, Phil had hired a woman to take care of the house, the cooking, and Nancy. Best of all, the woman loved the kitchen. Nancy, she had treated sternly, compelling the child to go to bed on time, which Nancy had never done, being unable to relax until late at night. When Stella returned with her infant, she found the older child pale and sullen, clinging to her, avoiding the sleek kitchen.

This, the woman had said, as she finished putting away dishes and polishing off the sink, is my domain . . . Extending her arms, she included the stove. Stella was abashed by the woman's complacent tone. Like a child herself, during the woman's stay, Stella pretended to be neat, conspiring with Nancy to appear more domestic than she felt. Only after the woman left was Stella able to spend a few hours a day on the research that was to become her one book.

Nevertheless, cooking allowed her to express a taste for art that she could no longer pursue as a historian and critic; yet, in cooking French food she had told Nancy about the Impressionists, and Greek pastry brought to mind the Classical age. But in cleaning up she returned to the limitations of the present. Consequently, she tried to get through the kitchen as quickly as possible, pushed pots and pans into corners and left bits of food adhering to the stove or sugar or flour speckling the floor. Yet, even as she made haste, she thought, now, as she had many times earlier, that she was being punished for her resentment . . . If only Phil were back . . . she thought. I was a bad wife, she concluded; I am a poor mother.

Mack didn't seem to like anything she cooked. Lately she had given up asking what he preferred. Nancy would eat anything.

Stella made coffee, squeezed oranges and had a glassful ready when she heard Nancy's ponderous step on the stairs. As the scent of fresh coffee burst from the pot, the cats began scratching and mewing behind the basement door. Nancy came into the kitchen, smiling as though everything had been solved.

Mack! Stella called. Feed your cats! Nancy was preparing her own eggs and bacon, starting her breakfast ritual, cooking with a finesse that Stella envied. Once Nancy had spent eight hours following a pastry recipe in the *New York Times Cook Book*. She was a perfectionist at everything from guitar playing to learning a new language, and when she polished furniture she did so with the same attentive concern that she gave to sewing or drawing. Stella had never known anyone to do so many things well. Phil had been proud of the girl's abilities. They had talked together a lot that last year.

Mack! Stella called again. And then MACK! She saw Nancy jump, and went out to fetch Mack. He was in the same position, his brown-haired head bent over the comic book from which he glanced up briefly to stare at the screen.

Why don't you answer me?

I won't do anything if you yell.

Good lord, she muttered.

Lowering her voice, she told him to go upstairs and dress, which he did with the air of one abused. A few moments later he appeared, still with streaks of grey on his face and rumpled hair, in the same jeans and shirt he had worn for the past few days. Wearily she sent him back to wash, though she knew he would only splash himself with cold water.

After breakfast Nancy swallowed her arsenal of pills. Stella followed her upstairs to dress. Since she herself merely grabbed the same slacks and sweater she had worn the day before, she could say nothing about Nancy's choice, which seemed to have been arrived at arbitrarily, a splotched, tight skirt, a shrunken sweater, worn at the elbows. Stella wished she could get Nancy interested in clothes again.

Let's go, she sighed.

Dry, crackling leaves swirled over the walks, were lifted by the breeze and flew at their faces as they went down the steps and across the walk to the car. Mack brushed away blown dust as he opened the car door, but Nancy stared ahead, expressionless, a wool hat pulled far down on her face. Pushing her aside, Mack said: I'm getting in front.

You always ride in front, Nancy said.

Well, it's my turn.

No it isn't.

Go on, Mack said, pushing her, Get in back.

Mack! Stella scolded. Stop that!

It's my turn.

That's what you always say, Nancy asserted.

Stella could see the anger rising; Nancy's fists drew themselves together, opening and closing; the shaking had begun again, her eyes were narrowed, mouth pulled down.

Mack, Stella admonished, why do you treat her that way? . . . and could say no more, afraid that Nancy would perceive implications that might hurt her. It was so hard to talk to Mack at any time about Nancy's illness. He was another problem. Stella wanted to think of Nancy as the adult she was supposed to be, to appeal to her for help in raising this uncomfortable boy. Before she could stop herself, Stella was back in a previous year, when Nancy had been the reliable one.

Nancy, you're the older one. Does it matter?

He's spoiled. You give in to him.

You're the one who's spoiled! Mack said.

Nancy, you've been to college . . .

I never want children, Nancy said.

You used to love each other.

Nancy was trembling.

Please, Mack, Stella said.

He spun about and headed down the street, silent, insolent, grim, the strategy he had always taken (I'll run away if . . .) but Stella had never been able to take the chance of ignoring his threat.

You used to sing together! she called out. He kept walking.

Does it really matter? Stella implored.

Nancy gave her mother a glance of absolute disgust and slipped into the back seat, complaining: I always feel sick in back.

He's impossible! Stella said.

You spoil him . . . Nancy huddled in a corner of the back seat, hands opening and closing.

Again, Stella called Mack to say that Nancy was in back. The boy turned about, and with head lowered began to lope toward them, though he seemed to be aiming for a spot behind the car. At the car door he hesitated, glowering in challenge.

Well, get in.

Are you sorry?

Am I sorry? Why should I be. Oh well, all right. I'm sorry.

Just get in.

Stella headed north, toward the state line, twenty minutes from town.

Why are you going this way? Mack asked.

Because I want to. Because it's a nice day and I promised Nancy a ride in the country.

What about me? You're always doing things for her. I don't want to go to the country.

She ignored him.

Look, Nancy, there are still some trees with leaves turning.

Nancy impaled her face upon the back window.

Why don't you sing? I'd love to hear you sing, Nancy.

I don't want her to sing.

Why not? Both of you can do it. Remember how you used to sing when we took trips? Harmonized?

Well, I don't feel like it and I don't feel like hearing her.

Sing, Nancy, please.

Nancy began to sing: 'How shall your true love know from another one' . . . ?

Mack turned on the radio, but the girl continued.

Stella switched the radio off.

Shut up! Mack said to Nancy.

I can't stand this, Stella said.

Well, I can't stand her voice.

But you used to love it. Remember when the two of you sang: It was a lover and his lass? and: Full Fathom Five . . . ? I loved to hear the two of you.

Take me home, Mack said.

I promised Nancy.

Then stop somewhere for me. There's the stamp store. Buy me some stamps.

I don't have enough money.

Well, why did you make me ride with you?

Make you? Did you want to be left behind?

Isn't it beautiful? Nancy asked in a suddenly clear, devout tone.

Houses had fallen back and trees and fields spread before them, the intensity of colors startling in certain trees. Perhaps the air is better or the land more protected, Stella reasoned . . . But the color of the sky had faded; drops of rain spread over the windshield.

Like it, Nancy?

Beautiful, Nancy said again. Something in the way she said it reminded Stella of the last few months of her husband's life, when he looked out at any day, grey or sunny, with wistful delight.

You'd better close the window, Mack announced. It will rain in.

Nancy told him she had to have the window open a bit, that when it wasn't open she felt ill.

Finally, Stella conceded that the rain was coming down too hard: We'd better turn back.

No, don't . . . Nancy pleaded, please go on. I don't want to go back to town yet. It's so ugly.

Stella had already turned about.

Well, at least stop for me, Mack said. There's a taco place. You're always doing what she asks.

No. Go back to the country. I must see the country . . .

Why can't I have some snacks?

I feel sick, Nancy said.

All at once Stella felt cold air blowing on her neck. Slowing down, she turned to see Nancy trying to get out of the door, one leg already through.

What do you think you're doing?

If you won't take me, I'll go myself.

Stella groaned. Mack, help me . . . and pulled to the side of the road while they shut the door and shoved Nancy back into the seat. She slid over to the other door, and Stella locked it, keeping her hand on the button. Nancy started screaming, jumping up and thrashing about.

Please, Stella said, please. We'll go again. I promise. But it's raining now.

The girl quieted, slumping in the seat, staring ahead bleakly, and laying her face against the streaming window. She glanced over at Mack who had paled and was shivering.

Let's go home quickly, he urged. Don't stop.

Nancy moaned and her "voice" began to break in . . . I feel awful, I feel nauseous . . . she cried out once. Keeping her hands on the wheel, Stella drove as fast as she could, unnerved by every traffic light. Just as she pulled into their driveway, she became aware of an acrid odor. Nancy was vomiting. Sending Mack for a mop and a sponge and pail, Stella bent over the girl and held her warm, perspiring head.

What did you eat? Stella asked. You didn't swallow something again like that other time, did you?

No nothing . . . Nancy heaved . . . I want to lie down. I just want to go to bed. Stella supported the girl into the house and upstairs.

All Nancy's strength seemed to have gone, and with it her rebelliousness; she seemed weary, enervated.

Take a bath, Stella suggested. You'll feel better if you take a bath . . . Even while she said it some other knowledge mocked that old panacea. But she had to believe in cures. A nice warm bath. Nancy nodded and began to undress.

Returning to the car, Stella started to clean it, scrubbing more vigorously than usual, compelling herself to smell the vomit and sweat, the agony, not caring about the rain that soaked her slacks and jacket.

The house seemed strangely quiet when she re-entered it, the TV screen opaque. Running upstairs, Stella heard splashing in the tub.

Is that you, Nancy?

The girl answered in her lucid voice, as though untainted by illness. For a few moments Stella listened. She could hear water sloshing around the girl's body. Are you almost finished? she asked.

I'm washing my hair.

Oh . . . Stella knew how Nancy washed her hair, laying her head back and submerging her face.

Don't stay too long, she warned.

The girl murmured an assent, and Stella proceeded to Mack's room.

His tear-streaked, red-eyed face jerked toward her as she opened the door. For a moment she expected him to chase her out, but he merely stared at the ceiling. She touched his hand, in question. He did not respond. She brushed the hair from his forehead. He peered into her eyes: I thought she was only fooling, Mom. Honestly, until now I thought she was fooling. I'm sorry, Mom. I'm really sorry . . .

O.K. . . . Stella said, leaning to kiss him . . . it's O.K.

Hearing Nancy leave the bath and enter her own room, Stella moved toward the door.

Tell her . . . Mack said . . .

I will . . .

Seeming placid, Nancy lay in bed, wet hair spread on the towel over her pillow. Her eyes were closed, and the caked lips moved soundlessly. She opened her eyes as Stella approached.

I hope I never have a child, Nancy said.

You used to say you wanted a child like Mack.

It's so sad, the girl said, to find that someone you love doesn't love you.

Mack?

The girl nodded. Stella wondered if she did mean Mack.

But Mack does love you. He told me to tell you he was sorry and hoped you felt better. He wants to talk to you.

Oh? . . . The expression on Nancy's face changed. In one instant she had reclaimed the hopes of her girlhood. Suddenly, she was headed for fame and love again in a world without malevolence. She smiled as she had not smiled since her lost love, Benjamin, walked into the house to take her to a concert.

With a shy, remorseful tenderness, Mack appeared, asking to come in. Nancy responded in loving surprise, and Mack swaggered a bit and called out: Hello, beautiful . . . Nancy giggled, beaming as Mack sat next to her, lifting her hand, caressing it, as he began to relate one of his ludicrous stories.

Stella was reminded of the way Phil always said to her, each evening when he came home: Hello beautiful . . . Nancy laughed, the old raucous laugh. Her face was animated, pink.

I'm going to take a nap, Stella said, leaving. They didn't seem to hear her.

. . . Maybe she's getting better, she whispered to her pillow as she lay down. Although the doors were closed, she could hear through the wall their murmuring and laughter. Then they began to sing: It was a lover and his lass/ with a hey and a ho and hey nonnyno . . .

Stella tried to sleep. She was so tired. The tiredness extended from her head into her spine and her chest. Her heart banged as though suspended in a bell. Blood steamed in her veins and dread clung to her mind. She demanded sleep, demanded a return to that dark land where the woman lived who was herself and beloved, but some knowledge kept crashing through her consciousness, consumed her faith. There was nothing but chaos in the half-formed figures that slipped through her partial trance. Then once more the phone rang and it was the same woman who had called in the morning and wanted to know if they were coming to dinner.

. . . I don't think we can. But thanks.

When she hung up the phone she knew Mack had left Nancy's room and confusion had replaced him, heard once more the "voice" that spelled possession of her daughter's mind, saying in falsetto: Oh you lovely, berlovely girl . . Oh my brenancy . . . ganancy . . . you are a . . . wonderful . . . you . . . adorable . . . bre . . . engmig . . . silga . . . a gre-great . . .

She ran into Nancy's room, shouting: Be quiet, stay away from her! Leave my girl alone! . . . And Nancy's dazed face looked up, half gone, far gone, and the girl raised herself out of chains and said: I have a terrible pain down the center of my head. Oh! Oh! I want to die, Mother . . . And pounded her fists against her head: I want to die!

Transfixed by an iciness that spread through her, Stella had an impulse to give up, to say: I can't stand it any longer. If you insist on dying, die . . .

But the next moment, appalled at herself, and with tears in her eyes, she leaped toward Nancy, grabbing the hands away from that young head, saying: Don't destroy yourself . . . for my sake, don't destroy yourself . . . and held her close, murmuring things about the world, the dear world, the radiant world, to which she must, she had to return.

Voices

Somehow it feels right for me to transcribe this story of my mother's word for word, like a naughty child staying after school to write his crime on the blackboard.

"Boy, I was awful," I tell my mother on the phone after I finish this task.

"That's not you," she says.

"Yes, it is. That's me all right. I remember. What a brat. If I haven't apologized to you before, I want to do it now."

She laughs. "Listen, Robin, you don't need to. You were pretty sweet most of the time."

"You don't remember," I say. "That's me." She's the one who doesn't remember. Maybe she needs to think I was sweet. On the other hand, maybe I need to think I was awful.

"He comes around in the end," she says. "Mack redeems himself."

"Maybe," I say, unconvinced.

Of course, not everything happened exactly the way my mother depicts it in her story, but there are echoes. My sister's suicide attempt. Her voices. "Well if you won't take me, I'll go myself." I can still hear Nola saying that as she walked along the highway toward her Guru's telepathic voice.

"Really, I think it's a beautiful story," I say.

"I don't know if you remember this," she says, "but I couldn't talk when Nola died without crying. It took months. Finally, I wrote this story, and I knew I was getting better."

*   *   *

I examine my mother's story and focus on what Stella tells Nancy, "If I had thought my work was more important than those I loved I never would have married or had children. I wanted you to be born."

The people I love are part of my work, as they're a part of my mother's work. It's hard sometimes to separate the two.

270

Almost every line has something for me to decipher. I look again at the line about Nancy's voices: "the message garbled, idiotic," and I think that yes, this was especially terrible to all of us, my sister's voices.

As I reread the story, something nags at me, a line I remember reading, but one I can't remember transcribing. So I go back and read the original tearsheet of my mother's story against the version I've transcribed. Finally, I find the passage and restore it:

Nancy giggled, beaming as Mack sat next to her, lifting her hand, caressing it, as he began to relate one of his ludicrous stories . . .

My ludicrous stories. All of our stories are ludicrous whether we change the names or not. My sister tells me ludicrous stories, even now, through her autobiography, and it's these I'm drawn to because these stories are what we shared, what we believed. And I have to think there was something beautiful in our acceptance, our surrender to the fantastic. I want to believe in them. I want to say this was not all her imagination and my imagination, that magical things happened, that there were forces good and bad operating on us all the time, that Nola brought them into my life. Even with Nola's voices, what I remember as the bleakest period, it was not all bleak, and she reminds me of this in her memoir.

A very strange thing was beginning to happen whenever I looked at Guru's picture. Again I wondered whether it was my imagination and finally knew that this was impossible. I began "hearing" Guru's voice in my head, telling me to come to the Centre of Being . . . assuring me that I was being properly guided. One evening I sat down amazed at what had begun to take place whenever I looked at Guru, and decided that I was going to find out definitely whether he was communicating with me or not. I gazed steadily at the picture for half an hour, very careful not to let extraneous thoughts interfere or be mistaken for the messages. The voice of Guru, then other voices, began to emerge like some new exotic growth, from the picture; at the end of the half hour they were so loud and insistent that I could scarcely sit still in the bathtub (after my staring session), where I was trying to wash up before bed. I still remember the soap flying in between divine imprecations to do this or that, trying to scrub my body while they insisted on purifying the spirit.

"Nola!" one rich tenor voice commanded. "You will walk with

us in the Garden of the Spirit . . . you have chosen the Divine
Path . . . you are being helped . . ."

"Yes, all right, I hear you, but will you please wait until I get
my back washed?"

I was actually able to test my voices before entering the bathroom; they were screeching so benevolently at me that I thought
it would do no harm to ask them one or two practical questions.
"O.K., if you're *really* up there talking to me, tell me where I can
find the Listerine."

I had lost my toothpaste and was groping about for it in desperation. Sure enough, one of my impalpable friends bellowed
at me: "It's in the *bathroom* under the chair, silly!"

"Thanks,"I said, returned to the bathroom and quietly retrieved my Listerine toothpaste from under the bathroom chair.
I no longer questioned my hearing; the voices had answered me
and I was convinced.

Of my own ludicrous stories, I believed them when I told them, or
most of them. Sometimes I exaggerated. I made up a few poltergeist
hauntings. I told my mother that an apple in a dream materialized on
our kitchen counter the next morning. I told Nola of a chair flying
past me as I watched TV with a friend. But these are small transgressions, I think. This was simply the way we communicated. Even when I
lied, I was not so much lying as spinning tales, telling my own version
of fairy stories, acknowledging that everything around us does not
have to be seen to be believed, and everything believed does not have to
be real.

But most things I told Nola and my mother were true, or I believed
they were. When I told Nola about one of my past lives, I believed in it.
When I wrote my answers as Shiva, I believed something greater than
me was using me as a tool. And what was the harm in that, I wonder.
What was the harm in telling each other these ludicrous stories? As
long as we were talking, as long as we believed in each other's voices . . .
I don't know. I want to say something patently untrue, some sappy
bromide about surviving, loving one another, but that's the most ludicrous sentiment of all. The truth is that finally we couldn't believe,
that all of our stories break down, become ridiculous, that our voices
speak to us alone.

Still, I'd rather hear and disbelieve than hear nothing at all. No matter what Nola tells me now, I want to listen, to assure her that, even if I can't fully believe, I'll try, really, to at least listen.

*   *   *

I awoke in the middle of the night. Someone was talking in a voice I didn't recognize. I didn't know where I was. A strange, garbled voice spoke somewhere below me in the dark.

"Your heart is ashes."

This was 1984. Nola had been dead eleven years. It wasn't a dream and it wasn't Nola, but my mother.

"Yes, I'm Jewish and proud of it," my mother was saying in her sleep.

My mother and I were visiting Los Angeles, where most of my family lives now, staying with my cousin David in his Topanga Canyon home. He had put us both up in his studio, me in a loft and my mother on the main floor of the studio.

> *Who would you remember.*
> *That is a devil's smile.*
> *This is what we don't want.*
> *Only smile the way beautiful people smile.*
> *I can't.*
> *The longer you do this the stronger you will become.*

Listening to my mother babble like that woke me completely and I sat on my futon, mesmerized and slightly horrified, half the night. She didn't speak incessantly, but in bursts, and I wanted to wake her, to make her stop talking like that, but I was also fascinated because the voice sounded so peculiar—actually, not one voice but many, a roller-coaster sound. Sometimes she spoke in a falsetto, sometimes a couple of registers deeper than her normal voice. It sounded just like Nola's voices. And my mother reminds me that these are Nola's words, too, at least some of them. This is what she had told my mother about Ralph Haven's diet: "The longer you do this the stronger you will become."

> *Murder.*
> *Listen.*
> *Listen, Selma. Pray.*
> *Pray.*
> *Think of only the spiritual. Do not let them get at your mind. Don't pay any attention to that damn movie.*
> *Please.*

The voices sometimes seemed oddly sublime:

> *Be beautiful and calm.*
> *Be beautiful and calm.*
> *I'm putting a circle of spirituality around you.*
> *Orange.*
> *Full of white flowers and red flowers.*
> *Don't touch 'em*
> *Don't touch.*

Just as often, the voices said things that were obviously bizarre:

> *Don't go around insulting women of my age or stature or frame.*
> *Think about it and put a few weights on yourself.*

I decided not to wake her because I thought maybe I'd disorient and frighten her if I did so, like what happens to a sleepwalker if you try to wake them.

In the morning, I told her. She had no recollection of these voices, but she believed me.

When she returned home, she bought a microcasette tape recorder and placed it by her bed at night. The recorder was voice-activated, and it would record her nightly voices. Rarely did they have anything to do with the dreams she remembered. For years, she transcribed these voices in her journals.

> *Flowers are on your head.*
> *You smell sweet as a flower.*
> *Some hang down your ears.*
> *You are full of [incoherent].*

> *Just think: I am beautiful.*
> *I live at a beautiful time.*
> *I live in a beautiful house.*
> *Oh I see something really beautiful.*
> *If you see something beautiful let us know . . .*

She finally stopped recording these nightly babblings because there was something draining about them, something disturbing, and it was impossible finally, to make sense of what she was saying.

But in her first entry about the voices, she tried to make sense of some of what she had cried out:

Robin just recalled something else I said in my sleep—he told me I sounded very upset and said, "Your heart is ashes."

This must have been about E—whom I am not aware of dreaming about anymore—but I have probably buried him in my unconscious—so I am not entirely free of the trauma—although when I question myself I know there is still disturbance within me.

Still, I wish I would stop talking in my sleep. I know I said something aloud last night also because I was aware of it at the time.

Had I read her journal then, I wouldn't have known that "E" was Elliot Chess, whose name she had reduced over the years to one single letter, a vowel sound, code for all her pain.

But it was I who heard her say, "Your heart is ashes," not Elliot. I felt accused, uncovered. I felt that judgment had been passed. I wondered if it was true. I wondered if anything could be done. Ash cannot be rebuilt, I knew, but built upon.

*   *   *

My mother calls and tells me she's found a tape of Nola singing from 1972. I remember my mother recording this tape. This was the last year of Nola's life, after her mind had deteriorated, but her voice had not. We were barely on speaking terms, and only through songs were we able to communicate. I remember how lovely her voice still sounded.

The tape of Nola's singing is on reel-to-reel, and so my mother must convert it to a cassette. A friend does this for her, and she sends one copy of the tape to me and one to my brother. She doesn't listen to it herself.

I pop the tape in my cassette deck, wondering how my sister will sound after so many years. My own voice is so much deeper now, but I know that I will sing along with her and remember. I wonder what songs are on the cassette: "Full Fathom Five," I hope. "A Lover and His Lass?"

Sometimes I put on music and dance with Olivia and Isabel. Whatever is on, we swing wildly around the room. I twirl them around and whip them through my legs until I'm too tired, although they're always greedy for more, smiling with love at me, so easily satisfied, their eyes sparkling. "Do it some more."

"No, Daddy's tired now," I have to say eventually, disappointing them that this easy bliss cannot go on forever.

"Just one more time," Olivia says.

"Okay, one more time."

And if the music is slow, Olivia and Isabel mimic ballerinas, or more like Isadora Duncan, standing crane-like in the middle of the room, looking heavenward with such serious expressions I have to stifle my laughter, making Statue-of-Liberty gestures, or simply twirling in place till they're dizzy and tip over.

The other day, Olivia made up what she called her "Hanukkah Dance." She started by hugging herself. She said, "I was cold in the shadows. It was cold because the lights weren't lit yet," and then she opened her arms and said, "And when the candles were lit, I moved into the light and became warmed." And she pranced around and twirled, her own expressive flame.

"Do you want to hear some music?" I ask Olivia.

"Sure," she says, "What is it?"

"It's my sister, your aunt."

"Oh," she says. "Sure." She stands with her arms out in a kind of flamenco position.

I push "play," and what I hear is not my sister. It *is* my sister but it's not. Somehow the voice has become terribly distorted. It sounds hollow and false and ripply. It's out of tune. I recognize the song but not the singer. It's one of the loveliest folk songs I've heard, a ballad called "Silkie," about mermaids and transformations and magic, and those sour chords that so many folk songs have.

"Little know I thy child's father," I hear Nola sing. "Of land or sea he's living on."

I don't remember Nola ever singing this song. I'm fascinated as much by the distortion of Nola's voice as the subject of the song. There's not a true note here—it changes, irrevocably, my impression of her singing. It makes me doubt. Did she really have such a beautiful voice or do I simply choose to remember it as such? I was probably better off before I heard this tape.

Olivia covers her ears. "Turn it off," she says. "It's hurting me." I turn off the tape and I put it away somewhere safe. Why do I do this? I wonder. Why not simply throw it away. The tape is awful, and yet I could never throw it away now that I have it. There's something of my sister on that tape, even if I can't bear to listen.

Young Americans with Helpful Attitudes

Joan, a woman my sister's age, called me up one day and told me that she had heard about my organization, SPEC. She represented another organization of concerned young people, called YAHA, Young Americans with Helpful Attitudes, and wanted to know if I'd be interested in talking about becoming a member. I didn't like the sound of the name. Young Americans with Helpful Attitudes? It sounded Republican to me and my family was Democratic.

"What kind of helpful attitudes?" I asked.

"Right now YAHA is more concerned with drug education than the environment," she said. "We think SPEC will round us out."

"Drug education?" I said. How boring, I thought.

"Jerry told us about you," she said. "At Everyday People."

"What . . . did Jerry say about me?" I asked.

"He called you a dynamic and sensitive young man. He thought you could make a difference."

If that's what he thought and she believed him, then maybe YAHA wasn't so boring.

"I'd like to take you out to dinner to discuss this, if your mother says you can go."

"My mother isn't here right now," I said. "She's in New York." I don't know why I gave Joan that information. It just confused her.

"Oh, when will she be back?"

"Who knows?" I said. "She's gone to look for my sister."

Actually, she'd found my sister. Nola was in the psychiatric unit of Bellevue Hospital in Manhattan. She'd been picked up by the police and dumped there. She must have done something pretty fantastic to gain the notice of the Manhattan police. I never found out and my mother doesn't remember. Perhaps she stood in the middle of Fifth Avenue, stopping traffic, intent on the telepathic messages she constantly received from her Guru. Or maybe she was preaching to the cabbies, the business people, the shoppers:

"Oh poor, lost twentieth-century man, when will you recognize the Truth of your myths, your fairy tales, your arts!?"

Not now, they thought, hunched in their winter coats, used to ignoring such people. She was not their problem. She was ours, and the hospital wanted something done with her, so my mother flew back to New York to retrieve her. I was left hurriedly in the care of the first available student who'd have me, a woman named Robyn, which, in itself, seemed auspicious. Everything was a sign back then. Everything part of a pattern. Put Robin in the care of Robyn, the Universal Author seemed to say, and all will turn out fine.

"If you want dinner, I'm up for it," I told Joan. "Let me check with my baby-sitter."

Robyn sat in front of the TV with her boyfriend Phil. She had her legs in his lap and he had one hand in her hair and another in a bag of chips. The house was smoky from cigarettes and all our ashtrays were full.

"I don't have any money," I told Joan.

"It's YAHA's treat," she said.

"I'm going out to dinner tonight," I told Robyn.

"Okay," she said without taking her eyes off the set.

*   *   *

SPEC was a good idea and little more. I didn't have much in the way of follow-through at thirteen. We went out that one time and picked up trash in downtown Columbia and then another time cleaned up trash at Hinkson Creek. At least I cared a lot. At least I *intended* to care a lot.

For a while we met on Saturday mornings at Everyday People, but mostly we just talked and fooled around. The room where we met was also the room where a sex education group met, and one day, we discovered a stash of birth-control pills and condoms in the closet. Jill Brinkley and Jill Peters popped a handful each of the tiny pills and the boys in our group went to the bathroom and filled our condoms with water. Then we opened a window (we were on the second floor) and pelted people heading next door to Alfies Fish & Chips with the giant distended condoms.

I'd quit Alfies by then and when they complained to Jerry, he gave us a stern lecture (stern for Jerry, which was really pretty mild). I explained that we were trying to make a statement, attacking Corporate America's laissez-faire attitude toward the poor and hungry, the overpopulated, starving regions of the world. I used that word, *laissez-faire* (it was something my mother or Nola had said), and he was bowled over. He thought that was great, and that's probably why he recommended me to Joan. When backed against a wall, I could make up explanations like that on the spot.

Still, SPEC was in a kind of stasis since I'd started attending school at Mid-Mo. I was crazy and the word was out at my former school, Jeff Junior. The two Jills, both so enamored of me, were the first to leave SPEC. Then my locker mate. Then the other two or three members, all except for Sarah Skolnick, my neighbor. But I could just go over to her house if I needed to issue a directive.

At dinner, I must have lied to Joan.

I must have made SPEC seem more important to the community than it was.

Three weeks after my dinner with Joan, an article on me and SPEC appeared in YAHA's national newsletter.

Youngest Director
Making
Big Plans

Thirteen year old Robin Hemley, director of the YAHA Association SPEC (Society for the Prevention of Environmental Corruption) has big plans for his Columbia, Missouri group. YAHA/SPEC's purpose is to help the environment and charity.

Robin and other members are active in an effort to clean up Columbia's Hinkson Creek. In coordination with Stephens College, YAHA members are analyzing water samples to determine what pollutants are present in the stream.

Past activities of the association have included a litter clean-up campaign along a major street in Columbia, Broadway. The members hosted a banquet last Christmas to raise funds for an international charitable organization.

Members of the group Robin heads are between the ages of 13–15 years old. They make up one of the youngest YAHA groups in the country.

Robin's plans for the future—clean up Hinkson Creek.

Young Americans with Helpful Attitudes, 510 National Press Building, Washington, DC 20004

I don't know where I got the idea of the banquet. That never happened, nor did the water analysis of Hinkson Creek. I was always making up stories, always lying or at least stretching the truth—and it was so easy to be believed. All you had to do was say something with a straight face, and if caught in a lie, deny, shut down, refuse to back down, make the wronged party apologize for being wronged, threaten to run away.

*   *   *

When something *truly* unusual happened, I sometimes let it pass, uncommented upon. If it wasn't imagined, it was somehow less real.

The day after my dinner with Joan, Robyn's former boyfriend came over to the house—how he found out where she was staying, I have no idea—and kidnapped us. He drove us around town, then out into the country. I sat in the backseat while the two of them argued up front. "I love you so much," he said, his face enraged.

"That's insane," she said. "Listen to yourself."

"I don't know what else to do," he said, the muscles in his jaw tense.

I had a comic book with me. I read it carefully, pretended I didn't understand. If I didn't understand, no harm could come to me. Nola said once on a field trip from Mid-Mo a bus nearly ran over her group. They all started giggling. "You can't kill us," she shouted after the bus. "We're crazy!"

He drove us to a place miles outside of Columbia called Devil's Icebox. It was a small canyon that led to a cave with a brook trickling through. I looked at Robyn and she said I should do what he said, that she'd take care of things. I walked to the cave and stayed there, looking into its mouth. The legend was that Jesse James and his gang had been cornered there after a robbery, and taking their chances, had run into the cave. Weeks later, they emerged in Kentucky. No one knew where the cave led, there were so many different chambers. It just went on and on.

I heard both their voices, his loud, hers calm. I thought about running into the cave, taking my chances too, but I was too scared. I thought I'd rather be killed in the daylight than disappear forever into some dark hole where I'd never be found. I listened to the pitch of their words, tried to concentrate only on that, not on what the words meant. I thought of what Jerry had told me right before I picked up the fake suicide call at Everyday People. "You've got to learn to listen," he told me. "Let go of your ego."

"What I think I'm hearing," I mumbled to myself, but that incantation did no good. There was no mirror and no one on the other side, and even if there was, they were just observers.

I didn't hear the footsteps behind me until I felt the hand on my hair. The hand could have been this man I didn't know who wanted to kill this woman because he loved her, but it was the woman instead. I didn't know her either, and it didn't matter that she had the same name as I. There was nothing special in that. Coincidence couldn't protect me. There was no cosmic alignment in that stupid fact. I turned around and looked at her and she took my hand and led me back to the car, silently.

After he let us go, Robyn made me promise not to tell my mother. "Why not?" I asked.

"You're all right, aren't you?" she said.

"Sure."

"Then why make her worry about something that's already happened, that she can't change?"

That made sense to me. And so I never told. Not for twenty years. I almost forgot it myself. Someone had told me to forget and so I forgot.

*   *   *

When Nola returned from New York, she had stories to tell. She said that she and her traveling companion had thirty dollars between them and that they'd lived for a week on those little cans of Vienna sausages (she had long since given up being a vegetarian, and as her mind worsened, so did her diet). She said she'd been attacked by a trucker and had barely escaped. My mother didn't say anything, but she told me later she was a little doubtful. She knew how Nola liked to dramatize.

Nola and the boy had split up in New York. "They chained me to my bed at Bellevue," she told me. "They wanted me to have shock therapy, but I wouldn't let them. So they chained me. I couldn't move. It was the worst thing in my life."

I believed her and I didn't want that to happen to me. I was a different person now.

*   *   *

I made remarkable improvement in Group Therapy. I was like a stool pigeon in an old crime movie. You want me to sing, I'll sing. They had never seen such a stoolie, such a talker, ready to deprecate himself at every turn. As long as I was willing to say terrible things about myself, they were ready to listen, to embrace me in a big fat hug, to say how good I was at heart.

"We have some visitors today. Does anyone mind?"

I raised my hand. "I'd just like to say that I don't mind at all. I used to mind, but not now. I see that I was using the observers behind the mirror as an excuse, that what I was afraid of all along was inside me, not outside."

I wasn't completely lying. There was a kind of truth in this. The lie came in the tone, in the devious goal of my self-disclosure. I was the con telling the parole board how remorseful he is, admitting his heinous crimes, while holding a hard part back, tight-fisted, away from exposure.

"And what is that, Robin? What were you afraid of, inside yourself?"

"I was afraid of letting other people inside." This was the patter of self-help. Like the wisdom of Shiva, it was a matter of rhythm.

I turned slightly toward the mirror, in profile, so they might see my watery eyes.

The Group leader nodded.

"I see how selfish I was . . . maybe I was a control freak, do you think so?"

"What do you think, Robin?"

"I don't know. I think so. Yes, I was. I am!" I looked down at my lap, remorseful. The secret was never deny, always accept. If you said anything in your defense, you were being Defensive. If you denied, you were In Denial. If you acted upset, you were Acting Out. Once you brought up an issue, you had to run with it. If I had said, "I wonder if the leper's head in the jar downstairs is trying to tell me something important," the Group leader would have urged me to go on.

"Yes, I think it is trying to tell me something."

"And what is that, Robin?"

"Don't let them cut off your head and stick you in a jar."

I never brought up the leper's head. Had I, they would have seen through my ruse, would have realized I was trying to fool them at their own game. No, I stayed with safe subjects. I told them about my father. I told them that I still felt anger at his death, that things had started going wrong after he died. Big insight. They loved that.

Jan raised her hand, "When do the rest of us get a turn?"

After a few weeks of this circuit, my act was growing stale. Time to take it on the road.

The only way to get out of Group was to suggest it to the Group, and see what they thought. This was a pure Democracy of Mental Health. In my months of therapy, I'd yet to see someone successfully bring up their rehabilitation and leave the Group. I practiced my words over and over before Group that evening. I even practiced my facial expressions:

humbled, thoughtful, slightly weary, wise. I thought, Abe Lincoln. That's the persona we're going for.

The big night. No Ghosts of Christmas Past, blubbering Cratchetts, or autistic Tiny Tims were going to ruin my performance this time.

I stayed silent most of the evening. I put my chin in my hand. I listened to the others, looked like I was considering everything carefully, nodded enthusiastically at the appropriate moments.

Finally, the Group leader said something. "I couldn't help noticing how quiet you've been tonight, Robin." That's all he needed to say.

"I'm kind of sad," I said, haltingly.

"Oh?"

"I've just been thinking how much you all mean to me."

He tilted his head like a dog when you say, "Outside?"

"And that makes you sad?"

"No, not that, well yes. I guess what I'm trying to say is that you all have helped me so much over these months. You've helped me see what I've been afraid to face in myself, and I'm so grateful. I feel like you're my own family."

"We feel that way about you, too, Robin," Jan said.

"I think I'm ready," I said.

"Ready for what?"

"I think I'm ready to deal with the issues in my family that I've been afraid to deal with. I think I'm ready to talk honestly to my sister and mother, to let them know the love I feel, and face our problems together, with courage. I'm going to carry you all in my hearts. You've given me the strength I need."

"You've found it in yourself," the Group leader said.

"I think I'm ready for the next step, to try it on my own," I said. "I'm not saying I'm all better. I just think I'm stronger now that I'm able to face my problems. And . . . I'm wondering what the rest of you think?"

I looked around the room. They were silent. They were looking at me. Jan smiled wryly. Maybe I hadn't fooled her. Everyone else looked so sad—they all wished it could be them.

"What do you think?" the Group leader asked them. "Is Robin ready to leave us?"

The first one to speak was a boy named Duke, who was always sullen and sneering. He had his legs stretched out in front of him. He was in the Children's Ward for spraying laughing gas he'd stolen from his dentist father in a Fannie Mae candy shop one afternoon. He thought it would be funny to see the old ladies behind the counter keel over, but he was so stupid he hadn't bothered to wear any kind of protection. He'd keeled over, too, and had awakened to the police standing over him.

Duke answered the Group leader by uttering a string of inventive, graphic, and vile curses. Mostly, they had to do with his claims that he had sodomized a large number of my family, clan, and species. He ended with a relatively mild, "You can lick my crusty ass!"

"The question is whether Robin is ready to leave. What do you think, Duke?"

"Sure, why not. I won't have to look at him and his booger-crusted nose." He had a thing about crust.

This was not the most promising opening. After him, came Jan.

"Robin has grown a lot. He's like a brother, someone you care about, someone you want to protect, to look out for. But we all have got to look out for ourselves eventually. Right, bro?"

I nodded slowly. Maybe she wasn't fooling. Maybe she really cared.

Jan set the tone for nearly everyone else. The only one besides Duke who didn't respond positively was Mary. She didn't seem to be buying my little spiel. She sat arms crossed, legs crossed, eyes tight, withdrawn, like someone had said, "Jinx" and she wasn't going to talk till they freed her. Like she'd jinxed herself. She was hard. I didn't think she'd ever give in. She was still playing our game. After Group, maybe she'd head for home base, but I wouldn't be there. Her numbers were filling up my head when I looked at her. "Minus ten, minus twenty." She was never going to get better. So I looked away.

*   *   *

My mother promised Nola a trip to England the summer of 1972, a kind of desperate mental-health bribe to encourage Nola to get better. She obviously couldn't take the trip if she was in Mid-Mo, and my mother knew how much Nola had loved England, Scotland, and Ireland. Nola had never been able to manage the trip to India—Sri Ramanuja had dissuaded her from the India trip, in fact. He'd told her that she shouldn't try to run away from America, even if she despised the country's material values. If she wanted to study with a guru, she should study with him. She wasn't in any shape to travel on her own, in any case. This trip to England would be a reward for Nola staying alive another year—it would give her reason to stay alive, show her once again the beauty of the physical world. Perhaps my mother and she both imagined Nola doing Irish jigs in the foliage as she had on her last visit.

The trip was also a kind of reward for my mother, who had never been overseas. She had been denied reappointment at Stephens—she was a witch, after all, according to one of her students, her children were crazy, she was a woman—who could blame the college? At the last minute, she'd found a new job at a branch campus of Indiana University, Indiana University at South Bend, and we were going to move to South Bend at the end of the summer. Good riddance to Columbia, we all thought, which had been better than Slippery Rock, but that wasn't saying much.

I wasn't going on this trip to England. I had bigger plans.

Joan from YAHA had offered me a job. She said that I was just the kind of involved young person YAHA was looking for to come to Washington, D.C. for the summer and help them in their lobbying efforts. Part of the summer would be spent at their offices in the National Press Building, and part would be spent on the road, raising money for our organization and visiting various YAHA groups. She said they'd pay me $1000 and my room and board. I could buy a lot of comic books for $1000. And traveling around the country sounded like fun, too. My mother said yes. Not only was she out of practice saying no, but I'm sure being rid of me for the summer was at least a partial relief. She'd be able to focus all her energies on Nola.

*   *   *

I returned to Jefferson Junior High for the last month of the school year. I'd been in Mid-Mo when the yearbook photos were taken, but even though my photo wasn't included, I still wanted to share in the

Yearbook Experience. On the day the yearbook was published, the students ran through the halls finding their friends and favorite teachers to sign. Even hated teachers were sought out. A general amnesty was declared and fellow feeling reigned—the first seeds of nostalgia as the students started remembering the year with relief that they had survived, the first seeds of myth-making as they recounted stories about themselves in heroic dodgeball situations.

I had little difficulty finding willing people to sign my yearbook, although everyone knew I was crazy.

This is the only yearbook I own, and why is a complete mystery to me since it was a miserable year. Why then, have I kept this yearbook with inscriptions from people I don't remember and no inscriptions from those I do?

To a real sweet acting guy. Good luck with the girls. It's been fun having you in the same class in 6th hour. See ya next year. Bye!!! Cyclone Power !!! Dorcas Worthington.

Sure thing, Dorcas. Cyclone Power.

I ran into Jill Peters outside, waiting for the bus.

"Jill," I said. "Will you sign my yearbook?"

She looked at me almost as though she didn't recognize me. I had bestowed my Sigma Alpha Mu pin on Jill Peters. She'd lost it within the week, but had said she cherished it. She'd been in SPEC. We'd even gone steady. She'd shown me a few things. Now she was afraid of me, because of what happened to my sister, because of what happened to me. It was easy to see.

"What's your name now?" she said.

"What?"

"Peter or Robin?"

She took the book from me and flipped through it. "Robin," I said.

"What do you want me to say?"

I looked at her. I probably looked pretty pathetic. She was wearing round tinted glasses, which were popular then, but made everyone who wore them look like some wide-eyed marsupial.

She put the yearbook close to her, the protective gesture of someone used to others looking over her shoulder for the answers to some test. She wrote a long, involved inscription, and I was grateful.

"Thanks a lot," I said.

She smiled and said, "See you 'round."

After she left, someone shouted my name. "Mr. Hay-mee-lee! Mr. Hay-mee-lee!"

My name had never sounded more like some invective. Mr. Sputz stood on the top step of the school, and I rapidly flipped through the previous minutes to see what I'd done wrong. Yes, I'd been running through the halls, but so had everyone else, and it was the last day of school so I figured as long as I stayed outside of his reach, he couldn't hit me with Betsy.

"You told them I beat you?" Mr. Sputz said calmly, although he was clearly enraged.

"What?"

"Did you tell them I beat you?"

"Who?"

"That's what your mother said, Mr. Hay-mee-lee. She says I beat you."

"I never said that," I told him, and that was true. I think. Perhaps I said he beat me, but just a little. I didn't remember. Was it *that* important? Water under the paddle, as far as I was concerned. "I never said that, Mr. Sputz." I told him. Not that exact word, at least. Smacked? Thrashed? Bashed? Struck?

"Don't you go telling stories on me, Mr. Hay-mee-lee."

"Okay," I said. I wasn't going to argue with him. He was halfway down the front steps toward me. His prickly hair was on end (nothing unusual) and his face was red. He leaned toward me, one long leg on one step, the other two steps down, pointing his finger at me. He looked like someone reaching across a precipice to pull someone to safety or push him off a cliff, or a Marine Corps version of God in the Sistine Chapel, reaching toward Adam while yelling at him. "Adam! Adam! Don't you go telling stories on me!"

But I don't think I told any stories on him, not until this one.

"Will you sign my yearbook for me?" I asked.

He smiled at me, the smile of one at peace with his station in life. He was the assistant principal after all. He could afford to act munificent toward me.

He signed his name boldly across his picture, which showed him at his desk smiling like someone who's poked his head through one of those cardboard mock-ups of someone in pioneer or cowboy dress. He was relatively new at his job. I always assumed people were born assistant principals, not appointed. The caption beside his photo reads:

Mr. Jay J. Sputz

In his first year as assistant principal at Jeff Jr., Mr. Jay J. Sputz feels the purpose of his position is to "help maintain order and school morale at Jeff Jr. so that the process of education can be carried on in a cooperative atmosphere." Outside of his work he enjoys hunting, fishing and doing things with his son.

Looking through my yearbook now, I see I was clearly a different person to almost everyone who signed the book. Opinion on my character seemed . . . divided, although not sharply. I seemed pretty strange to everyone, and whether you liked me or not depended on your tolerance for strange people. The signers of my yearbook can probably be split into three groups, Semi-Pro, Largely-Con, and Negatively Non-committal, including the large margin of Undecideds or Diplomatics, teachers who didn't particularly like me but figured they had to sign my book at least. Almost everyone by this time was back to calling me Robin. Only one inscription refers to me as "Pete."

To Robin,
You were an asset to our class in all our plays and comic strip writing. I hope that you continue writing and have a busy summer with your exciting job. Mrs. Vogel

Robin,
To a real cool guy! I like you a whole lot and I'll sure miss you when you move!!! Take care of yourself and please write. See ya! Megan Foss

Robin,
I enjoyed talking with you very much and I'm glad you were in my homeroom. Good luck with the many things you've become involved in, and have a good life in Indiana! Mrs. Johnson

To a Guy we tease in my music class. Do you or don't you talk to yourself?
Star Rush

To a very carzy boy in Science – Jim Houle.

Dear Robin,
You are about the nicest person
I ever met. Keep being a liberal,

intelligent feminist. Good luck and have
fun this summer. Chisolm for President.
Love, Judy Goldman

Pete
Good luck and always stay out of truble.
Matt Cottingham

To a goony person who ruined all my classes by being in them!!!
But you really weren't that bad. Adios, etc., Susan Beller

To Robin
The guy that is always talking.
Gary Scott

To a Strange Kid in My Social Studies Class. Good luck and
keep up being so strange! Christina Olson (The Grape)

Don't let people get you down, just sit back and laugh at all the
crazy people! Lynn Kilpatrick

Robin,
Stay the way you are and you'll always collect comics
Jim Brotherton

All of these inscriptions seem more or less unintelligible to me now,
written in a foreign language by people I don't know, about someone
I vaguely remember:

Why I collected signatures from people who obviously hated me, I'll
never know. I guess I was hopeful.

Later that night, I flipped through my yearbook looking for Jill
Peters' inscription. I couldn't find it. She hadn't written near her picture or anywhere else. I couldn't believe it. She'd been so convincing. I
thought she was writing something, but she wasn't. She was just making motions with her pen. It amazed me that she wouldn't even give
me that much, not even her name. I must have looked on every page of
that yearbook a dozen times wondering if somehow I'd missed it, if it
might someday miraculously appear.

*   *   *

I'm still baffled about YAHA. I wonder why I was invited along, why
they chose me, what I was supposed to do. Eighth grade was the year
we were supposed to study government in Missouri, but I'd been

studying mental health and mind control instead, so I barely knew the branches of government. Joan told me I was going to be a lobbyist. That meant nothing to me. What that turned out to mean was going to McDonalds and Kentucky Fried Chicken a lot, sitting in the backseat of a station wagon, and waiting to do something.

The mastermind of YAHA was a twenty-six-year-old named Dale, who, in matters of fashion and grooming, looked like he was apprenticing himself to be a son-in-law of Richard Nixon: geeky glasses, blue blazer, the pastiness of David Eisenhower, and a slick hair flap with a perfect part.

I flew down to Raleigh, North Carolina, to meet Joan and Dale for my first important assignment: junk-food detail at a YAHA coffeehouse in Durham, the inappropriately named Gathering Place, designed to keep kids off the streets and off drugs. Either there were no kids on drugs in Raleigh/Durham/Chapel Hill that summer, or the drugs were a lot better than our coffee. No one ever came in. Sometimes, we took jaunts to downtown Durham, which was hot and half deserted. Eventually, we'd head back to the Gathering Place and wait hopelessly for someone to wander in, someone we could rescue and keep off the streets.

From Durham, we headed north in Dale's station wagon to Chicago, where YAHA lobbied Marshall Fields the Fourth or Fifth or Something or Other. The three of us sat across from him at his big desk while Dale, as usual, did the talking. For a while, Marshall Fields looked just about as distracted as I, until Dale brought up the subject of railroads, by chance, and we learned that Fields was a railroad buff.

"I know this doesn't have to do with railroads," I said, "but I just bought a book of photographs by Matthew Brady, the Civil War photographer. Do you want to see them?"

Marshall Fields stared blankly across his desk at me, and Dale turned to Joan. "Why don't you and Robin go outside and wait. We shouldn't be much longer."

That's what lobbying was to me.

*   *   *

While YAHA hadn't lived up to my expectations in other respects, I couldn't at least fault the location of YAHA headquarters in the National Press Building in D.C. That impressed me. I liked putting on my coat and tie every morning and driving with Joan and Dale to

YAHA HQ, then riding up the elevator, and opening the office. After I entered the office, there wasn't much for me to do. The office had two rooms, a front area with a typewriter and spare furnishings, and a back room with a seminar table and a printing press. I wasn't allowed into the back room and had nothing to do in front. Most of my time, I spent sight-seeing, wandering alone around D.C., buying souvenirs. When I complained that I had nothing to do, Dale gave me YAHA flyers to hand out.

"Where should I hand them out?" I asked.

"Go to the White House."

"You brought me here to hand out flyers?" I asked.

"It's called paying your dues," he said.

Okay, maybe he had something there. I was reminded of my eagerness to handle the suicide lines back at Everyday People. Maybe I wasn't ready for any more responsibility. But if this was lobbying, I was already an expert. I'd paid my dues with SPEC flyers. And handing out flyers didn't really accomplish anything besides killing trees. SPEC flyers. YAHA flyers. They were written in generalities:

YOUNG AMERICANS with HELPFUL ATTITUDES
YAHA

A non-profit organization dedicated to helping solve many of the social ills that plague American Youth:

⇒ DRUG EDUCATION
⇒ REHABILITATION
⇒ ENVIRONMENTAL RESPONSIBILITY
⇒ FIGHTING DISCRIMINATION

Nowhere in the flyer was there any mention of the Vietnam War, nor any solutions to anything. These flyers, Dale said, were meant to raise awareness, but that didn't hold much weight with me. We were all aware. The society bristled with awareness. No one needed more flyers.

Still, I had nothing better to do, so I went to the White House to hand out my flyers. Dale loaded me down with 1,000 of them. I guess he wanted me gone all day. A small group of war protesters were picketing there. Actually, only a couple were picketing. About twenty protesters sat in small clusters by the fence as if they were spending a few days in a KOA campground, had just returned from a day of hiking, and were comparing notes.

Not long after I sat down, a film crew from Sweden showed up, and they headed straight for me, apparently the youngest war protester in the bunch.

"What brings you here?" a man with a microphone asked me.

"My conscience."

"Did anyone close to you die?" the man asked.

"My father," I said. "I'm here because of him. My father loved the photographs of Matthew Brady, the Civil War photographer. Matthew Brady took all of these pictures of corpses on battlefields, and I want to give my copy of the book to President Nixon so he'll stop the war. But I'm embarrassed because my dog Mamie peed on it, so I can't give that book to the president."

The man seemed moved by my story and after he was done filming, he took out twenty dollars and handed it to me. "For another book," he said.

I protested feebly and then took the twenty. He had my face on film. I had told him a story. It seemed like a fair trade.

*   *   *

My mother still believes a bridge collapsed under me that summer. Every time I bring up YAHA, this is what she says, "Remember when that bridge collapsed right after you crossed it?" And I say, "I remember," instead of saying, "No, Mom, I lied to you. That didn't really happen." But sometimes I almost believe it, too. I can see the bridge falling into the Potomac as Joan and Dale and I rush to safety. I've always been a little afraid of bridges, so I think that's why this image still seems real enough to me. The White Bridge disaster happened when I lived in Ohio, and I remember watching the news reports, the stories of all the people drowning in their cars. I imagined these cars on the bottom of the river, rolling along, still powered somehow as they tried to find a way back to the surface before their breath ran out. The causeway over Lake Ponchartrain into New Orleans affected me similarly. For years, I dreamed about the boat ramps on the causeway, which I mistook for exit ramps, as though a car might decide to take an exit underwater. My fear simply had to do with escape, being trapped, unable to breathe, and that's still my fear, although not so much with water in particular.

But no, a bridge didn't collapse after I had crossed. What happened is the sky opened up and the rain poured down. And Joan and Dale and I ran through the swelling streets. We crossed a bridge and saw the Potomac raging beneath, and the next day, we saw the bloated Potomac and a car floating by in the river.

I couldn't tell my mother I was in that car, although I would have if I thought she'd believe me.

*   *   *

Homesick, I quit YAHA early and went with Nola and my mother to England that summer. For them, this wasn't much of a reward. Nola suffered my presence and my mother tried to balance her attention between my emotional blackmail and Nola's mental disintegration. This was my arena of power. Here, I was an expert lobbyist.

The trip wasn't a complete mess, but if I'd been older than fourteen, I might have seen that I wasn't giving them a chance. Sometimes they spent time away from me. I made friends with a young boy named Nicholas near Salisbury Cathedral, and spent a couple of days with his family, and another time, they left me with the Russian landlady of a bed and breakfast who made strudel for me and told me stories of her escape from Russia with her daughter across Siberia.

The things that really impressed me in England were small and dislocated like me, with secrets no one could pry except through an imaginative effort. In Salisbury, we ate at a restaurant called The Haunch of Venison, where a severed hand holding an ace of spades had been discovered during excavations. I loved that. I stared at the hand, brightly lit in an alcove, still holding the card, while Nola and my mother ate dessert.

The Rosetta Stone in the British Museum with its key to understanding the garble of different tongues fascinated Nola and my mother, but not me. I was drawn to the severed foot of an extinct Dodo bird, mummified in a glass case. The plaque by the case stated that this was the only remnant of a Dodo bird, that all the millions of Dodo birds that had once existed had been distilled to this one little foot, the accidental gift to science and humanity of some Dutch sailor who only wanted a souvenir, not a record.

When I wasn't horrible on this trip, I could act pretty nice. I hated to see my sister so upset and depressed, to know that I only added to her depression, so I told stories to make her laugh, and sometimes it worked. I told my mother and Nola about YAHA. I told them about picketing in front of the White House, how a Swedish film crew mistook me for a young protester, and how a bridge collapsed in a flood as I passed over it.

And maybe that's why I still can't bear to tell my mother that this bridge didn't really collapse. Even though it happened, or didn't happen, so long ago. I suppose it's passed an imaginative statute of limitations, has passed from make-believe into truth, because there aren't many people around who can say for sure what happened when I crossed that bridge, what structures really collapsed and which ones held, who was driving that car I saw during the flood, mostly submerged in the Potomac, but still moving ahead as though guided in some rational direction.

The Greater Joy

. . . For the first time since my miraculous vision at thirteen, my life seemed to be making sense, the pieces were finally falling together, and I was at last able to justify every act, every move that I made. I knew Christ had intended me for service, but at the time I was first receiving his Message I had no idea how this was to be accomplished or in what form—I only felt a vague longing for a life of utter surrender, relinquishment of attachment, possessions, enjoyment of the senses—without being able to formulate the direction or goal I wished to follow. That night, I looked to Guru's picture, called seven times upon the Supreme, and wept. I knew that he heard me: a few moments later, when I stood before my bedroom mirror to put my hair back before I went to sleep, the soul of Alo-Devi, the Divine Mother of Guru's flock of followers, *entered* the mirror and began speaking to me with her own voice, mannerisms, and expressions, through my reflected image. "Do not be afraid, dearest Nola. You have chosen the right Path, in accordance with his Will. We will lead you to Joy, Light, and the highest Bliss. You will be *one* of us; you will walk with us in the company of the Supreme!" I jumped; the words that poured out of my reflection in the mirror were exactly the words that had emerged from Guru's picture; the voices had said: "You will be *one* of us. You will *walk* with us." I saw Alo's deep brown eyes glittering out of my own; her sublime voice turning my mouth in a smile. After her first words I could scarcely tell the color of her eyes, which blazed with such rapturous intensity that all colors, all the whims and forms of terrestrial change vanished into them as if reabsorbed in the Higher radiance of their source. I could hardly tolerate it for a few moments; it almost threatened to knock me down with the outrageous happiness it bestowed. "I adore you, Alo-Devi," I said

aloud to the mirror. "Your beauty murders my senses. How much love can a human tolerate, Mother?" I said goodnight and withdrew, inexpressibly happy, from the mirror.

The following morning I was again ravaged by all kinds of doubts. I was tormented by the urge to run to India, to cast off everything I owned and live in the streets, sleep in the gutter or in the open air by the Ganges. "It is a hard request you have made of me, Lord," I cried, looking toward the ceiling. "I have a terrible passion for the East, and I don't know how it can be squelched." I chanted Supreme again seven times and looked at Guru's picture. "Please resolve me in this" I pleaded to his face. "My mind is still in confusion." After gazing at him for some moments I put the picture down. Immediately afterwards I had a resurgence of the feeling that had overwhelmed me as a child, after my monumental dream. I knew, finally and decisively, that the Greater Joy lay in surrender, real surrender, the kind that requires neither place nor habitat nor external stimulus to give off its exuberance of light, The Light of the Inner World, the imperishable Truth which needs no earthly transportation to exotic retreats, for it holds that retreat abundantly within Itself. I no longer had to pursue Love and Light. I had discovered with Christ that they were within me and had only to let Love do its own work in my impassioned soul. For the first time I knew the significance of Charles Williams' words in his novel, *The Greater Trumps*: "That man has the right and the power to possess all things, with the sole provision that he is himself possessed." My living mind was at peace. I knew what to write to Guru, whom I recognized as the Embodiment of God. I have just committed my life to the spreading of His Kingdom.

All in the Family

Less than two months before my sister died, she received a letter from her Guru's spiritual partner, his shakti, Alo Devi. I have had this letter and have held onto it for many years. I don't remember where I found it or what made me want it. Like the court documents about the circumstances of my mother's relationship with Elliot Chess, this letter fills in some of the gaps in Nola's story and at the same time, adds new mystery to it. The only two documents about my sister that I kept for myself, in complete secret, for fifteen years or more (secret even to myself in a sense), are the two documents that best act as bookends to her life. All the other documents of my sister's life, including her memoir, have been sent to me by my mother. The court papers tell me how she was born, the pain and fiction of it. The letter tells me why she might have died. I can only guess that I took these documents because I knew on some intuitive level that someday I'd need to look at them, that someday they'd tell me as much about myself as they told me about Nola. That's one explanation, at least.

The letter, dated April 16th, 1973, is a four-page-long plea from Alo Devi to Nola to surrender herself entirely to Sri Ramanuja, to put herself completely in his care. The forces that were trying to pull her down were, according to Alo Devi, not so much psychological as spiritual. Alo Devi told Nola in the letter that Nola was far from insane, but that "little (but persistent) entities" had found their way into her being during her university years, and that explained everything: her voices, her nervousness, her confusion:

GURU SAYS HE WILL BE FULLY RESPONSIBLE FOR YOUR
MENTAL AND EMOTIONAL HEALTH IF YOU WILL OFFER
HIM YOUR FULL AND ENTIRE SURRENDER.

This line, all in capital letters and underlined, as I have written it, baffles me. I thought that Nola had already offered him her complete emotional and mental surrender, that she already considered herself a disciple, and that he considered her one, too. Apparently, she wasn't convinced; even one so spiritually and psychically inclined as Nola thought her cure might not be a spiritual one as she had always hoped. What despair this must have caused her, to believe she was simply mad, that all that was in her was sickness, nothing divine. She must have felt this way. She must have written this to her Guru, or else Alo Devi would not have written in this letter, "You are far from insane, believe me."

Alo Devi chided Nola in the letter for not following Guru's advice completely. The last time she had visited, she had taken a job as a waitress for a short time, and her mental health had worsened. Guru blamed this on the "lower vital forces" in the restaurant, that they had harmed her psychically. If she was to get better, Alo Devi said, she needed to follow Sri Ramanuja's advice completely. She needed to be with him. She needed to stop all psychiatric treatment: "The psychiatrists, as you have pointed out so clearly can only sedate and tranquilize the patient, but they really can't come to grips with the forces themselves." Alo Devi wrote that Nola needed to see only Sri Ramanuja, that she needed to be under his care entirely.

This would make her better.

And all disciples, of course, needed to stop taking any drugs or medication "or at least slowly diminish these."

"Come to Long Island as soon as possible," she wrote. "We shall give you great joy and affection, both inner and outer .... We shall take you to your Destined Goal. This is my *Promise*."

They kept that promise, in a manner of speaking.

*　　*　　*

A few days before Nola left for Long Island, she and I took a walk to Pandora's Books, a bookstore not far from our new house in South Bend. I clearly remember the walk, a mild day in April, up a wide tree-lined street. We so rarely did things together these days that this walk in itself was remarkable. Her mind, too, seemed lucid on this day, and I had let all my grudges drop, all my barriers. We were brother and sister. We could have been running away together in the way we had when I was five, running away at a leisurely pace, in no hurry, with no expectation of being caught, while she told me the myths behind the stars in the sky. But this was daylight.

It had been my idea to go to the bookstore. I wanted to buy a book on chess openings, my latest obsession. Nola had surprised me by asking to come along with me. "I need to get out," she told me. "We'll have a chance to talk."

Normally, this suggestion would have made me wary. I didn't want to talk about the things she wanted to talk about anymore. I didn't want to talk about spirits. I didn't want to talk about voices. I had recommitted my life to the Real, the actual, what I could see and touch. A rook, a knight, a pawn, a bishop. If I could put it out in front of me, if I could see my opponent, I felt safe, and only then.

Nola smiled at me, a benevolent smile. "I need to get out," she said. "It's such a beautiful day."

"Come along then, beautiful," I said and she laughed. She did look beautiful to me then, for the first time in months. Her hair was neat, not hatcheted, her complexion seemed less pasty, although her face was still puffy, but her eyes were clear and focused. She looked like someone who had awakened after a long midday nap, a little disoriented and disheveled, but readjusting. I wanted her to be with me.

That's what I want now, too, but the problem is that she just isn't. As much as I want her to walk with me, she doesn't. The problem is that I just don't remember what we talked about on that walk. I'd like to say we talked about her book, her memoir, that the walk to the bookstore spurred her to talk about the book she was working on. It would be so convenient to say that's what we talked about, and I'm tempted to lie, but I won't. I'm sure she knew I wouldn't understand, and if we ever spoke of her memoir, I don't remember doing so. And did we talk about her leaving for New York? Yes, I think so, but only in the most general terms. And did we talk about my mother and how glad we were she'd found a new job in South Bend? Yes, I think we did, but I can't remember a word we spoke, not a word. For me, this walk is soundless, wordless. We're moving through the atmosphere as though wading through water. We know that too much talk perjures the Real, that finally our love for one another can only be recorded in this wordless way, as a movement through time, through a dream, up this street, holding hands.

*   *   *

I wish that's all I remembered of Nola, but it's not.

That night, at dinner, she said she saw a spirit hovering near the dinner table.

"You're lying," I said. "You're just trying to get attention. It won't work anymore, so stop it, Nola. You acted normal this afternoon. Why can't you act normal now?"

"Robin," my mother said.

"You know it's true," I told my mother.

Nola didn't say anything, but just kept chewing her food. Chewing and chewing, eighteen times before she swallowed. Her pastiness was back. She disgusted me. I disgusted myself. What she reminded me of in myself I hated.

"I can't wait till you leave for good," I told her.

Still, Nola said nothing. She looked down at her food and chewed and I took my plate and left the room. I climbed the stairs two at a time, anxious to be alone, to hide away from everyone and everything, to feel nothing for anyone, to watch TV. I went into my mother's room. My grandmother had bought us a color TV, our first, and that's where my mother had installed it. *All in the Family* was on, my favorite show. I lay down on my mother's bed and started to watch the show, balancing the plate of food on my stomach.

Edith was talking to Meathead, who had just been insulted again by Archie. She was trying to make him feel better, saying that there was plenty of good in Archie, but sometimes you just needed to coax it out. Meathead raised his finger, about to respond as an incredibly loud toilet flushed offstage. He raised his eyebrows at Edith and smiled. She shrugged and the audience laughed.

I didn't hear Nola coming. She must have flown up the steps. The door banged open and I sat up, spilling the plate of food. She leaped on me and put her hands around my throat. I kicked at her, but she was too strong. Her face twisted close to mine, but she said nothing. There was simply hate and destruction in her eyes. She was nearly twice my age. I didn't stand a chance. She just kept choking, tightening her grip on my neck until I couldn't see, and then I landed a kick in her stomach and she backed off. That gave me a chance to stand. My shirt and pants were covered with the sauce from the goulash that my mother had made for dinner.

Nola regained her balance and found my neck again. My hands were flying, hitting her in the chest, the neck, the face, but she wouldn't stop. She wasn't just making a point. She wanted to kill me. And there was something in me that cut free from her at that moment. I didn't know if I was going to survive or not, but I was dead to her and she was dead to me. She was not someone I recognized at all.

We danced our way out into the hall, Nola silently choking me while I tried to gasp air. The only sounds we made were our heavy footsteps as we fought. The TV provided a laugh track in the background. Archie was still up to no good, still insulting and alienating people, but they loved him anyway.

And then my mother was there, and sound came back and so did air. She yelled, "Nola, stop. What are you doing? Get off him." But Nola wouldn't respond. She kept her fingers around my throat, on my shoulder, pressing hard, and my mother thrust herself between us.

Nola stopped and I stood behind my mother. Nola was gasping for air, too, as though someone had been choking her. "I want him to die," she said.

"You're not even my sister," I yelled at her. "You're crazy. I really hate you."

She turned away from us and ran to my room down the hall. She opened the door. She couldn't destroy me so she wanted to destroy any gateway I had to her. Right above my bed, I had hung the poster she had given me when my appendix ruptured in Columbia. The picture showed that peaceful jungle scene, all the animals gathered around one of the gods, who smiled serenely outward. So many times I had imagined myself entering that picture, drinking from the pool in the foreground, not speaking a word but understanding and being understood, finding a haven, a place to rest. She ripped it in half off the wall and I screamed. I understood, deep inside me, and I started to cry. My mother thought I was crying because Nola had hurt me, and she hugged me. "You know she loves you," my mother said, but I knew no such thing.

"What were you thinking?" my mother asked Nola, who simply headed downstairs without another word.

And that's the last mental picture I have of her, sick and angry beyond belief at me, angry enough to try to erase me from this world and her mind. I wish I could erase this image from *my* mind, but I know I can't, that it will always be there.

Beyond this, my memory fades and Nola becomes a story.

Riding the Whip

A short story by Robin Hemley

The night before my sister died, a friend of my parents, Natalie Ganzer, took me and her niece to a carnival. I couldn't stand Natalie, but I fell in love with the niece, a girl about fifteen named Rita. On the Ferris wheel Rita grabbed my hand. On any other ride I would have thought she was only frightened and wanted security. But this Ferris wheel was so tame and small. There was nothing to be afraid of at fifty feet.

When we got down and the man let us out of the basket, I kept hold of Rita's hand, and she didn't seem to mind.

"Oh, I'm so glad you children are enjoying the evening," said Natalie. "It's so festive. There's nothing like a carnival, is there?"

Normally, I would have minded being called a child, but not tonight. Things were improving. There was nothing to worry about, my mother had told me over the phone earlier that evening. Yes, Julie had done a stupid thing, but only to get attention.

Still, something was wrong, something bugged me about that night, where I was, the carnival and its sounds. I was having too much fun and I knew I shouldn't be. Already I had won a stuffed animal from one of the booths and given it to Rita. And usually I got nauseated on rides, but tonight they just made me laugh. Red neon swirled around on the rides, and barkers yelled at us on the fairway. Popguns blew holes in targets, and there were so many people screaming and laughing beside us that I could hardly take it in. I just stood there feeling everyone else's fun moving through me, and I could hardly hear what Natalie and Rita were saying. "Come on, Jay," shouted Rita. My hand was being tugged. "Let's ride the Whip." The whip. That didn't make any sense to me. A whip wasn't something you rode. It was something to hurt you, something from movies that came down hard on prisoners' backs and left them scarred.

"You can't ride a whip," I shouted to her over the noise.

She laughed and said, "Why not? Don't be scared. You won't get sick, I promise."

"Aren't you having fun, Jay?" Natalie said. "Your parents want you to have fun, and I'm sure that's what Julie wants, too."

I didn't answer, though I was having fun. Things seemed brighter and louder than a moment before. I could even hear a girl on the Ferris wheel say to someone, "You're cute, did you know that?" One carny in his booth stood out like a detail in a giant painting. He held a bunch of strings in his hand. The strings led to some stuffed animals. "Everyone's a winner," he said.

The carnival was just a painting, a bunch of petals in a bowl, which made me think of Julie. She was an artist and painted still lifes mostly, but she didn't think she was any good. My parents had discouraged her, but I bought a large painting of hers once with some paper money I cut from a notebook. A week before the carnival she came into my room and slashed the painting to bits. "She's not herself," my mother told me. "You know she loves you."

Now we stood at the gates of the Whip. Rita gave her stuffed animal to Natalie, who held it by the paw as though it were a new ward of hers. The man strapped us into our seat and Rita said to me, "You're so quiet. Aren't you having fun?"

"Sure," I said. "Doesn't it look like it?"

"Your sister's crazy, isn't she?" said Rita. "I mean, doing what she did."

I knew I shouldn't answer her, that I should step out of the ride and go home.

"She just sees things differently," I said.

"What do you mean?" Rita said. She was looking at me strangely, as though maybe I saw things differently, too. I didn't want to see differently. I didn't want to become like my sister.

"Sure she's crazy," I said. "I don't even care what happens to her."

Then the ride started up, and we laughed and screamed. We moved like we weren't people anymore, but electrical currents charging from different sources.

In the middle of the ride something grazed my head. A metal bar hung loose along one of the turns and each time we whipped around it, the bar touched me. The metal barely hit me, but going so fast it felt like being knocked with a sandbag. It didn't hit anyone else, just me, and I tried several times to get out of the way, but I was strapped in and there was no way to avoid it.

At the end of the ride I was completely punch drunk, and I could barely speak. Rita, who mistook my expression for one of pleasure, led me over to Natalie.

"That was fun," said Rita. "Let's go on the Cat and Mouse now."

My vision was blurry, and my legs were wobbling a bit. "I want to go on the Whip again," I said.

Natalie and Rita looked at each other. Natalie reached out towards my head, and I pulled back from her touch. "You're *bleeding,* Jay," she said. Her hand stayed in midair, and she looked at me as though she were someone in a gallery trying to get a better perspective on a curious painting.

I broke away from them into the crowd and made my way back to the Whip. After paying the man, I found the same seat. I knew which one it was because it was more beat up than the rest, with several gashes in the cushion, as though someone had taken a long knife and scarred it that way on purpose.

Danger, Pills

. . . I began to be aware of a presence standing over my right shoulder in a majestic red cloak, from a height of about seven feet. It was trying urgently to tell me something. My mother was seated at a small table with the British girl, and the girl's husband, a skeptic and pessimist, sat to my left on the sofa. The board was rocking excitedly, as if shaken by the urgency of a message that had to be received at once. "Nola . . . Nola . . . Danger!" it spelled out so quickly that my mother and the girl could hardly follow the moving disc with their fingers. The board became very agitated and the disc started to move about wildly. At this moment I felt the figure at my right rise up a few inches into the air (this seemed to be a characteristic preparation of these spirits for entering a human mind to convey messages), glide towards my right ear and finally enter my brain from the base of my skull. I *heard* a voice repeatedly insist "Danger . . . pills . . . PILLS." My mouth spontaneously flew open and I said "pills" to the surrounding company without knowing what I was doing or why; at that precise moment the same word was spelled out on the board, and the room shook as if some psychic earthquake had destroyed its equilibrium . . .

The Space between Contradictions

Little know I thy child's father
Of land or sea he's living on.
"Silkie" (traditional ballad)

I came home from school one day to find the door open and the house quiet. One of my mother's students, a woman named Lara, stood in the living room, hands in her pockets, looking awkward, disoriented, as though she'd just dropped into our living room from another dimension.

"Where's my mother?" I asked.

"She's gone to New York," the student said. "Nola tried to kill herself. She's in a coma."

"How?" I asked.

"Pills. She OD'd or something. I'm not sure, but your mother told me to meet you. You're going to stay at Norma's tonight."

"I can't."

"Sure you can," she said. "What do you mean, you can't?"

Lara was one of my favorites among my mother's students. I liked her because she talked to me as if I were a human being, not some crazy kid, and she always said what was on her mind. She wasn't the most sensitive person in the world, but I liked her directness, and she had a friendly nature that made her easy to get along with.

"I just can't go away from my home," I said. "If I do, Nola will die."

"What kind of talk is that?" she said, and laughed. "Nola's not going to die, and anyway, it's out of your hands. I can't stay with you. I'm going to Arizona for the summer in the morning. You have to stay with Norma."

Norma was another friend and sometime student of my mother's. Norma was an older student, about my mother's age. She was the widow of a coroner whose hobby it had been to take photos of the people he had performed autopsies on. One time, Norma showed me these photos as though flipping through a family album: a man who had died of a heart attack, a boy about nine whose snow-laden porch roof had collapsed on him. Of course, I couldn't take my eyes off these photos.

But this was not the place I wanted to go while my sister lay in a coma. Still, I was helpless, and eventually Lara talked me into going there.

Norma didn't talk to me about Nola. She wanted to talk about cheery things. A carnival was in town and she decided the best medicine for me would be to go with her and a niece about my age, to take my mind off my sister.

I went and I forgot about Nola. I spent the night going from ride to ride, thinking myself in love with Norma's niece, drunk on the carnival lights, the sounds, the realness of it all.

The next morning I awoke to the telephone ringing beside my bed. I let it ring until it stopped and then I stared at it until I couldn't ignore it any longer. I picked up the phone and at that moment heard my mother tell Norma, "Nola's dead. She died this morning."

"What?" I said.

"Get off the line, Robin," my mother said, and I did. I hung up.

*　　*　　*

Over the years, I've asked my mother time and again how Nola died. "Did she kill herself?" I asked, and my mother has always told me no. What happened was that her doctor prescribed too large a dose of Thorazine for her, and her body couldn't handle it. She had kidney failure, went into a coma, and died. She was at my grandmother's house when this happened, in Long Beach, New York. My grandmother had tried and failed to awaken Nola one morning, and that's when she'd called for an ambulance.

This was always the accepted version in my family. Even though she had tried to kill herself before, this time it was pure accident, a mistake, someone else we could blame. I always wondered, as did my brother, why my mother never sued the doctor who prescribed Nola's medication. My mother told me that at the time she couldn't, that it would be too painful, and I understood this. More recently, she's told me that another doctor told her she'd lose a lawsuit because the amount of Thorazine the doctor prescribed was high, yes, but within acceptable limits. Acceptable limits varied from person to person.

Still, I always believed that if I asked my mother enough times, she might someday tell me something different, not because I thought she was lying, but because I thought the truth could be remade, that perhaps I had heard wrong, that maybe I had remembered wrong, just as I had once hoped that my father would one day be cured of death, that someone would tell me he hadn't died for good.

I don't think I'll ever stop believing that Nola killed herself, in some way, no matter what anyone tells me. Even if it was an accident, as everyone else believes, I believe that she could have lived if she'd wanted to. I don't think she wanted to live. I think that all human recourse had failed, that she had lost her faith in this world and was ready to move on to the next.

I know now, from piecing the story together through my various documents, that Nola left South Bend for New York in April 1973 in response to a letter from Alo Devi, to be with her Guru, to commit her life entirely to him. She died barely two months later, at my grandmother's home. But that's all I know, except that something must have gone wrong at the ashram. Otherwise, wouldn't she have been at the ashram when she died, not at my grandmother's house? And they wanted her to stop taking medication, so if she'd been following her Guru's advice, she would have been taking nothing. As Alo Devi wrote in her letter, Nola had a stubborn streak, and maybe she had disobeyed her Guru once again, had tried to keep taking her medication against his wishes, much as she had worked in a restaurant against his wishes. Maybe her confusion, her visions and voices kept up, despite his assurances, and so finally, she left. I'll never know for sure. But it's plausible.

I call up my mother and ask her these difficult questions. "Why did she leave the ashram?" I ask.

"I don't know," my mother says. "Maybe she felt herself getting sick again."

"That's what I think," I tell her.

"The last week of her life, Nola was trying to get into the hospital," my mother tells me. "That's what Ida told me. They kept telling her there were no beds."

"Wait a second, back up," I say. "What hospital? You've never told me this."

"The Long Beach Hospital."

"You mean she was trying to commit herself again?"

"Yes."

"Mom, are you sure . . . Nola didn't kill herself?"

"Yes," my mother says, definitively. "Ida said she seemed to be happy and she was doing a lot of artwork. There was an art fair and she was supposed to have her art in the exhibit the next day."

"But . . ."

"The doctor told me she didn't kill herself," my mother says.

"How did he know?" I ask.

"Because he was in Long Beach. He was Ida's doctor."

"But how did he know she didn't kill herself? How would he know? I mean, there was too much Thorazine in her system. How would he know how it got there, what the intention was?"

"I guess he just assumed it," my mother says.

He just assumed it. This statement knocks me out. I imagine this doctor, this friend of my grandmother's perhaps trying to save her the extra pain of knowing her granddaughter took her own life.

"She was planning to be in the art show the next day," my mother continues. "She wouldn't commit suicide if she was planning to be in a show. Ida said she was happy."

"But she was trying to get into the hospital and she couldn't," I say. "They wouldn't let her in."

"Yes," my mother says. "She wouldn't kill herself if she was trying to get into the hospital."

I don't see the logic in that, but I don't say anything. I see it as just the reason she might have killed herself. I let it rest.

"Did they do an autopsy?"

"Yes."

"And they found too much Thorazine."

My mother pauses at the pain of this. "Too much Thorazine," she says softly. "The doctor had been prescribing too much from the beginning, 600 milligrams or something like that."

I think about that. I'm probably just dramatizing. She probably didn't kill herself. Like my mother says, it was an accident.

"I don't think I'll be able to read your book," my mother tells me.

"I know," I say.

"But I admire you for doing it."

*   *   *

I didn't want to go to the funeral. I asked my mother if I had to go. I just couldn't bear it, I told her, but she said she wouldn't be able to bear it without me.

On the drive from Colum-
bus to Athens, I sat in the
backseat, looking out at the
sparkling sun and trees, the
natural beauty of the day, and
I heard Nola talking to me.
I swear I did. But what we
talked about was between us,
unrepeatable, irretrievable.
To voice it would be to lose it.

Nola was buried in a grave
next to my father in Athens,
Ohio.

*   *   *

I go downstairs and talk to Beverly. "I just had the most remarkable discussion with my mother. I don't know, maybe my sister *did* kill herself."

I tell Beverly about the conversation and she agrees with my mother that Nola sounded too happy to kill herself. "Someone who's that sick wouldn't be able to fake their happiness," she tells me. "Your grandmother said she seemed happy, and she was going to be in an art show the next day."

"Yes, but Nola loved Ida. She would have felt protective of her, I think. You've heard about people, who seemed happy, killing themselves. If you're going to kill yourself, I don't think the plans you make for tomorrow are that important. It's only the moment. I've always felt as though she killed herself. I always wondered if I kept asking how she died, if I might eventually get a different answer."

"From yourself?" Beverly asks.

"From my mother."

"Intuition can be pretty powerful," Beverly says, "but there's no way you'll ever know. Your sister was such a writer, you'd think she would have left a note."

"There was no note," I say. "If there'd been a note, I'd have my answer."

"Sometimes people need a reason," Beverly says. "To know that it was willful, maybe that's easier for you than thinking it was just some senseless accident."

"I don't know," I say. But I know she's right. I guess I need to believe that she wrote this end to herself.

"I don't know either," Beverly says sadly. "I can't imagine what it must be like to have that illness."

I can, but I don't say anything.

Beverly asks me about Nola's father and my father. "How did she feel about her real father?"

"She didn't know him," I say. "When he died, my mother came to her room and said, 'I hope this doesn't upset you too much,' and Nola said, 'Why should it? I never knew him.'"

"That makes sense. And how did she get along with your father?"

"Toward the end of his life, they had these great philosophical discussions. But he treated her terribly most of the time."

"That's too bad. Because she wasn't his child?"

"Right."

I can see Beverly gently probing, making this argument of abandonment and betrayal as the cause for Nola's problems. And perhaps this is the only sound argument one can make. Abandonment and betrayal can leave a pretty large wake.

"Did her Guru want her to stop taking her medication?"

"Yes."

"Maybe that's why she left the ashram then. Maybe she stopped taking her medication, but she felt herself getting sick again, and she needed it, so she left."

"Yes, that's plausible," I say. "That sounds right. That's what I think."

"I guess we'll never know," she says, although she doesn't say it dismissively, but in a tone of voice that suggests that *not* knowing is an answer, just as much as knowing is an answer, the way we say the words of a prayer, and sometimes we don't understand the words of the prayer or its true meaning, but we know what to say at the end of the prayer. We say amen.

"Thanks," I tell Beverly softly, feeling happy she's entered into this final mystery. I've thought before at times that she didn't care, but I think it's not that at all, that I was afraid that she would tell me truths I didn't want to face. Sometimes Beverly brings me up hard against myself in a way I don't always appreciate at the moment. But that's not the same as not caring. At one point in our conversation, when she suggested I might look up hospital records about my sister or interview anyone still alive, she told me, "You don't really want to know," not harshly, not as an accusation, but gently, just as a matter of fact. And I said, "No, I don't."

The next morning, right before I awoke, I dreamed of words, round and crystalline, like fortune-teller balls, descending slowly through the depths of an ocean, and coming to rest gently on the bottom without shattering. As they settled in the silt, all that decayed life and dirt fluttered upward, enveloping the balls. But even though I couldn't see them anymore, I knew they were still there, that eventually things would settle again. The dream had no one in it, not even me. I felt peaceful, serene even. I felt somehow reassured that the words had finally touched bottom.

Rita

I had a girlfriend named Rita in graduate school—we met the summer after my first year there when I was twenty-three, and I think what attracted us were our mutual quirky sensibilities. During the first weeks of our infatuation, we would write strange little cards to each other full of malapropisms and leave them anonymously in our respective mailboxes. She worked at a convalescent center that summer making salad for the residents, and somehow we came to call this job "Salad Control." "Are you going to Salad Control tonight?" Like me, she had grown up spoiled and had a lilting, kind of decadent laugh, a little like Liza Minelli in *Cabaret.* Rita had been adopted at the age of four and was doted on by her mother, tolerated, I think, by her stern father.

"No, Robinito. Tonight, Salad Control must scrape by without me," and she laughed. "Tonight I am going to take a bath and luxuriate."

She had been married already, for about ten days, and I'm sure I saw her as worldly. And she was an older woman, twenty-five at the time. This was my worldly phase, when I was trying on worldliness to see how it fit.

After grad school we moved to Chicago. How much happiness we found those next few months in the city, I can't recall. I remember some of those moments, a street festival, going to movies, out to eat. But, everything, even our entertainments from that time, seem out of kilter, as though everything we did together was slightly insane: We had a barbecue one night on the tiny porch of Rita's apartment, and the smoke from it flooded into the hallway—an angry neighbor, invisible, but enraged apparently, stole the grill and our food from the porch when we went inside to fetch some water to douse the flames. A man in tattered clothes came to the window of a restaurant where we ate one night and pressed his face to the glass and made grotesque chewing motions. The movies we saw: Woody Allen's *Zelig,* about a man without a personality, and *Frances,* the film with Jessica Lange about Frances Farmer, the actress with too much personality, driven mad, and then lobotomized. One day, we went to a Cubs game, and the Cubs weren't doing well. "You'd think in a city as large as Chicago they could find better players," Rita said. That made me laugh, that kind of loopy comment.

Rita had a friend named Stephanie, her only other friend in Chicago besides me for a while. Stephanie was a recent transplant, too, although she had grown up on the city's South Side. Rita and I met Stephanie on the same day—I remember her sitting on my apartment floor. She didn't say much, but she seemed gentle and smart, and she and Rita became friends, although Stephanie seemed to need Rita more than the other way around. Rita borrowed twenty-five dollars from Stephanie once, saw her once every couple of weeks, sometimes avoided her. Stephanie called one day at work and asked if she could meet with Rita, but Rita was bored by her and made some excuse. The next day, Rita called me at work—she had stayed home. "Robin," she said in a stricken voice. "Stephanie killed herself this morning." I left work and went to Rita's apartment to be with her—she blamed herself for not meeting up with Stephanie. I tried to console her—a few days later, after the funeral, Stephanie's mother told Rita that she had been mentioned in Stephanie's suicide note, that she had asked her mother to collect the twenty-five dollars Rita owed her. The mother wasn't asking for the money, only wanted to call Rita because she thought Rita might be able to give her some clue to her daughter's unhappiness. Rita couldn't give her a clue, and that night wrote her a rambling apologetic letter with a check for her debt. After that, her behavior started to change—Rita was overcome with guilt, and nothing anyone said could help her through it.

She told me one day that she thought Stephanie's mother blamed her for Stephanie's death, that Stephanie's mother was trying to have her killed.

Although Rita had said some strange things before, she'd never said anything quite so bizarre, and I was silent a minute before I spoke. "You know, maybe it would be a good idea if you talked with someone about this."

"I'm talking to you," she said.

I took her hands and said as firmly as I could, although I could feel myself trembling, "Rita, no one is trying to kill you. No one blames you for Stephanie's death but yourself. What I want is for you to see that, that's all."

"Get out of here," she told me. "You're not my friend."

So I left her apartment, but the next day, she called me to apologize, just made me promise that I would not suggest a psychiatrist again. Reluctantly, I promised.

Later that week, we were taking the El back home from work when she suddenly told me to get off at the next stop. It wasn't our stop.

"Why do you want to get off here?"

"Please, Robin," she said. "Do you see those men?" and she indicated two black men who weren't even looking in our direction. "Stephanie's mother sent them to kill me."

Stephanie was African American. "You're afraid of anyone who's black now?" I sounded cold. It didn't make any sense. Couldn't she see? But she couldn't. She was terrified, and so I got off at the next station with her.

A week later, she told me that she had seen a ghost, that early one morning she'd gone to a deserted hallway at work and saw something heading toward her, a light. She thought it was Stephanie, and it was cold. It passed right through her body.

For much of the summer, she stayed in her apartment and ate and watched TV. She didn't want to go anywhere outside, but she stopped talking about Stephanie's mother trying to kill her.

I seemed entwined with her in a strange way—I loved her and cared for her and saw her losing a sense of herself. Against her warnings, I suggested a couple of more times that she talk to someone, that she find some help, but each time she reacted angrily. I couldn't let her go—I felt even more attached, pulled toward her, asked her to marry me at a restaurant one day. She touched my cheek. "Don't say something you don't mean."

We chose the wrong things to do—that night, we went to see *Zelig*, the next night *Frances*—the man pressed his face to the glass, or maybe it didn't happen in that order. Maybe there was none. Maybe I'm imagining all of this.

"My mother called me," she told me one day.

"Your mother?" She had a gin and tonic in her hand. I knew she wasn't talking about her adoptive mother—something in the way she said it.

"My real mother."

It always comes down to identity, I guess, that fruitless, endless search. We see ourselves in relief against our parents, our siblings, ourselves, our children. I think of the Eleusinian Mysteries, Persephone kidnapped by Hades from her mother, the Earth, tempted by a few

pomegranate seeds, condemned to spend part of each year in his shadowy kingdom. I think of Orpheus leading Eurydice out of the underworld and looking back, condemning her to remain forever, or Lot's
wife looking back, and being frozen in that backward, heedless glance.
We always accept these stories, or at least I do, without really asking
why it was so important for them not to look back. Wasn't it enough
that they were leaving? I suppose whenever we look back on trauma,
on misery and degradation, we risk being stuck there, back in the past,
unable to find our way to safety again. We risk, or at least I do, being
pulled under. The journey backward, to retrieve something, or the
journey forward to escape, is always going to cost you something you
love, something you might not have risked had you known.

And Rita's mother had called—just called—after how many years?
This was not good timing. This was not a good time for Rita to find
her real mother, and this mother was not a good mother for Rita at
this moment. The reason she had given up Rita for adoption in the
first place, it turned out, was because she had been hospitalized. She'd
spent most of her life in and out of hospitals. Rita's mother had
been diagnosed as schizophrenic, and this was the time it had to be
revealed.

This was perfect timing.

I wonder what I was thinking. I think I was just frightened.

*   *   *

I awoke in the middle of the night, aware that I was alone in bed in
Rita's apartment. Her front door was open to the hallway, wide open.

"Rita," I called, but there was no answer. I searched her small apartment, but she was gone. What had drawn her outside at three in the
morning, so frantically that she didn't even have time or desire
enough to close the door? To say I was worried is an understatement—
I was frantic, uncomprehending, unsure of what to do, and unable to
make a move. It seemed too soon to call the police, but walking alone
in the middle of the night in the city was dangerous, for a man or a
woman. There were gangs—the Latin Kings often lounged on the
stoop of my apartment building; once I witnessed a drive-by shooting.
A man had been shot and killed a block away while walking around
our neighborhood late at night a couple of weeks before Rita disappeared. She had left no note, nothing. I was in her apartment, alone,
with no explanation.

I sat on the edge of the bed and waited. An hour later, I realized I hadn't closed the door. Something stirred in the hallway. I poked my head out, but saw nothing, which spooked me, so I shut the door. Had she taken her keys? I couldn't find them. The door locked automatically, so I waited in the living room.

At 6 A.M., the door opened, and Rita stood there looking as radiant and joyful as I'd ever seen her. She had been so depressed, so horribly shaken by the events of the past few months, I had hardly seen her smile. There was something fierce and wild in her eyes, and she had a look of abandon, of complete ecstasy. I was taken in, drawn to her, and stood up from the bed to give her a hug, but she didn't even seem to see me. She walked past me and knelt down on the floor, and clasped her hands together, mumbling something unintelligible. I stood over her, and put out a hand, touched her shoulder.

"Rita," I said in a soft and terrified voice, probably no more intelligible to her than her words were to me.

She seemed to notice me then and looked up, through me, above me, beside me. "Robinito," she said. "The Lord promised he'd protect me. He found me wandering."

"What were you doing outside?" I asked, nonsensically, as though she should have known better to be out late at night where the Lord might find her.

She said that God had told her to walk to the Lakeview Covenant Church, a name that I didn't recognize at first, but she told me its location, and I could visualize it, a large squat hall with a parking lot as huge, near a bowling alley I sometimes went to with friends. I had walked past the church on several occasions, the doors closed. I'd like to say I heard the shouts of the preacher over his microphone, spitting words about the Lake of Fire and eternal damnation, but I didn't. I'd like to say something that could dismiss the congregation as a bunch of kooks, but I can't, not if I'm being honest with myself. I do still believe that churches like this prey as often as they pray, but that's all the condemning I'll do, because I wasn't there with Rita that night she was saved, and *I* certainly couldn't save her. I don't know what the preacher told her that night, or I've forgotten, although I remember he knelt with her in prayer and exorcised her demons, tapped her on the forehead, and out they fell, writhing back to the underworld where they belonged and not in her head anymore.

I dismissed her experience, didn't want to hear it, wanted her back the way she had been, tried to convince her that what she had experienced wasn't real. She, in turn, tried to convince me that what I was experiencing wasn't real, and wanted me to come back to the church with her because she didn't want me to go to hell.

"You're acting crazy, Rita," I told her.

Rita kicked me out of her apartment and I didn't see her for a week. She wouldn't answer my phone calls. The next time I saw her was on Broadway in New Town, standing beside her preacher, answering his fierce exhortations with a raised Bible, like Lady Liberty, shouting "Hallelujah!"

That week I probably spent a couple of hundred dollars in phone calls, to friends across the country, people I trusted, people who knew Rita. None of them could quite comprehend what was going on. Like me, they were astounded, in awe, could offer me no advice, though some suggested that Rita had always been a bit off kilter, and others focused on me, trying to assuage my guilt. "You're not responsible for her, Robin. She's making her own decisions."

True enough. But this was too sudden a change in her, one borne from desperation, and being a goal-oriented American male, I wanted solutions. I wanted her fixed, which meant the way she was before, not someone new. I didn't want her to believe in something that I couldn't believe in, and this frightened me as much as what I perceived to be her illness, I think. And I was thinking of Nola, dead for ten years, every bit as touched as Rita, whom I had abandoned and renounced because she believed in things I could not believe in, because she, too, was unrestrained, wild in her ecstasy and her pain.

Rita called me early one evening and asked me to come over. She told me she loved me and she was sorry for pushing me away. I told her I missed her and she said she missed me, too. She sounded normal to me, and I wondered, I hoped that maybe she was coming to her senses finally.

When I arrived, her door was locked—she'd demanded I give her back her key after I had tried, once again, to get her to see a psychiatrist—I could hear her mumbling behind the door, and then she screamed OHGODOHMYGOD as though she was in great pain, and I had no idea what was going on behind that door. I pounded, asked her to let me in, but she wouldn't, so I started pounding on the neighbors' doors. I wanted help, I'm not sure what kind of help, but I couldn't go through this with Rita alone anymore. No one answered. They were all frightened probably by the madman knocking on their doors. That hallway was always deserted anyway; people locked their doors behind them quickly as though they all had outstanding warrants. Or perhaps they were all still angry at us for our barbecue experience gone terribly wrong.

"Go away," Rita said. "You're trying to hurt me."

"You invited me over," I said through the door.

She opened the door and went back to praying, mumbling, kneeling over a stain on her wood floor. She turned to look at me, her eyes fearful. I knelt down beside her and touched her shoulder, hugged her. She pulled away and said, "That stain just appeared. It's the Devil's mark."

I didn't want her to kick me out, to yell at me and accuse me of trying to hurt her. I told her as much and then added, "This stain has been here since you moved in."

But she ignored me. Her expression changed and she opened up her Bible. "I found us in here," she said. "You and me." She opened up the book, seemingly at random and started to read a passage.

> Nebuchadnezzar the king of
>   Babylon has devoured me,
> he has crushed me;
> he has made me an empty vessel,
>   he has swallowed me like a
>   monster;
> he has filled his belly with my
>   delicacies.

I listened, wondering what she meant, trying to make sense of her words, and the words she pulled from the Bible. Did she see me as a monster, had she been crushed, had I devoured her? She closed the book and I whispered, "I don't see."

She looked at me tenderly, touched my cheek and opened up the Bible to another passage:

> But that same night the word of the Lord came to Nathan, "Go and tell my servant David, 'Thus says the Lord: You shall not build me a house to dwell in. For I have not dwelt in a house since the day I led up Israel to this day, but I have gone from tent to tent and from dwelling to dwelling . . .

"You and I, Robinito. We are both dwellings," she said. "Not empty vessels."

She wouldn't let me stay with her any longer, although I wanted to.

I was impure. She loved me still, but in a different way. She felt sorry for me, she said. She felt sorry that I was going to hell. I felt that someone should be with her always, that something was building in her, applying a volcanic pressure.

I'm not sure how long this period lasted, a week, two, maybe a month. After a while, the psyche adjusts to any behavior, any situation; what seemed abnormal before became the norm. Rita had become a new person, truly born again into someone I couldn't recognize or understand. Maybe all of these events only took place over a period of four or five days. I'm not sure anymore, and I'm not sure it matters. What matters is that one day I discovered her with the door to her apartment open again, and this time she was in it. She said various people had been up to see her, people she didn't know. She was giving them her possessions, a Walkman I'd given her she presented to some kids. They told a man who came up to her apartment.

"His breath smelled," she told me and laughed.

"What happened? What did he do?" I asked.

"He told me we should have sex, that he was my husband, but I told him no, that he was the false husband. He said it didn't matter, but I screamed and I kicked him and he left, but he said he was coming back. He wants to kill me. He's going to kill me at nine tonight. That's the deadline. Nine tonight."

"No one's going to kill you," I told her, but I wasn't sure. I had no idea what had happened, if the man was real, but he seemed to be real. She described a real man to me.

I told her to pack her clothes, she was leaving this apartment. I told her to bring only the things she needed, and one or two things she cherished. She asked me where she was going and I told her she was going home, to her parents.

Of course, now, many years later, I wonder why I didn't call her parents earlier, and I don't have a precise answer for that, except that it seemed to me the last option, one of utter desperation. She rarely talked of her parents, except negatively, especially her father. When she talked of them at all, it was in terms of material goods—her father was supposed to deliver a used car to her that summer, but she doubted he'd come through on his promise. Her mother, who had moved out West, was, according to Rita, self-absorbed and frivolous. But, of course, I was getting Rita's perceptions of her parents. I had never met them, never even spoken to either one. While she had never portrayed either one as evil incarnate, and she clearly cared for them both, she also seemed emotionally removed from them. They were out of the picture, at least until I started wondering about the accuracy of any of Rita's perceptions. Rita was twenty-seven then, and had lived away from her parents for nearly ten years, but I finally realized that this was too much for me. Something terrible had happened to her emotionally, psychically, and I clearly couldn't help her in this. Now, if something physical happened as well, I wouldn't be able to do much more than call an ambulance. Ultimately, I had so little influence.

I retrieved her suitcase from the back of her closet, set it on her bed, and asked her to help me help her pack. But she could hardly focus. She knelt beside her bed, praying frantically, asking God to forgive her, to protect her from the devil. She looked at me as though I were a stranger, as though I might hurt her, too. The day was steaming—late summer—she hadn't even turned on her window fan, no it was gone. The Devil had taken that, too, apparently. Her hair was matted, her face drenched in sweat, her skin red. I'm not even sure what I looked like.

"There's nothing you can do," she told me. "You can't fight the Devil. If he wants me, I'm his."

I gathered up all the knives in the apartment and threw them in the back of her closet. She seemed so sure of her own death, that I knew she'd hurt herself if no one else did.

I packed a suitcase, alone, without her help, filled with the clothes I thought she might need, a hairbrush, toiletries, essentials, although she wouldn't help me with any of this. Didn't she want to take anything with her?

There's nothing I'll need. She didn't say that, but that's the look she gave me. There was one memento of hers that I made sure she carried with her, something I knew she valued, a pocket watch made of rose gold that had belonged to her grandmother. I simply wanted her to have something that she associated with goodness, with safety.

When we left the apartment, it was 8:30, thirty minutes before the deadline the Devil had given her.

At my apartment, she only grew more agitated, pacing, mumbling to herself. I had also taken her address book, and with Rita in the living room, I dialed her mother from my bedroom. I hardly gave the woman a chance to answer.

"Rita has to come home," I told her. "She's acting . . . There's something really wrong with her, and she needs to come home. Right away."

I really hadn't prepared the woman at all, and we had never talked before, so she doubted me.

"Rita's always been strange," she told me and laughed. "If you'd seen some of the things she did . . . she's always been a handful."

"No," I said.

"Well, her father's coming to Chicago in a couple of weeks. He can see her then."

"No," I said, my voice probably edging toward hysteria. If Rita's mother wasn't going to help, I didn't know what I'd do. "She really needs help now."

"Is she there? Let me speak to her."

I went into the living room and told Rita her mother was on the phone and wanted to speak to her. Rita took this as though I was informing her of a business call. "Is it nine yet?" she asked me.

"Speak to her," I said, and handed her the phone. She went into my room and closed the door. It was nearly nine when she entered the bedroom and I could hardly hear her. I almost imagined that I'd find her gone, a ring of ashes on my bed, the phone bleating by my pillow, but she emerged twenty minutes later, whole, more or less, and handed me back the phone.

Rita's mother sounded completely different now. Her voice was hollow, terrified, like mine, but a little calmer than me. We were fellow initiates. We understood one another now. We had become new people. "Can you buy her a ticket?" she asked.

"I can't," I said, which was true. I had one credit card, with $1000 in credit, and two dollars remaining before I went over my limit. Rita's mother told me she'd see what she could do, and I told her that it was important for Rita to get some help as soon as possible, to find a flight as soon as she could.

To be truthful, there was a part of me closing off to Rita at that moment, learning to care less about her. I felt relief that someone else had some inkling now, and I also couldn't wait to put her on a plane. I know that's not a generous feeling. I know that's selfish, but I was exhausted. I wanted her to find help, yes, but I didn't necessarily want to be part of that help anymore. I don't think I was consciously thinking these things through, but I'm sure a part of me felt relief that Rita, finally, was someone else's responsibility.

A half hour later, Rita's mother called back. The earliest flight she could find left O'Hare the next day at four in the afternoon.

I had no idea what to do with Rita until then. I wasn't even sure she could survive that long. Now that the initial deadline had passed, Rita made a new deadline. Ten o'clock. There was no reasoning with her.

Instead of feeling happy that the Devil hadn't killed her, she seemed more convinced than ever. With every hour, there was a new deadline, and so we spent the entire evening. I stayed up with her that whole night, sitting on my back porch, which was a hundred and fifty feet from the tracks of the Ravenswood line of the Chicago El. The track curved around my apartment building, screeched and sometimes sparked as it made its way through the city. I tried to distract her and kept time by the slowly lightening sky and the train going by every thirty minutes. The passengers, one or two in the middle of the night, couldn't see us as they passed, but we could see them, and I always stopped in midsentence to look at them, to wonder who they were and if they were happy and sane—just seeing other human beings that night seemed like a kind of lifeline. Throughout the night Rita prayed, babbled, chanted, made up holy songs, wept, and even screamed as though her flesh were being rended. I tried to comfort her, argued with her, sang other songs, more down-to-earth, tried to get her to join in. The neighbors, if they heard, never made a sound—other than the sounds of traffic and the occasional train passing, we were alone. And the Devil, wherever he was, kept us dangling.

At seven in the morning we left the apartment and took a cab to the airport. This is undoubtedly the earliest I've ever arrived for a flight, but Rita kept getting more and more agitated, and I just couldn't deal with her alone anymore. I thought that perhaps if she were in a public place she might keep some semblance of composure—at least we'd be somewhere where others might notice, might offer me some assistance, I thought.

And I was right. At the airport, she seemed almost her old self. She talked about Chicago, how she didn't think she'd miss it, how she'd only miss me, and when would I come visit. "I don't know," I said. "As soon as I can, but I'll have to wait until I can get some vacation days."

"You can quit your job," she said. "Chicago is an evil place."

Easy for her to say. She was crazy, anyway. A part of me was thinking this. A part of me thought how much I loved her, and how horrible and twisted everything had become. A part of me didn't want her to leave. A part of me wanted her gone, evaporated.

O'Hare is a large airport, but not so large when you arrive seven hours before a scheduled flight. Things have changed since 1983—the new United wing, for instance, with its mad flashing neon sculptures, the jangling music that accompanies you on the moving sidewalk and the monotonous voice as you approach the end, warning you to step off carefully. None of that was there. And, at that time, the El still did-n't reach all the way to O'Hare, and many of the shops were different. But the travelers were there, almost the same, all moving forward, step-ping around us whenever Rita paused for a vision. I know O'Hare now. I know it as well as any place, and I never change planes there or arrive in Chicago without thinking of that day, trying to keep Rita safe and together, trying to lead her out of that burning underworld.

At two-thirty we sat in an airport bar. She wanted a drink, and al-though I tried to dissuade her, she did what she always did to get her way. She made light of my concern, made me doubt my own percep-tions, made me forget that I'd spent the better part of the last twenty-four hours trying to convince her that the Devil didn't want to kill her.

"Just a drink," she said. "Don't worry." She laughed lightly. "You al-ways worry so much."

Easy for her to say. She was crazy. But I followed. We sat down. We ordered drinks. One couldn't hurt. She ordered a gin and tonic. I or-dered a beer. The bar was small and dark, the requisite TV on in the corner, only three people besides us inside, including the bartender, a young guy in his twenties like us. She started making toasts, and that seemed fine to me. With every sip, she made a toast. "To us," she said. We drank. "To Chicago, this bloody city." We drank. "To our friends, may they always be safe and happy." We drank. "To Jesus." She drank. Hesitantly, I lifted my glass and drank, too. A look of alarm grew in her eyes and she started to rise from her chair, almost as though she were levitating.

"Should I have said that?"

"What?" I said, rising slowly, too.

"I shouldn't have said that," she told me.

"No, it's fine."

"It was blasphemy. Oh forgive me, Jesus, don't let them hurt me."

Her drink flipped over and spilled on the floor and Rita sank down, too, under the table. The guys at the bar turned around, for the briefest moment, and then turned back to their own brooding silence, the silence of the TV in the corner, as though they saw this every day, and perhaps they did. But I didn't. Rita was on the floor now, writhing and twitching, vomit starting to come out of the side of her mouth, her clothes wet with the spilled drink.

I ran to the bartender and looked into his impassive face. He held a bar rag as though this was the only assistance he'd offer. "My friend is sick," I said. "Call someone. Call an ambulance."

The man didn't move. "She looks fine to me," he said.

I ran back to her, knelt beside her, and held her hand. She looked up at me, and just like that, the seizure or whatever it was, left her.

She stood up and I left some money on the table. "I should have known better," she said. "I shouldn't have talked about Jesus that way."

"No, it's fine," I told her, nearly in tears. Holding her hand, I led her to the gate. "I'm sure he must understand."

*   *   *

In the years since I put Rita on the plane back to her mother, I have heard from her from time to time, but never again have I seen her. I don't know what she looks like anymore, although I imagine the years have devastated her, because she has devastated herself, and the world has been even crueler. I tell myself I would have joined her on that flight if I could have, and I think I would have, but now that so many years have gone by I can't be sure of my own actions, my own motives. I think that if I'd loved her enough I would have found a way to join her, but her mother didn't offer to pay my way, I didn't ask, and I had no means of my own. Rita and I spoke by telephone, at first frequently, when she returned. She told me of the visions she'd seen out the window the entire three-hour trip home, how the flight attendants had left her alone. She called me from a hospital. She told me that her mother had met her with a straitjacket, how she had been chased in the airport parking lot and tackled, how humiliated she was. I don't know whether this is true or not. It's possible, although she was always embellishing, like me. We talked about visiting, and it seemed likely somehow, at first.

Every year or so, I'd get a letter from her. She talked about Jesus and what he did for her, how she'd be sitting at a bar with her glass empty and then miraculously, he'd fill the glass again. I didn't keep one of these letters, although there weren't many, maybe four. And sometimes, she'd call me up. She roamed around the country for a while, dropping unannounced among friends, many of whom had been close to her, and after every visit, I'd get a call or hear about it later, how shocked they were to see her, how different she was, how she didn't make any sense, how she was still selfish and demanding, but demented, too. She was pregnant when she dropped in on my friends, Jack and Julia, who lived in Baltimore. No one knew who the father was, but she said she was giving birth to the Jehovah and she was going to stop in at the White House to deliver an important message to

President Reagan before going on to Israel to give birth to another Jesus.

She never made it to the Holy Land, but gave birth to a little girl, of whom the little girl's grandmother, Rita's adopted mother, not her real one, won custody. Every once in a while I hear from Rita now, but not in the last three years, not since I moved out West. She thinks we should get married, but I know we can't, not only because I'm already married, but because she's dead, because she died when she said the Devil would kill her, while I was on the phone to her mother, and she was in the living room, pacing alone, left alone, forever—what I didn't see then, but see now, is that I could have kept all the knives in the world out of her reach, that I could have kept the doors locked, but she had been killed in one way or another, by whom, I'll never be sure.

Quieted

"If this path is incomprehensible, then why do you compose
books combining natural science with the divine names?"

He said, "For you and those like you among the philoso-
phizers, to attract your human minds naturally. Perhaps this attraction will bring you to the knowledge of the Name?"

THE ESSENTIAL KABBALAH

Olivia and Isabel are always making drawings for Beverly and me.
Sometimes Olivia writes "books," drawings with jumbles of letters
around them—she can't spell or read yet. But she likes to draw pictures
and tell me stories that seem to fly into her head as she turns the pages.
They have little in the way of narrative order, but you can't fault them
for unpredictablity and imagination. Sometimes, she makes cards for
me and sings happy birthday any chance she gets, whether appropriate .
or not. Birthday songs and songs in general shouldn't be restricted to
one's birthday, she seems to think. One day, she's at the kitchen table as
I come in, and she quickly covers the paper she's been drawing on.

"Daddy, don't look."

"I'm not looking."

"Daddy, *don't* look."

"I told you. I'm not looking."

"It's a surprise for you."

A few minutes later, she hands me her card with a heartfelt "Happy
Birthday." It *is* a surprise, more than she knows. On the front of the
card is the figure of a woman with her arms outstretched, no features,
but a blank face, all yellow, and yellow hands, brown hair and a blue-
and-red-striped shirt. And on the inside of the card is the word NOLA
surrounded by other letters that make little sense: WON, WOA, WO.

I suppose the word could read "Nova," not "Nola," but I show it to
Beverly, and she sees what I see, too, my sister's name surrounded by
the incomprehensible. It seems the perfect birthday present from

Olivia; coming as it does, not on my birthday. And yellow was Nola's favorite color, my mother tells me. Yellow is Olivia's favorite, too.

I look at my children sometimes and I wonder what they've inherited from us, from me, from people they've never even known. What combinations of letters will throw them off? What combinations will guide them?

*   *   *

My mother tells me she's working on a new novel. What's this one about? I want to know. "Mexico," she tells me. "My time in Mexico." She says she was always afraid of the material, but now that I've delved into it, she's been able to face it. I'm happy for her, of course, and over the coming weeks and months, she tells me she's become obsessed with her book, just as I've become obsessed with mine, and here we are, writing about the same thing.

At first, I feel proud of myself in a way, that this action of mine that I've felt so guilty about, uncovering my mother's past, my sister's past, bit by bit, has led my mother back into her life, has made her able to face the pain in it. But then, I come to realize that I've got it backward. My mother has uncovered the past for *me*, by granting me these documents. She's made *me* face pain and responsibility I didn't want to face. She's faced her own pain every day in the private/public realm of her stories. And me? I have started to reconcile who I am with who I was and who I want to be. For a while, I thought this was all about Nola, preserving her, bringing her back from the Valley of Ednah. Now I see that this isn't about saving Nola.

"He comes around in the end," I hear my mother say about the fictional me in her story. "Mack redeems himself."

"Maybe," I say, less unconvinced.

*   *   *

My mother is still worried that I somehow see her as dishonest, which I don't. She's worried in particular about the lie she told about her fictional marriage to Elliot Chess.

Tuesday, Sept. 3, 1996

Dear Robin,

IT'S ABOUT 2:00 a.m. and you can tell from my typing. I must do this quickly and go to sleep . . . but have been thinking about Mexico, especially since I found another story, unrewritten, in absolute 1st draft, about Elliot and the situation. I hadn't liked it and just buried it. Now I think I might restore it. Could the novel bear another fictionalization of a vital part of its makeup?

I keep thinking of the incidence of my "lie" and how I felt then. I was so weakened, so exhausted by the whole thing. I was very grateful to Ida, but that feeling (which she encouraged) also did much to increase my sense of guilt. I felt more and more that I had wronged Nola by not pursuing E. to El Paso, and that I should take the consequences. I felt that I owed her something, and therefore I listened to Ida, even though I decided long before to let him go. I understood him pretty well and didn't think we could possibly live together. In Mexico I drifted along in some kind of post-war romantic nimbus that we romantics expected to be due us after five years of darkness and dejection and juggling with absolutes.

Your father saved me, saved both Nola and me (for a while). But life is no fairy tale and one only marginally inspires one's own fate.
    Love,
    Mom

Could the novel bear another fictionalization of a vital part of its makeup? That's my central question, too, perhaps everyone's, but in a more generalized way. What memories to restore, what drafts to revise, what self, what relationships to resurrect, what to bury deeper?

One day I tell her I'm writing about the ghost that Jonny and I saw when we were kids and she says, "Oh, I've already written about that. It's in my novel."

"But I thought your novel was about Mexico," I say.

"Part of it. But I'm done with that part. Your ghost is in there, too. I've been working on it, on and off, for years. No, the main character is a Shelley scholar. It's a book about Romanticism, and the Romantic act in the lives of Shelley and Mary Shelley."

"Great," I say. "Isn't it wonderful how we appropriate each other's lives," and we both laugh.

The next day we're talking she lets slip that she's been reading some old letters from her father to her mother, my grandmother, Ida. The letters are from 1920, when my grandmother went to the Mayo Clinic for a goiter operation, and my grandfather stayed behind in New York with the kids, my mother and my uncle Allan. She tells me that what's interesting about the letters is that they start off very warmly, with him signing each letter "Affectionately," and the letters end coolly with him just signing off, "Sincerely." The cause of the estrangement was money. On the one hand, Nelson's mother Fanny was pressuring them to pay back a loan. But Ida's mother, Hannah, who was with her at the Mayo Clinic, kept pressuring Ida to ask Nelson for *more* money, and he kept writing back that he couldn't send any more.

"Where did you get the letters?" I ask my mother.

Here, she hesitates and says, "I found them in a drawer at Ida's."

"You took them!" I scream. I can't believe she stole them from Ida, that my own thefts were not even original, that, as a thief, I've apprenticed to my mother my entire life.

"I'll send them to you," she says, and in fact, she does.

I don't interpret these letters the same way my mother does. She looks for the tension in the words between her parents, but what captures my attention are the references in the letter to my mother, at that time the same age as Olivia is now. Her father writes:

> *Sylivia [what she was called as a child] is surely all there, physically and mentally. She easily holds her own with her five and six year old playmates. She is just as busy and mischievious as ever . . . . Yesterday evening I took them both for a walk and just while we were passing a group of people she tells me at the top of her voice, that "she (sic) made poo poo twice yesterday." I put my hand over her mouth to shut her up and she pulls my hand away and yells it twice as loud. We haven't been able to impress her yet with the importance of just whispering this kind of information.*

Isabel says embarrasing things, too, in public, which is normal. Rather than clamp our hands over her mouth, Beverly and I laugh and don't make a deal out of it, afraid of stigmatizing her. A few days ago, Beverly was with Isabel and Olivia at Olivia's music class. During one of the rectitals, Isabel looked up at Beverly and yelled out, "Mommy, I tooted!" "Well, that's quite an announcement," one of the other parents said.

I find Beverly in the kitchen with Isabel.

"Listen to this," I say. "The more things change, the more things stay the same," I add in a goofy voice.

"Great saying," she says. "You should write that down."

I read her this passage from my grandfather's letter.

"So it comes from *your* side of the family," Beverly says, "yelling out embarrassing things in public."

*   *   *

The weather is terrible this fall in the Northwest. We've been having record rainfall, and floods have been washing out communities from Northern California to our own county. And what have Beverly and I decided to do, but take a vacation? Figures, but who can predict the weather, and I had to book a vacation rental for us months in advance. We're going down to a coastal Oregon community called Yachats. We've rented a beachside house with the romantic name Sea Grass Cottage. When I called the manager of the the rental in July, I asked him what late October is like in Yachats. "It's the best time of the year," he assured me.

The night before we leave, it rains ferociously. As we're chatting in the kitchen, the four of us, we hear a loud crack.

"My God," Beverly says. "The tree by the swingset just fell."

I go outside with a flashlight in the wind and rain and inspect the fallen maple. It fell in the best possible way, just missing the swingset and missing our house, but falling partially into our neighbor's yard. I go next door to tell our neighbors what happened, and that we'll take care of it when we return from Yachats.

This is not the most auspicious beginning. We should probably just forget the trip, and lose our deposit, but it's been so long since we've taken time away together as a family, and who knows, maybe the weather will clear up.

It doesn't. The next morning, we pile into our car in the rain and head down to Oregon, where none of us have been before. But maybe the weather will clear up in Oregon.

It doesn't. What's more, I'm not especially known for my planning of trips. The drive takes us much longer than expected, partly because I get us lost in downtown Portland during rush hour and partly because we get into a mysterious traffic jam an hour later in the middle of what can only be described as a village. We stop for coffee here, and the woman at the counter tells us that we should be careful on the road to the seashore. "It's treacherous."

Great. And it's getting dark, and the kids are tired, and we're not having much fun. An hour later we're crossing the mountains on a deserted road in blinding rain. Beverly peers out into the dark, helping me make sure I don't drive us off into a ravine or a river.

Finally, we make it across the mountains, and we've still got two hours to drive down the seashore. We stop for groceries, utterly exhausted, and press on.

We can't see much, though the rain has let up, but as we approach

Yachats, Beverly points out the darkness of the ocean. We can hear its impressive rumble, and even though it's taken us a while to get here, Beverly's love for the ocean takes over, and I'm happy that we've finally been delivered out of the elements to a place where we can safely view.

And when we make our way down a rutted dirt road to Sea Grass Cottage, we feel elated, probably more so than if we'd just had an easy drive of an hour or so, or if we had always lived here. The boom of the ocean presses palpably against the house, but we're not afraid anymore. We build a fire in the fireplace. We take out our groceries and eat and the girls play with the cat who comes along with the house, a cat named Ocean. After dinner, Beverly reads the journal entries of the people who've come before us to Sea Grass Cottage. It's tradition to record your thoughts about this place and leave it for the next guests to arrive.

The next day the storm worsens and we contemplate staying indoors for the entire weekend. But we don't care. The girls play games and watch videos while Beverly and I play a game of Scrabble. Nine times out ten, she slaughters me, but this time, I'm lucky. I go first and I'm able to use all my letters, every one, with hardly even trying.

Q-U-I-E-T-E-D

She comes close to beating me, but I hold onto my lead, barely.

By noon, the sun is out and we go exploring. We drive up and down the coast, visit all the tourist stops: Sea Lion Cave, Heceta Head Lighthouse, the town of Florence. We return to Sea Grass Cottage in time for some play time at the beach. Olivia and Isabel dig in the sand for a while, and then Isabel and Beverly return to the house. Olivia wants to keep playing, so I stay out with her. We walk to the edge of the water where a crane poses against a brilliant sunset. Over the cottage, the moon has already appeared, full and glowing, seeming to take up half the sky. Olivia has a little camera with her, and I take pictures of all this, wishing I could preserve it, but knowing that there's really not enough light for her camera—but still, hopeful.

We let the waves chase us into shore and then we take a walk together. We walk about a mile and as we're heading back, Olivia says, "I want to run, Daddy."

She goes ahead, every once in a while turning back and waving, then running some more, turning and waving. As long as she stays in sight, I don't mind. But then she runs past the house, and she keeps running, without turning around, without waving, and I call after her, into the wind, but of course, she can't hear me.

What made us want to bring her and Isabel into this world? What made us want to care and risk such loss? I'm not sure. All I can say is that I know I am not alone.

I am not only myself, but all the people who pass through me, insubstantial as ghosts, solid as the sand on which I'm running now. Olivia is so far off, her figure diminishing the more I love her. I hope she'll finally turn around and notice.

And she does. We've overrun the house by quite a bit. This time, I take her hand and don't let her go. We walk slowly back to the house, lit up by the moon, lit inside. I can see Beverly in the cottage. I can see Isabel sitting on a stool by the counter.

Olivia and I find a rope in the sand. "You know what this is?" I tell her.

"What?"

I remember doing writing workshops for elementary school kids, asking them to imagine a trapdoor under their beds, and to describe where it leads them. "It's a door to another world," I say.

"No it's not," she says.

I pick up the rope and tug on it. I can't budge it. "Here, you try."

She's suspicious, but she takes the rope in her hand and tugs. "You can go there later, without me, in your dreams," I say. "Okay?"

Love them now, wildly, a voice tells me, sings. If there is fate, it resides in this moment, the crack between fiction and dreams, between pre-science and presence, *our* presences, flashing brilliantly, already gone.

"Okay." She knows what I say is real, that it sometimes takes more than one try and an effort to get there, even if we don't know where there is.

We climb the steps to Sea Grass Cottage and Olivia bursts into the kitchen. "Mommy, we found another world under the sand."

"You did!" Beverly says, ready to believe almost anything.

A Dark and Ageless Voice

. . . I was in a white robe, and had bright yellow hair. Grim mountains surrounded the world ~~like impenetrable prehistoric beasts~~, and behind them ~~the mountains~~ a dark and ageless Voice, which I knew was God. The earth was covered ~~filled~~ with people in agony: The ground ~~earth~~ quaked and opened ~~its great maw and poured~~ pouring out streams of fire, ~~which leapt out of the core of the troubled planet and~~ swallowed everyone ~~in its midst~~. One after another people I had known for years were swept ~~into these wells of~~ death before my ~~stricken~~ eyes. ~~I was petrified.~~ The earth had been turned into an ~~infernal~~ oven from which it seemed there was no escape. No patch of ground was ~~sure or~~ stable; the moment one stepped anywhere on ~~its~~ the surface ~~it would give~~ gave way, ~~and the screaming victim would be buried alive in its crust~~. I was certain that I was going to die like the rest. Suddenly I heard the Voice speak to me from the mountains: "No, you will not die, you are my bright and selfless child, and I love you." I listened and my hope for life was ~~slightly~~ raised, although I awoke from the dream feeling ~~very~~ disturbed, since I thought that God was ~~surely~~ overestimating me and that I ~~would, in the end, also~~ too, would be consumed. It seemed to me a matter of spiritual strength whether or not one was destroyed, and I *knew* that for this reason my faith and love had to be kept pure . . .

Acknowledgments

I have had so much help writing this book, in ways that are hardly fathomable. First, I want to thank my mother, Elaine Gottlieb Hemley, without whose personal courage and integrity, Nola's story and the story of my family would have been impossible for me to write. I'm also grateful to Beverly Hemley and my daughters, Olivia and Isabel, who gave me a reason for writing this. I'm indebted to Bruce Beasley and Suzanne Paola whose wise counsel, encouragement, and criticism buoyed me. And to Nola, whose words I've rediscovered.

I also want to thank Lisa Bullard, Anne Czarniecki, Dale Gottlieb, David Gottlieb, Jennifer Hengen, Fiona McCrae, Mark Sherman, David Shields, Linny Stovall, Kate Trueblood, for their friendship, help, and collective *joie de vivre*. And grateful acknowledgment is made to the Bureau for Faculty Research at Western Washington University for two summer research grants that helped free my time for writing, and to Elizabeth Fox for helping me with the many pages of transcripts.

Portions of this book were published in slightly different form in *Prairie Schooner* and *Hawaii Review*. My story, "Riding the Whip," appeared originally in *ACM* and *Twenty Under Thirty* (Scribners), and my mother's story, "The Woman Who Was Absent" appeared originally in the *Southern Review*.

Family photographs, court documents, and journal entries are reprinted by permission of Elaine Gottlieb Hemley.

Excerpts from "In Dreams Begin Responsibilities," by Delmore Schwartz. Copyright © 1961 by Delmore Schwartz. Reprinted by permission of New Directions Publishing Corp.

"The Papers of a Poet" by Chad Walsh. Copyright © 1967 by The New York Times Company. Reprinted by permission.

The illustrations are the work of Nola Hemley.

Some names have been changed, but otherwise, everyone is as real as I remember.

R O B I N   H E M L E Y is the author of several works of fiction and nonfiction, including a popular book on form, *Turning Life into Fiction,* the novel *The Last Studebaker,* and the collections of short stories, *All You Can Eat* and *The Big Ear.* His work has also been published in Great Britain, Germany, and Japan, and his awards include first prize in the Nelson Algren Award competition from the *Chicago Tribune,* two Pushcart Prizes, and the George Garrett Award. His work has been heard on NPR's *Selected Shorts* and *The Sound of Writing.* He presently teaches creative writing at Western Washington University in Bellingham, Washington.

This book was designed by Will Powers and set in type by Stanton Publication Services, Inc., and manufactured by The Maple-Vail Book Manufacturing Group on acid-free paper.